"An excellent work and very much needed. It is architecture for every man, and it not only is a useful field guide, but is a thorough introduction to American architecture, the easy way . . . I want more, more, more."

—Arthur P. Ziegler, Jr., *President*
Pittsburgh History and Landmarks Foundation

"A FIELD GUIDE TO AMERICAN ARCHITECTURE, written for all ages, will quickly become an indispensable tool for those who care deeply about the stewardship of the built environment. It is a triumph."

—Robert McNulty, *President*
Partners for Livable Places

"The facts of American architecture are all there, yet the book is so clear, well organized, beautifully written, and totally absorbing. It represents a real breakthrough in architectural education literature."

—Susan Reichman, *Director*
Museum Education Program
Bank Street College of Education

"This book is an original, not a duplication of any other book on American architecture. It will be an indispensable reference for anyone interested in the subject, and armed with it we will all be instant experts. It's an inspiration to revisit every city I've seen with the benefit of rich background knowledge."

—Margot Wellington,
Executive Director
The Municipal Art Society of New York

"A very useful reference companion, especially for its broad coverage of buildings, by type and geographical setting, its clear and informative drawings, and the author's skill in relating architectural innovation to the changing social and economic scene."

—Bayard Still,
Department of History
New York University

ABOUT THE AUTHOR:

CAROLE RIFKIND, who teaches at the Graduate School of Architecture and Planning at Columbia University, is also a consultant on historic preservation and tourism planning. Her previous books are *Mansions, Mills, and Main Streets* (with Carol Levine) and *Main Street: The Face of Urban America.*

ALSO BY CAROLE RIKFIND

Mansions, Mills and Main Streets
(with Carol Levine)

Main Street: The Face of Urban America

A Field Guide to American Architecture

by

Carole Rifkind

A PLUME BOOK
NEW AMERICAN LIBRARY
TIMES MIRROR
NEW YORK, LONDON AND SCARBOROUGH, ONTARIO

NAL Books are available at quantity discounts when used to promote products or services. For information please write to Premium Marketing Division, The New American Library, Inc., 1633 Broadway, New York, New York 10019.

PLUME TRADEMARK REG. U.S. PAT. OFF. AND FOREIGN COUNTRIES
REGISTERED TRADEMARK—MARCA REGISTRADA
HECHO EN FORGE VILLAGE, MASS., U.S.A.

SIGNET, SIGNET CLASSICS, MENTOR, PLUME, MERIDIAN and NAL BOOKS are published *in the United States* by The New American Library, Inc., 1633 Broadway, New York, New York 10019, *in Canada* by The New American Library of Canada Limited, 81 Mack Avenue, Scarborough, Ontario M1L 1M8, *in the United Kingdom* by The New English Library Limited, Barnard's Inn, Holborn, London EC1N 2JR, England

First Printing, March, 1980

Library of Congress Cataloging in Publication Data

Rifkind, Carole.
A field guide to American architecture.

(A Plume book)
Bibliography: p.
Includes index.
1. Architecture—United States—Handbooks, manuals, etc.
2. Decoration and ornament, Architectural—United States—Handbooks, manuals, etc. I. Title.
[NA705.R53 1980b] 720'.973 79-29651
ISBN 0-452-25224-5 pbk.

3 4 5 6 7 8 9

PRINTED IN THE UNITED STATES OF AMERICA

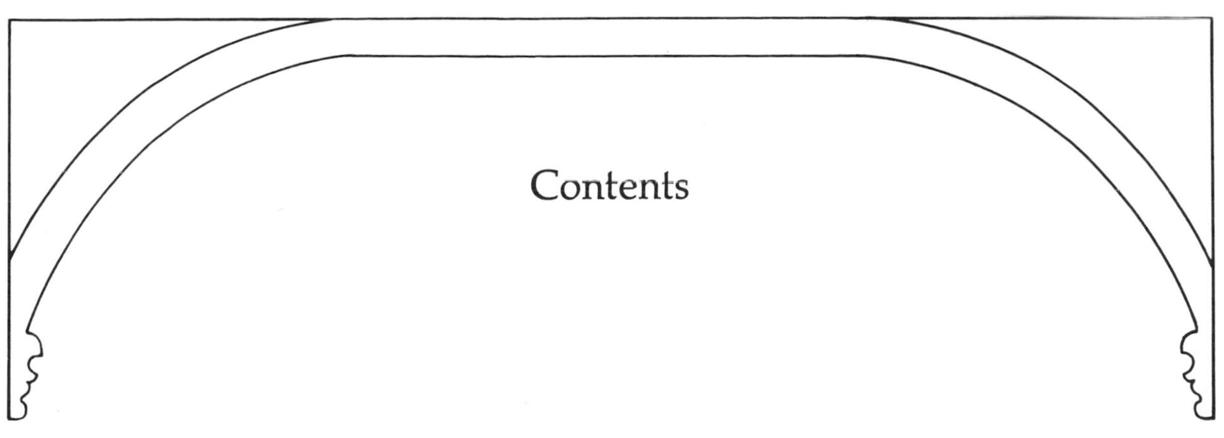

Contents

Part IV

Utilitarian

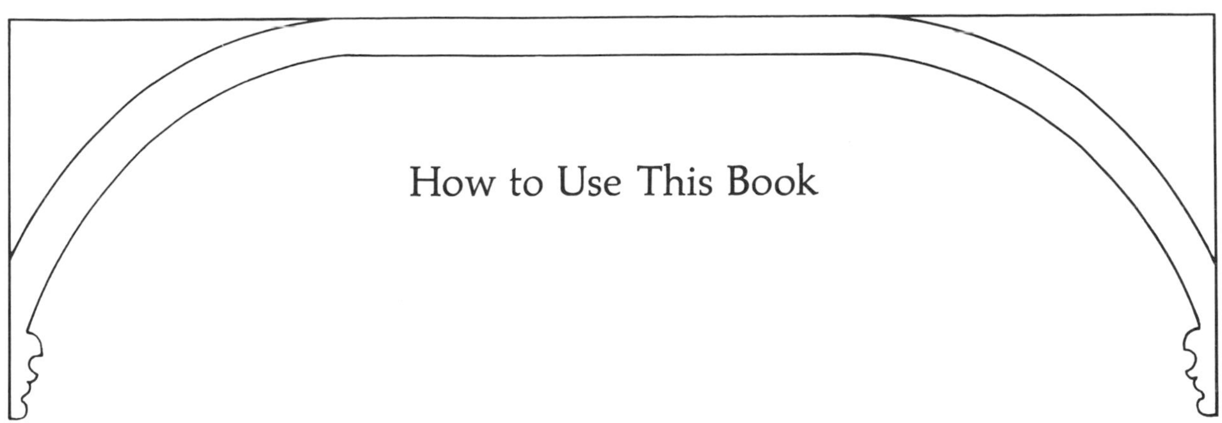

How to Use This Book

THIS is a guide book for the traveler who thrills to novelty, the student in search of a tangible record of culture, the lover of art and history. Discoveries are to be made anywhere and everywhere—they are the heritage of three centuries of American history. The worker's cottage, merchant prince's palace, and utopian planner's housing project; the corner drugstore and corporate office building; the riverside mill and the electric power station; the meetinghouse on the green and the downtown city hall—on all sides, buildings, streets, and landscape configurations speak of history and culture, art and technology, time and events. We must learn their language.

Included in this book are more than 450 line drawings which illustrate representative examples of American building up to about 1940. Because of their clarity and precision, these drawings are particularly revealing of how the builder's vocabulary—scale, shape, mass, proportion, rhythm, articulation, ornamental trim, and material—is used to fulfill function and convey meaning. No detail is too small or insignificant. Like brush strokes on canvas, details express personality, technical capability, the conventions or style of the period, and the spirit of the age.

A few photographs are included as well. They should serve as reminders of the sensual and emotional qualities that drawings cannot convey—the texture of surface, the heaviness and density of mass, the patterns set in motion by light and shadow.

The drawings are divided into four sections according to building type: residential; ecclesiastical; civic and commercial; and a "catch-all" category of utilitarian buildings grouped by function—agriculture, transportation, and industry.

Since this volume is intended as a field guide, attention is focused on building exteriors. However, there are also many plans, and in any case the observer should certainly make every effort to enter and experience the interiors of buildings that are open to the public—from the serene spaces of a Quaker meetinghouse to the Jazz Age splendor of an Art Deco office building.

For each building type, drawings are arranged to convey an understanding of sequential development, successive stylistic phases, and the relationship between "high" and "low" style. The reader should be aware of regional variations and observe that a structure will reflect distinct characteristics if it is in a city or a small town, designed for a richer or poorer owner, built to the plans of an architect or carpenter. Almost by definition, utilitarian buildings lack "style"—but, inevitably, function, form, proportion, detail, material, and construction reflect the individuality and personality of the time. Architects' names are given only when they are of national, rather than local, significance.

While it is generally true that all building types pass through the same succession of styles, although at somewhat different times, the length of time that a style remains popular and the number of buildings constructed vary a great deal. Some building types are closely associated with certain styles—for example, the Gothic church, the Italianate commercial structure, and the Neoclassical public building. And certain styles, peculiarly appropriate to their locality, linger much longer there than elsewhere—the southern plantation house, for example, perpetuated Greek Revival style through several generations.

Examining the Contents on pages v and vi, the

reader will observe that both chronology and stylistic names may vary from one building type to another. This is as it must be; buildings are not so neatly categorized as birds.

Every style does not begin or end at precisely the same moment for all building types. For example, the inception of the Victorian era can be glimpsed in churches built as early as the 1830s, but not until the 1840s in the case of dwellings. The durability of a mode also determines how it is characterized. The long-popular Greek Revival stands as a discrete category for dwellings, but seems more appropriately considered a stage of Early Victorian in the case of civic and commercial structures.

One building type may seem to be more aptly described by one stylistic name than by another, so that Federal describes the dwelling style of 1790–1820, while the more general characterization of Neoclassical seems appropriate for the churches of that era. The impact of a style is dependent on its survival rate: for example, the Georgian church, relatively rare today, is simply included within the Colonial era, rather than standing in its own category.

Although these and other distinctions may be cause for puzzlement, this flexible approach is intended to help the reader and the viewer to understand structures as being similar or different for inherent historical, cultural, and aesthetic significance rather than to see them in pigeonholes which are too rigidly defined.

The point of view taken in this book is that the ordinary can be as fascinating as the extraordinary. In the selection of illustrations, a typical building has been considered to be as important as a special one. Even so, there are a number of "fine" buildings—probably a disproportionately large number in view of the very small fraction of the total built environment that they actually represent. However, each chapter does have a wide variety of buildings, including "high-style," vernacular, and provincial examples. These terms should be understood to mean the following: high-style buildings are the creations of trained designers; vernacular buildings are the work of craftsmen who might prefer to follow local tradition rather than the latest vogue; provincial examples are the efforts of builders who lack a complete understanding of high-style design and thus reproduce its idiosyncrasies rather than its spirit. Generally excluded in this selection are styles or types that are extinct or rare—for example, dwellings in the Egyptian or Moorish Revival, pioneer dugouts, or the sod houses of Nebraska.

Most of the structures illustrated are extant. Many are listed in *The National Register of Historic Places*. But because this is a guide to style and type rather than to particular buildings, precise information regarding status, location and accessibility is not given.

Alterations

Buildings that have been altered or enlarged during the course of generations defy precise categorization, yet are particularly fascinating as they reveal history's richness, complexity, and continuity. The observer with a discerning eye and some knowledge of local history will begin to see the significance of alterations sustained by buildings of every type, period, and place.

For dwellings, the addition of a wing is a simple solution to space needs. Often this is expressed frankly, and is recognizable because of deviant scale, proportions, fenestration, chimney position, and materials. A typical device is the unification of mismatched sections by the addition of porch or eaves trim. A sufficiently large addition may dictate remodeling the original section. Revealing clues are complicated massing, change in foundation material and sheathing, substitution of window for door, and variation in ceiling heights and rooflines. Alternatively, space may be gained simply by adding dormers or an extra story. Usually a major alteration occasions minor changes as well—particularly on eaves trim, porch design, size and type of window opening, door, and roofline.

Generally, major alterations are most likely during prosperous times—the years preceding and following the Civil War, the Centennial years, the mid 1880s, the turn of the century, and the late 1920s. Kitchen additions were particularly popular during these times.

Taste as well as practicality generates renovation. Particularly beloved modifications include steep cross gables in the 1850s, mansard roofs in the 1870s, wide verandas in the 1890s, enclosed porches in the 1910s, colonialized doorways in the 1930s, picture windows in the 1950s.

Because remodeling was often an economical way to accommodate growing religious congregations, church buildings tend to be cumulative in character. The date on the cornerstone, or of the congregation's founding, may have little relevance to the final appearance of the church. Typical modifications of church buildings are a lengthening of the nave and the addition of transepts or a new tower. Space is also gained by joining another building to the existing church. Observation of the foundation material is often revealing in these cases. A double tier of windows sometimes may be evidence for the horizontal division of a church auditorium, the lower half converted to a parish house.

Commercial buildings were not usually as permanent as churches—speculation and changing business practice spur construction of larger, more efficient, and more profitable shops and office buildings. Characteristic modifications include raising the roof and shop restyling. Civic buildings, generally high-style and expensive, were less often tampered with. Additions are likely to be modest and pallid interpretations of the original style.

Adaptive use of utilitarian buildings has always occurred in a pragmatic fashion, often with as little exterior change as possible. For factory structures, the mass and silhouette of new construction usually reflect new industrial processes and technological specialization. In our own time, the growing practice of redesigning industrial spaces for nonindustrial purposes is reconditioning our expectations of building types. A railroad station may be a restaurant or art gallery; a cannery becomes a retail mall; a trolley depot engenders an entertainment complex.

Unfamiliar Terms

No doubt, knowing how to name the parts of a building helps to see and understand them. But because these drawings represent the building parts so clearly, the use of technical names has been limited as severely as possible. When it has been necessary to use a term that may be unfamiliar, its first use has been followed by a simple definition. These words are listed in the index, so if the reader is puzzled by them elsewhere the definition may be located within the text.

A Note on the Drawings

The *plan* is the basic element of a measured drawing. It shows the outline of a building on the ground plane, and its interior spaces. The *elevation* is a projection onto the page of the elements that are perpendicular to the plan—that is, the façade. Necessarily, all lines are drawn on the same plane, so one must look closely to see what parts of the building actually lie in different planes. Similarly, since measured drawings only reveal edges of buildings, not their bulk, it takes a little imagination and some practice to understand the organization of volumes, or massing. The photographs may be helpful in this respect.

Almost all of the drawings are from the Historic American Buildings Survey (HABS) or the Historic American Engineering Record (HAER), under the auspices of the Heritage Conservation and Recreation Service (formerly under the National Park Service), Department of the Interior.

HABS and HAER drawings are the public record of structures and sites associated with the nation's architectural and industrial heritage. Together with written data, photographs, and other documentation, they form an extraordinary archive of the art of building in America.

While drawings are intended to record the actual appearance of a building, later modifications or additions may have been ignored if they transform the character of the building. The conjectural original, then, is indicated by broken lines.

When HABS began in 1933, as a Works Project Administration project to put unemployed architects to work, it focused on the seventeenth and eighteenth centuries and on endangered structures. Since the passage of the National Historic Preservation Act in 1966, the scope of HABS has been considerably enlarged.

Among the criteria for inclusion in a HABS survey are that a structure be the work of a major architect or craftsman; representative of a type or period; important in the development of construction, building type, or style; significant in the development of modern architecture; interrelated with others within an area so that their sum has a significance exceeding that of individual buildings; representative of the contribution of cultural or ethnic groups; or endangered by demolition or deterioration. There are measured drawings for more than 16,000 buildings, and HABS has also developed methodology for conducting landscape, area, and other environmental studies.

HAER drawings emphasize industrial structures, including rare early types and those that are the work of major designers or have significance in the history of engineering and the economic or industrial development of an area. In addition to individual sites and structures, technological networks, such as railroads and canals, are also included in HAER surveys. More than 500 sites have been recorded by drawings or photographs since 1969, when the federal government established HAER, recognizing the importance of our technological heritage and the threats posed to industrial buildings by rapid obsolescence.

Fundamental to the HABS-HAER philosophy is that projects are undertaken on a shared-cost basis. Groups that cooperatively sponsor the survey projects are municipalities, industries, historical societies, and preservation organizations, including the National Trust for Historic Preservation. Professional associations have played an important role in both HABS and HAER—in fact, cooperative arrangements with the American Institute of Architects, American Society of Civil Engineers, the American Society of Mechanical Engineers, the Institute of Electrical and Electronic Engineers, and the American Society of Engineering Educators have been essential.

All of this means that aware and concerned citizens have the opportunity to aid in the documentation of the built environment and to spur its preservation. An unfortunate corollary, however, is that areas with a low level of environmental consciousness are least likely to participate in survey projects, yet are most in need.

Because so many buildings completed in the late nineteenth century and first part of the twentieth century are large and complex, and are therefore difficult and expensive to record, I have had to go beyond the HABS and HAER archive to achieve representative examples. These have come from several sources, and credit is given where appropriate. Because structures completed within the last fifty years have generally been excluded from survey projects, there can be relatively few included here.

Acknowledgments

For assistance in the preparation of this book, I am very grateful for the help of John Poppeliers, Chief of the Historic American Buildings Survey; Eric DeLony, formerly Chief Architect of the Historic American Engineering Record; and David DeLong and Theodore Prudon of Columbia University, all of whom read the manuscript and offered valuable advice and suggestions. My appreciation also goes to Mary Farrell, Christine St. Lawrence Taylor, and Alicia Stamm of the HABS staff, Mary Ison and Ford Peatross of the Prints and Photograph Division of the Library of Congress, and Steven Bauer for their kindness and courtesy in making the illustrative material available to me. The staff and resources of the Avery Library, Columbia University, have been of great assistance. Special thanks are owed to John Thornton and Ted Johnson for their patient editorial guidance, to Irene Pink and Helen Richards for their careful attention to every detail of copy and production, and to Julian Hamer for his very special interest in this book and his creative approach to difficult design problems. For their encouragement and for help of many kinds, my deepest gratitude is to my husband and to my daughters, Barbara and Nancy.

PART I

Residential

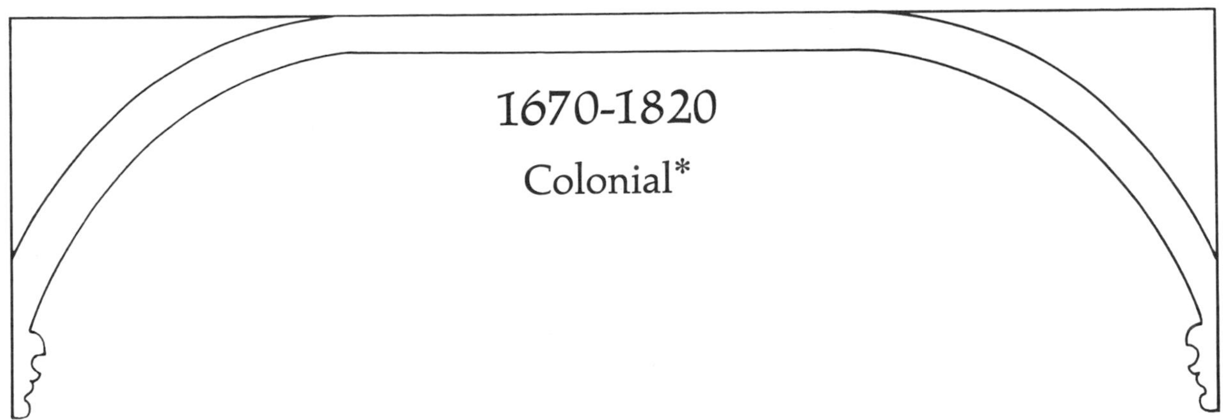

1670-1820
Colonial*

"FIRE and water are not more heterogeneous than the different colonies in North America," wrote an early visitor, struck by the New World diversity of settlement patterns, agricultural practices, climatic conditions, local economies, and ethnic, religious, and social-class backgrounds.

The continent was vast, travel was difficult, populations were isolated. Through a century and more, the colonial experience tempered the building traditions brought by English settlers, and by the Dutch, Flemish, Huguenots, Swedes, Germans, French, and Spanish.

Though as different from each other as they were from their European antecedents, the homes of these wilderness orphans were, nevertheless, recognizably American. With rare exceptions, colonial economy, colonial life-style, and colonial technology dictated that dwellings be of a similar modest scale and elaboration. Without difficult detailing or time-consuming finishes, materials were used frankly and bluntly.

With apparent willingness, the contemporary aesthetic accepted unornamented exteriors, asymmetry, the awkwardness of added sections, enlargements, cut-in doors and windows, steep roofs, and abrupt gables. All in all, very pragmatic decisions governed building practices.

Regional characteristics emerged in the use of local materials, such as clapboard-sheathed wood frame in New England; fieldstone or local quarry stone in western Pennsylvania, northern New Jersey, and the Hudson River Valley; and brick in southern New Jersey, Philadelphia, and Virginia.

Distinctive forms evolved through adaptation to climate: the raised Gulf Coast cottage, with its first story open to cooling breezes and safe from flood; the south-oriented Dutch dwelling protected from the coldest winter winds; the Virginia homestead with detached kitchen; the continuous house-barn-shed that served well for cold New England winters.

Prevailing conditions within seaport cities, agricultural towns, plantation headquarters, and wilderness settlements each impressed a distinctive stamp on the Colonial home.

Materials

Materials are used in a fairly simple state. Fieldstone, split shingles, and handmade bricks are among the earliest colonial materials.

Clapboard was a sawmill product widely available even before the eighteenth century. Reflecting social and ethnic background almost as much as the availability of materials, the use of brick is concentrated in the cities and on southern plantations, the use of stone in Pennsylvania and the Hudson River Valley, the use of wood—originally unpainted or painted in earth tones—in New England. Hand-forged iron serves for hinges, handles, and nails.

* The term "Colonial" is used here to refer to dwellings with little or no stylistic pretensions. It should be understood in a developmental more than a strictly chronological sense. In some areas, Colonial traditions may persist until the 1840s or later.

Plan

Reflecting an incremental process of construction over an extended period, the plan of Colonial dwellings may be irregular and complex, with visible additions and enlargements.

Since the primitive house probably included no more than a single room (perhaps with a sleeping loft above) and a chimney, the development of the Colonial plan is concerned with the placement of additional rooms and their relationship to the chimney(s). A later stage has two major rooms on the main floor, on either side of a massive central chimney, with an entrance into a stair hall (leading to a full second story) in front of the chimney this applies particularly to the dwellings of English settlers. A more developed plan includes rooms across the rear of the house [5]. When this addition is one story in height, on a two-story main section, the resulting roof slope is described as a "saltbox" [4]. The saltbox is most frequent in New England; under the name a "cat's slide" it survives in the South as well. Variations also exist [12].

In New England and the Middle Colonies—later—the chimneys are paired and are pushed nearer to the end walls. The plan may be two rooms wide and two rooms deep, with a stair hall at or near the center of the building. Additions, smaller in size and lower in height, may be aligned to the side or to the rear [8; 14, 15].

The house plan with German or Dutch antecedents has rooms that are approximately equal in size arranged laterally with separate entrances into each and without a central stair hall [18]. Chimneys are at the end walls, often placed in a catercorner position.

The early southern house plan has two rooms, side by side or flanking a central hall. Some examples have projecting porches front and rear that create a cruciform plan. Characteristically, the chimneys are against the exterior side walls [7]. The log cabin—found from Carolina to Texas—may have two rooms side by side against a central chimney. Alternatively, a breezeway connects the rooms and exterior chimneys flank the outside walls [27].

Localisms are sometimes confined to very discrete regions: for example, the Providence vicinity "stone-ender" with stone end walls with wood-frame front and rear [6] and the Hudson Valley "Dutch Colonial" [19, 20].

A characteristic French dwelling in the Mississippi River Valley has a steeply sloping roof that projects far enough beyond the walls to form a roomy porch [24].

In the Southwest, under Spanish influence, the primitive one-room plan of an urban dwelling may be incorporated into a continuous row facing a plaza [30, 31]. As a hacienda, the rural dwelling extends around one or two rectangular courtyards [32, 33, 34].

Elevation

Low, yet steeply vertical in proportion, bluntly plain, lacking symmetry, the late-seventeenth-century Colonial dwelling reveals its past in the medieval tradition brought by colonists [1].

Typical features of the eighteenth-century house display the persistence of this medieval outlook. There is a steeply pitched roof with gable ends. The eaves (edge of the roof that projects beyond the wall) are close to the windows. Dormers (windows placed vertically in a slanting roof) have shed roofs. Asymmetrically placed windows have a sash with as many as nine or twelve small lights (panes) and wide muntins (wooden frames for the lights). The composition is complicated by successive enlargements [8].

Eighteenth-century modifications are gentle yet definite. Among them are a lower roof slope, regularly placed and proportionately larger door and window openings, paneled doors and shutters—especially in the Middle Colonies—transom light above the front door, and gabled dormer windows [7]. Advanced southern taste creates modest refinements—door and window openings headed by flat brick arches; gable ends hipped (sloped inward) to reduce apparent steepness; and eaves with detailed moldings [9]. Otherwise, there generally persists an absence of ornamentation or formal organizing devices to set off door, window, floor level, and roofline.

In provincial areas these characteristics persist in dwellings that were built as late as the early nineteenth century.

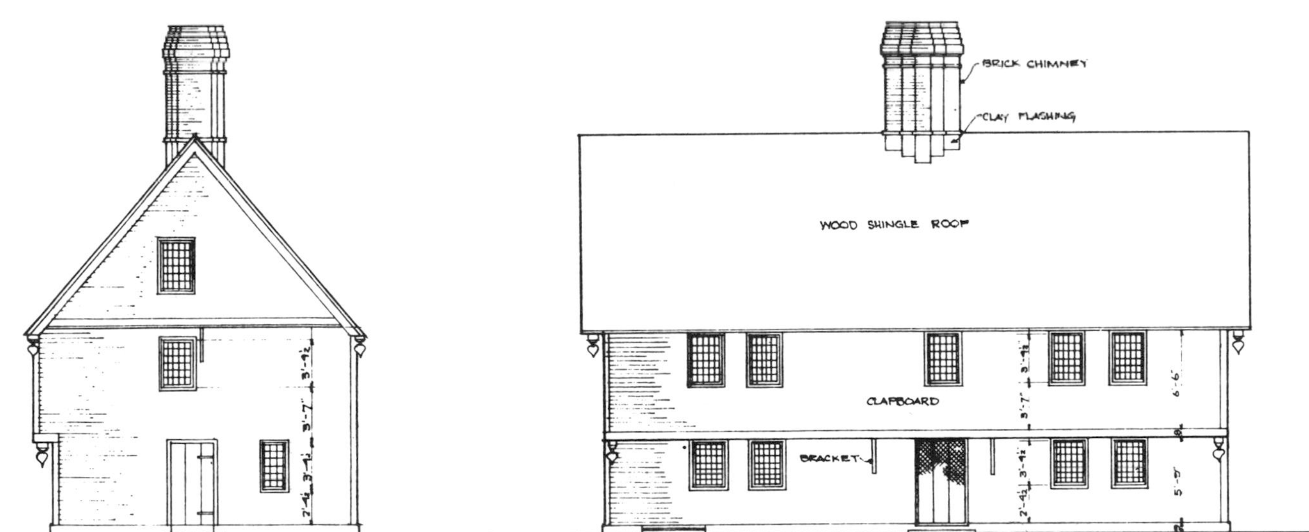

1, 2 Parson Joseph Capen House. Topsfield, Massachusetts. 1683. Lingering medievalisms on the early Colonial dwelling are the grouped chimneys, second-story overhang, fixed sash with many small lights.

Old Ogden House, Fairfield, Connecticut; c. 1700 (see 3, 4, 5).

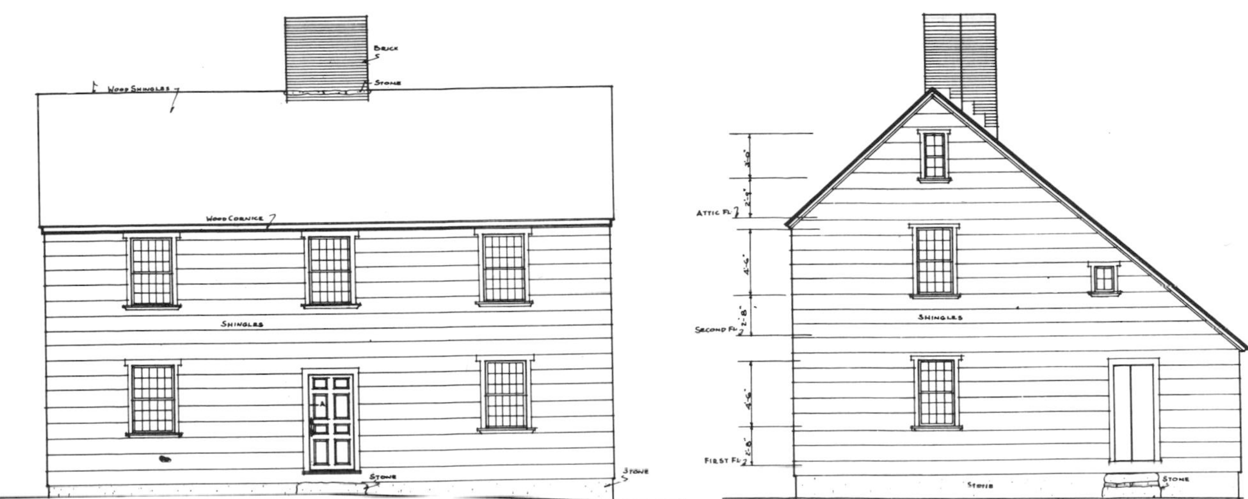

3, 4, 5 Old Ogden House. Fairfield, Connecticut. C.1700. Characteristic of this period in Connecticut and elsewhere in New England: massive central chimney, plank-framed window openings, twelve-over-twelve sash, saltbox profile.

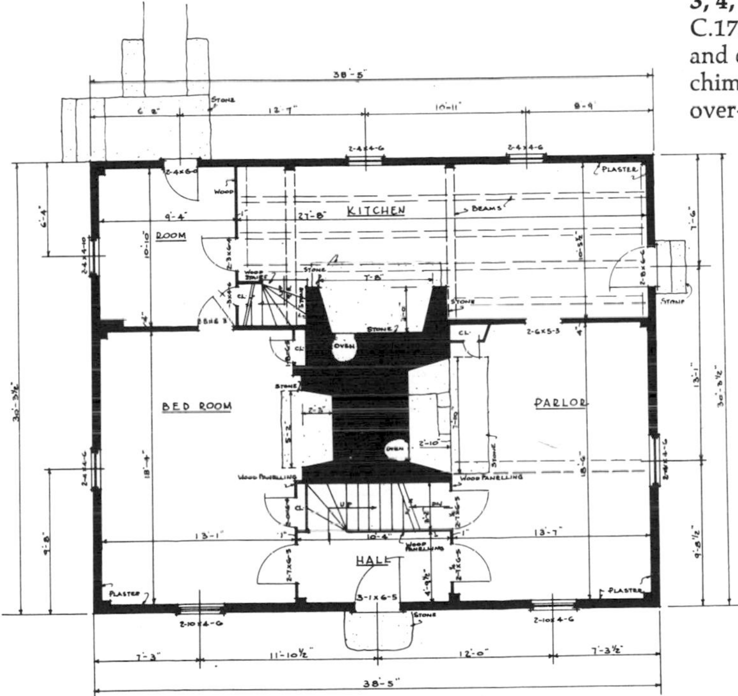

FIRST FLOOR PLAN

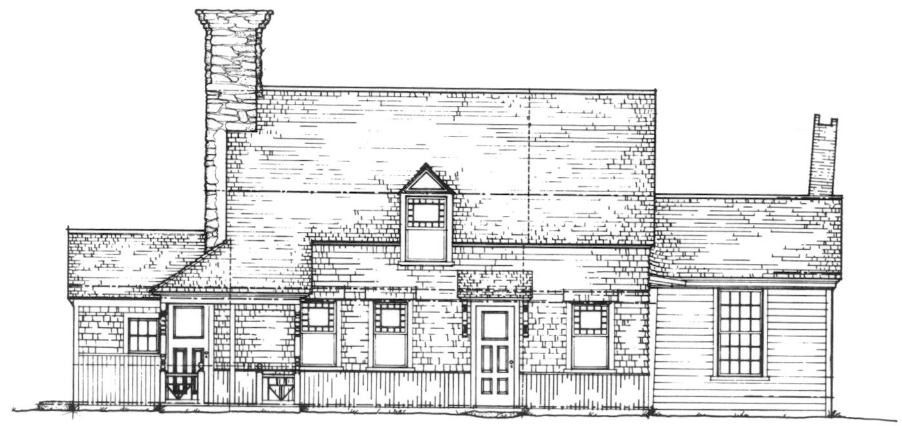

6 Clemence Irons House. Johnston, Rhode Island. 1677, with later sash, dormers, and wings. A type native to the Providence area, with the stone chimney built into the stone end wall, and shingle-clad frame wall front and rear.

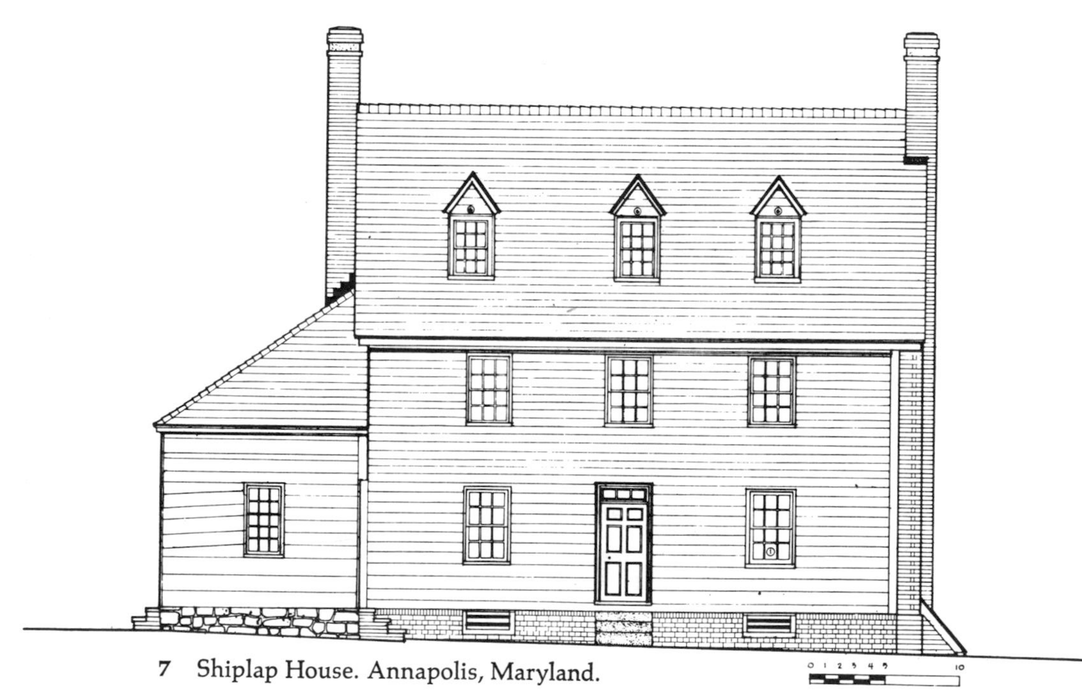

7 Shiplap House. Annapolis, Maryland.

8 Glen Fern. Philadelphia, Pennsylvania. 1733–1739, one-and-one-half-story height; c.1765, roof raised; 1853, ells added. A fine example, in the Delaware Valley vernacular, built of locally quarried schist, with balcony in place of the more typical pent roof.

9 Mayfield. Petersburg vicinity, Virginia. Mid-eighteenth century. A stylish example, with fine proportions and subtle refinements—the molded water table, flat-arch brick door and window openings, eaves detail, and pedimented dormers.

10, 11 Hollingsworth House. Winchester, Virginia. Main section, 1754; door and windows set within cut-masonry relieving arches. Addition, c.1840; openings headed by flat stone lintels.

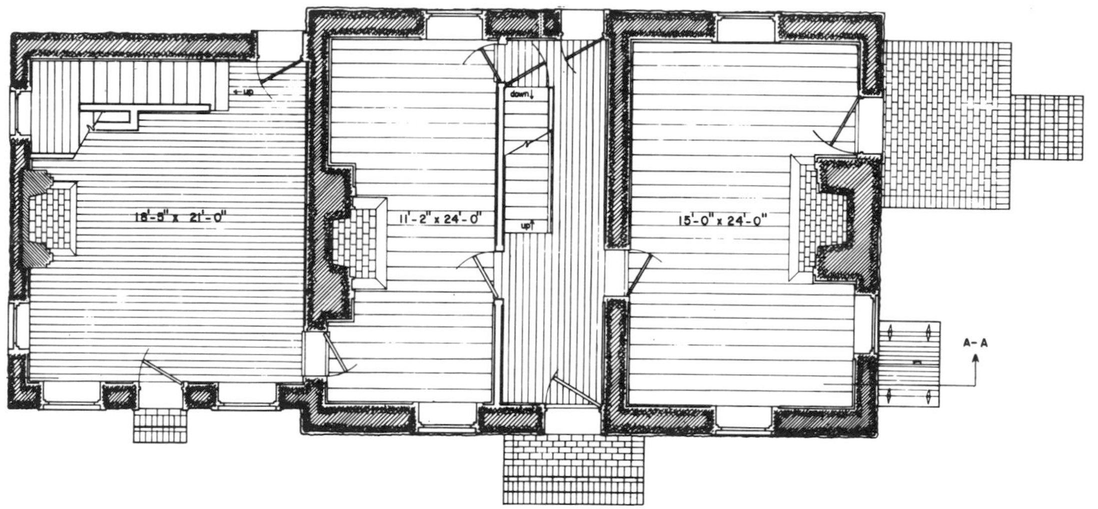

FIRST FLOOR PLAN

12, 13 19 Hussey Street. Nantucket, Massachusetts. 1758; door trim and six-over-six window sash date from the early nineteenth century. The four-bay width of the main section is a Nantucket localism.

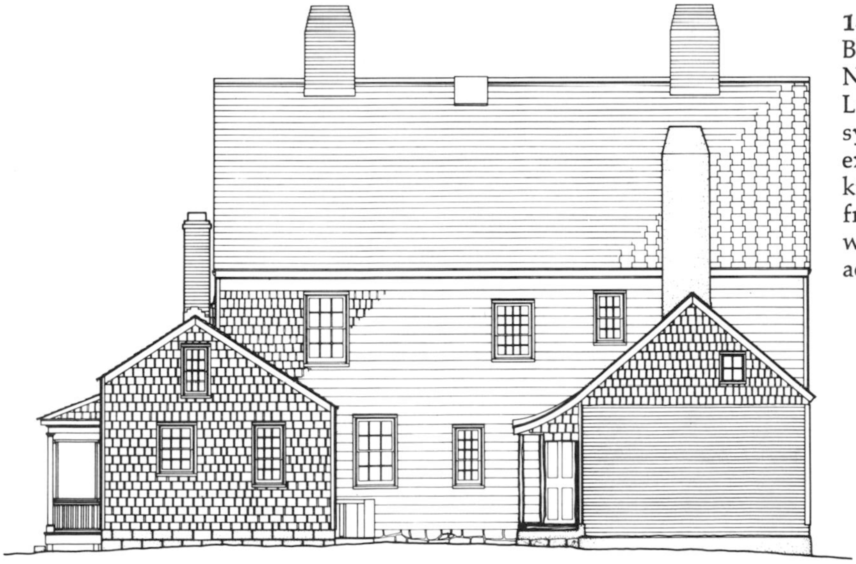

14, 15 Sayrelands. Bridgehampton, Long Island, New York. C.1775. A familiar Long Island type, symmetrically composed except for the protruding kitchen wing, visible on the front elevation. The other wing is a nineteenth-century addition.

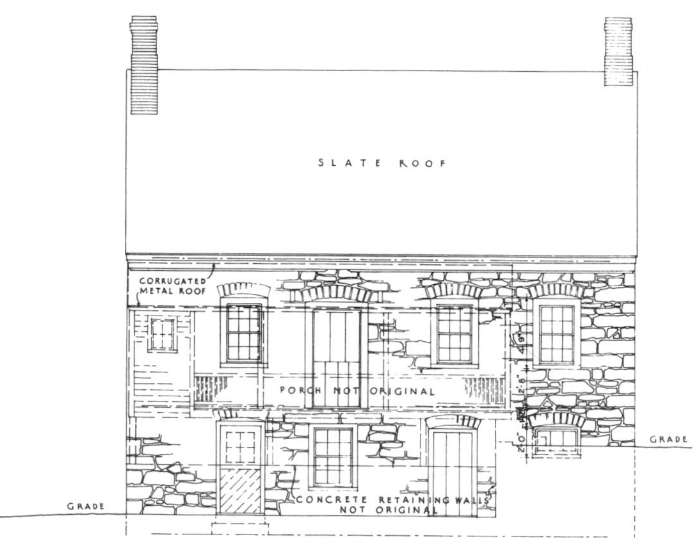

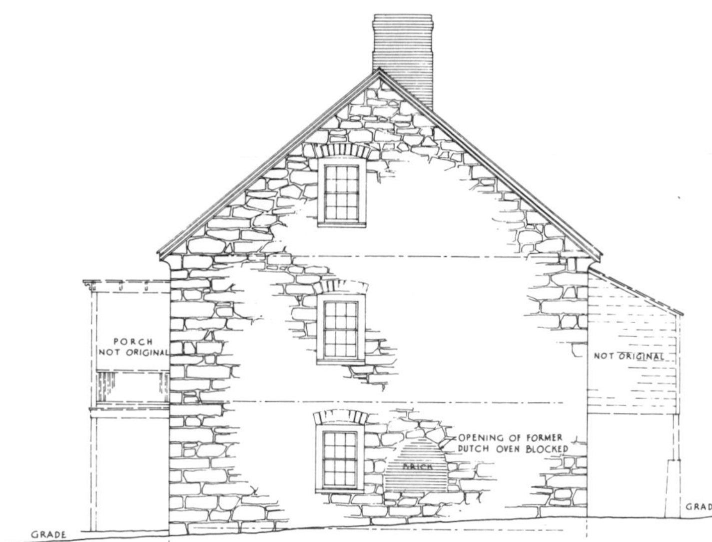

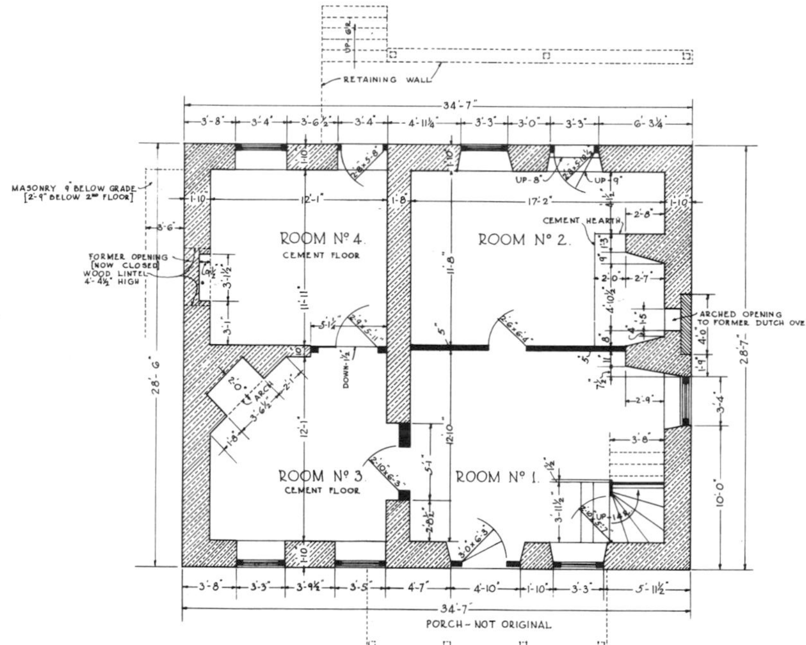

FIRST FLOOR PLAN

16, 17, 18 Moravian Farmhouse. Hope, New Jersey. C.1780. Reflecting German origins are the high attic, thick stone walls, segmentally arched door and window openings, rooms arranged side-by-side without a stair hall.

19, 20 Dyckman House. New York, New York. 1783 rebuilding of an earlier structure; the section at the left built as a bakehouse in 1725. A Dutch Colonial feature is the broad gambrel roof flaring at the ends and extending over projecting porches.

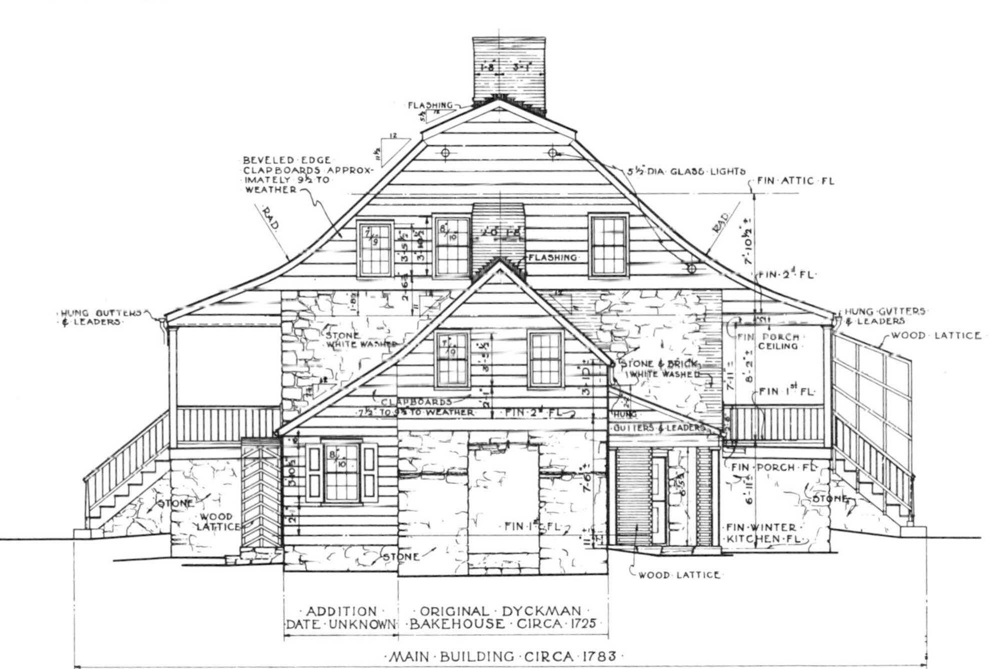

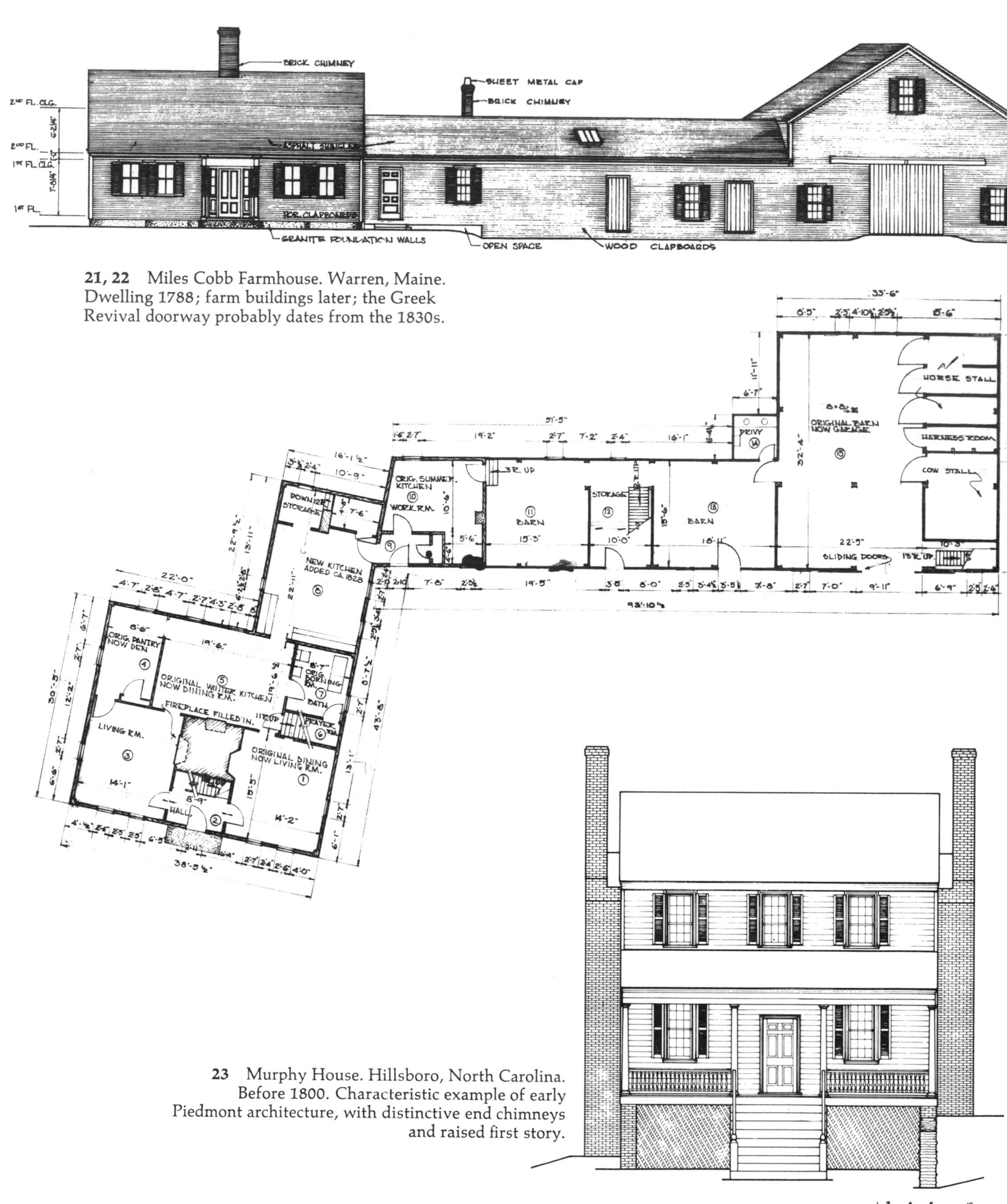

21, 22 Miles Cobb Farmhouse. Warren, Maine. Dwelling 1788; farm buildings later; the Greek Revival doorway probably dates from the 1830s.

23 Murphy House. Hillsboro, North Carolina. Before 1800. Characteristic example of early Piedmont architecture, with distinctive end chimneys and raised first story.

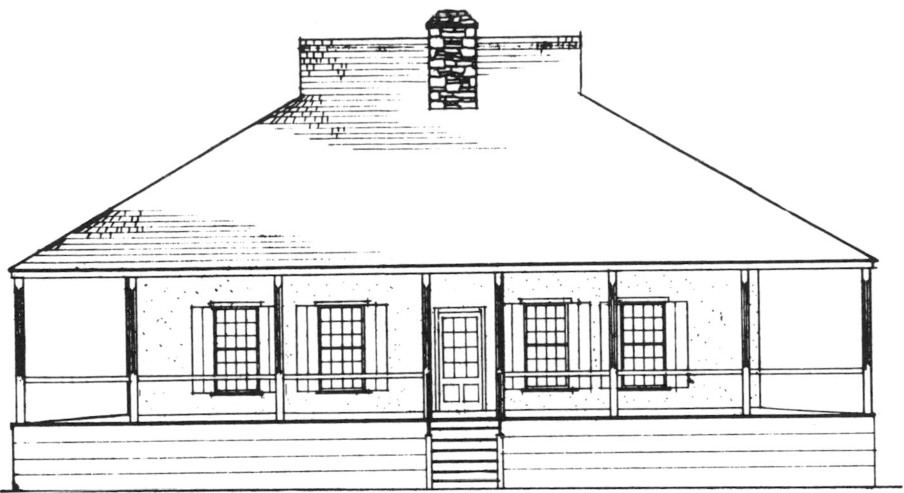

24 J. B. Valle House. Ste. Genevieve, Missouri. C.1800. The high hipped roof, spreading like a parasol to create an encircling porch, is evidence of the French presence in the Mississippi River Valley.

25 Charles Lavalle House. Pensacola, Florida. C.1803. A Gulf Coast cottage, with a deeply recessed porch, gable roof, French windows, brick-pier foundation. The standing-seam sheet-metal roof covering replaces original wood shingles.

26 Washington Historic District. Washington, Kentucky. 1800–1820. Vernacular forms that would appear at home in almost any locale.

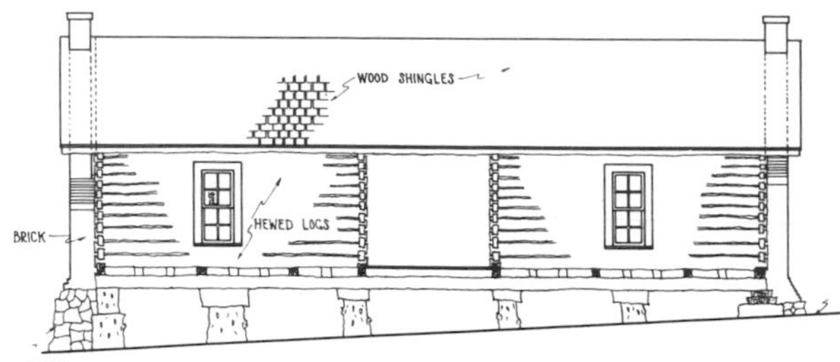

27, 28, 29 James Innes Thornton Plantation servants' quarters. Watsonia, Alabama. 1833. The central breezeway and elevation off the ground are regionalisms that respond to the climate and culture of the Deep South.

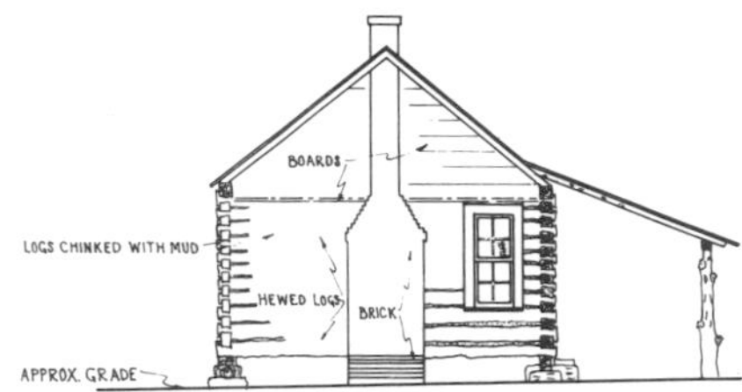

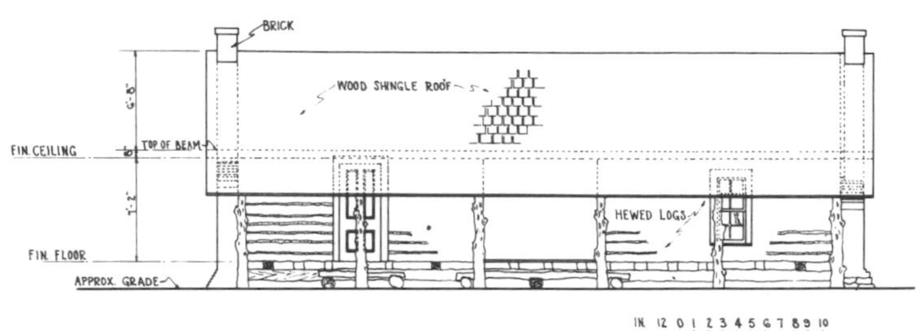

30, 31 El Cerrito. Upper Pecos River Valley, New Mexico. 1810 and later. A fusion of native Indian, Spanish, and American forms, with plaza orientation, stuccoed adobe brick walls, small and irregular wood-framed door and window openings, pitched-roof replacements of original flat roofs.

SHINGLE ROOF
FLOOR LINE
CEILING LINE
TILE ROOF
WOOD SHUTTERS
PLASTER ON ADOBE
CONCRETE STEPS
FLOOR LINE
GRADE LINE

MODERN BRICK CHIMNEY
MODERN BRICK CHIMNEY
MODERN CONCRETE CONSTRUCTION
WOOD SHUTTERS
ARCADE FL. LINE
FLOOR LINE
GRADE LINE
12 6 0 1 2 3 4 5 6 7 8 9 10 11 12 13 14 FT.

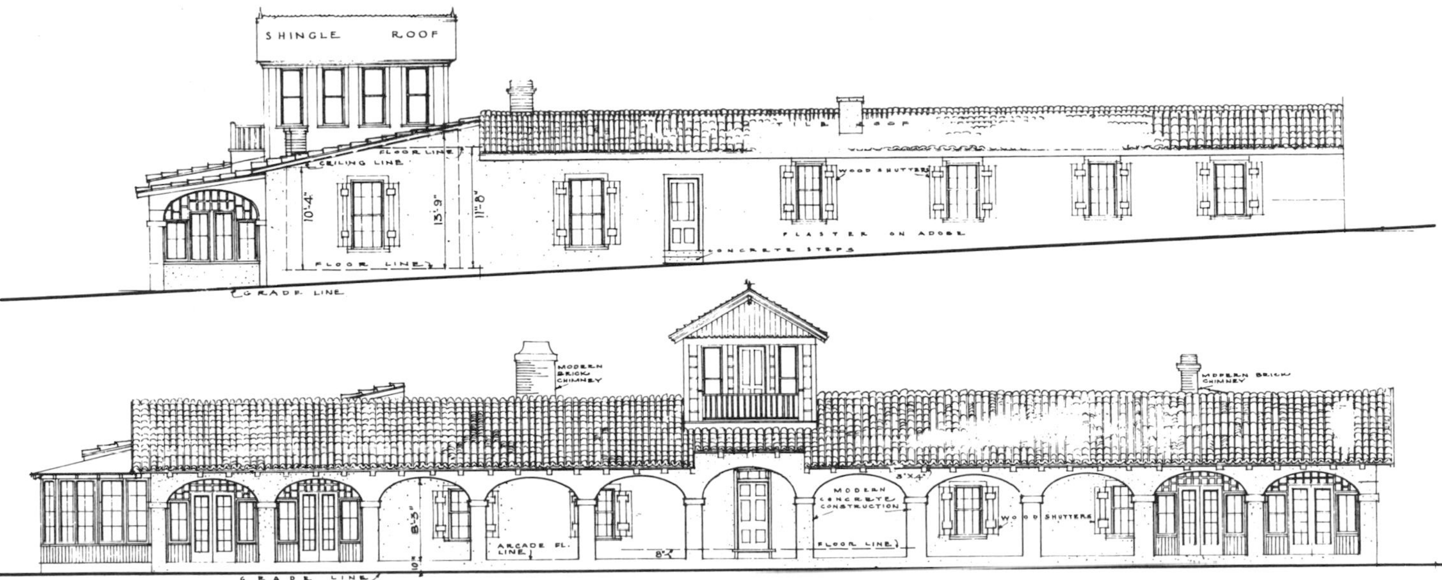

32, 33, 34 La Casa del Rancho. San Luis Rey, California. C.1851. Spanish Colonial features—one-story, patio plan, arcaded veranda, stuccoed adobe walls, and tile roof.

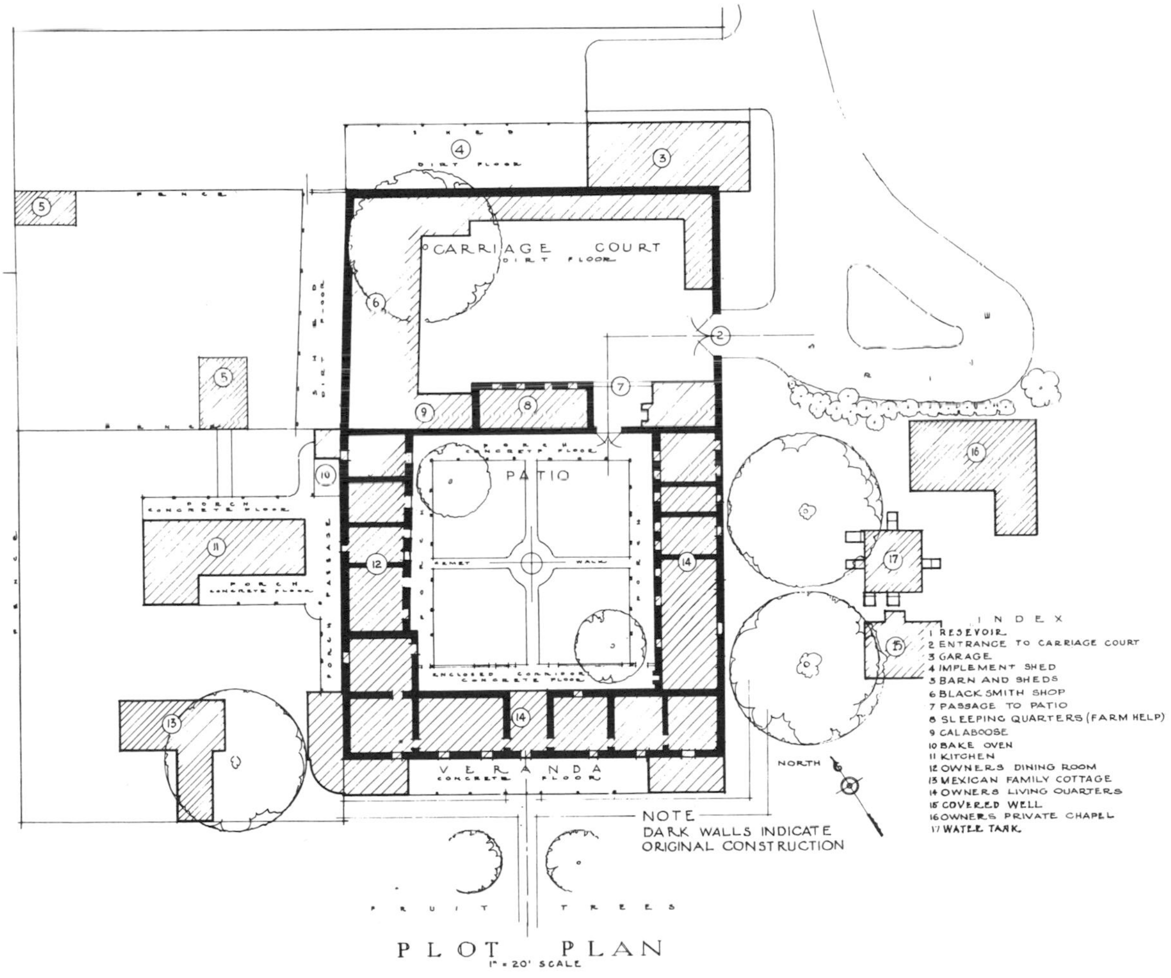
SHED
DIRT FLOOR
FENCE
CARRIAGE COURT
DIRT FLOOR
PORCH CONCRETE FLOOR
PATIO
PORCH CONCRETE FLOOR
PORCH CONCRETE FLOOR
ENCLOSED CORRIDOR CONCRETE FLOOR
VERANDA
CONCRETE FLOOR
NORTH
NOTE
DARK WALLS INDICATE
ORIGINAL CONSTRUCTION
INDEX
1 RESEVOIR
2 ENTRANCE TO CARRIAGE COURT
3 GARAGE
4 IMPLEMENT SHED
5 BARN AND SHEDS
6 BLACKSMITH SHOP
7 PASSAGE TO PATIO
8 SLEEPING QUARTERS (FARM HELP)
9 CALABOOSE
10 BAKE OVEN
11 KITCHEN
12 OWNERS DINING ROOM
13 MEXICAN FAMILY COTTAGE
14 OWNERS LIVING QUARTERS
15 COVERED WELL
16 OWNERS PRIVATE CHAPEL
17 WATER TANK
FRUIT TREES
PLOT PLAN
1" = 20' SCALE

1735-1790

Georgian

DURING the eighteenth century, having achieved fair mastery of the *essentials* of living, America turned her attention to the *arts* of living. That time was "most honorable to human nature," wrote John Adams to Thomas Jefferson. "Knowledge and virtue was increased and diffused; arts, sciences, useful to man, ameliorating their condition, were improved more than in any former equal period."

Principles began to govern pragmatism. Urbane and sophisticated architecture was nourished by a venerable literary tradition that extended back to the first-century Roman architect-engineer Vitruvius, whose *Ten Books of Architecture* recorded ancient principles of construction, proportion, and ornament. Popularized in the Renaissance by Palladio and Serlio, and revived by the English architects who flourished during the reigns of the first three Georges, this tradition found a receptive audience in America. Books such as Colin Campbell's *Vitruvius Britannicus* (1716) and James Gibbs' *A Book of Architecture* (1728) could be found in the gentleman's library.

Providing simpler designs, Batty Langley's *City and Country Builder's and Workman's Treasury of Designs* (1740) was more likely to be owned by a carpenter. Reports from abroad as well as a midcentury wave of immigrants—artisans and craftsmen among them—further fired popular enthusiasm and demand for an architecture with "style."

Mirroring the civilizing changes in American society since the first breaching of the wilderness, the new dwellings were well proportioned, composed for formal effect, and—from plinth to pediment—embellished with robust ornament.

This was the style for cultured and comfortable Americans—city dwellers in Newport, Boston, New York, Philadelphia, Annapolis, Williamsburg, or Charleston and gentlemen farmers on riverfront plantations in Virginia and the Carolinas, on manors in Maryland and Pennsylvania, and on large estates in New York and New England. And, in a more modest scale, in a simple form, and with cautious embellishment, this was the style for artisan, trader, and farmer.

Most significantly, from the Savannah River to Ipswich Bay the spread and success of the new style were clear signals that America would no longer be satisfied with second-class status.

Materials

Clapboard (painted in cheerful tones of blue, green, salmon, or yellow) can be associated with early Georgian architecture. The hallmark of the mature Georgian style is its fine brickwork, rose or salmon in color against fairly wide joints of white lime mortar. Frequently, bricks are laid in the Flemish-bond pattern of alternating headers (ends) and stretchers (sides). Another popular decorative pattern is the English bond, formed by alternate courses of headers and stretchers. The trim is usually wood, vigorously carved to produce pleasant shadows.

In rural New England, clapboard—now cut in narrower boards—remains popular. Fieldstone is characteristic of rural Pennsylvania and the Hudson River Valley. Brass hardware becomes more common.

Dr. Upton Scott House, Annapolis, Maryland; 1762–1765 (see 41, p. 23).

Plan

Regional differences are diminished in importance. Determined by principles of formal composition, the house plan evolves to a compact and approximately square shape. The four rooms on the main floor—two front and two back—are of about equal size and flank a central stair hall that extends through the depth of the house [47]. In the largest houses the stairway may be in a hall perpendicular to the main hall [36].

The urban dwelling (particularly as a row house) may be only one room in width with a side stair hall, and two, three, or more rooms in depth [50].

Elevation

In the evolution of the Georgian style in America, a novel vocabulary of ornament, a sophisticated system of proportions, and reasoned principles of design are introduced (circa 1735–1760), assimilated (circa 1760–1775) and developed (circa 1775–1790). It should be recalled that "Georgian"—as opposed to "Colonial"—is essentially a high-style tradition.

During the early phase, new ornamental vocabulary is displayed like a trophy. The doorway has an insistent emphasis—set off within a central pavilion (projecting element) [35], and/or by a Classical enframement consisting of columns or pilasters supporting a pediment [37; 38]. The basement, usually low, may be indicated by a water table (sloped horizontal ledge) [35]. Floor levels may be indicated by courses, although they do not extend as far as the corners of the building. As on the Colonial dwelling, the eaves are close over the second-story window, but now they are decorated with fuller moldings.

The development progresses toward even bays (division of space between windows or doors); five bays are typical. Windows have nine-over-nine or twelve-over-twelve lights, and are headed by segmental arches [38], stone lintels with carved keystones [35], or triangular pediments [37].

The dwelling is less vertical in character. The roof has a lower pitch, a gambrel shape (double pitch from eaves to ridge) [38, 39], or is hipped (sloped inward on all four sides) [35]. Chimneys (there may be as many as four) are symmetrically placed, usually at the end walls.

In the progression of style through the middle years of the eighteenth century, ornament is more fully integrated into the composition and proportions are more consistently horizontal. A rich visual effect is achieved by virtuoso wood carving and paneling. The entry is a major design element. Culminating a flight of steps [40], it may be set within a portico or a projecting pavilion which itself is crowned by a triangular pediment [40; 41].

An increasingly common urban form is the Georgian row house, three bays wide (with or without a passageway to a rear service wing) and with restrained ornamental detailing [48; 49].

For the freestanding dwelling, formal expression of structure may be an emphatic water table, coursing which continues to the ends of the building, and quoins (articulated stone or brick blocks at a corner) [40]. The eaves and the top of the wall are treated as a cornice (a crowning unit with multiple moldings that follow a Classical prototype). This may include emphatic modillions (blocklike brackets) [41], smaller dentils (toothlike moldings [44]), and carved ornament [43].

Windowpanes are larger and the progression is toward six-over-six lights. Window openings are defined by architraves (enframing mouldings) and are headed by flat arches in brick or stone, or by small, usually flat pediments [43]. Another stylish feature is a version of the Palladian motif (tripartite window or door treatment, consisting of an arched central element flanked by lower square-headed elements) [40; 42].

The hipped roof is the paradigm; it may be crowned at its apex by a balustrade [40].

The mature Georgian style of the later eighteenth century reduces ornament, refines proportions, and emphasizes harmonious relationships. The façade is flat, the doorway—reduced in size—is well integrated in the total composition. Decorative carving is restrained and simplified [48; 51; 52]. Over the door, a decorative arched (or sometimes a rectangular) light is nearly universal, even on the humble vernacular structure [53].

35, 36 Sabine Hall. Richmond County, Virginia. C.1735. Despite a lingering medieval verticality, this exceptionally fine residence has conspicuous early Georgian ornamentation: a formal entrance set off by rusticated stone; Flemish-bond brickwork; pediment at the eaves.

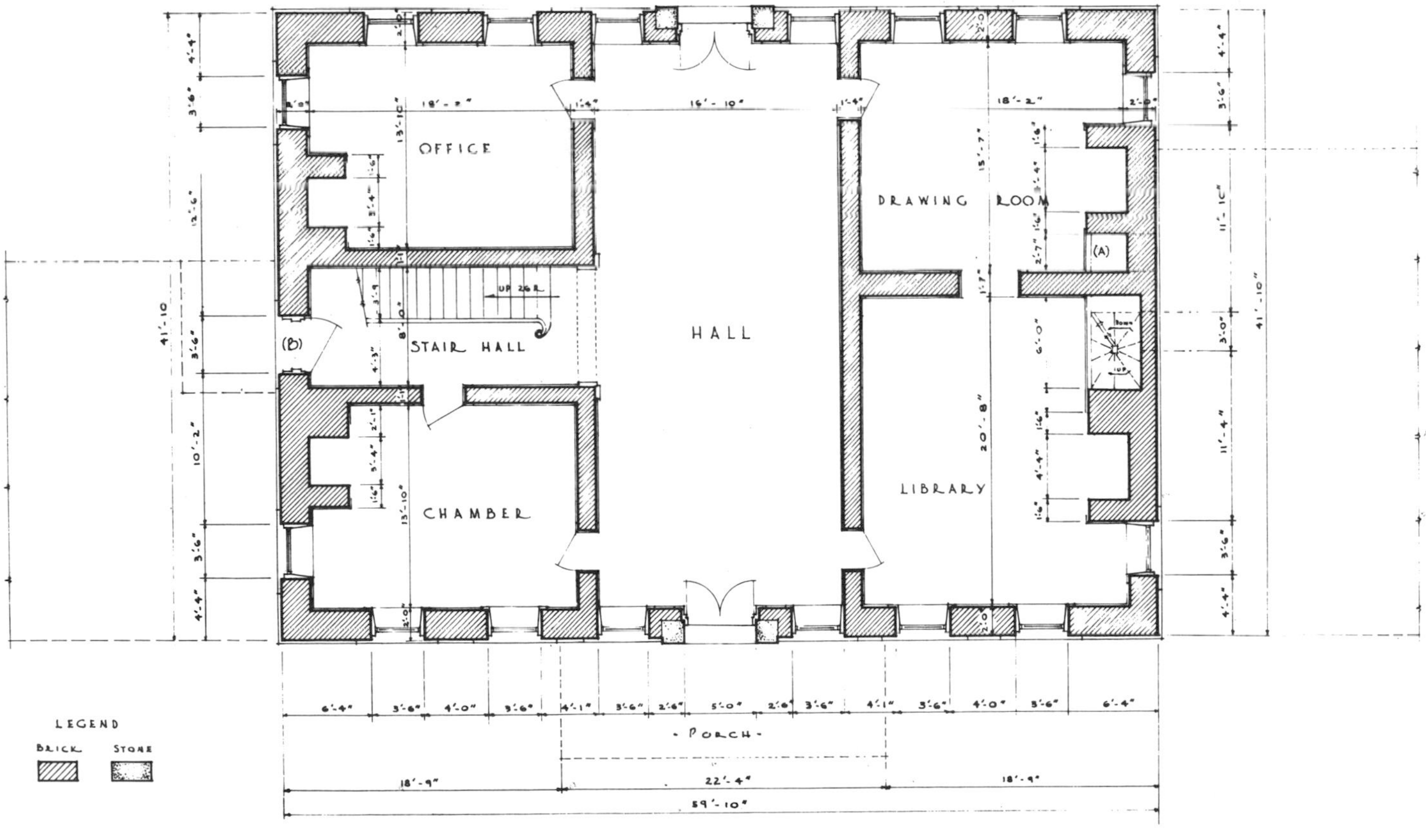

FIRST FLOOR PLAN

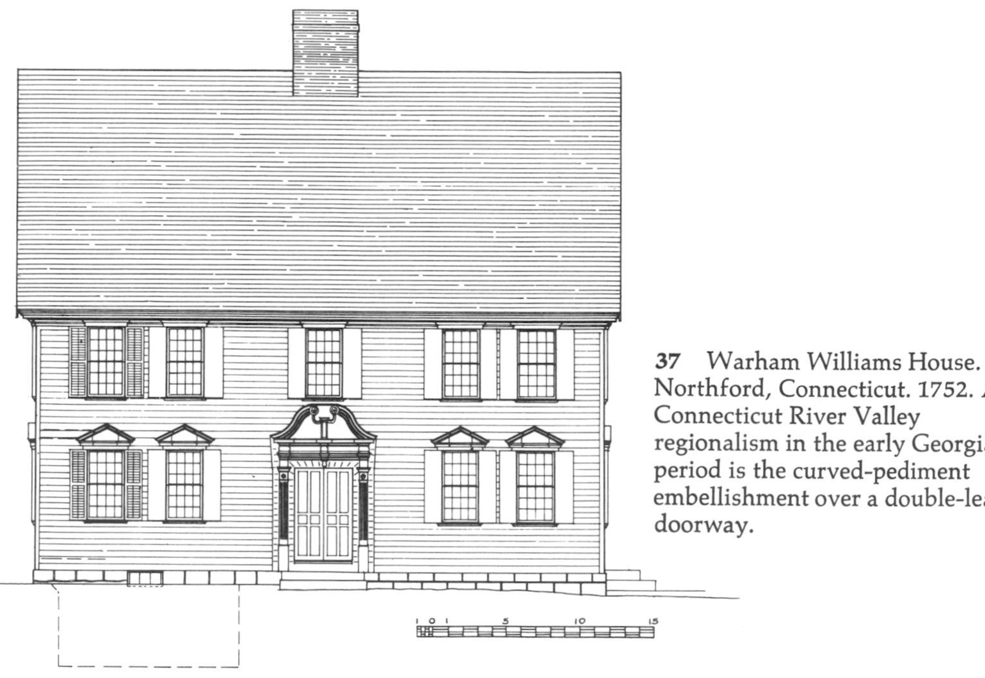

37 Warham Williams House. Northford, Connecticut. 1752. A Connecticut River Valley regionalism in the early Georgian period is the curved-pediment embellishment over a double-leaved doorway.

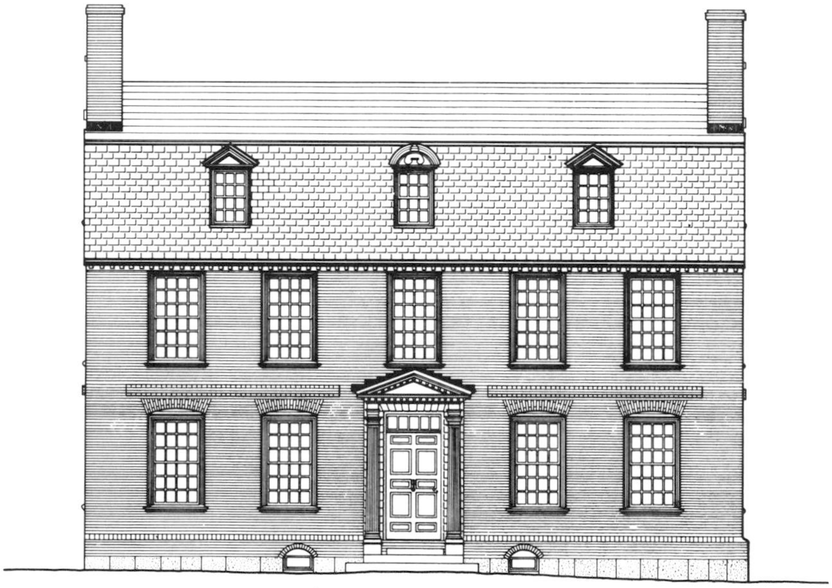

38, 39 Derby House. Salem, Massachusetts. 1762. An elaborate early Georgian townhouse, with pilasters flanking the entry, pedimented dormers, modillion blocks at the eaves.

40 Mt. Pleasant Mansion. Philadelphia, Pennsylvania. 1761. Philadelphia Georgian—the most elaborate in the colonies. Notable features are high basement, central pavilion, elaborate window heads, and roof balustrade. Fieldstone and brick are stuccoed to resemble smooth stone.

41 Dr. Upton Scott House. Annapolis, Maryland. 1762–1765. Attributed to William Buckland, a carpenter-architect noted for his masterly woodwork trim. Window sash is later.

0 5 10 15 20 FT

42 Ford House. Morristown, New Jersey. 1772. The horizontal proportions and wide entrance hall are characteristic of this date and locale. Although it would seem to be an addition, the kitchen wing is probably contemporary with the main section.

43 Rock Hall. Lawrence, New York. 1764. Note the elaborate Chippendale-design roof balustrade.

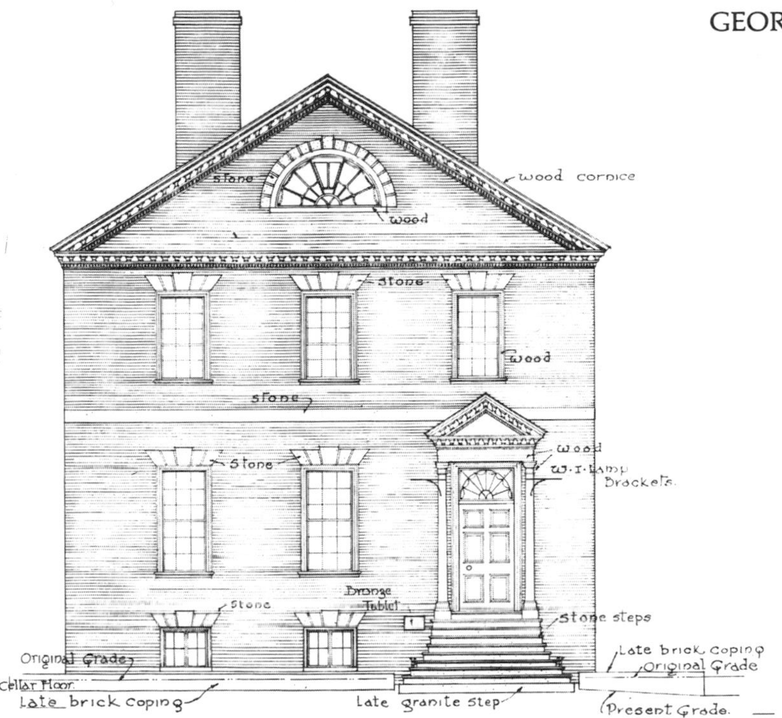

44, 45 Whittle House. Norfolk, Virginia. 1791. Sophisticated late-Georgian design is manifest in the pediment treatment of gable end and delicacy of ornamentation.

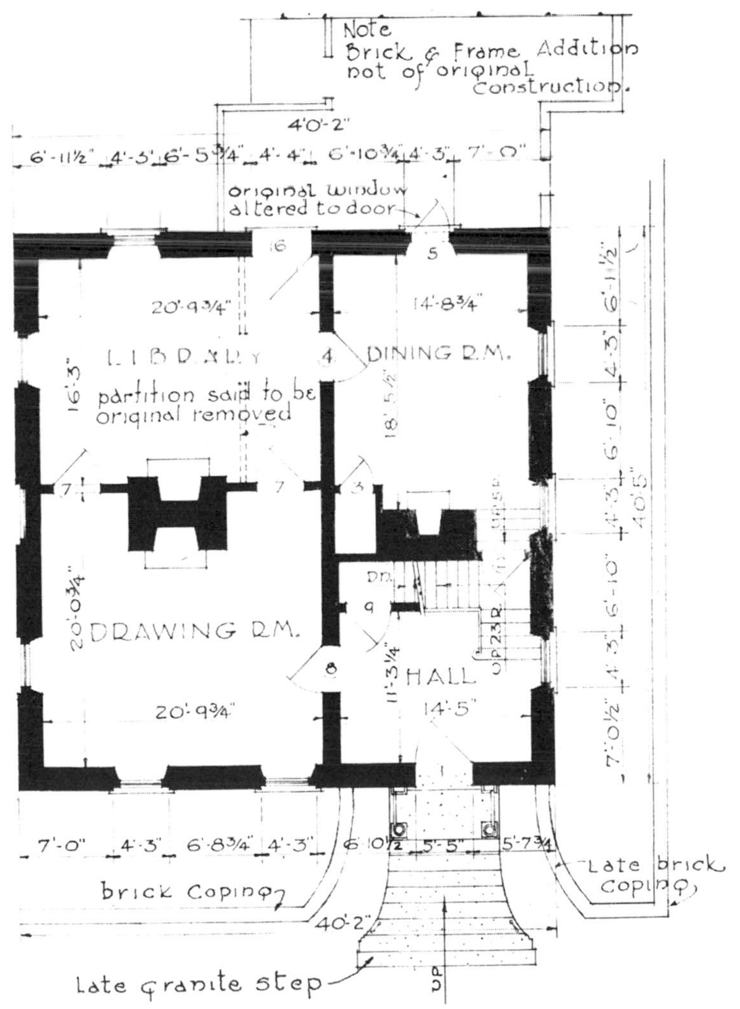

FIRST FLOOR PLAN

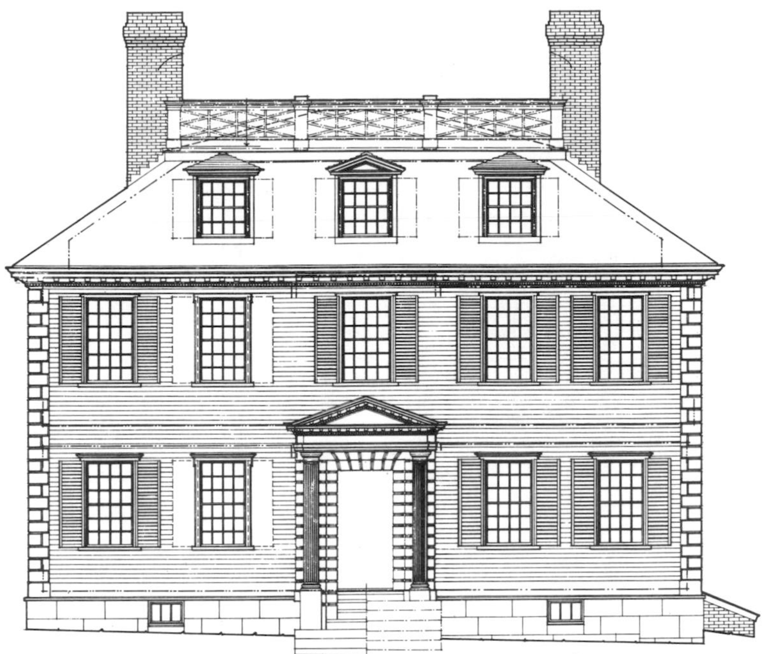

46, 47 Benjamin Hall, Jr., House. Medford, Massachusetts. 1785. Georgian style in a New England town: ample scale; high, cut-stone basement; wood-frame construction; columned, pedimented entry; corner quoins, with wood used in imitation of stone; cornice treatment of eaves; high hipped roof with balustrade at deck. The door, here missing, would have been paneled.

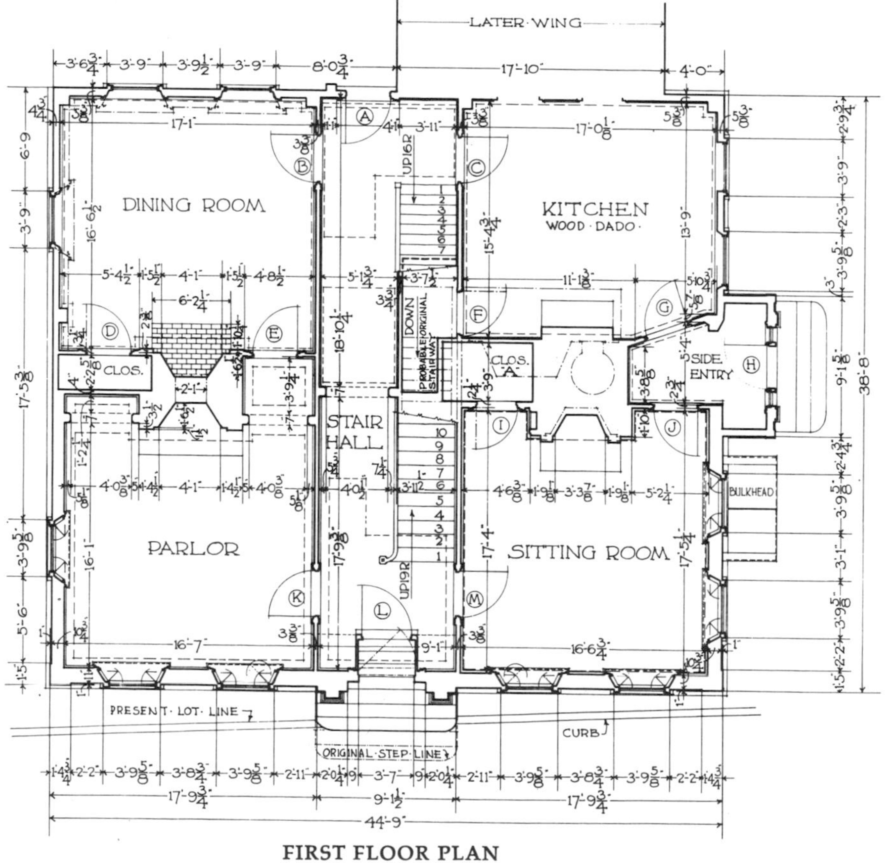

FIRST FLOOR PLAN

48 Wharton House, Hopkinson House. Philadelphia, Pennsylvania. Above left, 1790. Above right, c.1775. Two stages in Philadelphia Georgian row-house design.

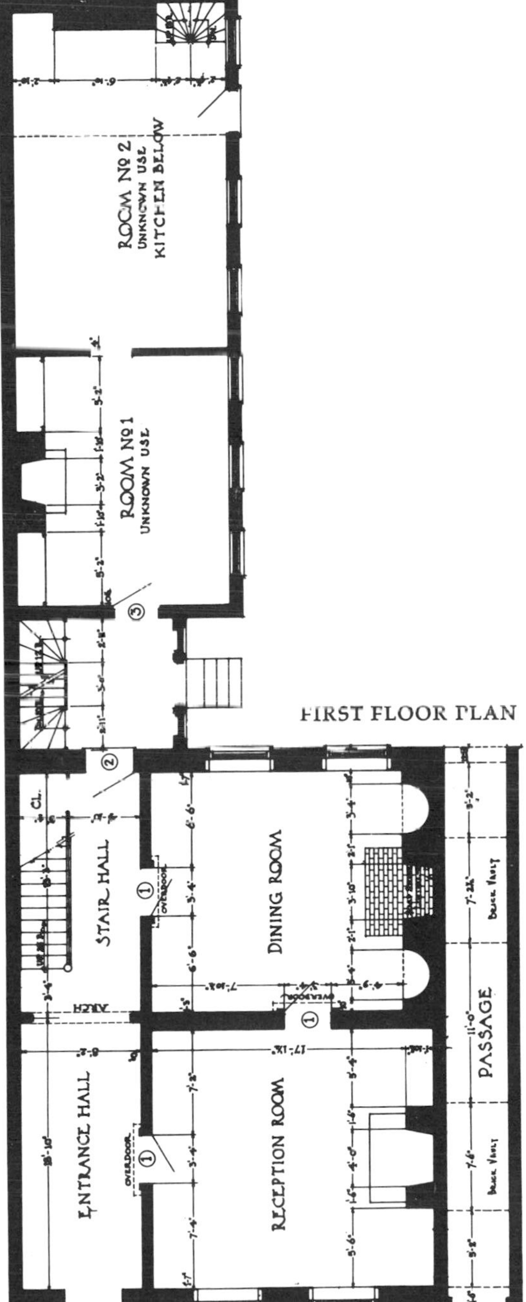

49, 50 1621 Thames Street. Baltimore, Maryland. 1798 remodeling of 1760s structure.

51 Chancellor Kensey Johns House. Newcastle, Delaware. 1790. A combination house and office, with handsome woodworking and Flemish-bond brickwork.

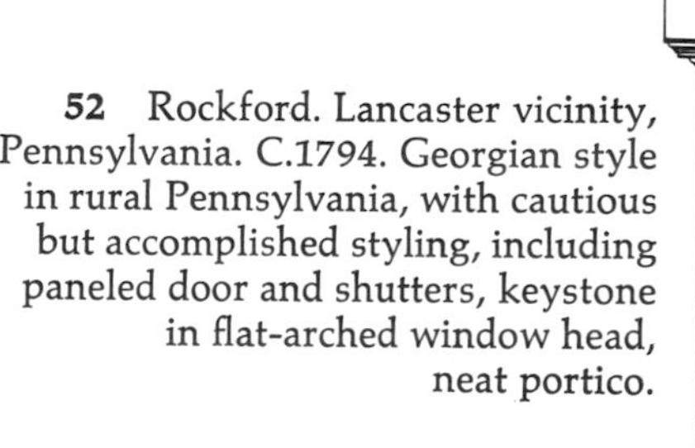

52 Rockford. Lancaster vicinity, Pennsylvania. C.1794. Georgian style in rural Pennsylvania, with cautious but accomplished styling, including paneled door and shutters, keystone in flat-arched window head, neat portico.

53 Vandenburgh-Hasbrouck House. Kingston, New York. C.1780. A Hudson River Valley vernacular townhouse with Georgian paneled door and fanlight.

1790-1820
Federal

"IN Baltimore, as in the other cities, merchants occupy the highest social position; the ship captains are just below," observed a traveler in 1800. "Many ship captains manage to accumulate huge fortunes, profiting from their dauntlessness and their willingness to risk their lives wherever there is a prospect of making money." But if daring in action, these self-made merchants, bankers, traders, and shipbuilders—principally identified with the Federalist party—were conservative in attitude. As before the War of Independence, they looked to England for cultural leadership.

So it is hardly surprising to see that the mansion of Salem shipbuilder, Philadelphia banker, or Charlestown planter-trader echoed the style popularized in London a generation earlier by architect-decorator Robert Adam. This refined the proportions of the Georgian house and borrowed ornamental motifs like the urn, garland, and festoon from the recently excavated Roman country houses in Pompeii and Herculaneum.

These dwellings—in the style known in America as Federal—are characterized by balance and symmetry in design, lightness and elegance in mood, delicacy and finesse in execution.

In these early years of nationhood the sense of American identity demanded an American architecture for the common man as well as the privileged. Though closely derived from contemporary English handbooks, Asher Benjamin's influential builder's guide, *The American Builder's Companion: or a New System of Architecture Particularly Adapted to the Present Style of Building in the United States of America,* published in Boston in 1806, declared American cultural independence and social egalitarianism. Architecture in America must be different from architecture in Europe, the author asserted. Americans had different materials to work with, less use for decoration, and a need to economize on labor and materials.

The goal for American architecture was clear: to bring comfort, dignity, and quality to *all* classes—in townhouses in eastern port cities, artisans' dwellings in new grid-plan towns, farmhouses in the hinterlands, cottages on the moving frontier. "Architecture is worth great attention," Jefferson declared. "As we double our numbers every twenty years, we must double our houses. . . . It is then, among the most important arts; and it is desirable to introduce taste into an art which shows so much."

Materials

Most high-style and many urban dwellings are built of brick, laid in Flemish bond. Frame dwellings are sheathed in overlapping clapboard or smooth-fitted matchboard, painted in white or pastel colors. Hardware is more delicate; brass and iron may be used in combination. Fence and rail—in wood or iron—are employed as decorative features.

Plan

The most elaborate residences, particularly in the South, are composed of a central block with flanking wings; the plan may also be laterally extended by the addition of connectors between the wings [54; 55]. But the simple rectangular plan is usual—long side facing the street with the entrance in the center when freestanding, short side to the street and the entrance on one side when in a row. The Charleston house is unique in plan—a single room in width with an open porch along its length [59].

Although the four-room plan, with two rectangular rooms from front to rear on each side of a central stair hall, remains typical, interiors show more variety in the shape, size, and location of rooms. The oval or elliptical shape—hallmark of the Federal style—sometimes appears as a stair hall or a projecting bay [55]. Dwellings may be two, three, or four stories in height.

Elevation

Compared to robust late Georgian design, Federal proportions and ornamental vocabulary are elegant and refined.

Surfaces are treated as thin, with shallow projections and delicate nonarchitectonic embellishments such as festoons [56; 63].

On the most elaborate examples, the basement is high, with graceful single or paired stairway leading to the entrance [54; 56; 57]. The doorway is wide and tall and the door is usually flanked by side lights and headed by a fanlight. There may be a portico with complete Classical order (column with base, shaft, and capital supporting an entablature, which consists of architrave moldings, frieze, and cornice). See p. 44 for illustration.

Window openings are spacious, lights are significantly larger, and muntins are thinly drawn. A characteristic Federal motif is the window set within a recessed arch [54; 56]. Cut-stone lintels have refined detailing, with splayed ends and projecting keystones [57]. Windows may also be capped by an entablature [56; 63].

The hipped roof is characteristic—tall in the South for coolness, low in New England and concealed by a balustrade for elegance [56]. The cornice barely projects beyond the eaves, and moldings are reduced in size and scale. Chimneys, smaller, narrower, and rectangular in shape, are located near the end walls.

The Palladian motif that belonged to the Georgian period finds its way to rural New England [63]. The simplest dwellings may be Federal in character, although ornament is minimal [60].

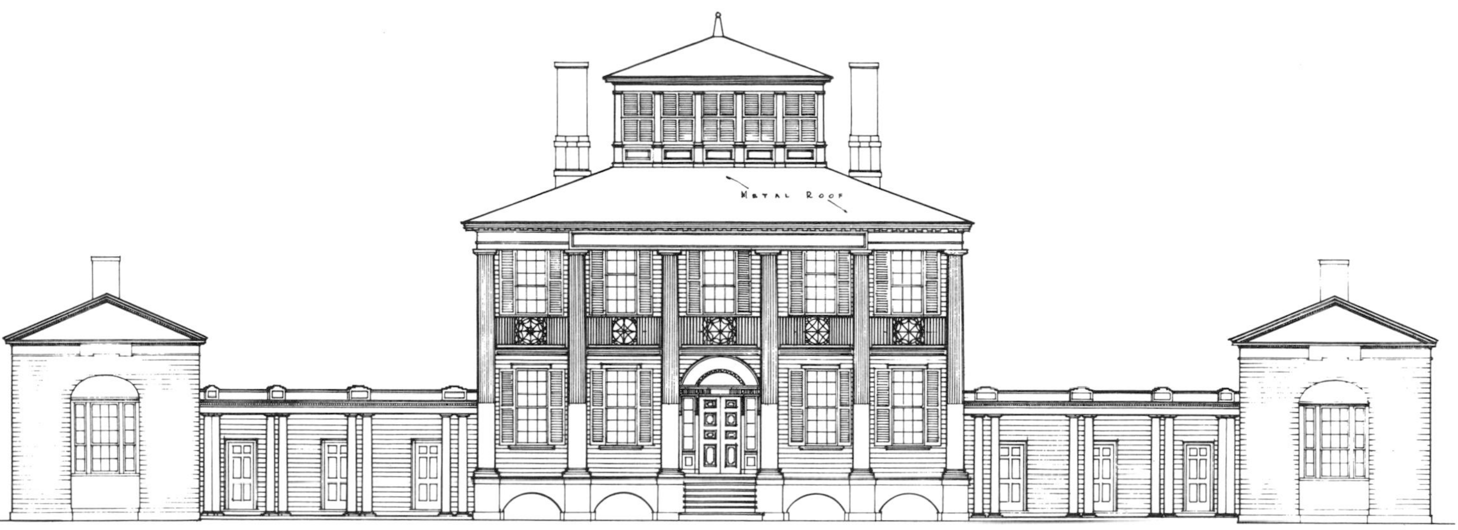

54, 55 Hayes Manor. Edenton, North Carolina. 1815. Lively rhythms distinguish Federal composition; note the alternation of flat and arched openings and the variety in room size and shape.

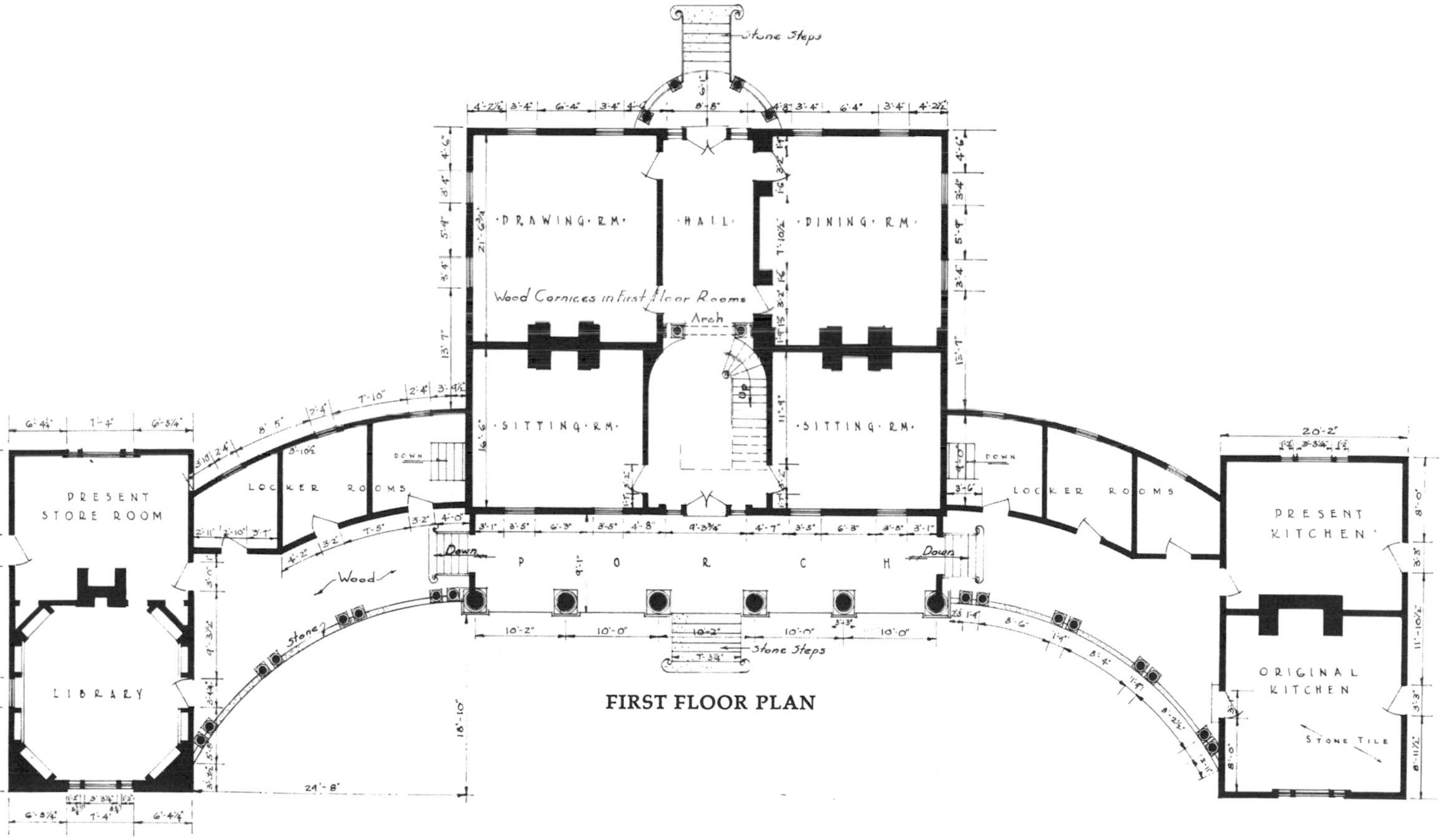

Stone Steps
DRAWING RM
HALL
DINING RM
Wood Cornices in First Floor Rooms
Arch
SITTING RM
SITTING RM
PRESENT STORE ROOM
LOCKER ROOMS
LOCKER ROOMS
DOWN
DOWN
PRESENT KITCHEN
Down
PORCH
Down
Wood
Stone
LIBRARY
Stone Steps
ORIGINAL KITCHEN
STONE TILE

FIRST FLOOR PLAN

56 Amory Ticknor House. Boston, Massachusetts. 1804. An impressive Federal townhouse: chimneys narrow and at the end walls, a pair of curving stairs, a well-proportioned portico at the entrance, fanlight above the doorway, first-story windows set within recessed arches, diminished ceiling heights at the upper stories, balustrade at the eaves.

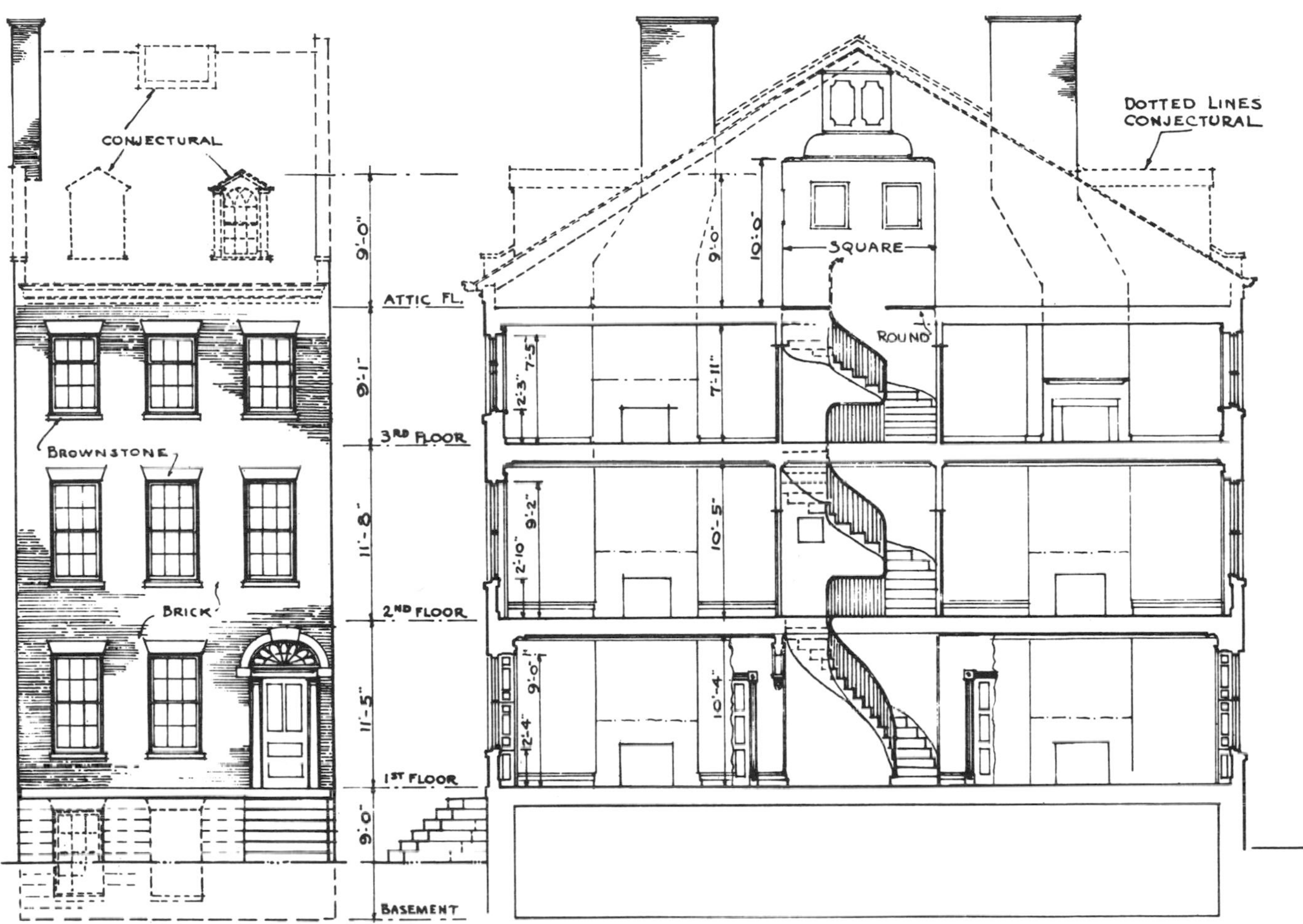

57, 58 8 Greenwich Street. New York, New York. 1807–1808. A Federal row house. Note the delicately curved stairs and rails that are seen in the longitudinal section.

59 Gadsden House. Charleston, South Carolina. C.1800. The tall windows at the second story indicate the location of the principal reception rooms—high enough to capture cooling breezes from Charleston's bay.

Gadsden House, Charleston, South Carolina; c. 1800 (see 59).

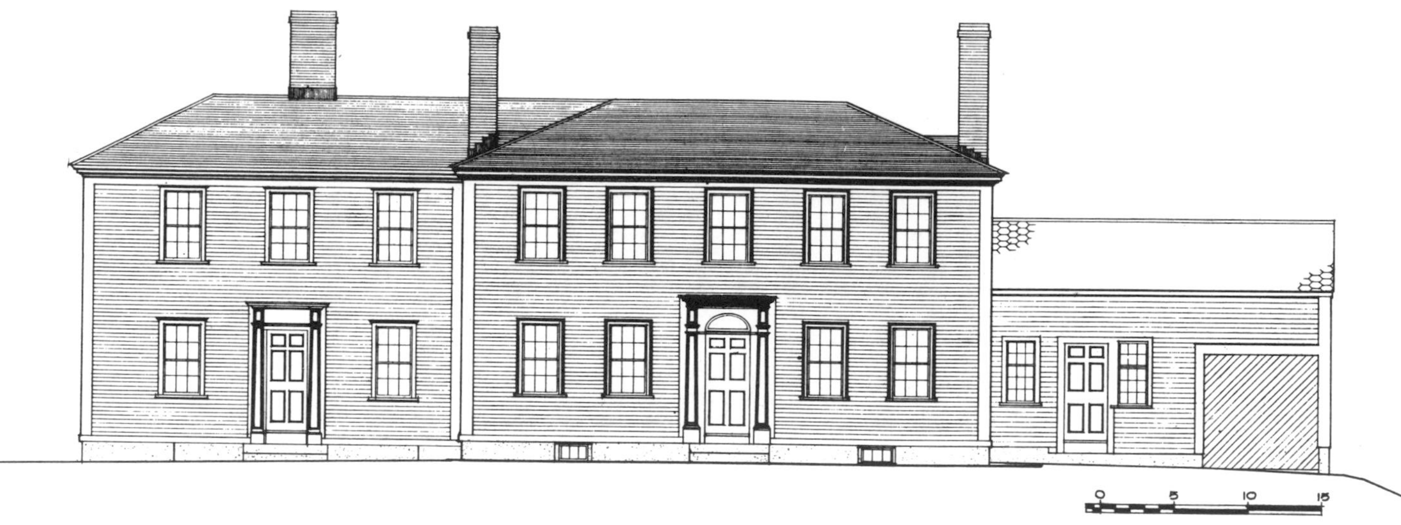

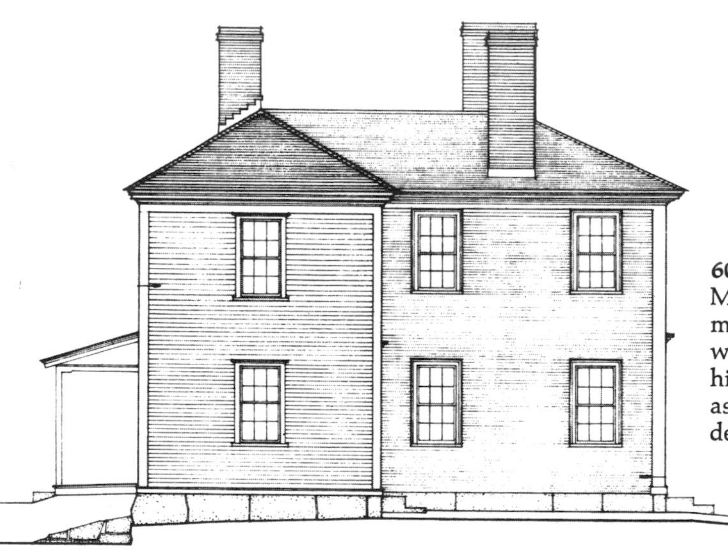

60, 61, 62 John Nelson House. Lincoln, Massachusetts. 1811 and later. A Federal mood can be detected in the narrow, well-proportioned end chimneys and low hipped roof, despite the additive, assymmetrical composition and blunt detailing.

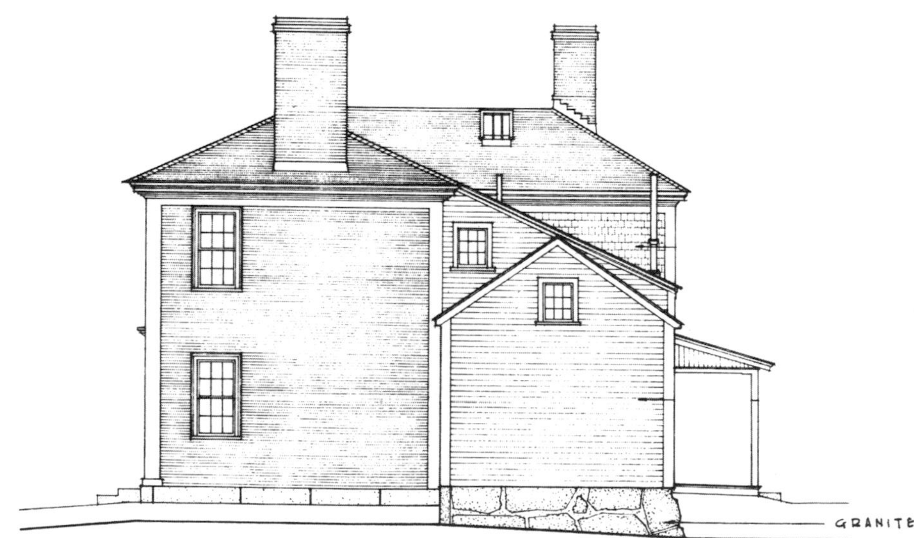

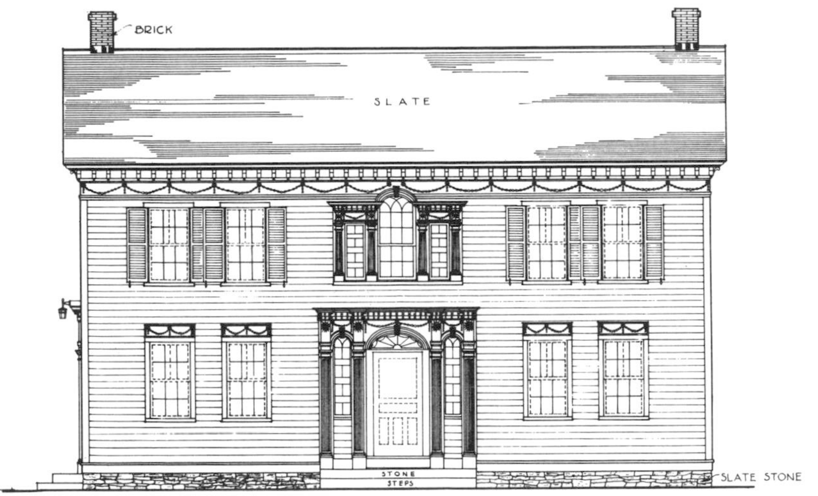

63 Harris House. Castleton, Vermont. C.1800. Garbed with Federal ornament, a dwelling whose uneven window spacing typifies the long persistence of older tradition in rural areas.

Josiah Harris House, Castleton, Vermont; c. 1800.

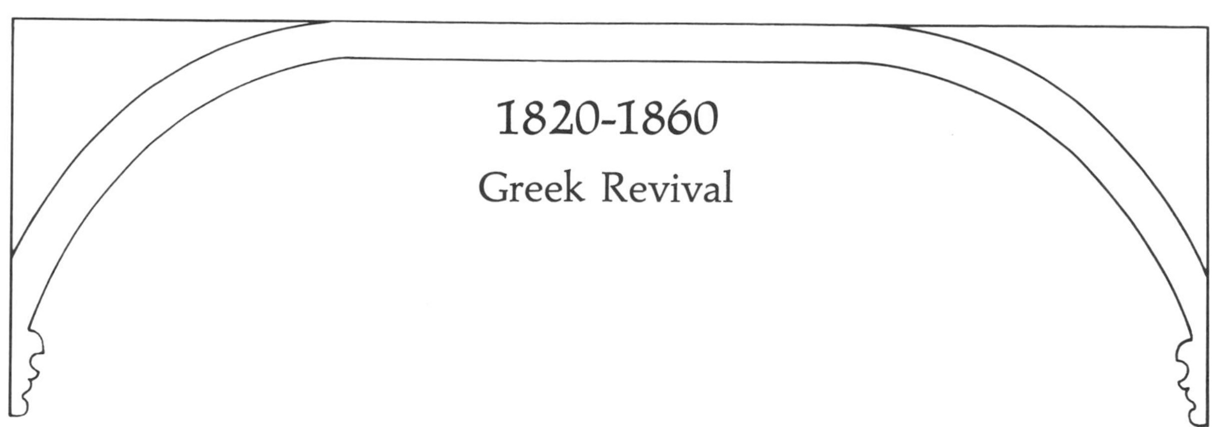

1820-1860

Greek Revival

IN the 1820s, American admiration for Greece reached a burning intensity—sparked by her valiant struggle against the Turks and fueled by a new understanding of the vigor of her ancient culture. In the spirit of Greek architecture Jacksonian America found its aesthetic ideal.

Minard Lafever (in his *Young Builder's General Instructor*, published in Newark in 1829 and one of the most influential of the many builder's guides that popularized ornament and construction details for Greek Revival architecture) extolled a temple in Athens—known to him only through books—for the "elegant base of the columns," the "grand" proportions of the entablature, the "spacious surface of the frieze," and the "strength" of its appearance.

To a nation that was optimistic, expansive, idealistic, and mindful of posterity, the Greek Revival brought an architecture of beauty, breadth, simplicity, and permanence.

Greek Revival architecture offered a Classical vocabulary that was versatile enough to express both regional vernacular and urbane design concepts, and a mood that was romantic as well as rational.

Above all, Greek Revival was the language of a nation that welcomed innovation and aspired to greatness. "Must man progress in goodness and wisdom? Then, must architecture also!" a Baltimore architect declared. "Architecture must manifest the changes that are taking place in society, the greater ones, we hope and believe, that are yet to come."

In these years, Texas, Kansas, Iowa, and Minnesota were opened to settlement. The nation's population grew from 10 million to 31 million; her western boundary met the Pacific. The Greek Revival style was written across the face of a continent.

Materials

The frame dwelling—painted white—is ubiquitous. The "better" house is brick, trimmed with wood or ashlar (square-cut) granite, sandstone, or marble.

Columns are almost invariably wood, usually hollow. Decorative cast iron appears in porch and stair railings.

Masonry craftsmanship is at a high level; surfaces are smooth, joints are fine and even. Masonry materials and techniques contribute to the character of regional types such as the cobblestone dwellings of western New York and the old Northwest, the stuccoed stone of German Texas, the cut limestone of Wisconsin and Minnesota, the fieldstone of Pennsylvania, and the ashlar granite of Massachusetts and Maine.

Plan

Whether high-style or vernacular, the detached dwelling exhibits ingenious solutions to the problem of containing differentiated interior spaces within a plan that appears geometrically regular on the exterior.

The basic house plan—freestanding or in a row and joined by party walls—is a rectangle, typically set short side to the street [66]. The corner unit in a row may be larger and have a side ell [73].

The freestanding two-story townhouse may be flanked by one-story wings [64]. When the plan is of the four-room five-bay type, entry is through the central stair hall, whether the dwelling faces the front [71; 76] or the side of its lot [67]. Rear wings create an L, T, or irregular plan [77, 78]. A porch is often integrated into the plan.

Forms perpetuating ethnic traditions and all but ignoring Greek Revival style include the Texas German plan with two rooms side by side [86], the Monterey type with laterally disposed rooms having individual entries and a second-story gallery [85], and the New Orleans courtyard-oriented house [88].

Elevation

The Greek Revival dwelling is bold in silhouette, broad in proportions, and simplified in details. The paradigm is the monumental two-story temple front with pedimented gable (trimmed by moldings along the base and sloping sides) [64]; or flat entablature [69; 71]. Columns may be freestanding or applied to the façade. Alternatively, when the eaves face the street, they are finished with a cornice [74; 75] and the gable side is embellished with a cornice return [78; 81].

A portico may also be employed to frame the entry [79] or the door may be framed by pilasters and an entablature [74]. Pilasters may also be applied to the façade [80].

Greek orders are modified to accord with American taste and carpenter skill—free rather than mechanical interpretations of their prototypes.

Doorways and windows are boldly delineated. Door openings are generally flanked by side lights and headed by an oblong transom light [64; 86]. Window openings set in masonry are marked by emphatic lintels, sometimes with carved keystones or endblocks [71]. Wooden window surrounds are heavily molded and may also emphasize a corner block [85] or a heavy pediment [69]. Windows are approximately the same size as in the Federal period and are typically six-over-six lights. Attic windows may be in a frieze beneath the eaves [79] or in the triangular pediment [66]. Dormers are not usual.

The roof, whether pitched or hipped, is lower than in earlier years; roof height is also minimized by a parapet at the eaves or a flattened deck at the ridge.

As a row house, the Greek Revival dwelling is differentiated from its Federal predecessor mainly in the character of its ornament at door and window and in a certain vigor of proportion and simplicity of mien [73].

A smooth wall surface provides an ideal background for robust ornamentation in wood, appearing as Greek-inspired foliate and geometric motifs and applied to portico, door surrounds, and eaves. Particularly fine examples of Greek Revival ornament are found in western New York State, Ohio, and Michigan [66].

Most impressive of all are the Greek Revival plantation houses that symbolized the Antebellum South and the border area [69; 71].

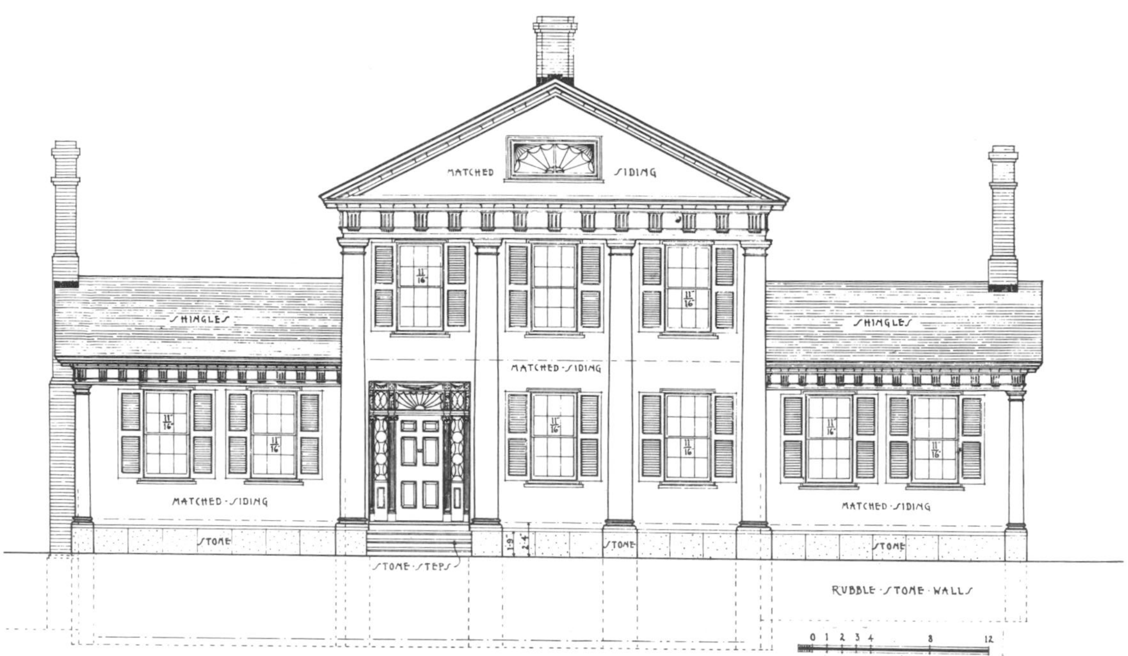

64 Dr. John Mathews House. Painesville, Ohio. 1829. A version of the Roman Doric order, with applied pilasters and pedimented gable. Although it is a curious feature on a temple front, the tympanum window does provide attic light.

Dr. John Mathews House, Painesville, Ohio; 1829.

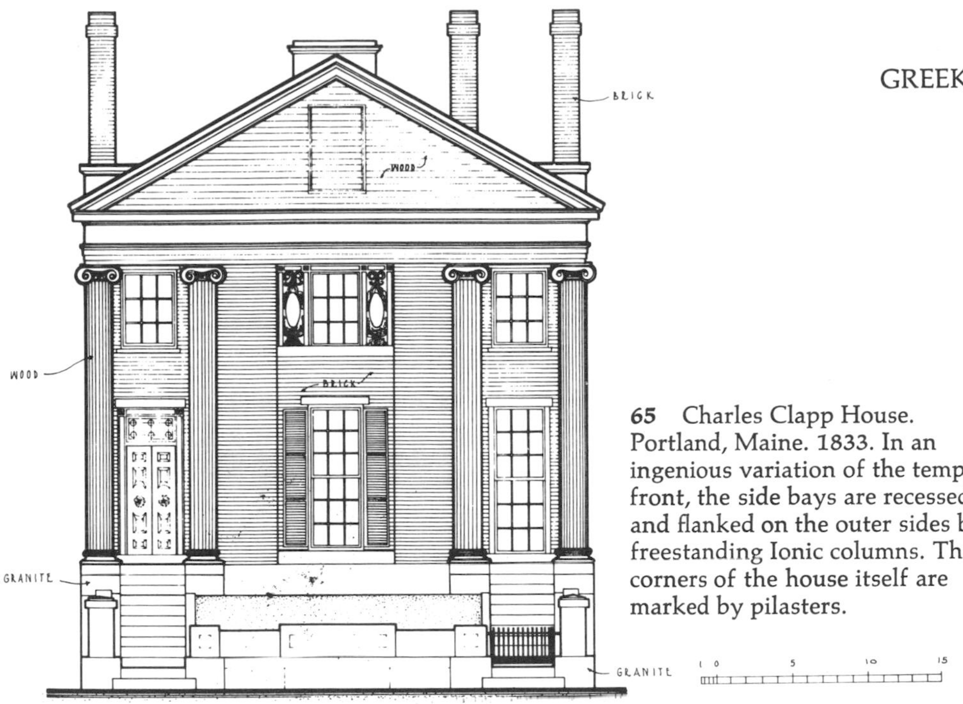

65 Charles Clapp House. Portland, Maine. 1833. In an ingenious variation of the temple front, the side bays are recessed and flanked on the outer sides by freestanding Ionic columns. The corners of the house itself are marked by pilasters.

Charles Clapp House, Portland, Maine; 1833.

66, 67 Whittelsey House. Rochester, New York. 1835–1836. Observe that this elaborate portico is embellishing what is actually the dwelling's side.

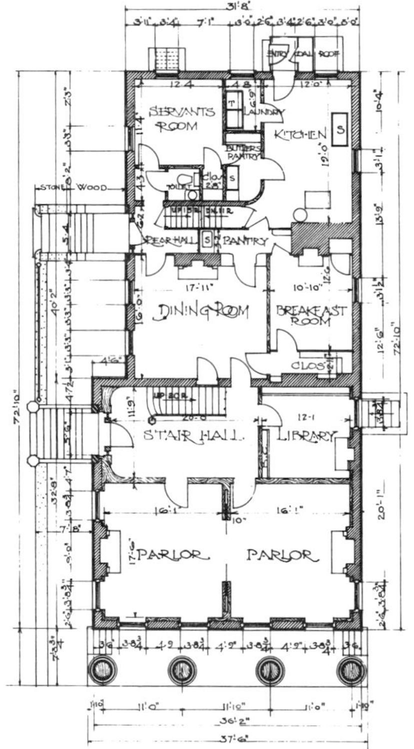

FIRST FLOOR PLAN

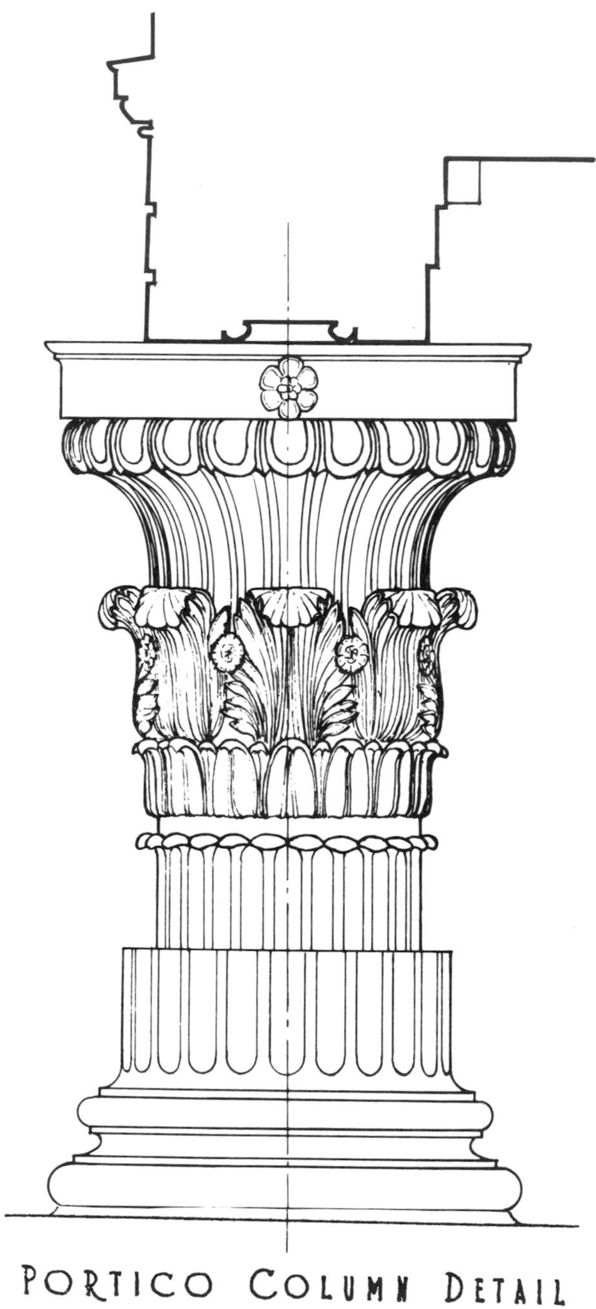

PORTICO COLUMN DETAIL

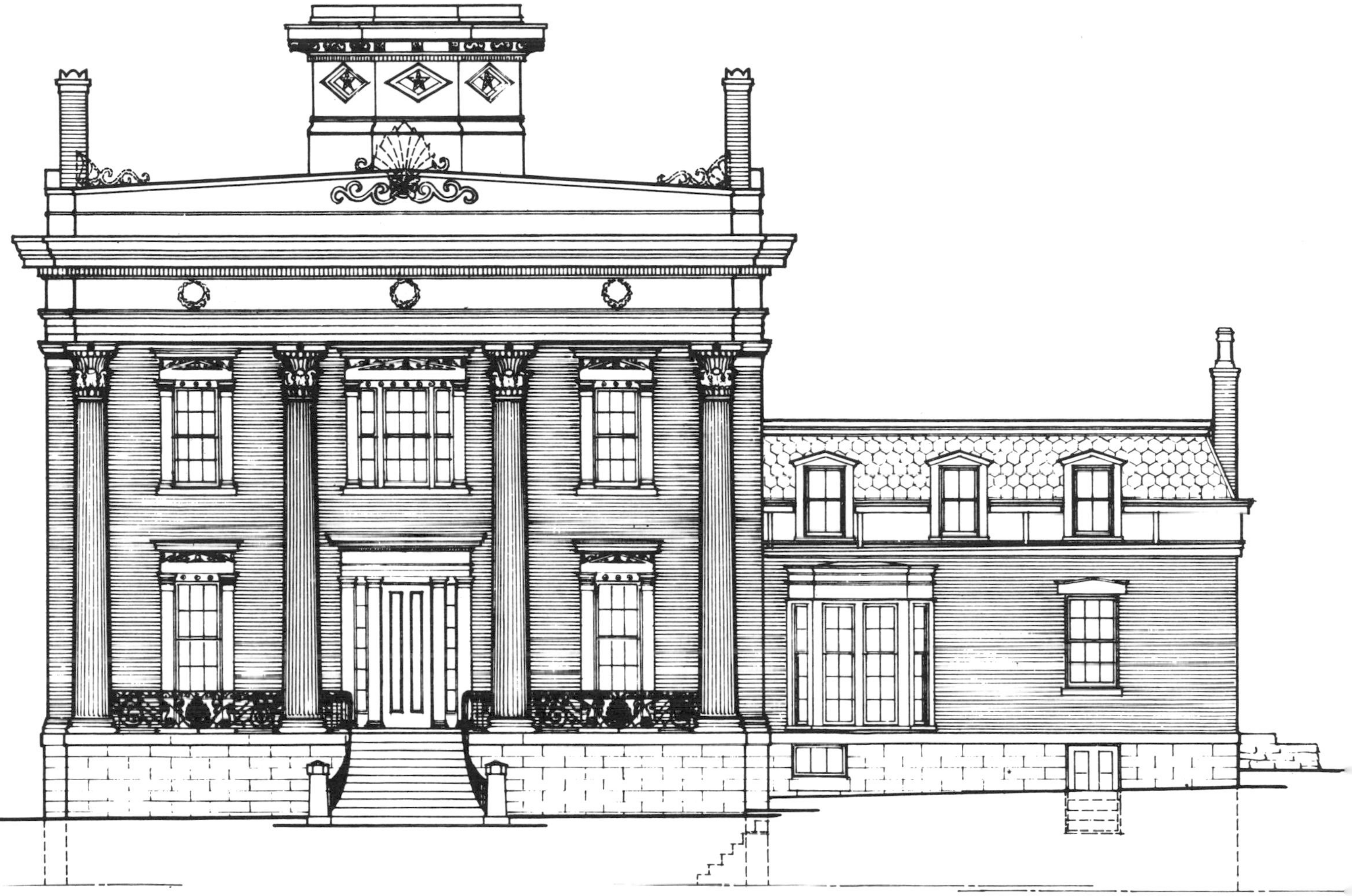

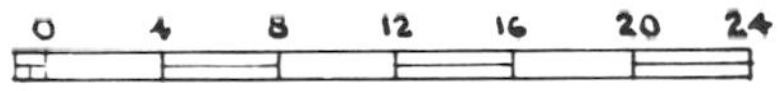

68, 69, 70 James Lanier House. Madison, Indiana. 1844; kitchen wing probably 1870s. Southern in character, this elaborate dwelling has a flat entablature with parapet and cupola above. Note the elaboration in the iron rail detail and in the lush foliage of the Corinthian column on the facing page (figure 68).

PORTICO RAIL DETAIL

71, 72 Shamrock. Vicksburg, Mississippi. 1851. Imposing in scale and demeanor, the Greek Revival plantation home becomes the symbol of the antebellum South.

73 William Remshart row houses. Savannah, Georgia. 1852. Typical late Greek Revival high-stoop Savannah row houses, with restrained detailing at cornice, window, and doorway.

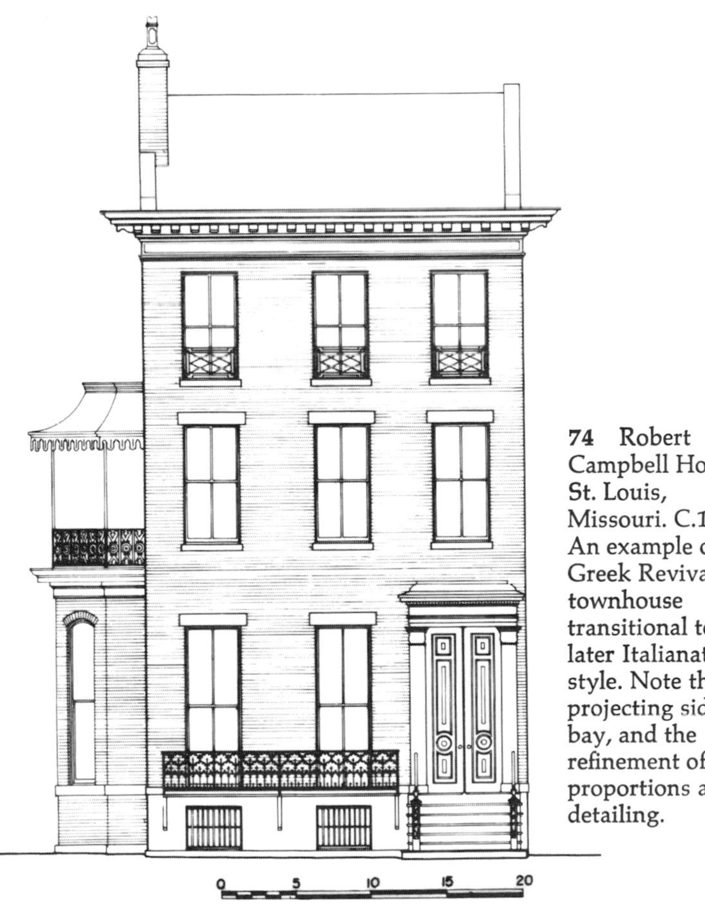

74 Robert Campbell House. St. Louis, Missouri. C.1855. An example of a Greek Revival townhouse transitional to the later Italianate style. Note the projecting side bay, and the refinement of proportions and detailing.

75 Frederick Stahl House. Galena, Illinois. 1844. A curious feature on this otherwise robust Greek Revival dwelling is the graceful Federal-style fanlight.

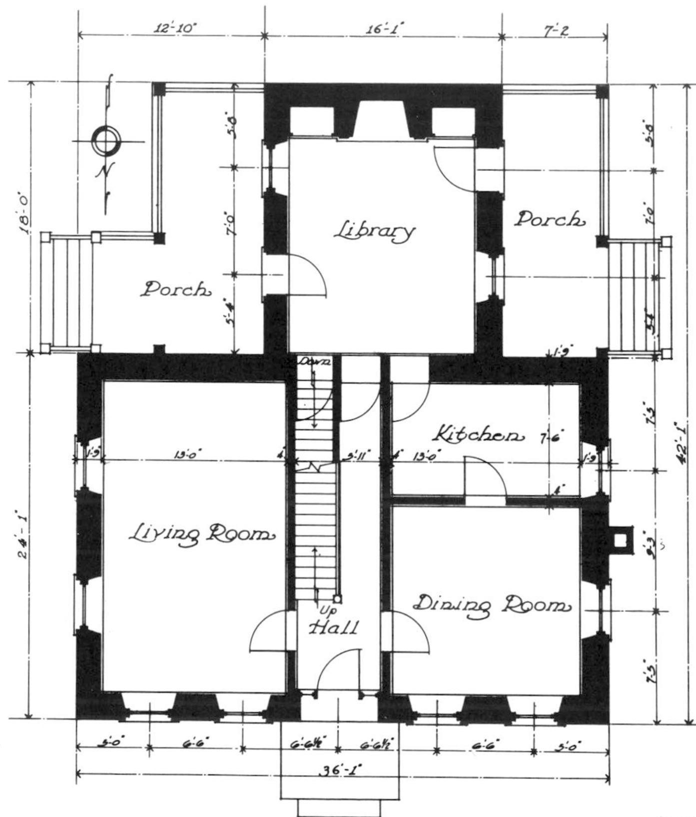

FIRST FLOOR PLAN

76, 77, 78 Charles Miller House. Menomonee Falls vicinity, Wisconsin. 1858. A midwestern farmhouse whose blunt plainness asserts a masculine character.

79 Isaac Crane House. Montclair, New Jersey. 1838 remodeling of 1795 dwelling. In place of dormers, the grille-covered frieze windows light the attic without adding to the dwelling's apparent height.

80, 81 James Fraser House. Honey Creek Falls vicinity, Wisconsin. 1855. With attenuated proportions and extravagant width, this rural dwelling has a delicate aspect.

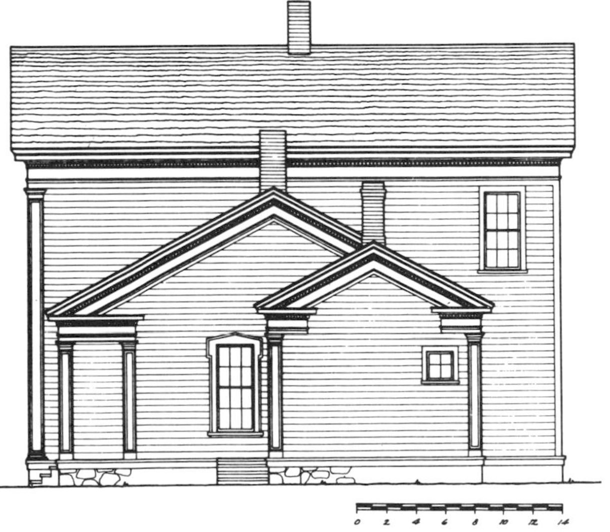

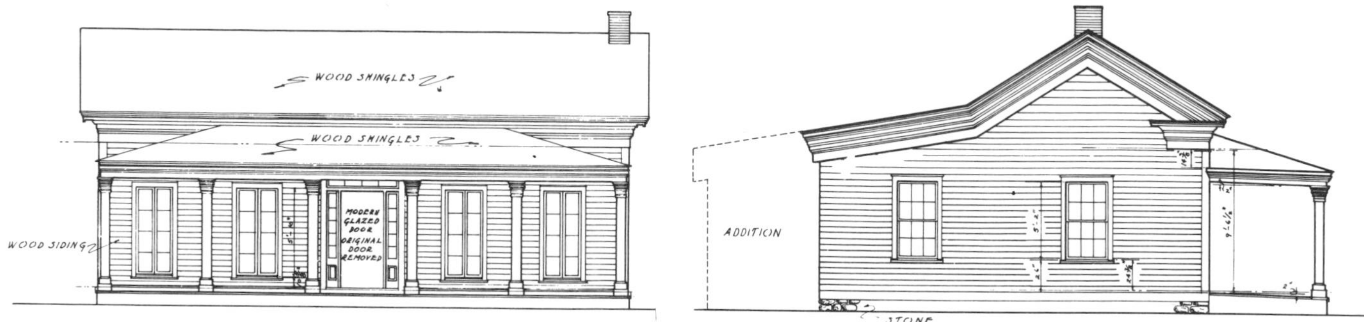

82, 83 Hiram Colver House. Phoenix, Oregon. C.1855. The multiplication of cornice moldings and the use of French windows are manifestations of a provincial independence.

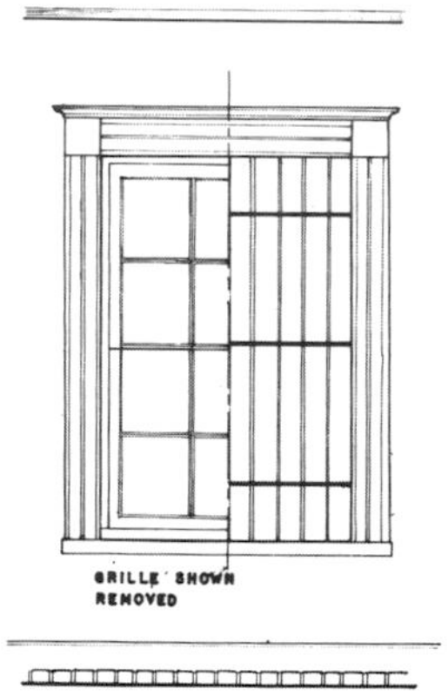

GRILLE SHOWN REMOVED

FIRST STORY WINDOW

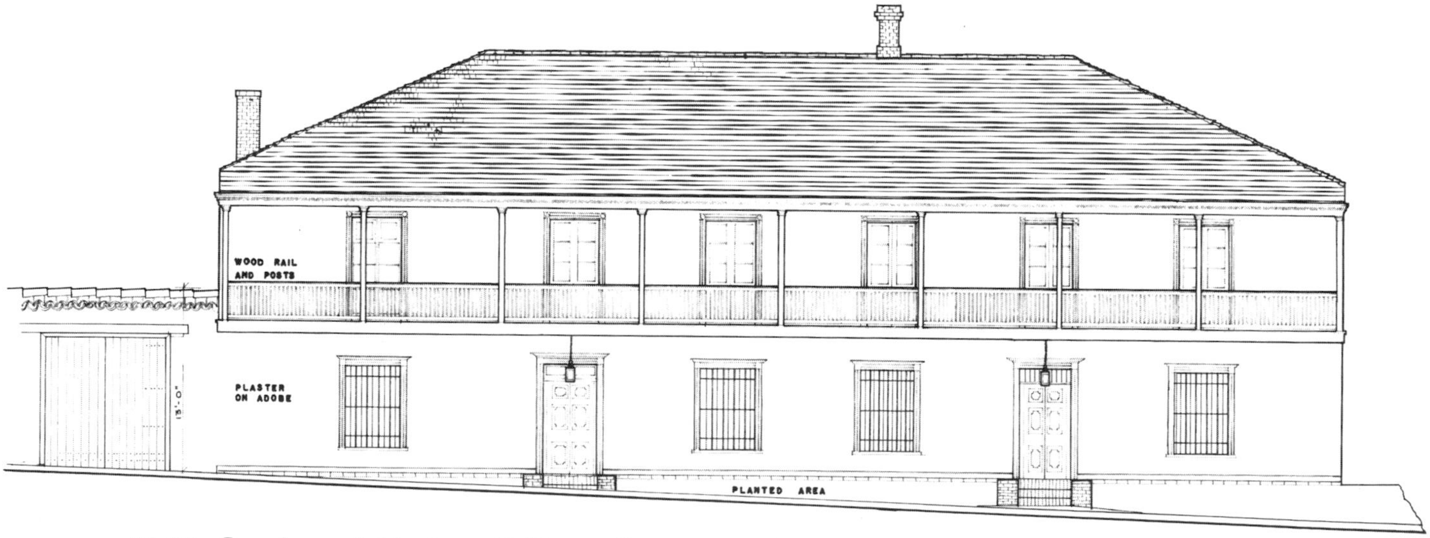

WOOD RAIL AND POSTS

PLASTER ON ADOBE

PLANTED AREA

84, 85 Casa Amnesti. Monterey, California. C.1834–1855. A type associated with Monterey, fusing Spanish Colonial and Yankee elements. From the older tradition, an extended plan, plastered adobe, iron grillework; from the subsequent Americanization, two-story height, hipped roof, and simplified Greek Revival woodworking. The doorways are a result of a 1919 restoration.

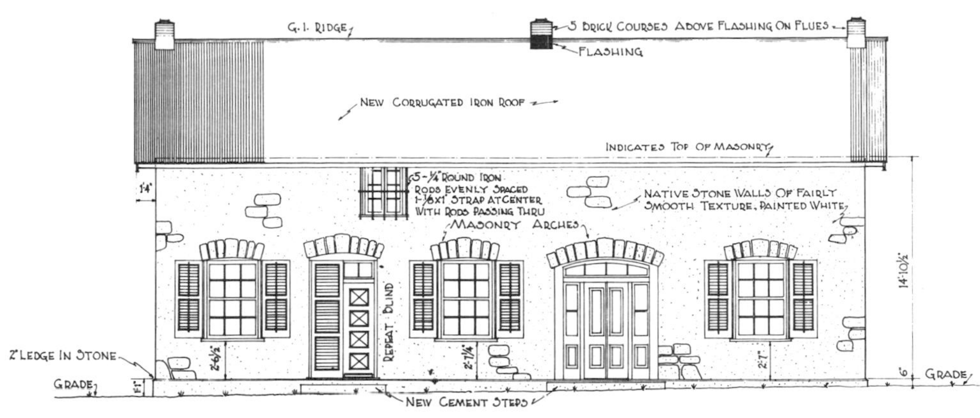

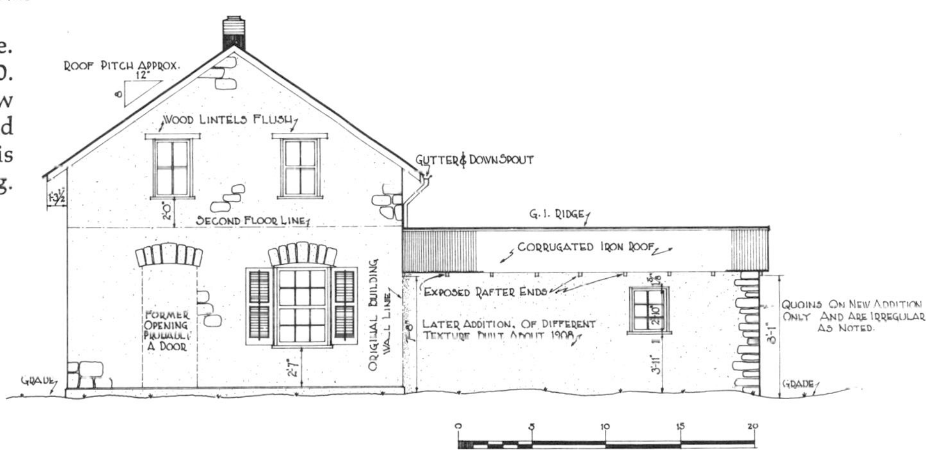

86, 87 Otto Pfeil House. Fredericksburg, Texas. 1845–1850. American woodwork—window sash, door enframements, and louvered shutters—embellish this thoroughly German stone dwelling.

88 Louis Lanoix House. New Orleans, Louisiana. 1818–1824. This French-type city house—with carriageway to rear courtyard, first-story service rooms, and iron balcony—supports the later Greek Revival tradition in New Orleans.

1840-1860

Early Victorian

Gothic Revival • Italian Villa, Romanesque

FOR the intellectuals of the 1840s, material prosperity could not mask the complexity and confusion of modern life. An enormous wave of immigration promised to mitigate the chronic scarcity of labor, but it also brought ethnic, religious, and class conflict. Expansion of the frontier opened vast lands for settlement, but provoked nostalgia for the passing of the wilderness.

Populous cities offered an urban life-style that rivaled the capitals of Europe in comfort and sophistication, yet the dangers of fire, epidemic, crime, and poor housing intensified. The increasing mechanization of food preservation and of clothing and furniture production prophesied women's freedom from drudgery, yet trend-setters like *Godey's Lady's Magazine* (March 1842) proclaimed that "the true dignity and beauty of the female character" is in the performance of household chores.

As living standards rose, the discrepancy between expectation and fulfillment was achingly apparent.

For a generation of European-inspired Romantics—led by Washington Irving, the Hudson River landscape painters, and their coterie of poets and politicians—the response to the contemporary challenge was a flight into the security of the past.

"It is in the solitude and freedom of the family home in the country which constantly preserves the purity of the nation and invigorates its intellectual powers," wrote Andrew Jackson Downing, landscape architect and author of *The Architecture of Country Houses* (1850), one of the earliest and no doubt the most influential of the house pattern books.

This new and enormously popular genre offered dwelling plans, perspectives, descriptions, and price estimates—not only to the carpenter or builder, but to the prospective homeowner as well.

In an ideal vision of a domestic retreat for every man—mechanic or millionaire—the rural, suburban, or small-town home had a significance beyond mere function. It was evidence of culture, an expression of individualism, a social, moral, patriotic, and democratizing force. The rules of ancient Greece were set aside. For the Romantic, the appeal of the past was the freedom it offered from the present.

"A blind partiality for any one style in building is detrimental to the progress of improvement," wrote Downing. A wide vocabulary of historic motifs adds novelty to architecture, creates variety, and bestows symbolic associations.

The lover of art and landscape can have a dwelling in the Tuscan style; the wealthy landowner, a castellated home; the leisured gentleman, a Tudor residence; the man of modest means and good taste, a dwelling in the bracketed style. A Swiss cottage in the Hudson or Allegheny Highlands; a Gothic dwelling in New England. In the middle states the Romanesque or Norman style; in the South the Venetian mode; in the West the manners of an Italian villa. For the artisan, a cottage; for the merchant, a villa; for the gentleman, a mansion.

"What, then, are the proper characteristics of a rural residence?" asked Downing. "The harmonious union of buildings and scenery . . . utility . . . expression of purpose . . . a style marked by irregularity of form and outlines, a variety of effect and boldness of composition."

In Philadelphia suburb or Nevada mining camp, Romantic Revival styles reflected diversity, expressed complexity, and responded to the challenges of the day.

Materials

The paradigm of the wooden Gothic dwelling is board-and-batten wall cladding (narrow batten strips covering the joints between vertically applied boards) [91]. Stone is usually rustic in character.

The Italian villa and its variations are more likely to employ brick or stone to create a smooth effect, sometimes using stucco that simulates masonry as a surfacing material.

Chunky cast iron may be used for Gothic-styled door hinges or hardware, roof cresting, and fence posts.

Plan

Freed from the confines of the simple rectangle, the Early Victorian house plan has a complicated outline with unpredictable projections and setbacks for wings, rooms, and bays.

Complex massing and a picturesque silhouette, allow practical advantages in variety in room size, convenience in layout, and multiple exposures for most rooms. Also characteristic are porches that extend from the plan and function as outdoor living rooms [94; 96, 97].

An L-shaped plan endows even a conservative dwelling with picturesque qualities, while no more than a projecting window bay will add a quaint touch [94].

Elevation

GOTHIC REVIVAL

The Gothic Revival dwelling has a strong character, a romantic disposition, and an expressive vocabulary. It may seem to be almost rooted in the ground, but it rises steeply, its aspiring verticality accented by board-and-batten siding [91], steeply pitched cross gables and wall dormers [89], sharp roof slope, and insistent chimneys. The chimneys, in fact, grouped and decorated as medieval symbols of hearth and home, are major design elements.

The cross gable in the center of the façade is a characteristic feature; its incline is usually decorated by a bargeboard (wood trim carved in a curvilinear pattern reminiscent of Gothic tracery) [91]. These bargeboards (whether original or added later) virtually may be the single distinctive stylistic feature [94].

Window openings are varied in size and shape and tend to escape symmetrical placement. Above, Gothic earred drip moldings are common [89; 94; 95].

ITALIAN VILLA, ROMANESQUE

A hallmark of the Italian Villa and Romanesque styles (and their close cousins, the Tuscan and Norman styles) is the three- or four-story tower with arched openings [96; 98]. The low roof, pitched or hipped, has a wide overhang and is often articulated by carved brackets ("bracketed style").

An Italian-accented decorative vocabulary includes modillion moldings at the eaves; flat, round, or shallow-arched window openings; and rusticated (rough-cut at the edges) masonry door surrounds [96]. The double-leafed door with heavy applied moldings is almost a requisite element.

Slight modifications—a steeply pitched tower roof and shaped gables, for example—translate the Tuscan into the Elizabethan style [100].

A Romanesque (Norman) version makes more consistent use of arch-shaped openings. A distinctive feature is the decorative arcading beneath the eaves [98].

There is variety in fenestration (window size, shape, and placement). Characteristic is the tall, narrow window with thickened mullions (dividers) that give a crucifix effect [96]. Typically, the two-over-two window belongs to the Villa [99] and the diamond-pane window to the Gothic dwelling [89].

Isolated stylistic elements "update" alterations or additions to basically conservative provincial dwellings [101].

89 The Meadows. Rhinebeck vicinity, New York. C.1848; veranda at south end, after 1893. References to medieval English domestic architecture include cross gables, Tudor-arched doorway, leaded casement windows, clustered chimney stacks, earred drip moldings above the windows.

90 Lyndhurst. Tarrytown, New York. 1838; tower and section to the left added 1864; Alexander Jackson Davis, architect. Quintessential American Gothic, with elaborate gables, windows, and battlements responding to the Romantic's appreciation for the picturesque, and a veranda to satisfy the pragmatist's regard for comfort.

Lyndhurst, Tarrytown, New York.

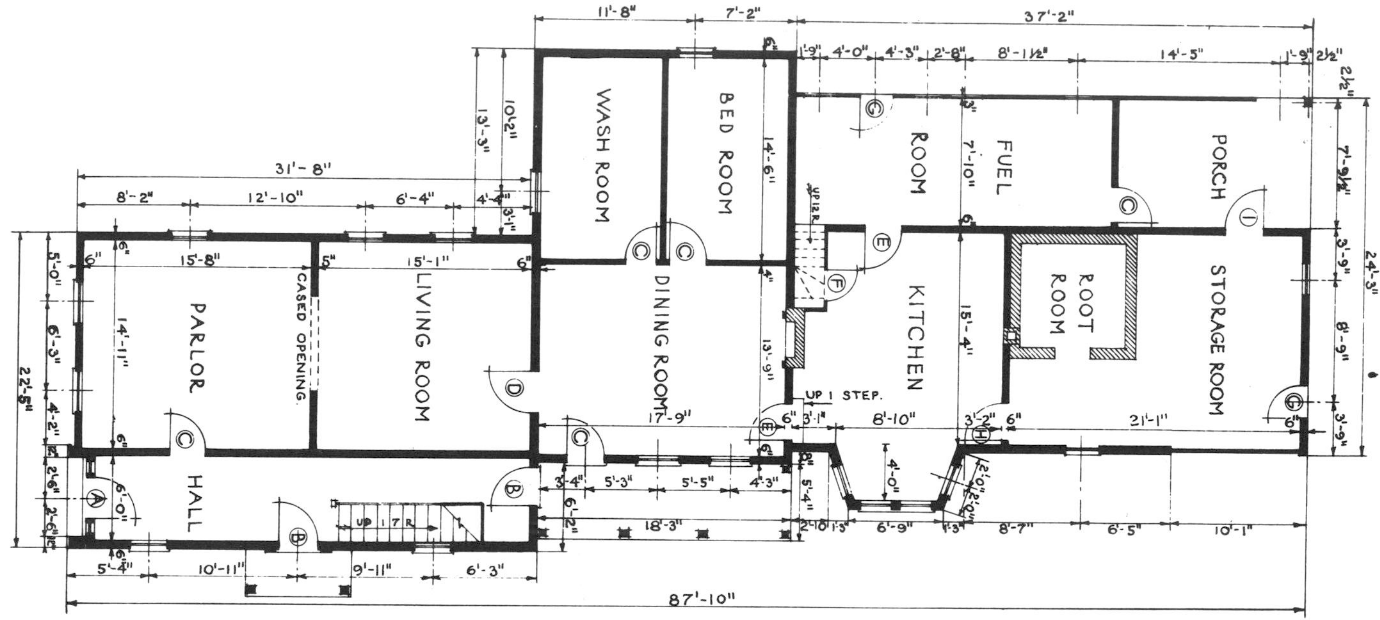

FIRST FLOOR PLAN

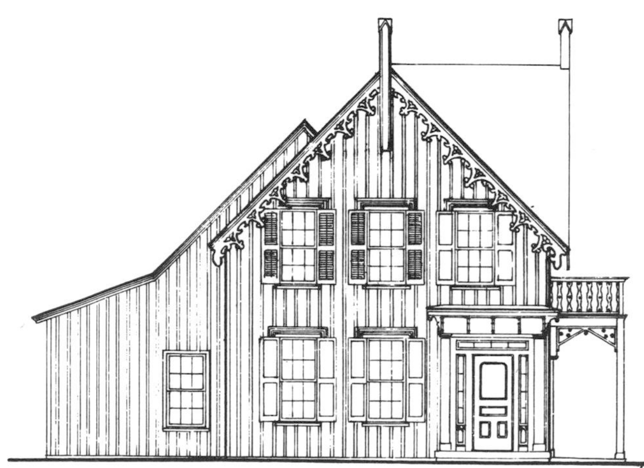

91, 92, 93 A. B. Austin House. Paris, Illinois. 1854. The gable over what is actually the farmhouse's side entrance, emphasizes the importance of cooking and eating areas. The delicate eaves decoration has a "gingerbread" quality.

A. B. Austin House, Paris, Illinois; 1854 (see 91, 92, 93).

94 General Pershing Boyhood Home. Laclede, Missouri. 1857–1858. A conservatively styled dwelling with restrained Gothic ornament.

95 Sunnyside (Washington Irving House). Irvington, New York. An eclectic 1837 remodeling of a seventeenth-century Hudson River Valley farmhouse. The stepped gable ends are nostalgic evocations of the Dutch presence; the wooden trim is Gothic in spirit; the tower, Italianate.

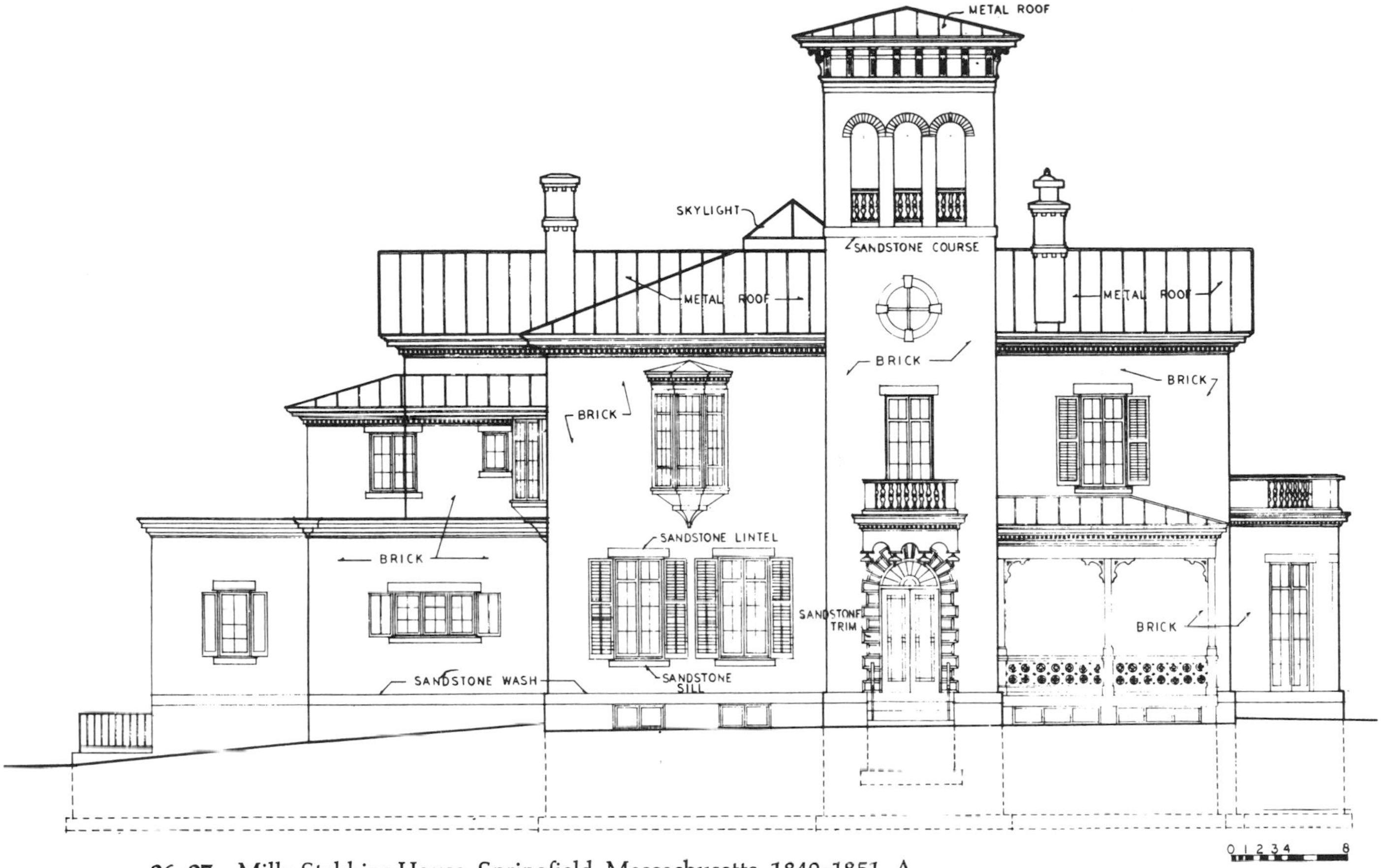

96, 97 Mills-Stebbins House. Springfield, Massachusetts. 1849–1851. A picturesque Italian villa with a lively, irregular silhouette.

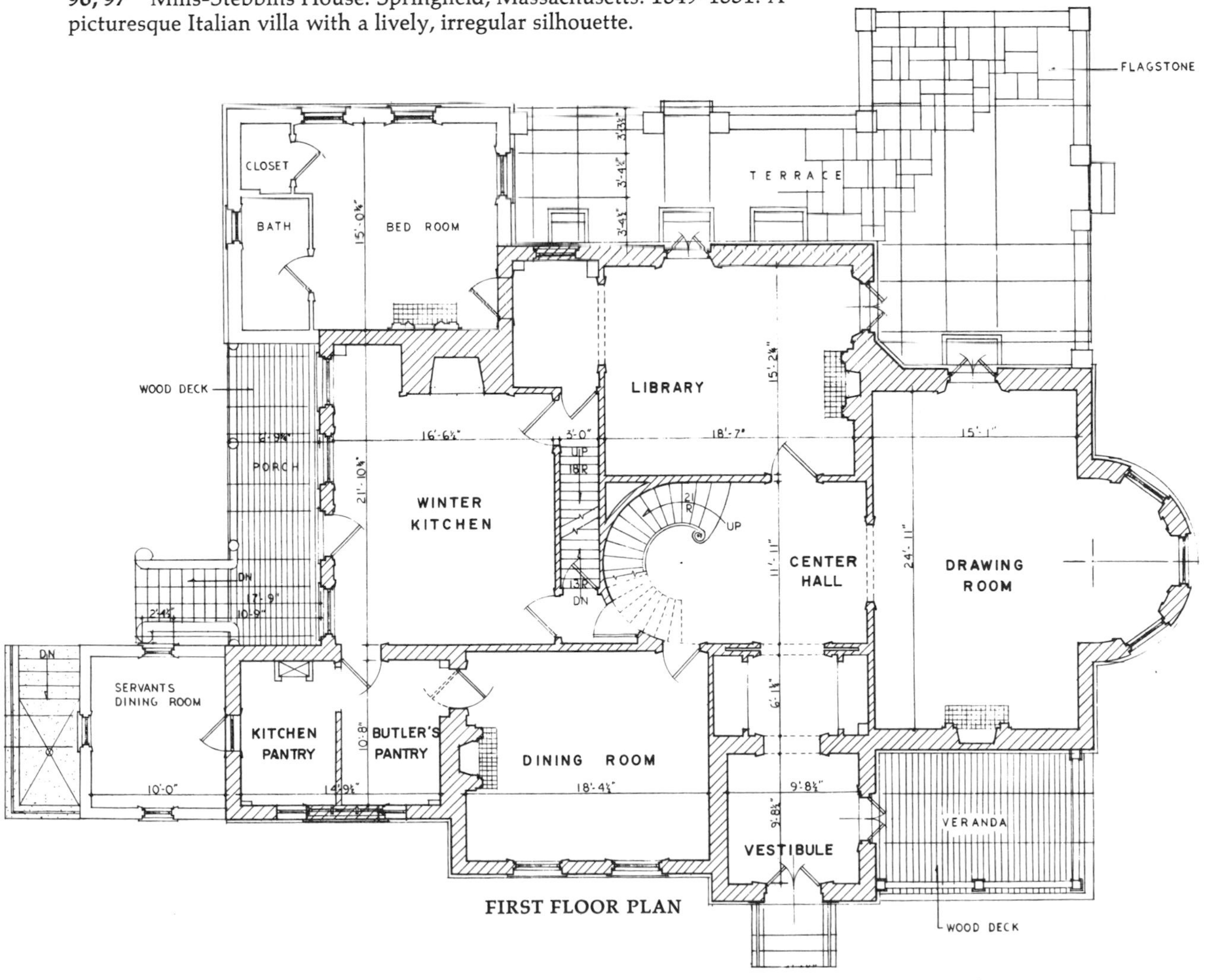

FIRST FLOOR PLAN

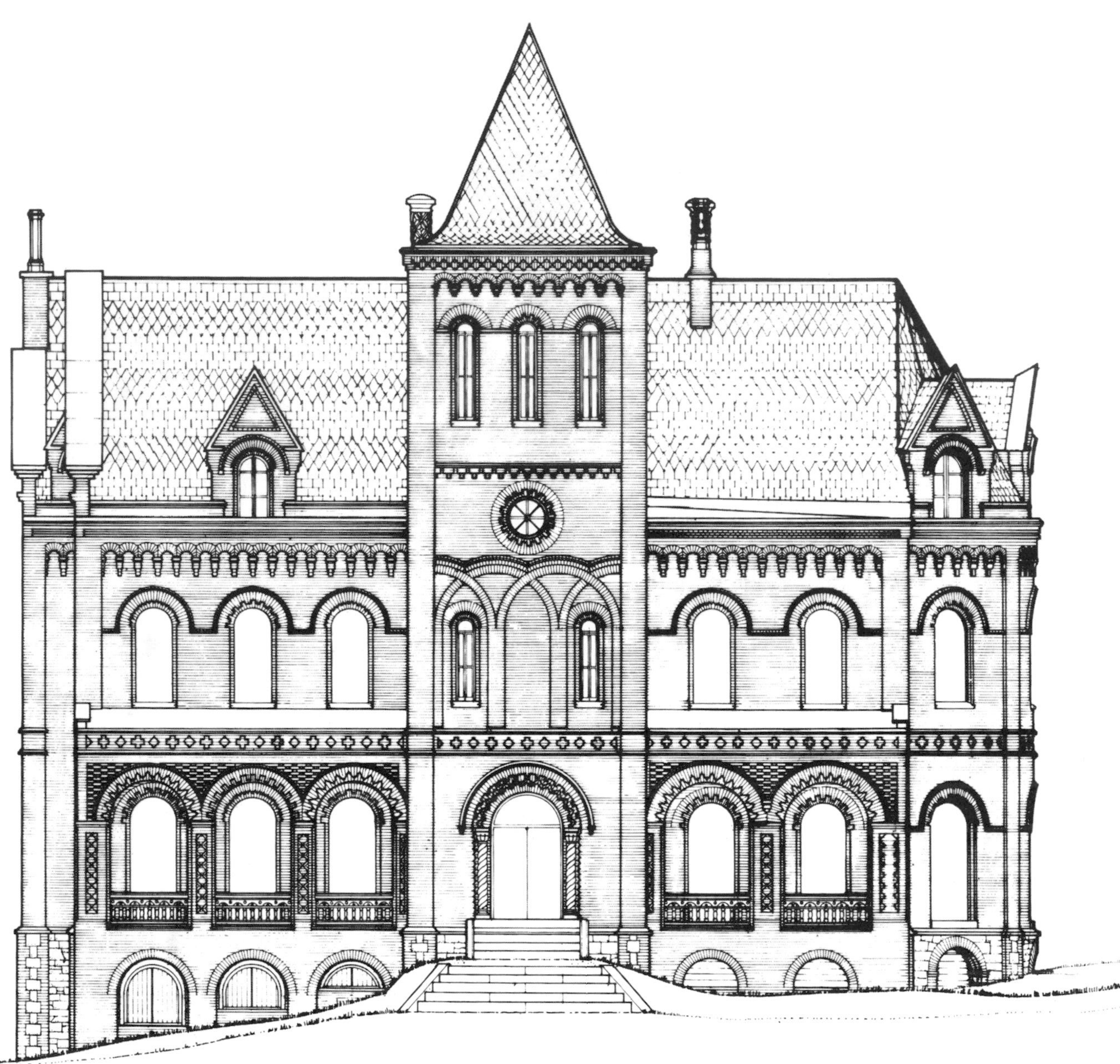

98 Wyndclyffe. Rhinecliff vicinity, New York. 1853. An inventive and extravagantly ornamented Norman manor house.

99 Superintendent's House, Tower Grove Park. St. Louis, Missouri. 1868–1869. Characteristic of Italian Villa in its later stages is the crisp contrast of ashlar masonry, brick, and wood trim.

100 Ebenezer Maxwell House. Germantown, Philadelphia, Pennsylvania. 1859. Fanciful stonework, woodwork, and gable patterns evoke medieval England. An early use of the mansard roof.

101, 102 The Wayside. Concord, Massachusetts. C.1860s. Italian Villa/Gothic Revival updating of an eighteenth-century structure added a tower, grouped chimneys, and cross gable. The wing with its veranda is an addition of the same period.

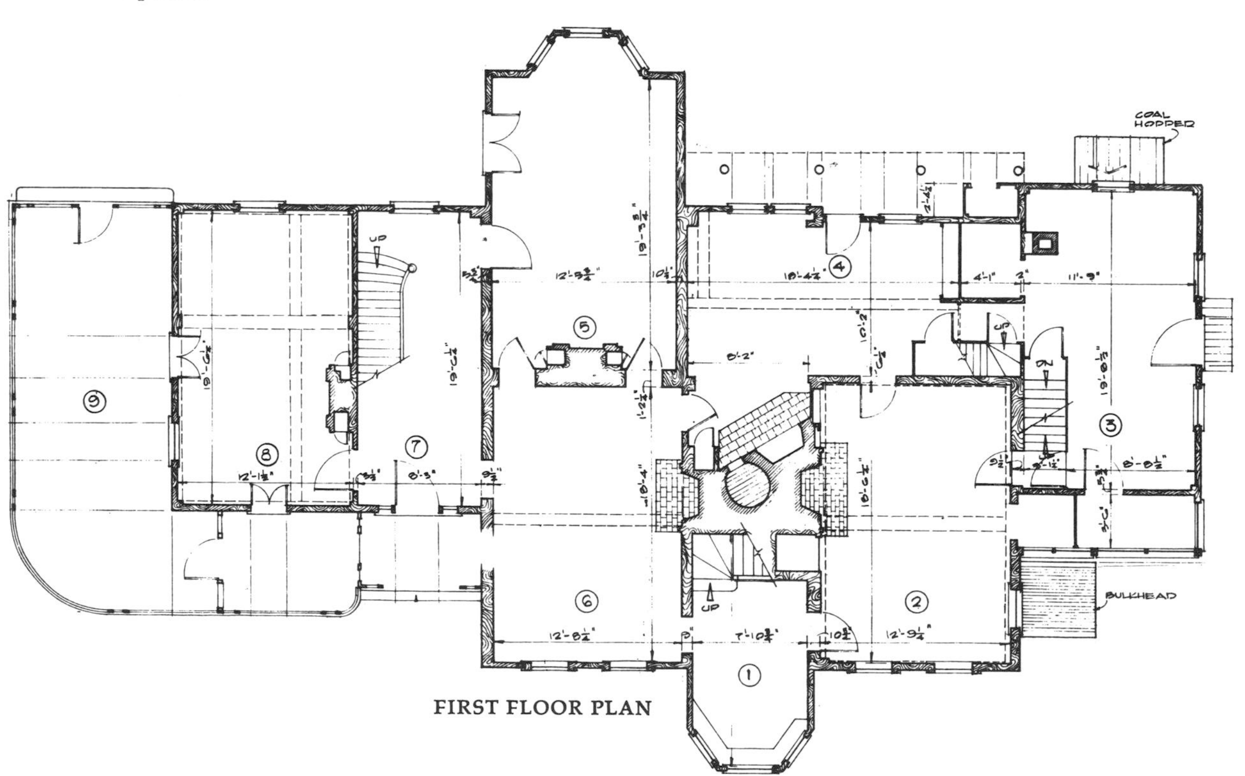

FIRST FLOOR PLAN

1860-1900

Victorian

Italianate, Second Empire • Victorian Gothic, Stick Style
Queen Anne, Chateauesque
Richardsonian Romanesque, Shingle Style
Classical and Colonial Revivals • Vernacular Victorian

VILIFIED as a gilded age, and praised as a golden age, this was, finally, an age of enormous energy. And, indeed, extraordinary efforts were required to keep pace with the housing needs of an exploding population.

Rural or European immigrant workers crowded into slums, back-alley shacks, five- and six-story tenement buildings, and boardinghouses. Others, more fortunate, dwelt in brick row houses or "triple-deckers." The well-to-do, in greater numbers than ever before, found comfort in spacious suburban villas, in substantial townhouses, in ostentatious hotels, and in the new "French flats."

But the American dream was an individually owned home on a lawn-fronted lot for every working man—as a testament to material progress and to family stability in a dynamic society within a transformed physical world. American husbands will work harder and longer than any other, an Englishman commented in 1869, "content to slave in business in order that their families may live in affluence."

Streetfronts of row houses or closely built detached dwellings ringed the increasingly specialized commercial downtown in larger cities. As a late-nineteenth-century observer noted, most "Americans do not live in the centers of great cities, but only do business there, while their families live elsewhere." With transportation by horse trolley, commuter railroad, or electric trolley, a man could live five, ten, twenty miles or more from the place where he worked. Along straight avenues, curving suburban lanes, or spacious parkways, fragile oak or maple saplings promised to soften the raw newness of these endlessly proliferating subdivisions.

Each residential neighborhood acquired a definite and distinct character and grew as a unique expression of social and economic forces. Just as neighborhoods expressed ethnic background, social class, and economic status, so too were they evidence of local custom, of the speculator's practices, changing taste, successive periods of prosperity and depression, the effects of growth, change, and time.

A vast volume of construction was realized only through increasingly industrialized building technology. Mass-produced components included pressed brick, cut stone, plate glass, cast iron, and jigsawed wood. A fully developed rail system permitted the transportation of materials for great distances from their source. And if the ever-present "servant problem" irritated the wife of the factory worker as well as the wife of the factory owner, then at least indoor plumbing, central heating, and gas light and refrigeration made housekeeping less onerous than ever before.

Perhaps it is that this raw and unabated energy found a safety valve in the stylistic excesses of domestic architecture—in dwellings of larger scale, freer plan, exuberant form, and elaborate detail.

Architects practicing in large cities—men of competence, even genius, such as Richard Morris Hunt, Henry Hobson Richardson, and the firm of McKim, Mead & White—set the pace. Architects also thrived in dozens of lesser communities across the nation.

And up-to-date builders' guides—such as Palliser's *Model Homes for the People* (Bridgeport, 1876) and Pierce and Dockstader's *Modern Buildings at Moderate Cost* (Elmira, 1886)—offered radically new styles, complete house plans, illustrative construction details, and cost estimates.

With breathless speed new styles flared and faded. During the Civil War decade the Gothic lingered, but a lush High Victorian Italianate became dominant. In the 1870s, the Gothic was rich and expressive, in both a high-style High-Victorian Gothic and a vernacular "Stick Style." The Italianate matured to the mansard-roofed Second Empire mode.

Late Victorian form drew on both traditions, and added an embroidery of Colonial detailing (inspired by the Centennial celebration), resulting in the coquettish, eclectic, and inventive Queen Anne style. This was also known as the Eastlake, Jacobean, and "free classical" style.

By the mid-1880s, no less adventurous in spirit if quieter in tone were the Richardsonian Romanesque (particularly associated with masonry dwellings) and the Shingle Style (its suburban or resort counterpart in wood).

Finally, as the century approached its end, dwellings were characterized more by the amplitude of their scale than the elaboration of their style. On Fifth Avenue or Euclid Avenue, in Palm Beach or in Newport, America's rising industrial princes paid homage to French or Italian Renaissance royalty or to English landowners in limestone chateaux, marble palazzi, and red-brick manor houses.

At the same time, in pleasant suburban neighborhoods and in remote vacation retreats, the middle class found its language of style in a revival of the American Colonial and Classical Revival past. It was clear that the restless and ruthless inventiveness of the previous decades had paused for breath.

Materials

Each substyle of the Victorian era selects and manipulates building materials to express its particular aesthetic.

For the Italianate dwelling, materials are handled to emphasize mass and heaviness and to create a surface rich with shadows and highlights. Enormously voguish, brownstone is used for bearing walls, facing, and ornament.

Wood, used in boards or scored to resemble masonry and painted in robust tones of red, blue, green, violet, or gray, gives an opulent effect.

Highly decorative on the eye-catching mansard roof are patterns of gray, green, or red slate tiles.

Stick Style dwellings are generally wood, and skeletal wood ornament may also embellish brick or stone houses.

For High Victorian Gothic dwellings, polychrome masonry is an essential element: brick is often of the dense, dark-red, industrially produced variety, sometimes set off by contrasting bands of black-glazed brick, and laid with thin white mortar joints. Blue, tan, and gray limestone—sometimes carved into rosette patterns or incised with linear motifs—are also typical.

A variety of materials, including brick, clapboard, ornamental shingle, and terra-cotta cast in decorative patterns, enlivens the Queen Anne façade. A striking accent is wooden decoration which is incised, chamfered, and carved in scroll shapes, or lattice work in basketweave, spindle, reel, or other patterns.

Rustic shingles (alone, or in juxtaposition with clapboard) in Indian red, brown, olive green, and deep yellow are characteristic of the Shingle Style.

The Richardsonian Romanesque may use shingle or clapboard on upper stories, but is essentially a masonry style, dramatically highlighting boulderlike fieldstone or dense, rock-faced granite, laid with wide joints of rose-tinted mortar.

In contrast, pale, smooth surfaces of marble, limestone, or sandstone are typical of buildings in the Chateauesque and Classical Revival styles. Pastel tones (gray, buff, blue, green, and yellow) also characterize clapboard and shingle dwellings in the Colonial Revival style.

The American vernacular Victorian is typically wood-frame, sheathed in clapboard and frankly revealing structural members such as sill and rafter.

Common in cities are simple brick dwellings whose sole ornament is the brick patterning or stamped metal cornice at the eaves.

Plan

The High Victorian freestanding dwelling is broader and taller than its Early Victorian counterpart, and rather more complex in plan. Recalling Classical origins, the Italianate plan is formal, symmetrical, compact, and squarish in shape [105].

The two-, three-, or four-story townhouse is of the familiar three-bay, side-hall type [124]. Toward the end of this period, the "English" plan, with a stair hall between the front and back rooms, achieves some popularity.

Tenements and apartment houses—as tall as six stories—have much greater depth and they experiment with interior cut-outs and light wells [118].

The Late Victorian dwelling—Queen Anne or Shingle Style—is inventive in plan, with cross axes, projecting wings, and voids in the form of porches, balconies, or porte-cochères incorporated into its main mass [126].

In their Late Victorian phase, Colonial Revival and Classical Revival plans, while expansive in scale, are symmetrical, tightly organized, and clearly defined.

Elevation

ITALIANATE, SECOND EMPIRE

In the Civil War decades, the Italianate dwelling preens like the stereotyped Victorian matron—well dressed, well behaved, and self satisfied. Proportions tend toward the vertical, and ornament toward the florid [103]. A robust and richly plastic decorative vocabulary includes carved and turned balusters as porch or balcony rail, repeating columns or pilasters at portico [106], wide and lavishly detailed window and door surrounds, and elaborately molded cornice with heavily profiled (often paired) brackets [104].

Paying homage to the Italian Renaissance tradition, room heights diminish at upper stories [106; 110], floor divisions are articulated by horizontal coursing, and corners by bold quoins [103; 107]. Doors are usually double-leaved.

With paired and grouped arch-headed door and window openings, the rhythm of solid and void has a dignified cadence [106; 107]. Window panes are either full [106—first story] or with a single vertical muntin [106—second story].

Italianate ornament—simplified and restrained

—also embellishes the octagonal-plan dwelling, something of a fad during the 1860s [108].

Most distinctive of the 1870s modifications that accompany the evolution of the Italianate to the Second Empire style is the mansard roof (steeply sloping sides that rise to a flat or shallow pitched deck) [109; 110]. Its profile may be concave [110; 111], straight [109], or convex. Cast-iron pinnacles or other decorative roof cresting draw attention upward, where complex massing and expansive height are most impressive [109; 110].

The segmentally arched door or window opening with emphatic hood molding is characteristic of the 1870s and early 1880s [110; 111]. Alternatively, the window opening is headed by a flat lintel with shaped or slanted upper edges [108].

In the Eastlake taste (named for an influential English theoretician who generally touted the Gothic) are elements such as decorative bosses on portico piers [109] and spandrels around windows [110]. Columns or piers may be drilled, incised, shaped, or proportioned for a novel aesthetic effect [109—portico; 110—at window and door surrounds].

VICTORIAN GOTHIC, STICK STYLE

More mature than in its Early Victorian phase, High Victorian Gothic remains lively and picturesque. Although it may lack certain typical Gothic features it is still irregular in silhouette, complicated in massing and attenuated in proportions.

In masonry, a "truthfulness" in expressing function and the nature of materials is the hallmark of the Victorian Gothic. (With pointed arches laid in polychrome masonry, this style is sometimes known as the Venetian Gothic, or Ruskinian, after the English critic who admired the mode.)

Typically, a variety of incised or patterned decorative materials and light-toned stone masonry against a dark brick or stone façade outline and articulate basement, entries and porches, door and window openings, floor levels, and rooflines [117; 119].

In wood—for its braggadocio display of skeletal structure—High Victorian Gothic is appropriately named the Stick Style. Dramatic rather than literal, "Stick" expression emphasizes on the skin of the building the vertical-horizontal relationships of its interior post-and-beam construction [113] and the spiky, angular quality of its diagonal bracing [112].

Exterior framing—such as porch or eaves supports, sometimes in intricate machined patterns—is dramatically overstated, as if to give tangible presence to hidden structural forces. Eloquent, too, is "Stick" elaboration of Italianate vernacular structures [114; 115].

Stick Style massing tends to be complicated by towers, wings, and intersecting volumes. The display is most effective at the roofline, with its multiplicity of gables which vary in size, shape, and pitch [112; 113].

QUEEN ANNE, CHATEAUESQUE

Although less emphatically vertical than the Victorian Gothic, the Queen Anne style perpetuates its picturesque qualities, making bravura display of original and historical motifs in arresting shapes, colors, and textures, combining clapboard, shingle, masonry, and terra-cotta for a vivid pictorial effect.

While Queen Anne names a contemporary English trend that looked to the great early-eighteenth-century manor houses, the style in America also evokes the simple dwellings of the colonial and early Republican eras. Decorative elements include grouped chimneys, small-paned windows, Palladian window motif [121], door opening with fan and side lights [123], turned balusters, intricate lathework, and the application of shingles to rounded or flaring surfaces [120].

Another version of this style, sometimes called Jacobean, emphasizes diagonal bracing and heavily carved trim [122].

The Queen Anne achieves a dowager maturity, emerging in a stately Chateauesque version (named for the steep hipped roof and the polygonal or cylindrical towers which are its dominant features) [125; 127].

The façade tends toward symmetrical organization. On the major stories, windows are tall, thin, and regularly spaced; a common treatment makes use of a heavy transom bar [125]. More capricious is attic fenestration, with its wall and roof dormers and tower openings which are single or grouped and headed by round, flattened, or Tudor arches.

Craft refinements of this period are stained glass windows at entry or stair hall. Ornament is usually a cautious mixture of Gothic, Renaissance, Romanesque, and Adamesque motifs.

RICHARDSONIAN ROMANESQUE, SHINGLE STYLE

Steps are few from Queen Anne to Shingle Style, but they cover the distance from nervous affectation to a mood of assured informality.

This is essentially a suburban and a resort style. The dwelling is ample in size and substantial in appearance, and spreads low against the ground on a heavy stone foundation. Generally, it has rounded contours and is sheltered by a broad and overhanging roof. The particular manner of using wood shingles—so that they appear to flow across surfaces, turn corners, and enclose deep loggias and entryways—is the style's chief hallmark [129; 131]. However, similar qualities are also achieved in clapboard or cut stone. As a resort style it serves equally well for pretentious and utilitarian structures [129; 130].

The Shingle Style reduces the number and variety of motifs, enlarges their scale, and complicates massing [133; 134]. Colonial motifs survive as isolated elements such as shingles, broad gables or gambrels, and small window panes.

Fenestration is generally regular and windows are frequently grouped in horizontal bands. The curving "eyebrow" dormer is distinctive [136].

In masonry, the style is named Richardsonian Romanesque after its most brilliant practitioner, the architect Henry Hobson Richardson. This is generally an urban style, hence it is more regular and self-contained in plan and elevation [135; 136]. Qualities of weight, density, and permanence are pronounced. Masonry is dark and rough-hewn. Entries are defined by heavy (often low) arches; columns are short and stubby.

CLASSICAL AND COLONIAL REVIVALS

Expansive scale, calm mien, and nostalgia for a younger America distinguish dwellings in the Classical Revival and Colonial Revival styles.

High-style residences, built for rich and knowledgeable families, are likely to be enormous in size and academic in spirit, borrowing motifs from a specific model or a single style, most commonly Renaissance, Georgian, or Neoclassical [137; 138].

On lesser dwellings, decorative motifs from several historical periods may be combined. Proportions are low and broad, their horizontal dimensions emphasized by widely spaced window openings, horizontal coursing, and strong (although shallowly projecting) cornice lines. Surface texture is generally limited to restrained ornament [139; 140]. An occasional phenomenon is a classicism interpreted with such originality to invoke a striking modernity [141].

VERNACULAR VICTORIAN

Vernacular architecture tends to reiterate local forms, adapting them to changing conditions over a long period of time. For economy, a compact plan is the rule. Hence, an agglutinative character results from the addition of service units and successive enlargements [142].

Older dwelling types persist: for example, the raised East Texas house [143], the porch-and-gable-fronted dwelling [152], the extended-plan farmhouse [144], and the flat-roofed urban row house [145].

Even the simplest dwelling has a modicum of ornament, though only patterning at the eaves [145] or door paneling [148]. For more ambitious houses, ornament is inevitable, but it is reduced, simplified, and abstracted. It is often a generation or more behind the times, exhibiting motifs from several periods [146; 151].

Streetfronts and neighborhoods assume distinct characteristics, based on lot size, building scale and expense, and stylistic range [152; 153].

Morse-Libby House, Portland, Maine; c. 1859 (see 103, p. 68).

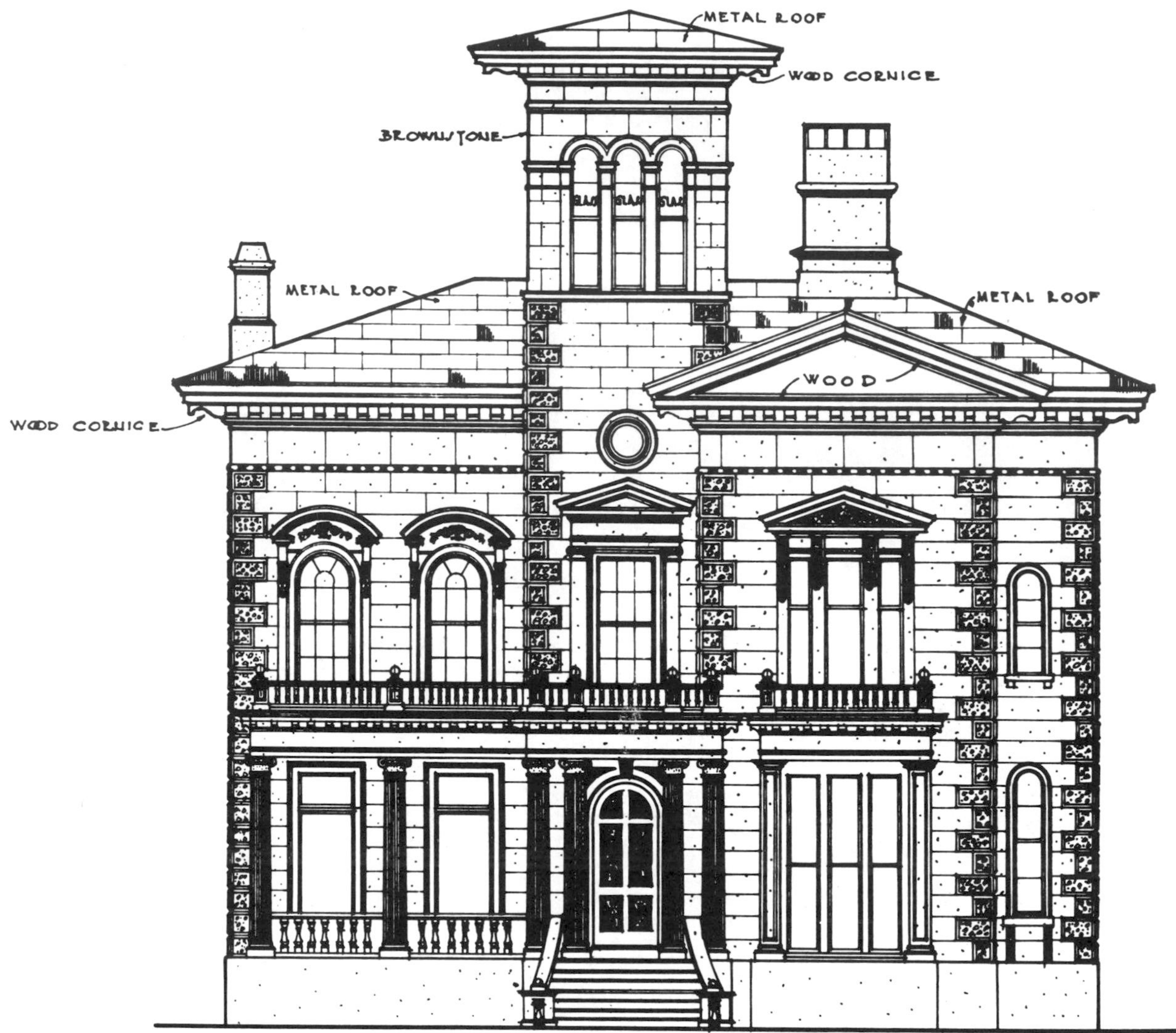

103 Morse-Libby House. Portland, Maine. C.1859. Descendant of the Early Victorian Italian Villa, the High Victorian Italianate dwelling is staid and opulent, rather than inventive and picturesque, with compact massing and imposing cornices, pediments, and quoins.

104, 105 Kinsey House. Milton vicinity, Indiana. 1871. A farmhouse of some opulence, with ornamental iron porch railings, cornice trim and roof cresting. Breaking from the compact plan, the extension at the right enlarges the space of the farmhouse kitchen.

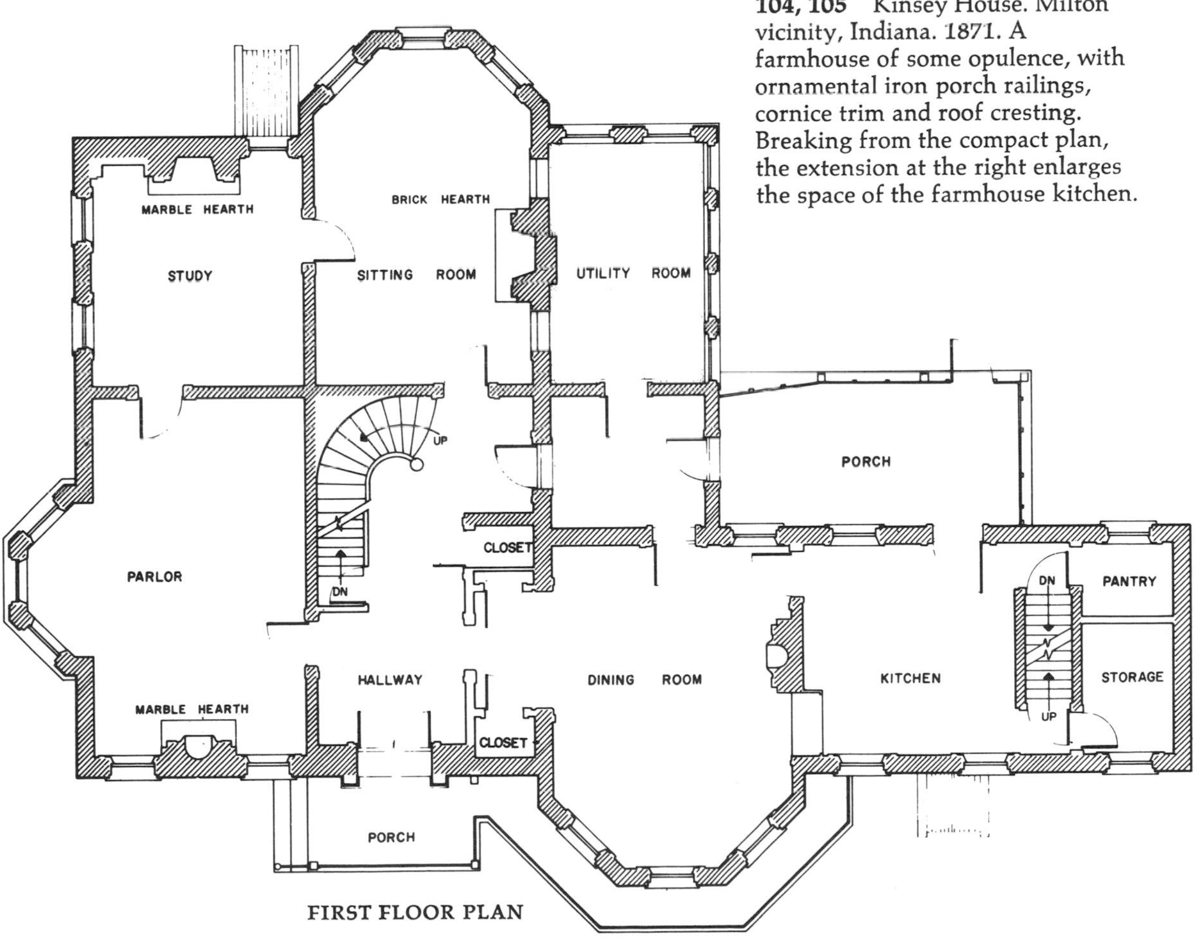

FIRST FLOOR PLAN

106 Albert Scott House. Petersburg, Virginia. C.1860–1861. Typical of the Italianate dwelling are tall windows, high ceilings, and cupola.

107 Dayton Street. Cincinnati, Ohio. C.1860–1868. Distinctive for their narrow lots, high-stooped entrances, and elaborate Italianate ornament, these freestanding mansions are midwestern cousins of New York City's brownstone rows.

108 1830 Phelps Place. Washington, D.C. 1865. A modicum of Italianate ornament and smooth stucco covering over clapboards dress this innovative octagon in the fashionable mode.

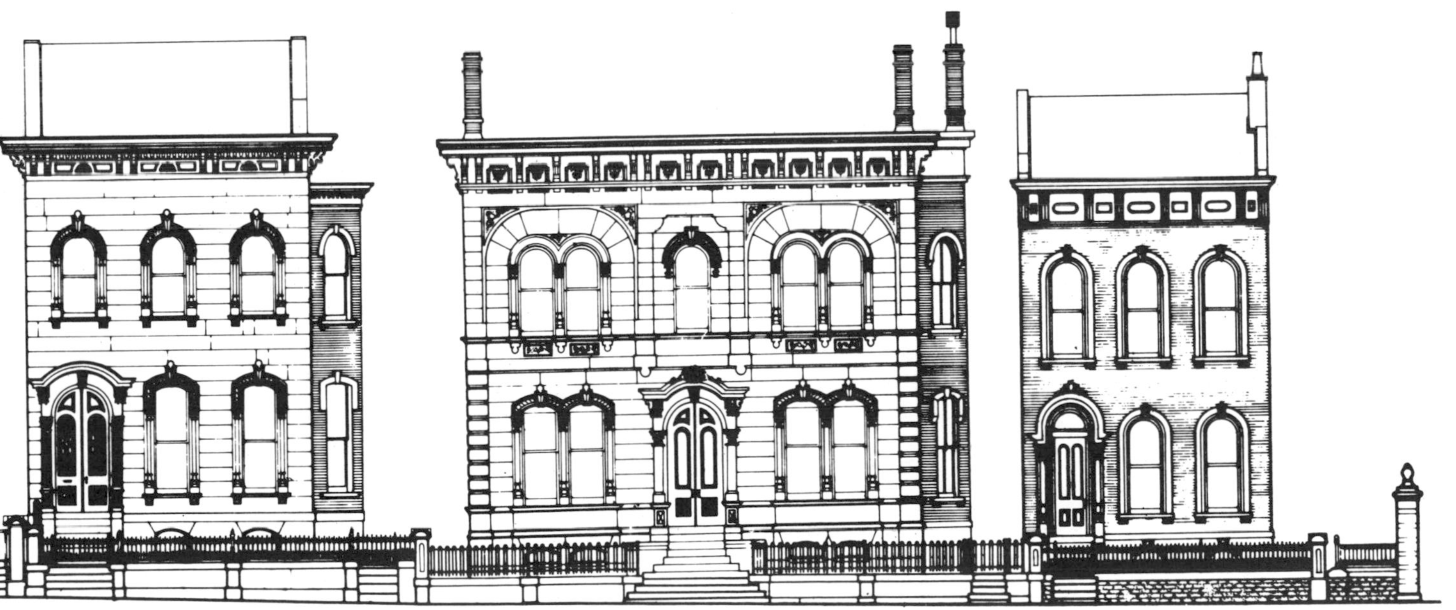

109 Chateau-sur-Mer. Newport, Rhode Island. 1871–1872 remodeling by architect Richard Morris Hunt of an 1851 structure. A bold mansard roof and imposing pillared entryways.

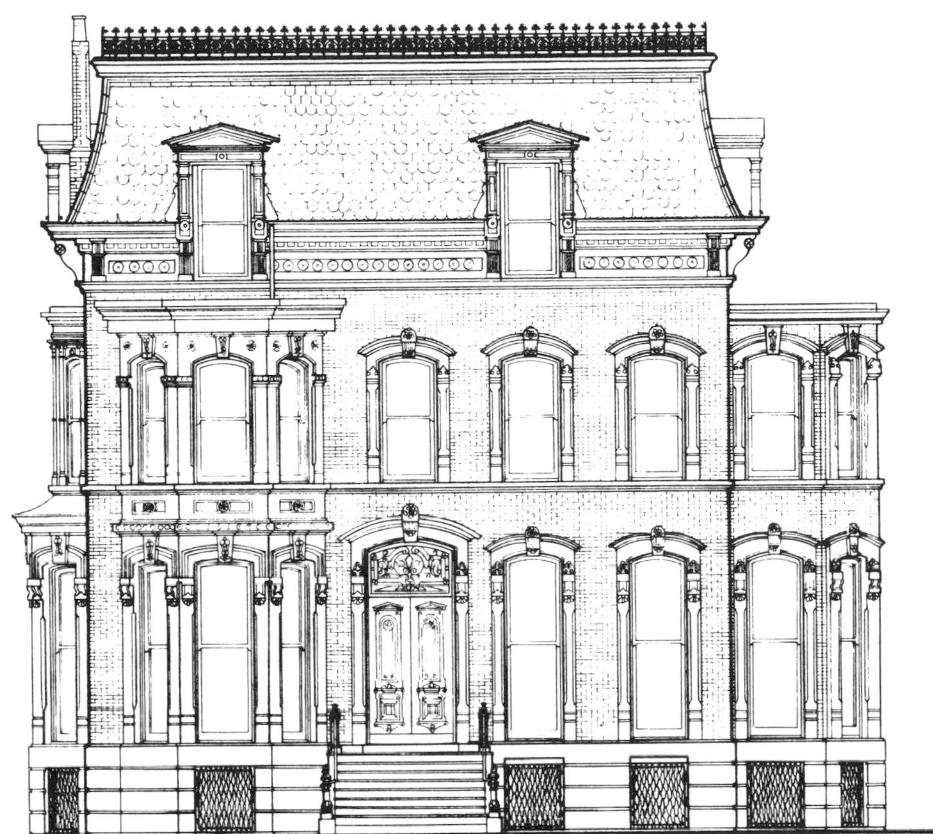

110 John DeKoven House. Chicago, Illinois. 1874. Sympathy with the florid French Second Empire style demands materials that enhance visual richness, particularly in the patterns of roof tiles and cresting, the details of door and window surrounds, and the rusticated masonry on basement walls.

111 Captain's Cottage No. 2. Sailors' Snug Harbor, Staten Island, New York. 1885; small, late, and provincial; nevertheless, a high-spirited version of the Second Empire style.

Emlen Physick House, Cape May, New Jersey; 1879 (see 113).

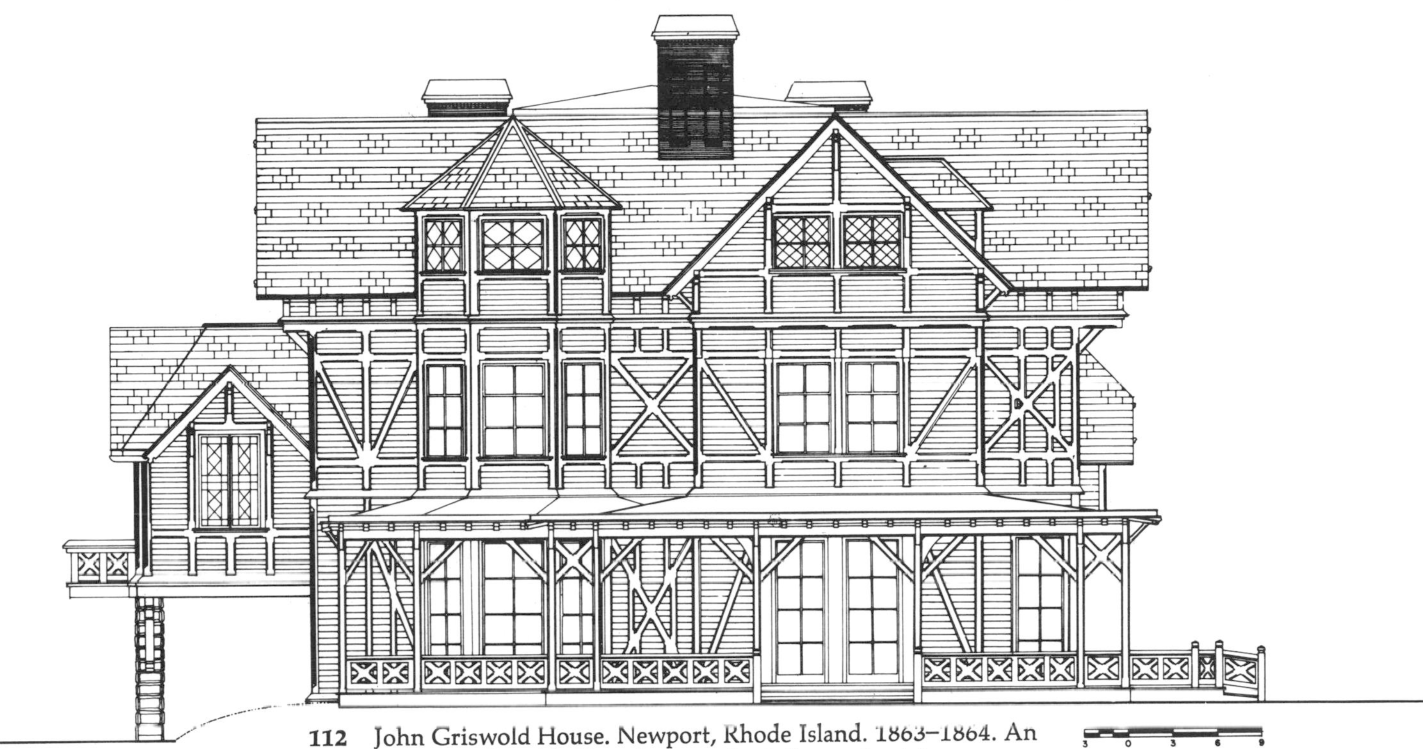

112 John Griswold House. Newport, Rhode Island. 1863–1864. An evocation of medieval half-timbering, playfully emphasizing horizontal, vertical, and diagonal framing.

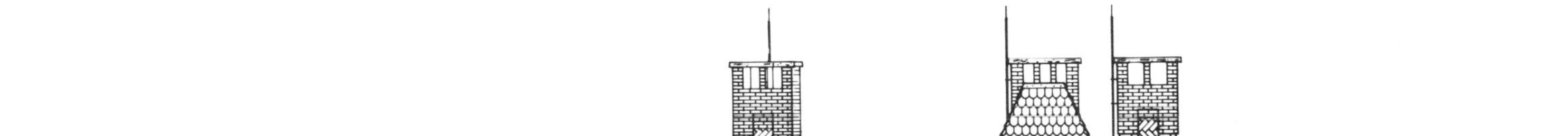

113 Emlen Physick House. Cape May, New Jersey. 1879; attributed to architect Frank Furness. The weblike porch supports and spiky roof silhouette lighten the dwelling's apparent mass.

114 Commandant's Quarters. Pensacola, Florida. 1874. Porch construction as a showcase for carpenter skill and originality.

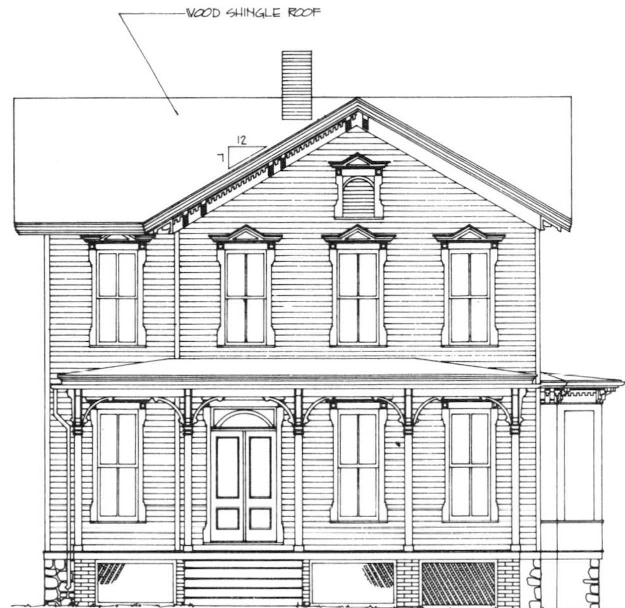

115 Morrow House. Lawrence, Kansas. 1870–1875. In the vernacular, a fusion of Italianate and Stick Style Gothic.

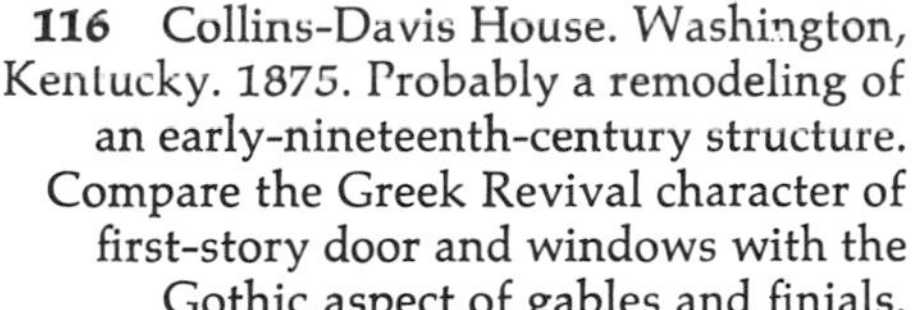

116 Collins-Davis House. Washington, Kentucky. 1875. Probably a remodeling of an early-nineteenth-century structure. Compare the Greek Revival character of first-story door and windows with the Gothic aspect of gables and finials.

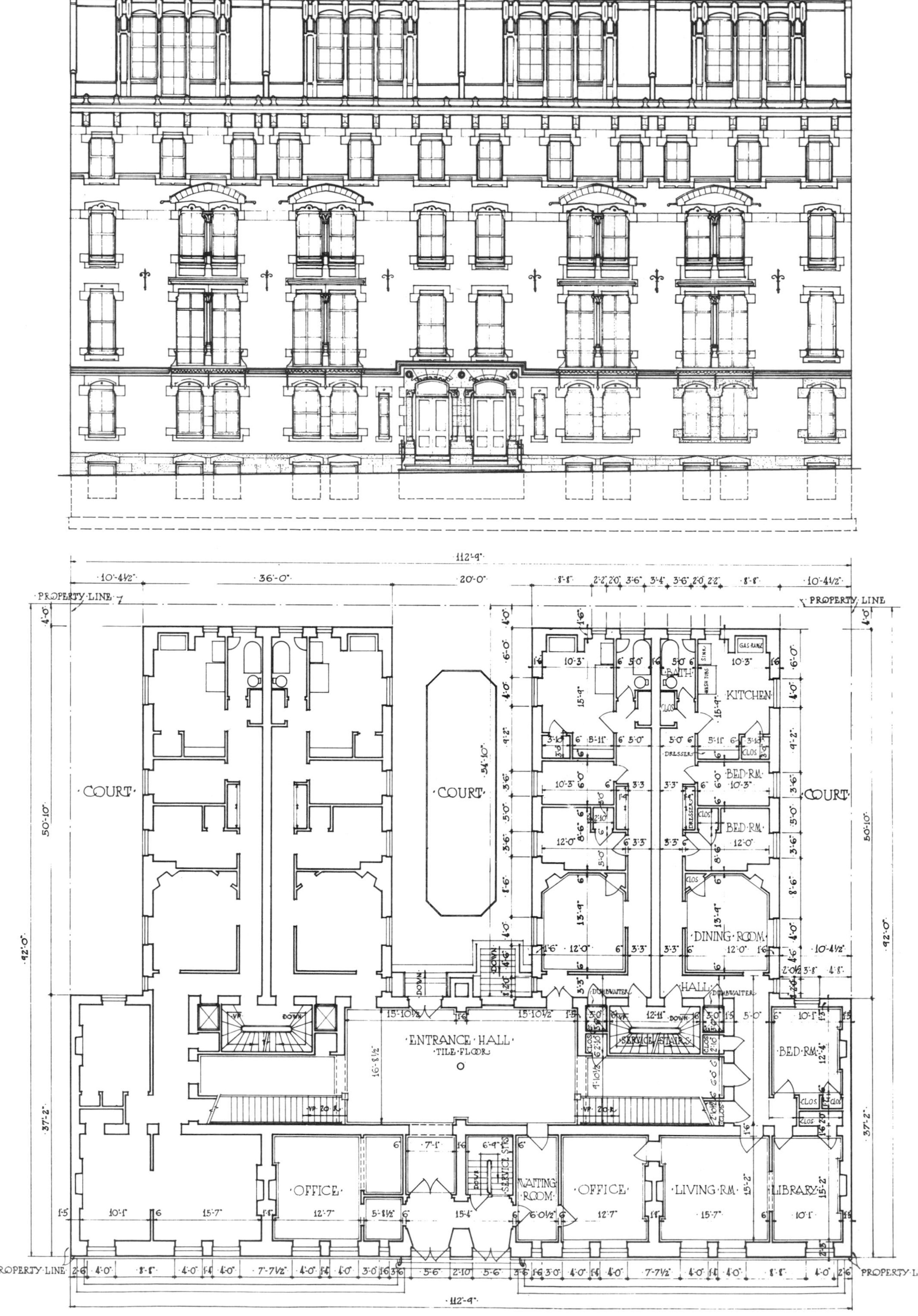

COURT
COURT
COURT
ENTRANCE HALL
TILE FLOOR
OFFICE
OFFICE
WAITING ROOM
LIVING RM.
LIBRARY
DINING ROOM
BED RM.
BED RM.
BED RM.
KITCHEN
BATH
SERVICE STAIRS
HALL
PROPERTY LINE
112'-9"

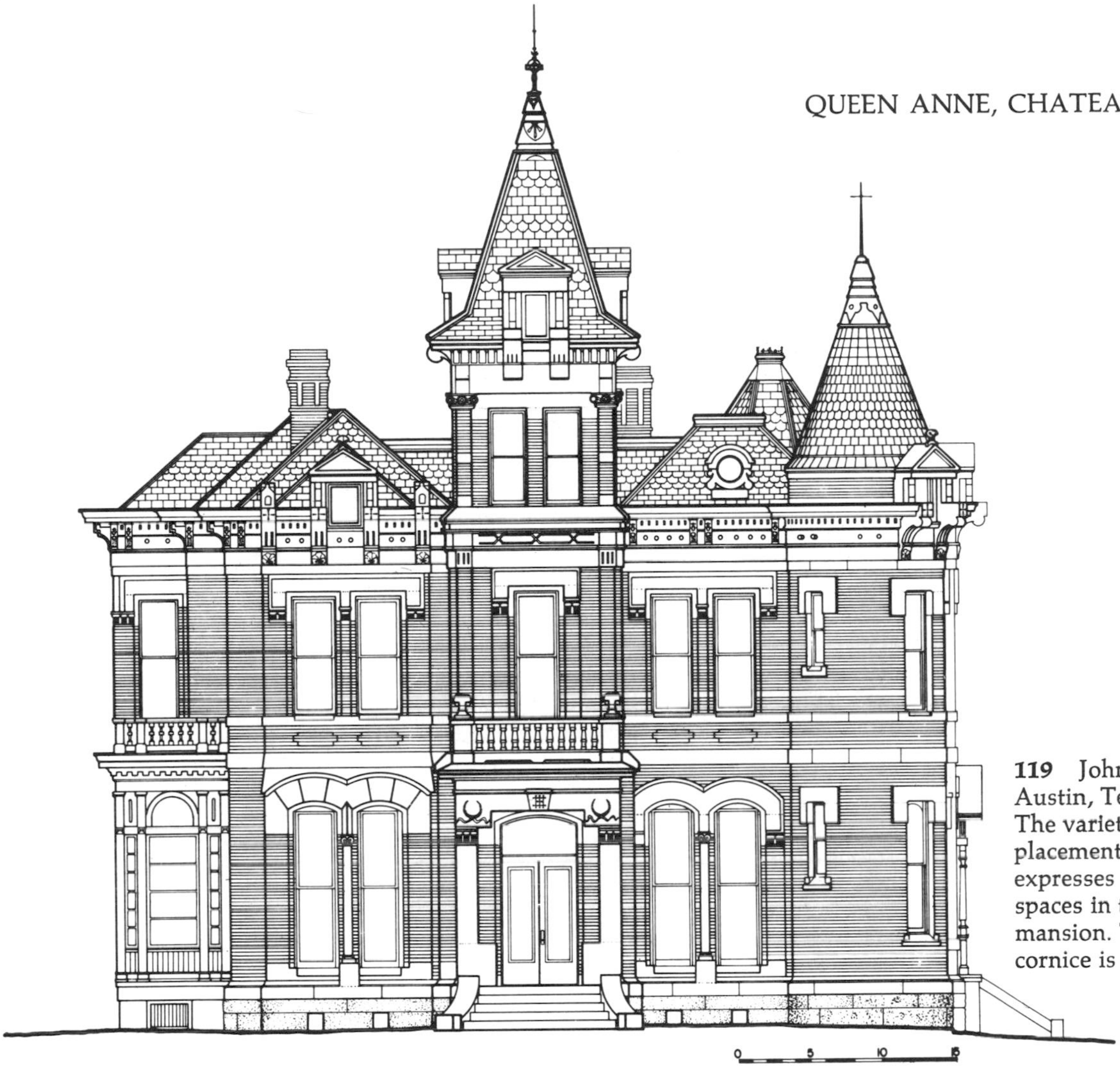

119 John Houghton House. Austin, Texas. 1886–1887. The variety in design and placement of the windows expresses variety in interior spaces in the Queen Anne mansion. The elaborate cornice is of sheet metal.

◀ **117, 118** Left: Stuyvesant Apartment. New York, New York. 1869; Richard Morris Hunt, architect. French in ancestry, this prototype apartment house assembles brick, stone, copper, and wood with vivacity and elegance.

120 Miss Parks House. Cape May, New Jersey. C.1876. Carpenter Queen Anne. Note particularly the display of wooden lathework.

121 Glenmont. West Orange, New Jersey. 1880; Henry Hudson Holly, architect. Queen Anne in its eclecticism. The broad gables and low verandas (not originally enclosed) emphasize the horizontal dimension.

122 Robert Machek House. Milwaukee, Wisconsin. 1893–1894. A Jacobean hybrid, built by a Viennese carpenter. Virtuoso woodcarving decorates gables, window surrounds, and railings.

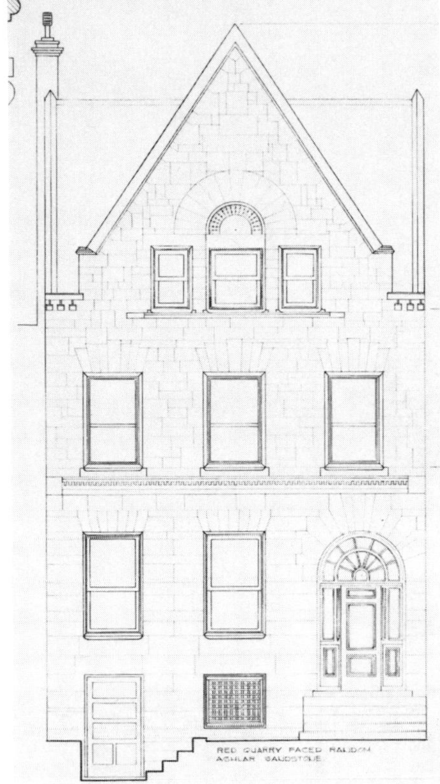

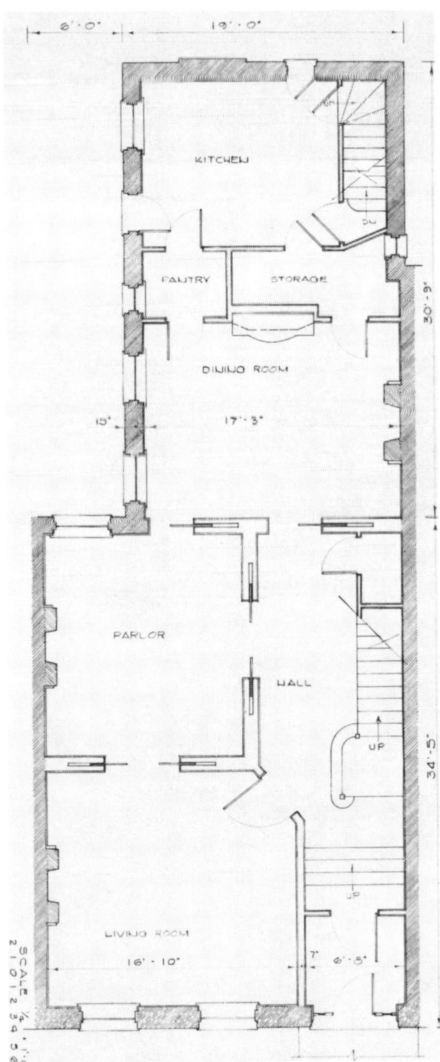

FIRST FLOOR PLAN

Ira Heath House, Chicago, Illinois; 1886.

123, 124 Ira Heath House. Chicago, Illinois. 1886; attributed to Sullivan and Adler. With overscaled fanlight, steep gable, and Palladian window motif, Queen Anne style transfigures the traditional row house.

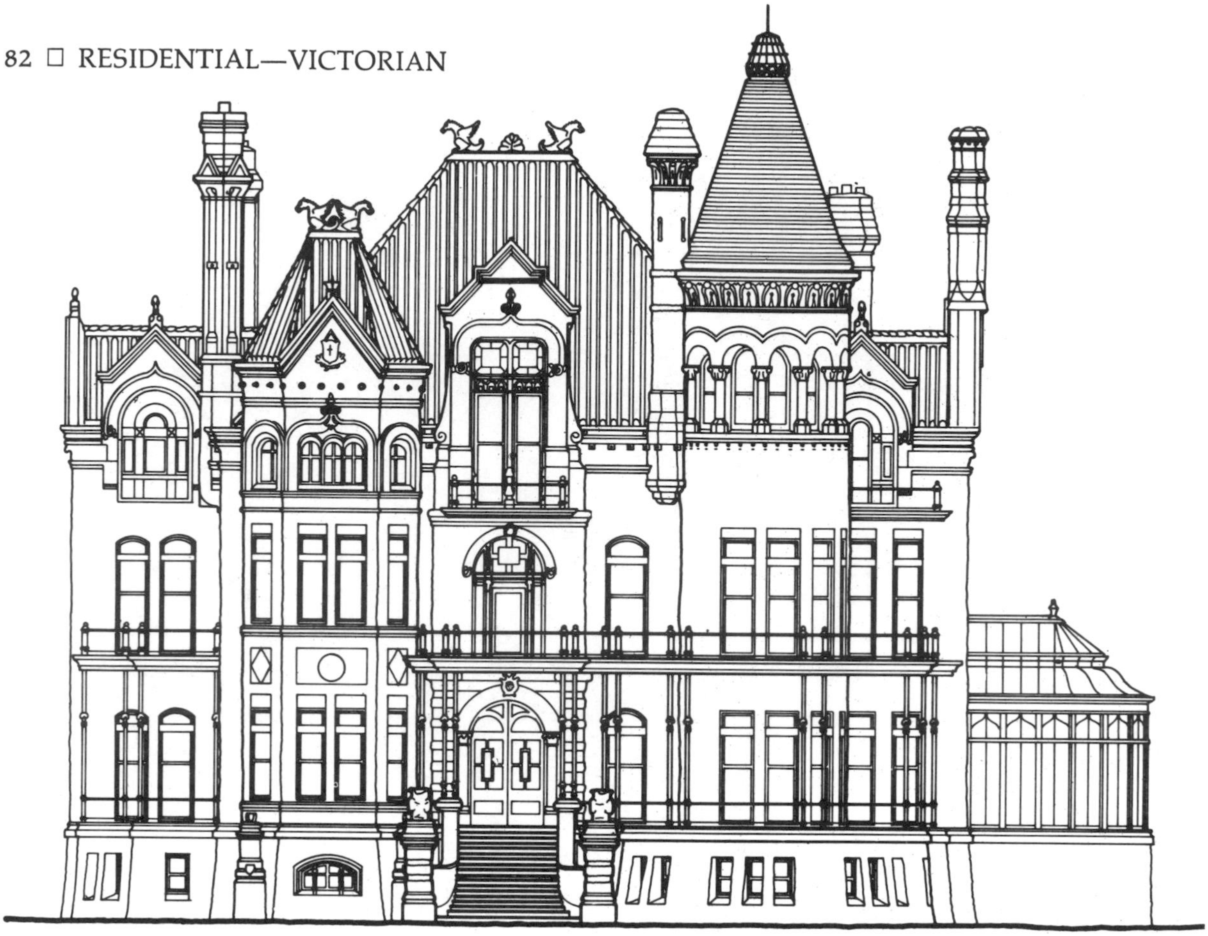

125, 126 Walter Gresham House. Galveston, Texas. 1886–1893. Renewed emphasis on height and verticality as Chateauesque forms emerge from Queen Anne.

0 5 20

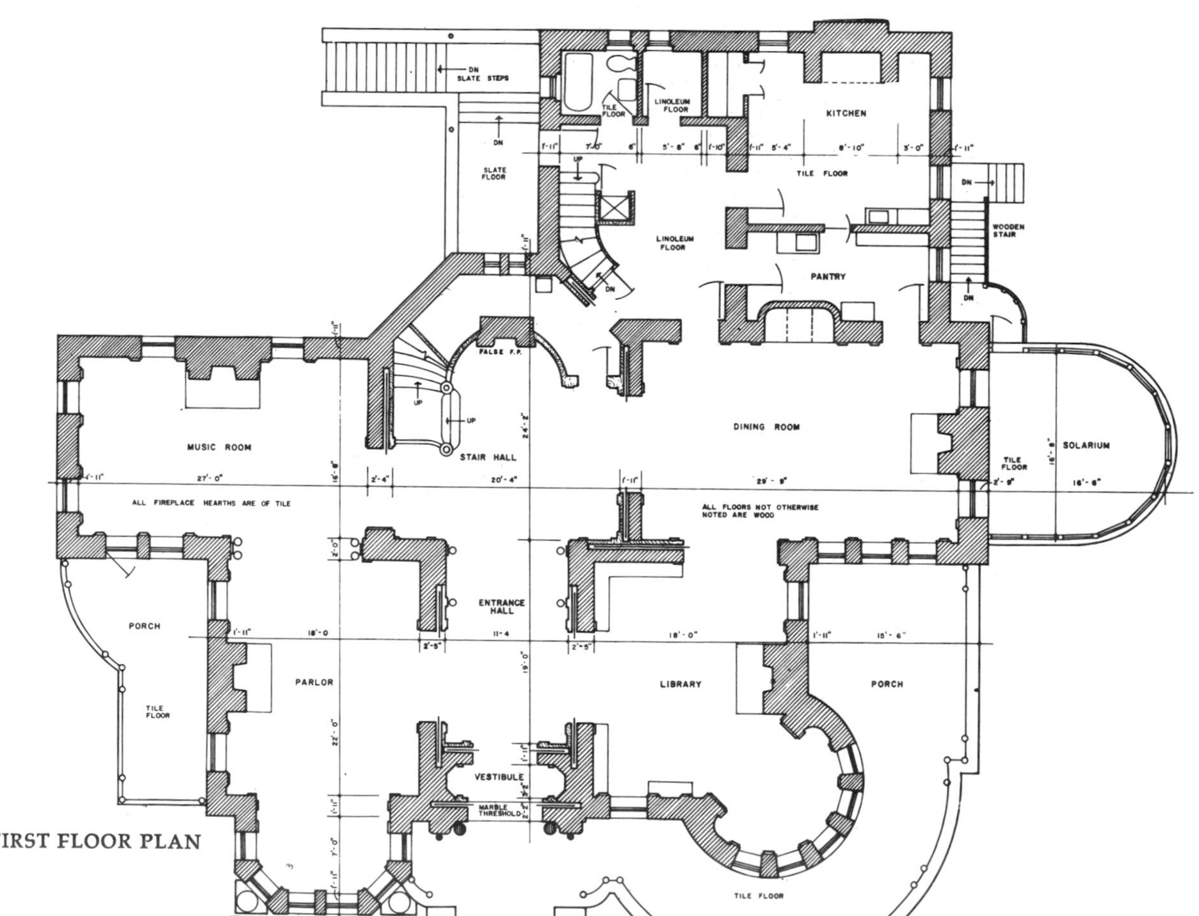

FIRST FLOOR PLAN

127 John Lindale House. Magnolia, Delaware. C.1900. Relative symmetry and simplicity characterize late and provincial Queen Anne.

128 Newton Mitchell House. San Antonio, Texas. 1880s remodeling of c.1860 structure. The Queen Anne doorway and second-story window are Late Victorian modifications of a Classic Revival dwelling.

129 Brown-Donahue House. Cape Elizabeth, Maine. 1885–1886. Boulderlike stone masonry conveys the boldness and vigor of the Shingle Style. The photograph at the right reveals the particular character imparted by the flow and pattern of shingled surfaces.

130 Caffey's Inlet Life-Saving Station. Outer Banks, North Carolina. C.1900. Shingle Style in the vernacular.

Brown-Donahue House, Cape Elizabeth, Maine; 1885–1886 (see 129).

131 Isaac Bell House. Newport, Rhode Island. 1882–1883; McKim, Mead & White, architects. The steps lead to a deep, encircling porch; note that the posts are shingle-sheathed.

132 Kingscote. Newport, Rhode Island. 1880–1881 Shingle Style wing (at the left) by McKim, Mead & White, was an addition to an 1839–1841 Gothic Revival dwelling by Richard Upjohn.

133, 134 The Reservation, Buildings 2 and 5. Long Branch, New Jersey. C.1900. Late examples, with Queen Anne affinities.

135 John Glessner House. Chicago, Illinois. 1886–1887; Henry Hobson Richardson, architect. Masterful handling of overscaled and heavily textured stone masonry.

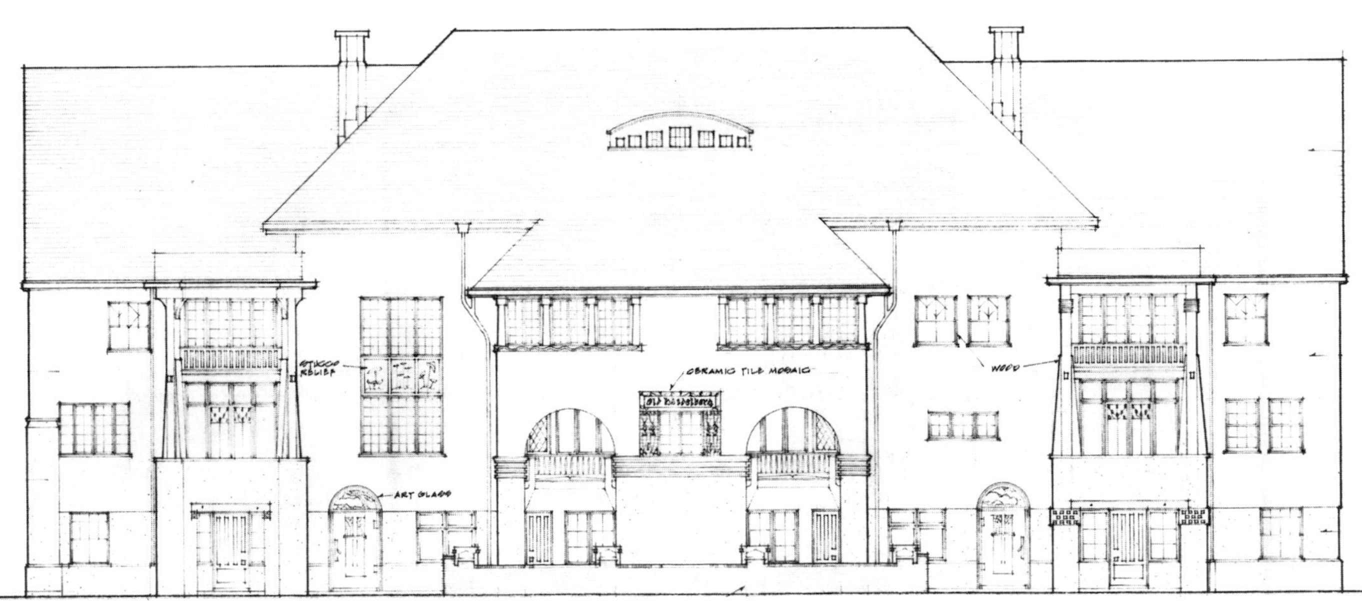

136 Old Heidelberg Apartments. Pittsburgh, Pennsylvania. 1905. Art glass, ceramic tile, and stucco surfacing reflect a turn-of-the-century interest in Arts and Crafts—but note the persistence of Richardsonian motifs.

137 Frederick Vanderbilt House. Hyde Park, New York. 1896–1898; McKim, Mead & White, architects. Classic Revival in the genre of the White House, but richer, with ornate Corinthian porticos.

Frederick Vanderbilt House, Hyde Park, New York; 1896–1898.

139 House. Plainfield, New Jersey. C.1900. Ample scale and a range of ornamental detail from a long and undifferentiated "Colonial" period distinguish this Colonial Revival. The dwelling is embellished with early colonial paneled chimneys, later colonial small-paned window sash, and such post-colonial Classical forms as pediments, cornice, Palladian motif, and urns.

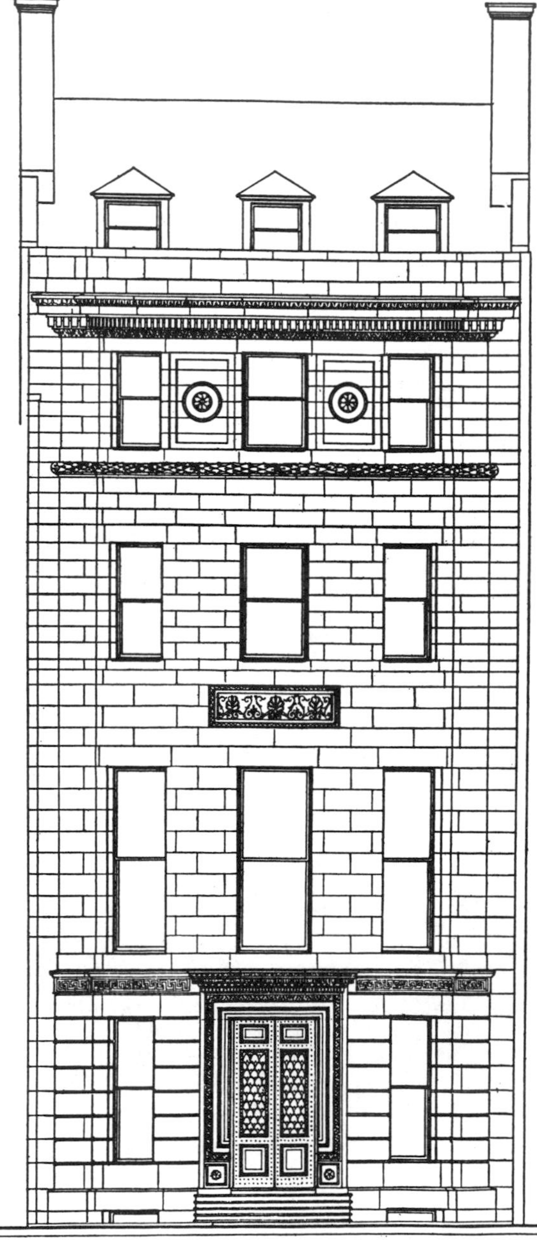

138 George Nickerson House. Boston, Massachusetts. 1895–1897; McKim, Mead & White, architects. The simple bowed facade evokes Boston's dignified Federal-era streets.

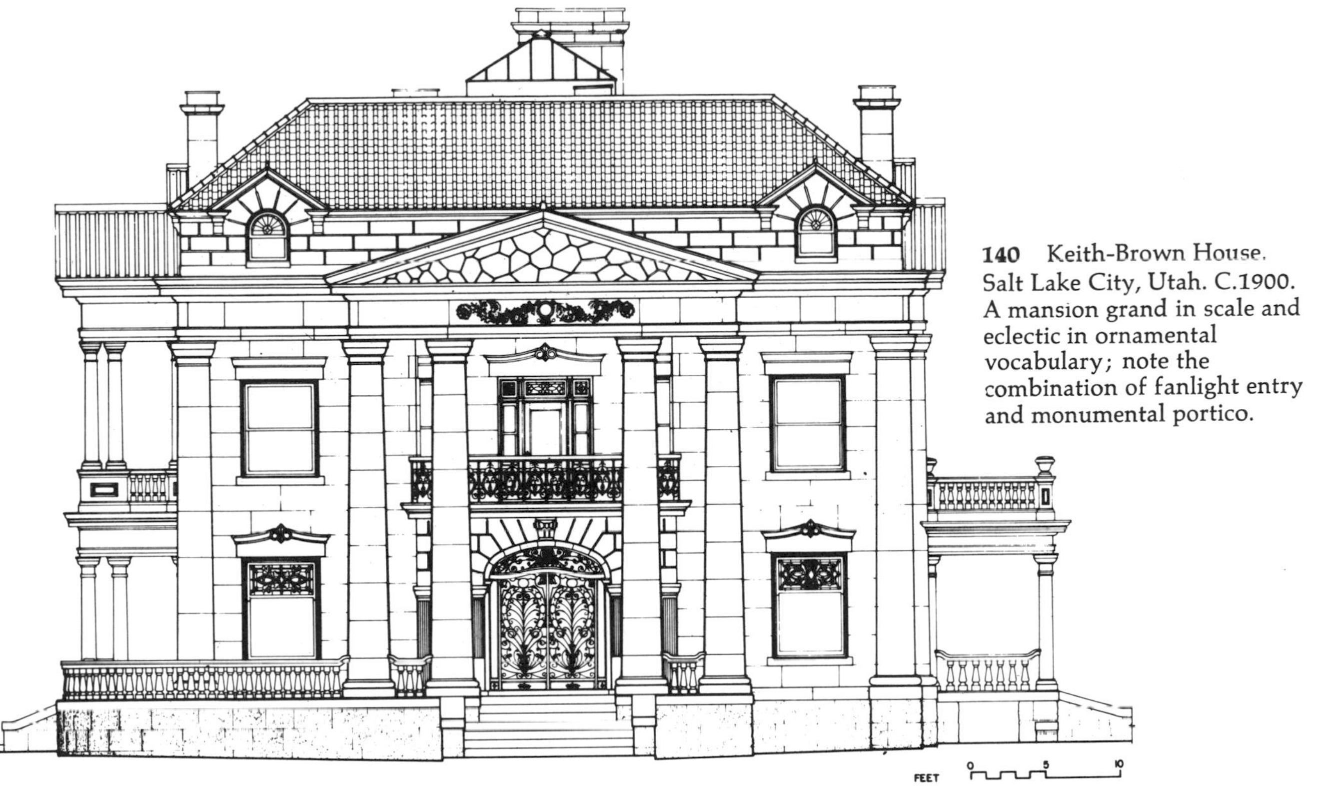

140 Keith-Brown House. Salt Lake City, Utah. C.1900. A mansion grand in scale and eclectic in ornamental vocabulary; note the combination of fanlight entry and monumental portico.

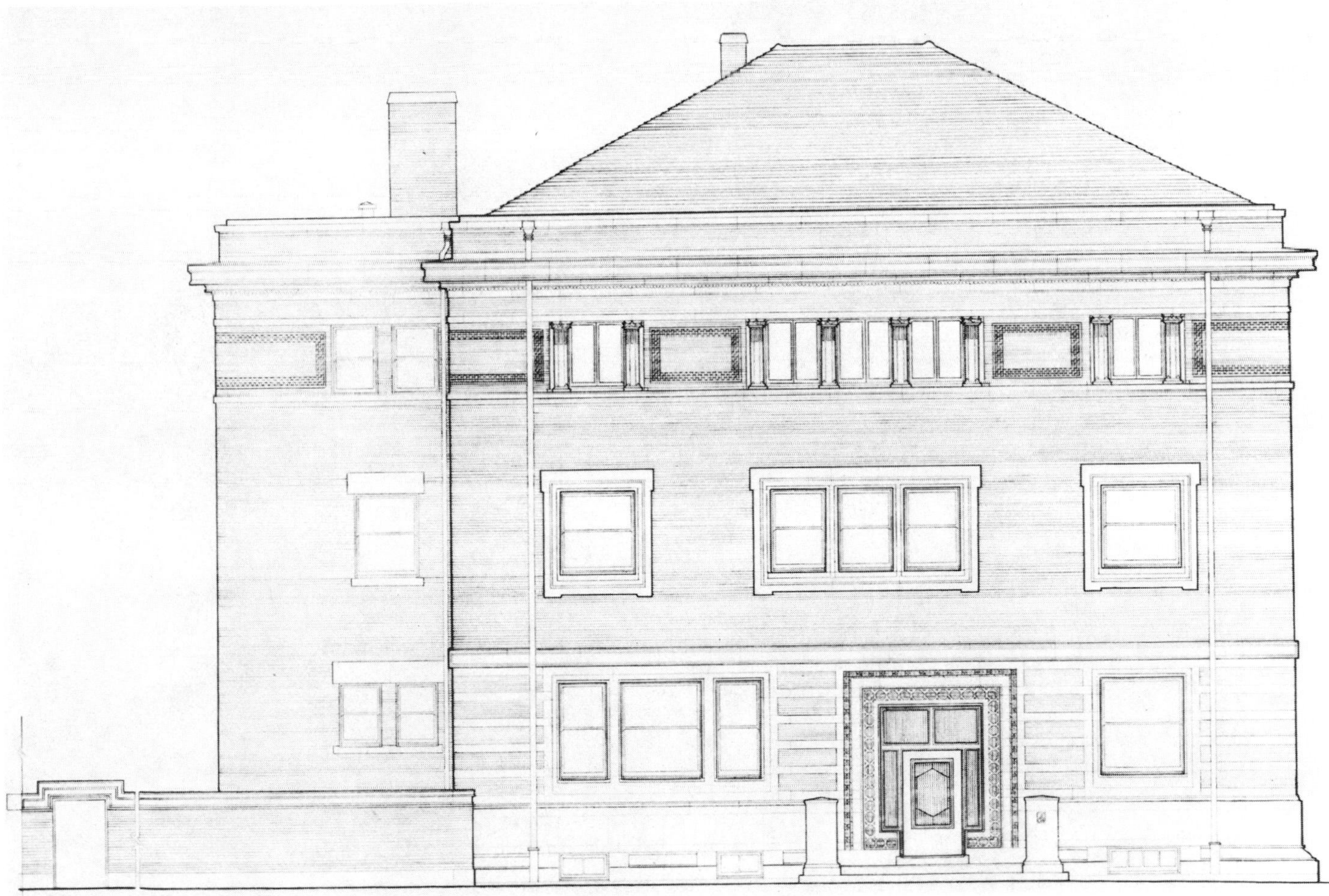

141 Albert Madlener House. Chicago, Illinois. 1902. With its non-historical ornament and boldly simplified geometric forms, this dwelling is decidedly modern. Nevertheless, scale and proportion do evoke the Colonial Revival.

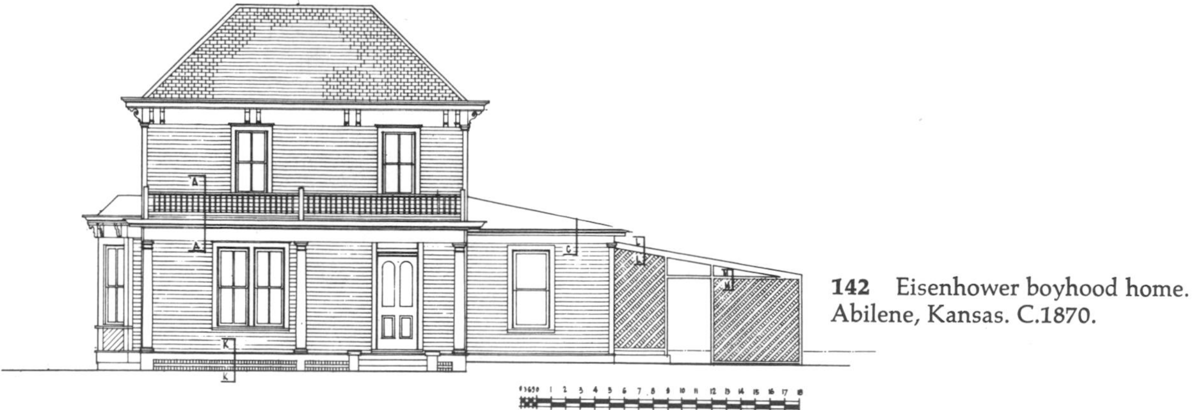

142 Eisenhower boyhood home. Abilene, Kansas. C.1870.

Eisenhower boyhood home, Abilene, Kansas; c. 1870.

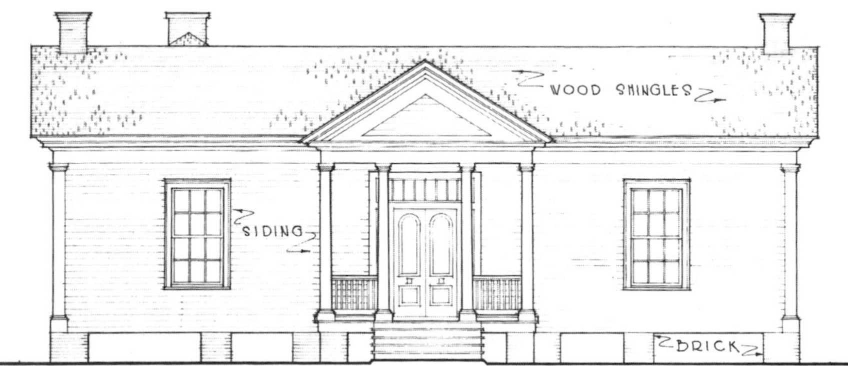

143 Governor Sayers House. Bastrop, Texas. 1868.

144 John Wentworth Farmhouse. Summit, Illinois. 1868.

145 Unidentified working-class house. 1877.

146 Kuntz House. Louisville, Kentucky. C.1890.

147, 148, 149 Orange Grove housing for industrial workers. Chattanooga, Tennessee. A long, thin, "shotgun" plan typical of the South. C.1888.

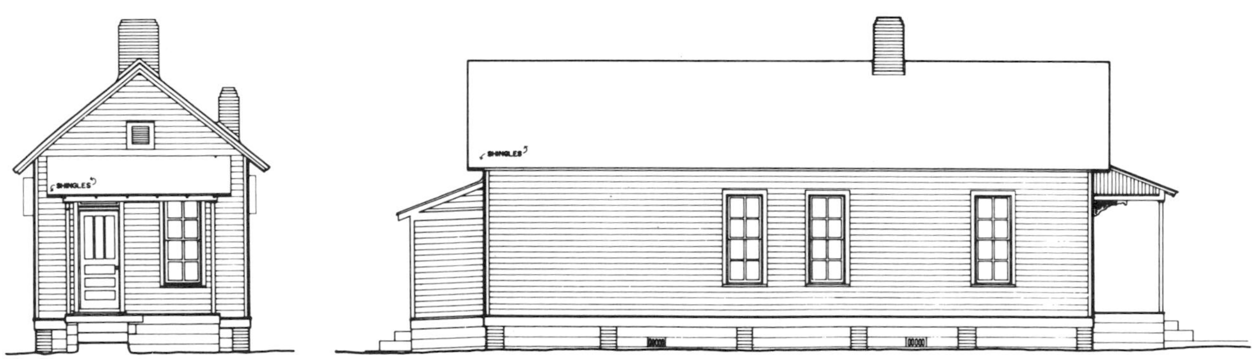

150, 151 President Kennedy birthplace. Brookline, Massachusetts. C.1908.

152 San Gregorio Street. Pescadero, California. C.1860–1890.

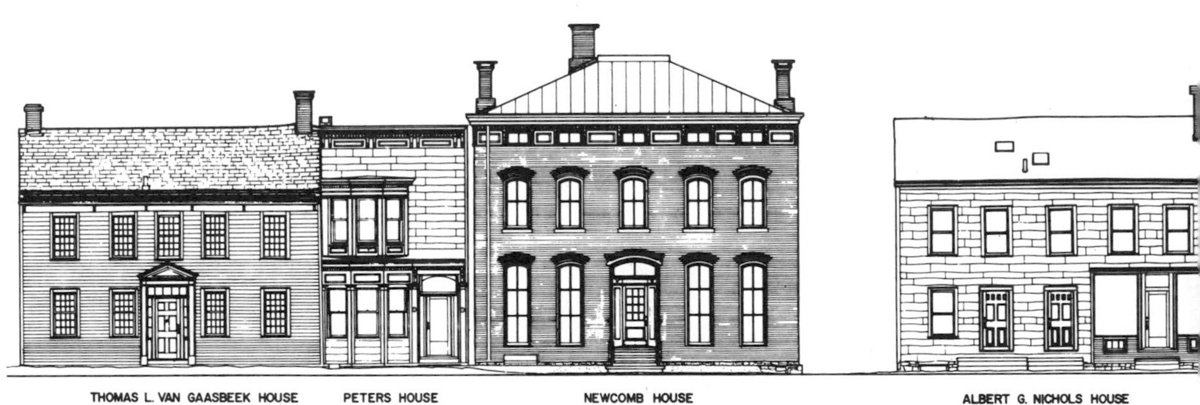

153 Clinton Avenue. Kingston, New York. A typical mid-Victorian streetfront. Van Gaasbeek, 1824; Peters, 1874 addition; Newcomb, 1872; Nichols, 1852, with c.1910 shopfront; Smith houses, 1831; Westbrook, c.1860.

5 10 20 FT

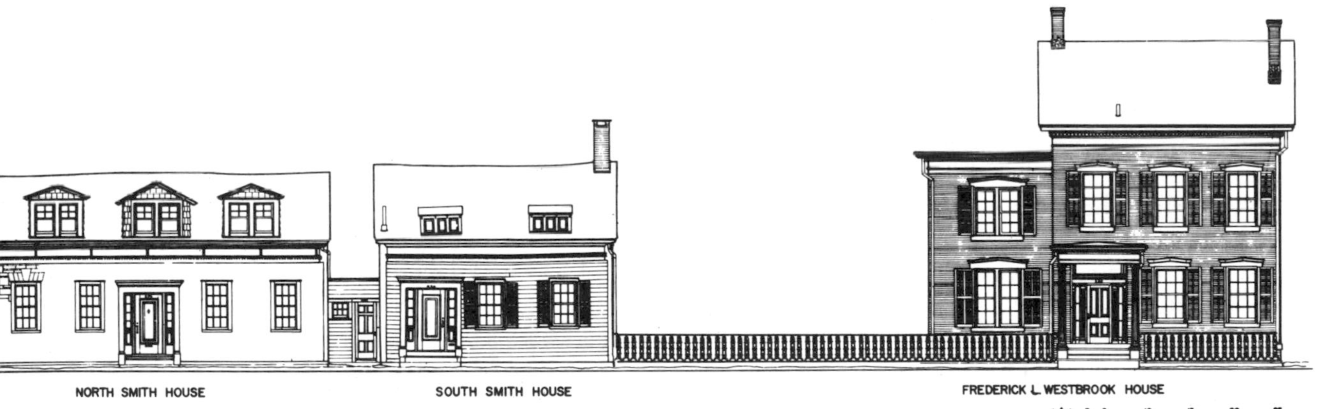
NORTH SMITH HOUSE
SOUTH SMITH HOUSE
FREDERICK L. WESTBROOK HOUSE
1 0 1 3 5 10 15 20 25

1900-1940

Twentieth Century

Prairie School, Bungalow
Period Revivals
Modern and Moderne • Multifamily Residences

THE new century promised the American family a new style of living. A rapidly expanding industrial economy burgeoned job opportunities in every corner of the nation, fattened workers' paychecks, and produced a consumer revolution. These were the years of the Ford car and the chain store, of installment buying and the mass-circulation monthly, of the movie palace, the telephone, and the country club.

The new life-style brought with it nostalgia for a pre-machine age and a revived and refreshed handicraft and decorative-arts traditions. In comfortable midwestern suburbs, the architect searched for forms to express both modern spirit and the deepest human values. He found new ways of relating interior and exterior space, new understanding of the nature of materials, novel ornament that expressed structure.

"Organic architecture," said Frank Lloyd Wright, "can live and let live because it can never express mere style." But the time was not yet ripe—the Prairie School scarcely survived the First World War.

Like the Prairie School house, the Bungalow house on the West Coast reflected diverse undercurrents—Arts and Crafts philosophy, the American Stick Style and Shingle Style, Japanese aesthetic principles and methods of wood framing.

The Bungalow also answered to a mild climate and an informal life-style. But with a few splendid exceptions (above all, the work of the Greene brothers), it was a mass mode, low in cost and small in scale. It was not spread by architects, but by published builders' plans that sold for only a few dollars apiece. In freshly reinterpreted versions of Stick, Shingle, Colonial, and rustic-log-cabin modes, the Bungalow—exported south, north, and east—had enormous vogue in the period from 1900 to 1920.

East Coast architects remained nostalgic for the past. "We are drawing upon all known motives for our information, changing, adapting, developing them to new uses and requirements, finding the new through the old," declared Aymar Embury, a prominent architect and critic.

In suburban Boston, New York, or Philadelphia, architects were inspired by local Colonial forms. So Florida, the Southwest, and California found their own heritage.

By the 1920s, revival styles broke geographic constraints; the Spanish Colonial sprang up in Scarsdale, the Dutch Colonial in Beverly Hills. In a Romantic spirit, styles that never were American—the English Tudor cottage, the French provincial farmhouse—became enormously popular.

The choice of material and the mood of the client determined style as much as anything else. Stuccoed hollow-concrete blocks created an Italian Renaissance villa, an English gingerbread house, or a Spanish hacienda; brick a Georgian manor house; clapboard an English Colonial farmhouse and rubble stone a Dutch one.

As today's observer will discover, it was Period Revival architecture that impressed the consumer in the first half of the twentieth century.

Pioneered by architect Irving Gill, one modern form grew out of the indigenous Spanish vernacular of California. This mode had a powerful simplicity. It was planned for machine-age comfort and convenience, and its dwellings were built in new ways, using poured concrete and metal framing. But it found only a select patronage.

It was after the Peace of 1919 that modernism found a place in America, with the importation of the International Style. This modern architecture made no claim to "style" but to modern planning, modern structural principles, and modern materials. Spawned by a crowded, industrial society, the Modern house answered the need for functional planning and the desire for a closer relationship to nature.

Architects who preferred traditional style also experimented with planning innovations. From coast to coast, there developed new standards for comfort, higher expectations for convenience, and a new ingenuity in devising solutions to old housing problems.

A home should be "at once practical and aesthetic," proclaimed *House Beautiful*, a monthly that held up the homemaker's viewpoint, in 1925. "A good house is one which exactly fits the needs of the family for whom it is built."

Thus, central heating, gas or electric refrigeration, electric wiring, gas stoves, tiled kitchens, shower baths, and concrete cellar floors became the norm for every new home.

Novel room arrangements put the kitchen of the servantless household in easy communication with both the front door and the children's play yard, and opened house interiors to space and light and garden views.

Suburb and country retreat newly accessible by automobile filled in the spaces around the nation's large cities. "To accompany a real estate man through his district is instructive," wrote a Czech journalist in 1930. "He is a founder of communities; beside him, Peter the Great is a small operator."

But the detached one-family dwelling was not for every famliy. The bungalow court, the garden apartment, and the two- or three-family home (as two- or three-decker) thickened development along trolley lines and new rapid transit systems. In larger cities, clifflike apartment houses built an almost solid wall from six to twenty stories high along long avenues from Riverside Drive to Lake Shore Drive.

Despite Depression, despite pockets of persistent poverty in rural areas, in the South, and in the cities, the American home—no matter its style—reflected the highest standard of living that history had ever achieved.

Materials

In the first two decades of the twentieth century, the Arts and Crafts philosophy guides selection of crafted materials for architectual elements —unpainted hand-carved and hand-finished wood, ceramic tile, leaded and stained glass, and wrought iron, for example. Period Revival and Bungalow structures persist in the use of these materials through the 1930s.

By the 1920s, however, the machine aesthetic more and more insistently dictates poured concrete, concrete cinder blocks, stucco on metal lath, steel framing, glass blocks, and other elements of industrialized technology. Nevertheless, it is safe to say that throughout this period, the majority of dwellings were built of traditional materials, and in traditional ways.

Plan

The conventional symmetrical plan of the Colonial Revival dwelling is the dominant form at the opening of the twentieth century, and is again at midcentury, but the intervening years are a period of profound innovation.

The ground-hugging Prairie house triumphantly exploits new spatial concepts and modern functional planning. The structure is formed by a series of interpenetrating horizontal and vertical volumes composed along several axes. Room partitions are reduced or eliminated, skylights and clerestories (windows at the upper zone of a high wall) flood interiors with light. Exterior walls are little more than an alignment of doors and windows—so space can flow easily from one area to the next and to the out-of-doors [154; 157].

The house is no longer boxlike, and its roof is not merely a cover, but an expressively low, hovering shape (pitched, hipped, or flat) anchored in place by a massive chimney. In a far less radical manner, the one- or one-and-a-half-story Bungalow house of the century's first decade, and as modified later, also attempts to link indoors and outdoors [155; 156].

With fewer but larger rooms and with more doors and windows, even Revival-style dwellings tend to be more open in character, frequently following a laterally extended plan that relates to outdoor living, with sleeping porches, patios, and terraces. Experiments to organize separate living, sleeping, and working spaces create plans of elaborately staggered shapes [169; 170]. Flexible planning permits two-story spaces, interior balconies, and areas designed for future expansion. Typically, the garage is integrated into the total plan and is located near the kitchen and the front entrance [169].

Elevation

Whether avowedly anti-historical or frankly nostalgic for the past, common attributes of early-twentieth-century houses are strong horizontality, emphasis on cubic volumes and their articulation, the use of window walls or horizontal window bands, and the reduction of ornament and detail or its redesign in the interest of modernity.

PRAIRIE SCHOOL, BUNGALOW

Essentially lacking ornament, the walls of the Prairie house are, nevertheless, "decorated" by long courses of smooth stone coping or dark-stained wood that enliven the building surface and exaggerate the pronounced horizontality [154; 157]. Strong corner piers also exploit structure for decorative effect. Similarly, materials are used for color and texture—the pattern of dark wood and shingle against stucco [157] or the tapestry effect of thin Roman brick [154]. Windows are framed in novel and simple fashion; colored and leaded glass is not uncommon.

Details distinguish the Bungalow structure's style, from log-cabin rustic to Swiss chalet, but the form is fairly constant [155]. Typically, the Bungalow has widely overhanging gables forming a porch at the front, supported by heavy battered piers. The natural quality of materials is emphasized: stone as cobble or boulder; wood in stained earth tones for its stick quality; shingle or stucco for tactile richness.

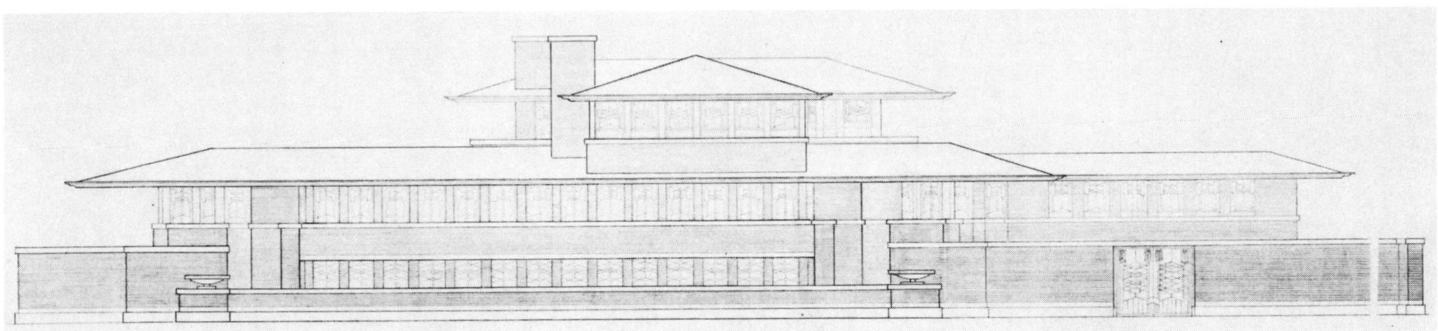

154 Frederick Robie House. Chicago, Illinois. 1907–1909; Frank Lloyd Wright, architect. Virtually an abstract composition in which expansive space-defining planes (parapets, window bands, balcony, low hipped roof) play against decisive vertical elements (urns, corner piers, chimneys).

PERIOD REVIVALS

The Period Revival dwelling of the period from 1910 to 1930 tends to be quaint and informal although carefully disciplined. It does, on occasion, reproduce historic precedent with accuracy, but more often it assimilates and combines diverse motifs for convenience, gracious living, and artistic effect.

Distinctive characteristics are a garden setting, an additive composition, irregular fenestration, and vernacular roof shapes like the gambrel or the shed to suggest an indigenous local style, such as Spanish or Dutch Colonial [158; 160].

Multiple-family dwellings, with no historic precedent, tend to borrow motifs to suggest a specific style—a heavy cornice, dentil moldings, and an iron grille for the Italian [179], a stucco surface and a tile roof for the Spanish Colonial [184], cross gables for the Tudor [181].

Ornament tends to be underscaled and carefully executed [161]. Fine effects are achieved through the handling of quality materials for color and texture—shingle or slate roofs with a weathered, hand-crafted appearance; dark-stained "hand-hewn" oak lintels, tapestry brick laid to create a richly textured surface.

In the decade of the 1930s, by comparison, the Period Revival dwelling has simpler massing, less lavish use of materials, cruder detailing, and more economical scale. Sparked by the spirit of Williamsburg, "Early American" styles predominate. Again, some are faithful reproductions. Others make no direct reference to historical precedent but merely suggest it by motifs such as paired end chimneys, porticos of exaggerated proportions [163], additive composition [166], or a saltbox profile. Not infrequently, a Victorian home is renovated in a Colonial mood [164].

In the Southwest, original forms are also rich in historical association: the one-story Pueblo house with undulating adobe (or adobe-like) walls and projecting vigas (roof beams) [170, 171]; the Spanish Colonial house with classically framed door, patio, and balcony, and low, hipped tile roof [165]; the Spanish Mission dwelling, bare of ornamentation, displaying smooth walls, arched openings, and tile roof. The most advanced among these are truly pioneers in modern design aesthetic [182].

MODERN AND MODERNE

The intricate composition and extended structure of the Modern house can defy precise identification of front or back, interior or exterior. Atticless and flat-roofed, the profile is low. The concrete floor is laid directly at garden grade, and glass walls and sliding panels establish continuity between interior and exterior space. Trellised roof overhangs further blur the margins of indoors and out [172, 173].

The Modern house rejects ornament yet draws heavily on surface and texture, employing reinforced concrete, insulating board, glass both in walls and windows, and redwood or other dark-stained wood for framing. The pattern of windows grouped in bands, either at full-room height or in the upper wall zones, is a major feature.

As American Modern merges with European

155 Bungalow. Tacoma, Washington. C.1910. Suggestions of handcrafting, such as exposed pegs and carved brackets, are part of the Bungalow aesthetic.

International Style in the 1920s, experiments become more radical and the product takes on a mechanical appearance [174, 175, 176]. But by the early 1930s, experimentation has generally run its course. The result is the Moderne dwelling, emphasizing simple geometric volumes, and plain wall surfaces set off by linear elements. The dwelling is sculptural in character, self-contained and basically symmetrical. Door and window openings, though large, do not violate the stolid character of walls [177].

MULTIFAMILY RESIDENCES

Stacking family units one above another, multifamily residences emerge in every style and scale [179; 180]. The four- to six-story walkup may be either a tenement with two or more family units on each floor sharing toilet facilities, or a garden apartment, with full amenities and a countrified setting [181; 183; 184]. Elevator-serviced residences of six to twenty stories have expansive floor plans for each apartment. An experimental plan groups low buildings around an interior court to provide each family unit with access to both communal and private recreational space [182].

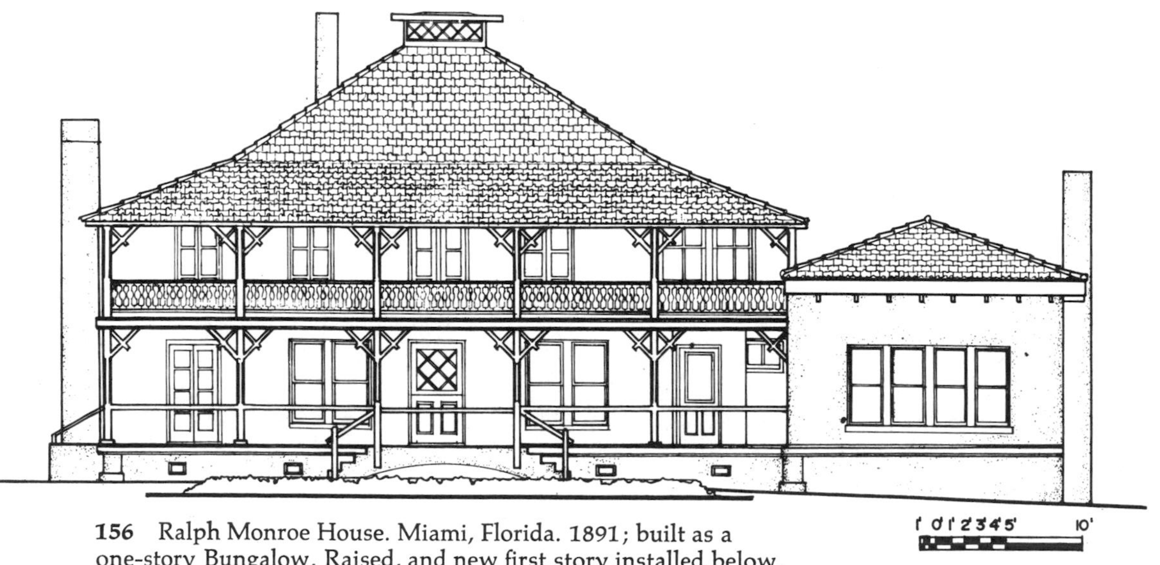

156 Ralph Monroe House. Miami, Florida. 1891; built as a one-story Bungalow. Raised, and new first story installed below, 1908.

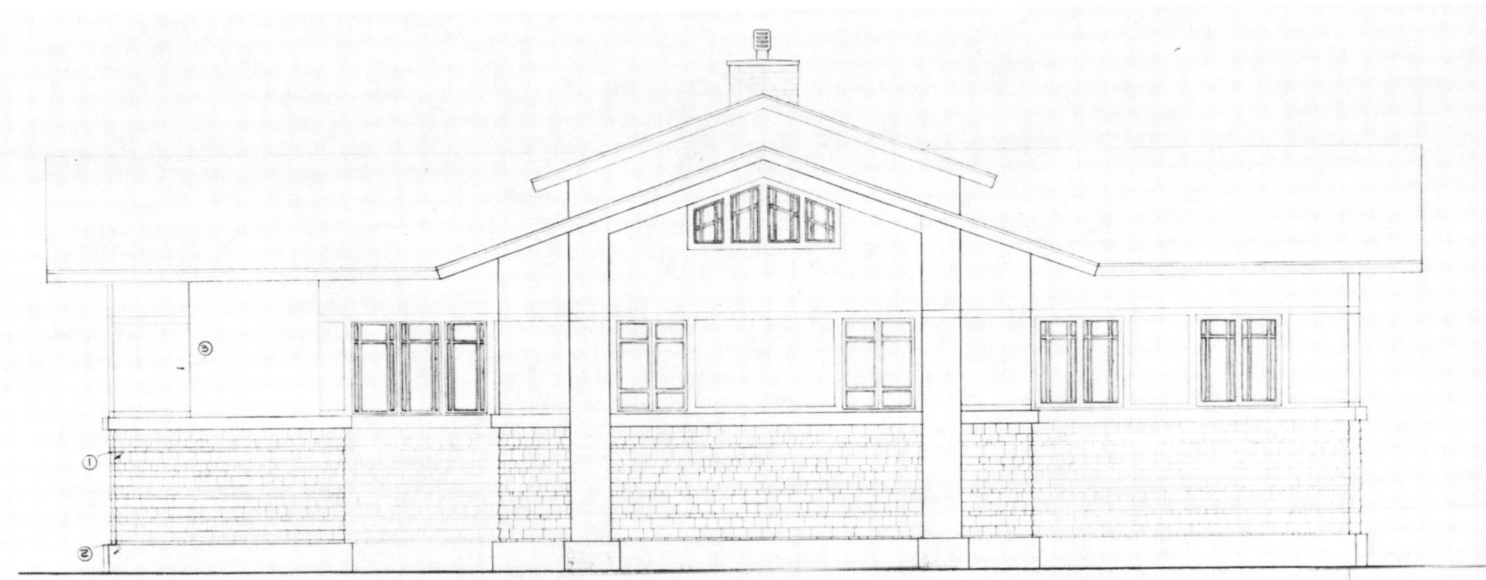

157 T. S. Eastabrook House. Oak Park, Illinois. 1908. A Prairie School house of modest character, with gently pitched roof, rustic stucco and board siding, abbreviated window openings, lack of historical ornament.

T. S. Eastabrook House, Oak Park, Illinois; 1908.

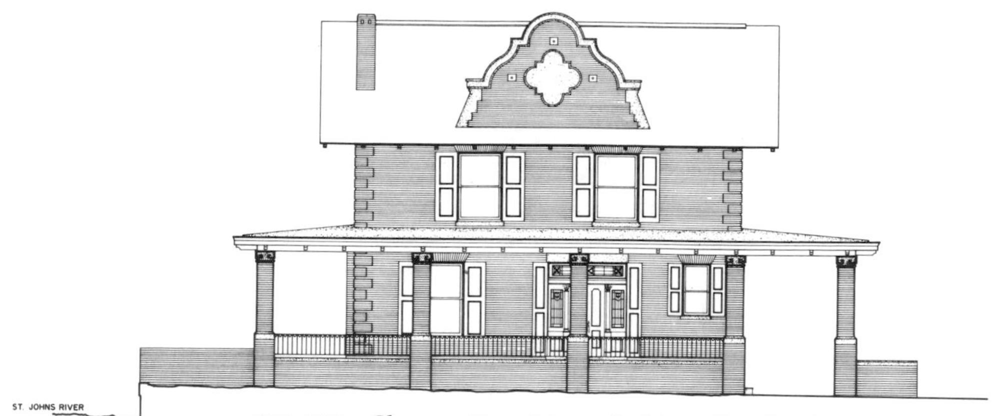

158, 159 Clarence Doty House. Jacksonville, Florida. C.1900. The shaped gable imparts a Spanish Baroque flavor to a Colonial Revival dwelling.

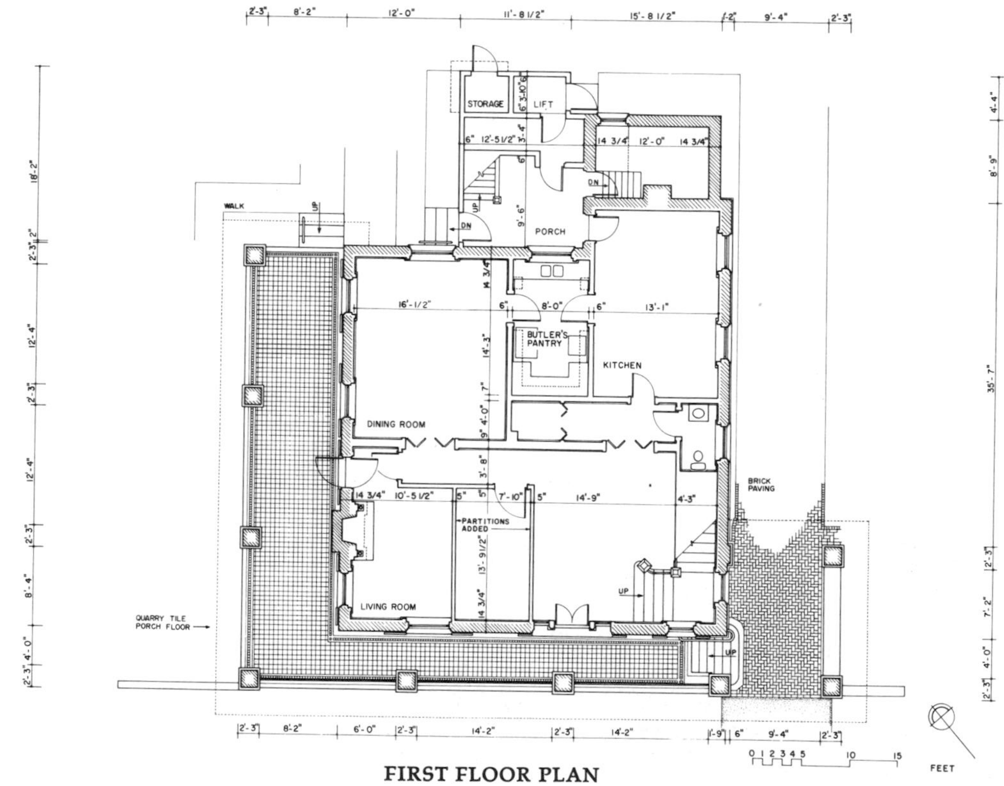

FIRST FLOOR PLAN

160 Marshall Morgan House. Philadelphia, Pennsylvania. C.1910. Despite quotations from colonial history—use of native fieldstone, louvered shutters, shed roof, and gambrel shapes—this residence is definitely modern in concept.

Marshall Morgan House, Philadelphia, Pennsylvania; c. 1910.

161 Alan Scaife House. Laughlintown, Pennsylvania. C.1920. Characteristic of post–World War I Gothic: essentially horizontal; simplified wall surfaces with restrained and finely crafted details; a combination of overscaled and underscaled window openings.

162, 163 Wilder House. Greenwich, Connecticut. C.1934. 1930s revivalism alludes to a historical period, but asserts the importance of geometry.

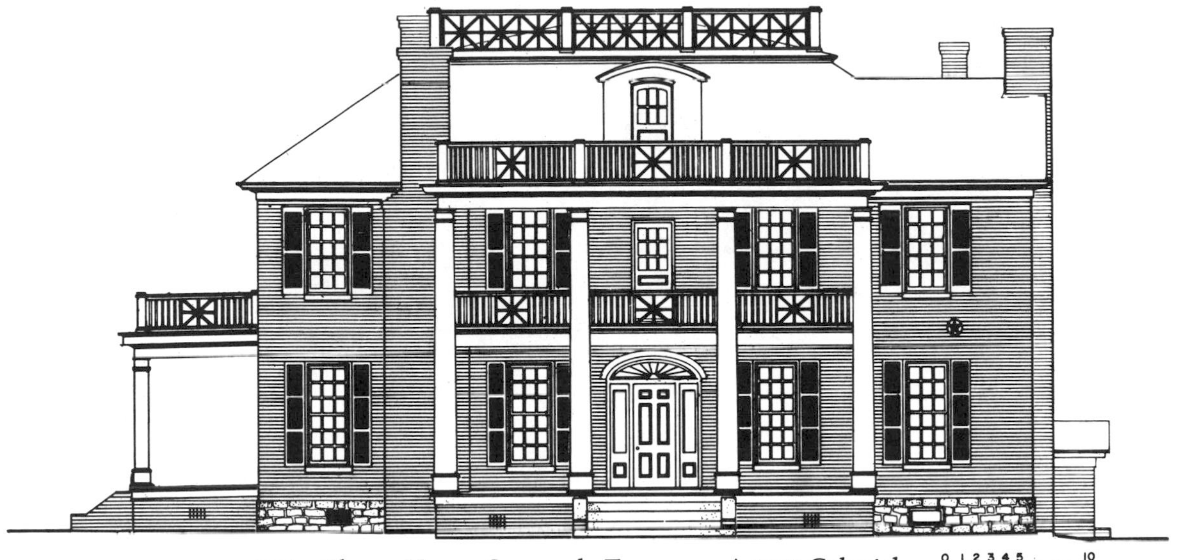

164 Cherry House. Savannah, Tennessee. A 1933 Colonial Revival mask on a dwelling first built in 1849.

165, 166 Helms House. Los Angeles, California. C.1933. Stucco and lath, cement block, concrete, low hipped roof with red clay tile, wrought-iron trim—hallmarks of the Spanish Colonial and Monterey revivals.

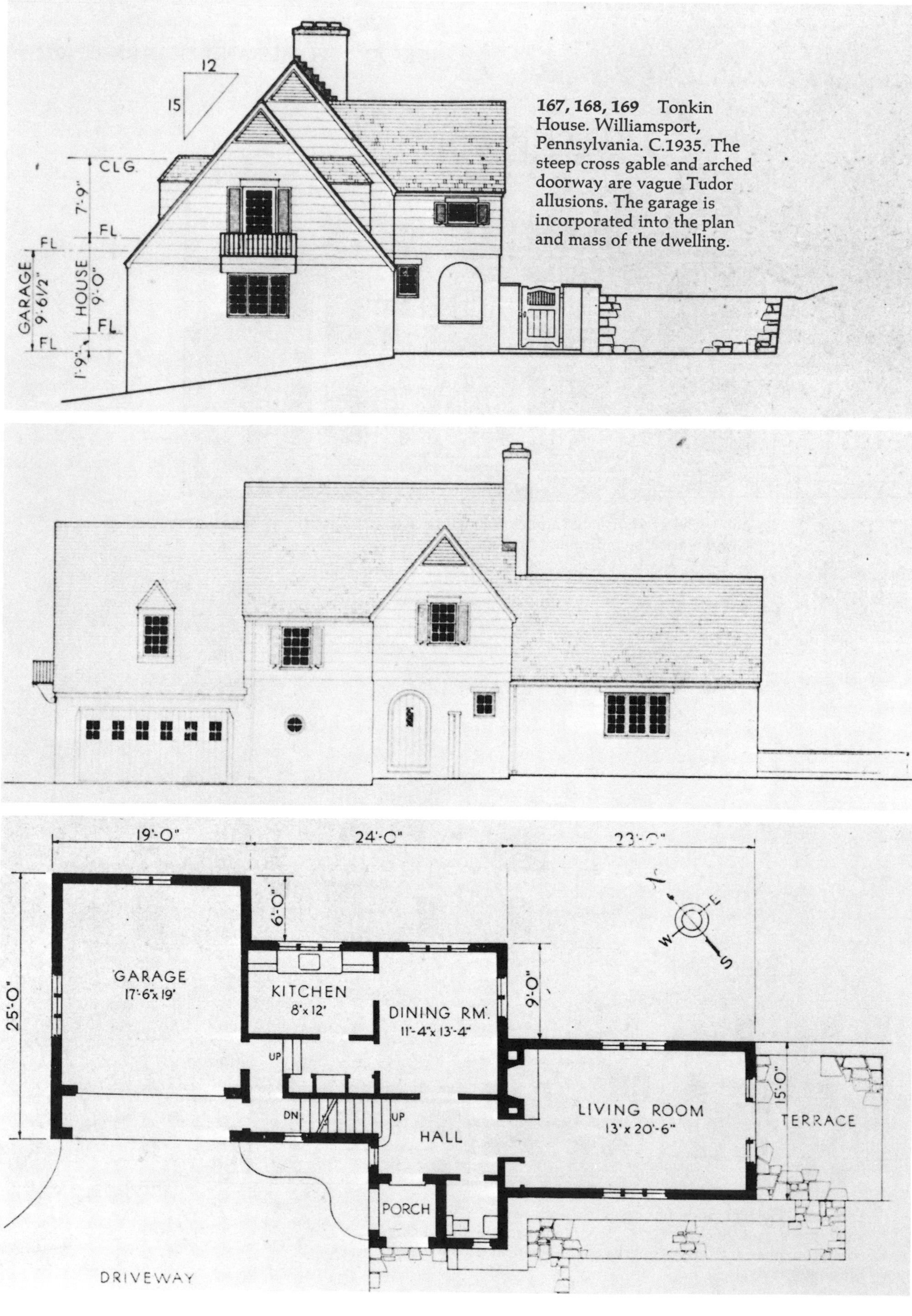

167, 168, 169 Tonkin House. Williamsport, Pennsylvania. C.1935. The steep cross gable and arched doorway are vague Tudor allusions. The garage is incorporated into the plan and mass of the dwelling.

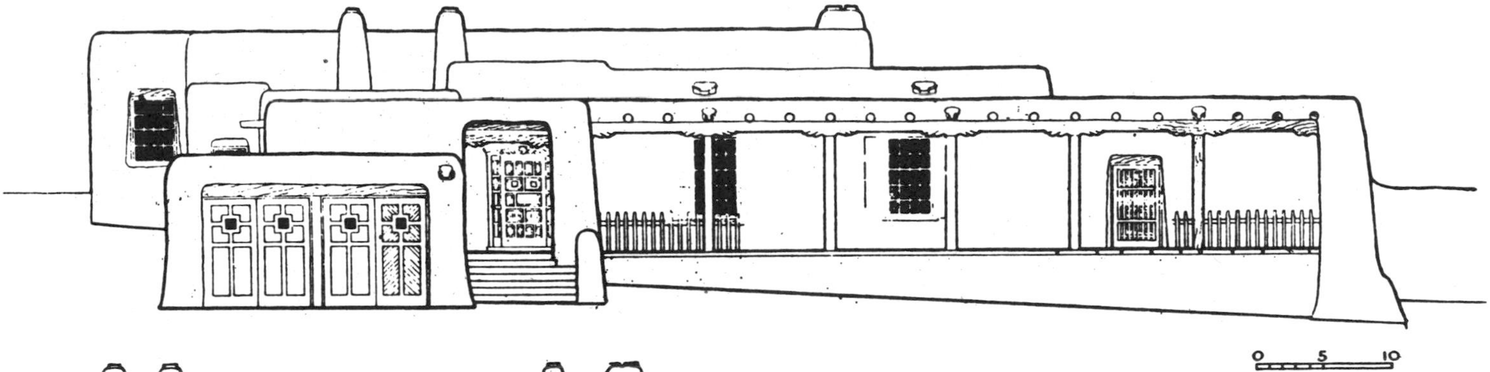

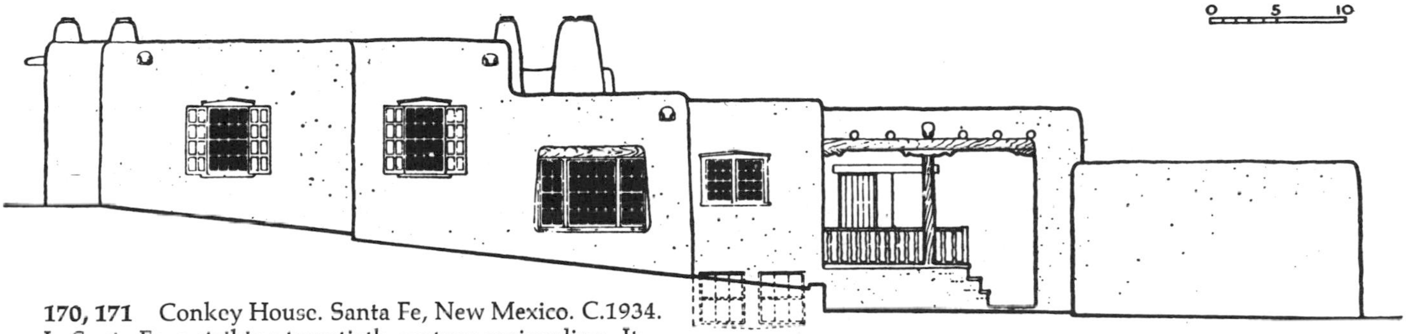

170, 171 Conkey House. Santa Fe, New Mexico. C.1934. In Santa Fe, a striking twentieth-century regionalism. It incorporates taste for both the old and the new, the familiar and the exotic. The front view (top) shows garage doors in a Spanish idiom.

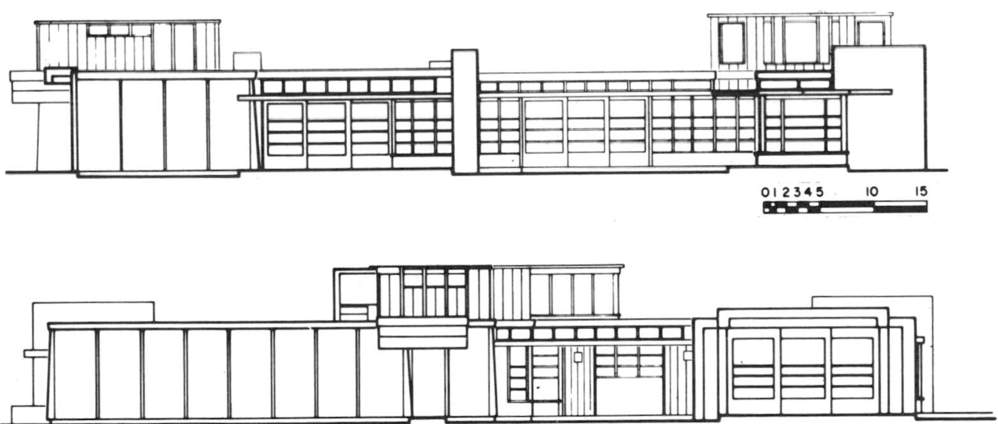

172, 173 Rudolph Schindler House. Los Angeles, California. 1921–1922; Rudolph Schindler, architect. Assertively modern, the dwelling is constructed of reinforced concrete panels, with screens and sliding doors of canvas, glass, wood, and insulating board. Here are a front and a side view, but note that this aesthetic downplays the importance of the front doorway as a design element.

174, 175, 176 Lovell-Health House. Los Angeles, California. 1928; Richard Neutra, architect. The complexity of site planning and room layout reflects the architect's fascination with the principles of modern engineering. ▶ ▼

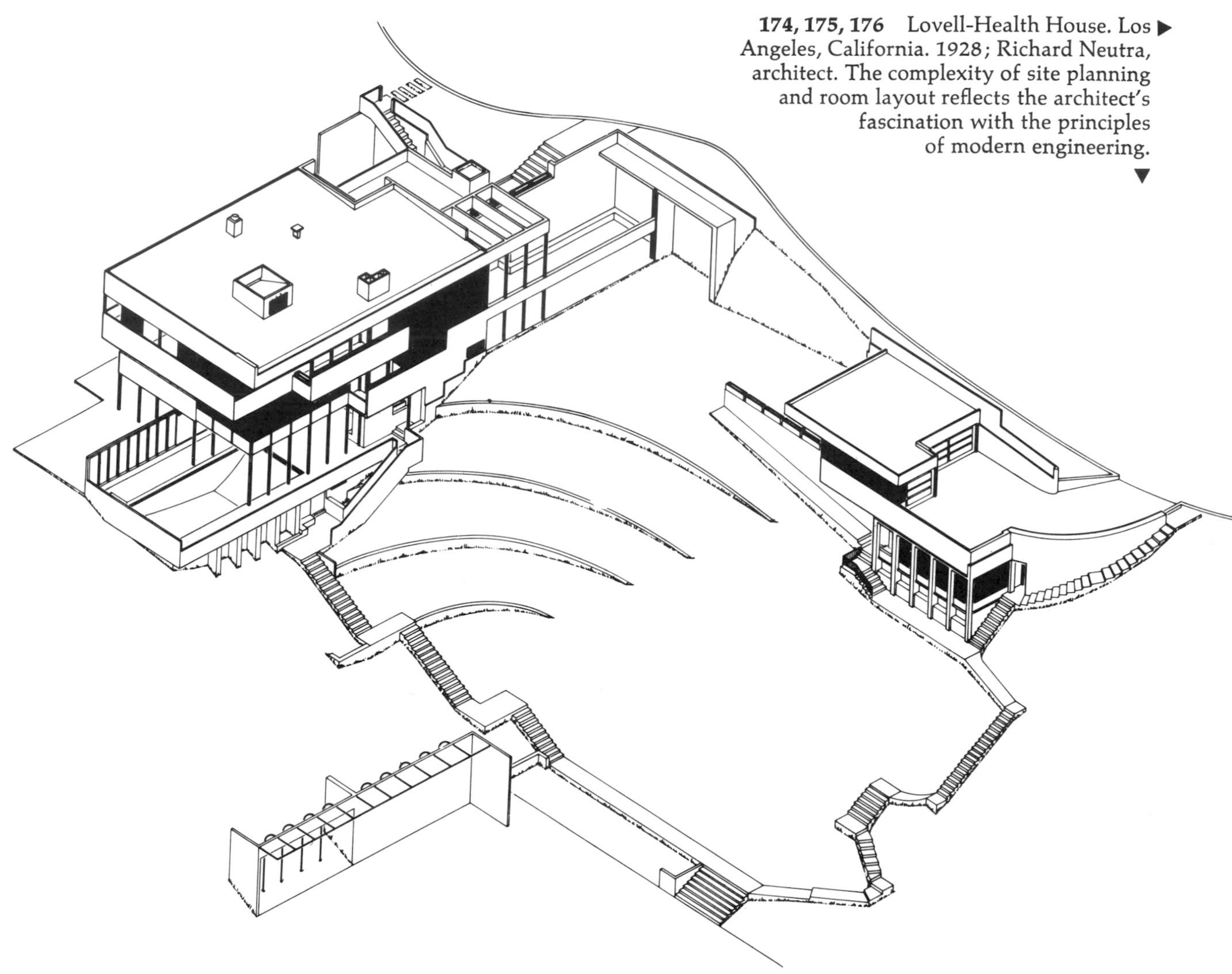

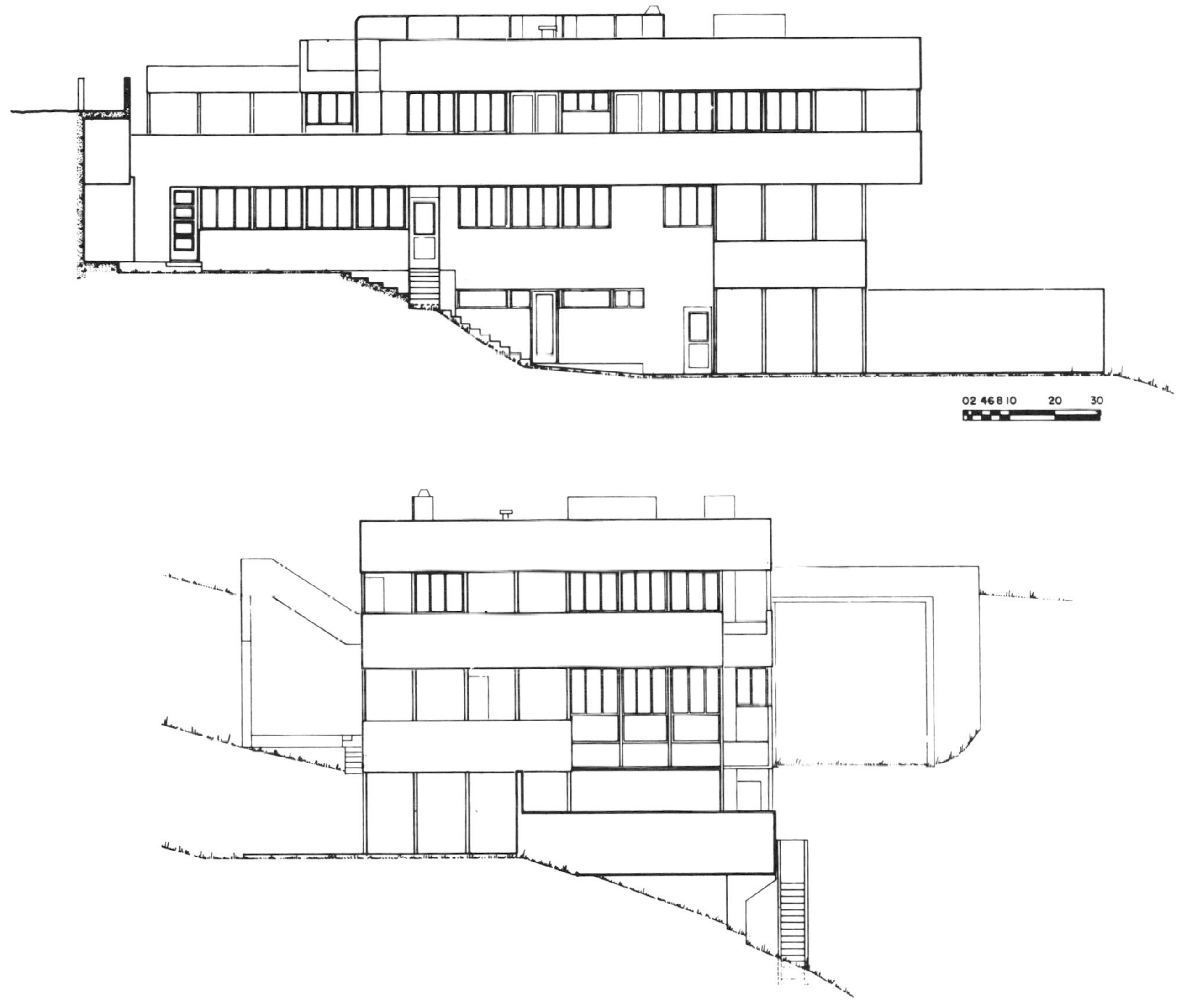
02 4 6 8 10 20 30

177, 178 Design for a modern house. C.1931. In a very simple dwelling, manifestations of Moderne style.

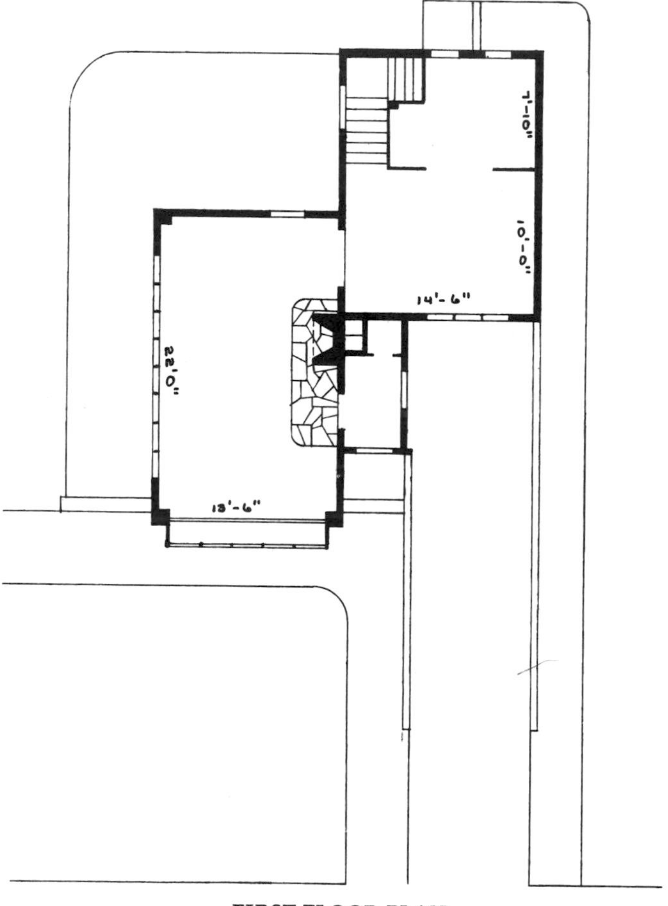

FIRST FLOOR PLAN

179 Radford's flat. C.1913. A very simple two-family house with a few historical details to dress it up.

180 J. Francis Kenna Apartments. Chicago, Illinois. 1916. An unusual design, the work of Prairie School architect Barry Byrne, with simple wall surfaces, bands of windows, novel plan.

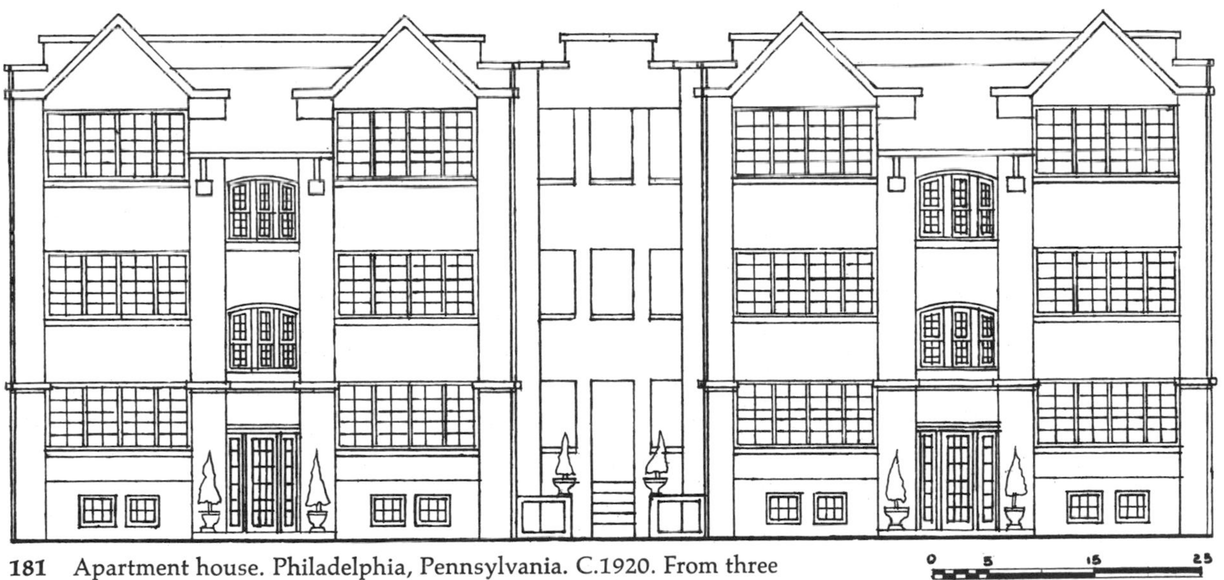

181 Apartment house. Philadelphia, Pennsylvania. C.1920. From three to twenty stories, typical of apartment-house design in the 1920–1940 era.

182 Horatio Court West Apartments. Santa Monica, California. 1919; Irving Gill, architect. Modern in style, this early garden-apartment complex preserves both the urbanity of the row house and the individuality of the detached dwelling.

183 Shelby Apartments. Kingsport, Tennessee. C.1926. Period Revival mannerisms lend variety to a multi-unit complex.

184 Carolyn Park Apartments. Mamaroneck, New York. C.1925. Spanish motifs at the roofline give character to an otherwise utilitarian apartment house.

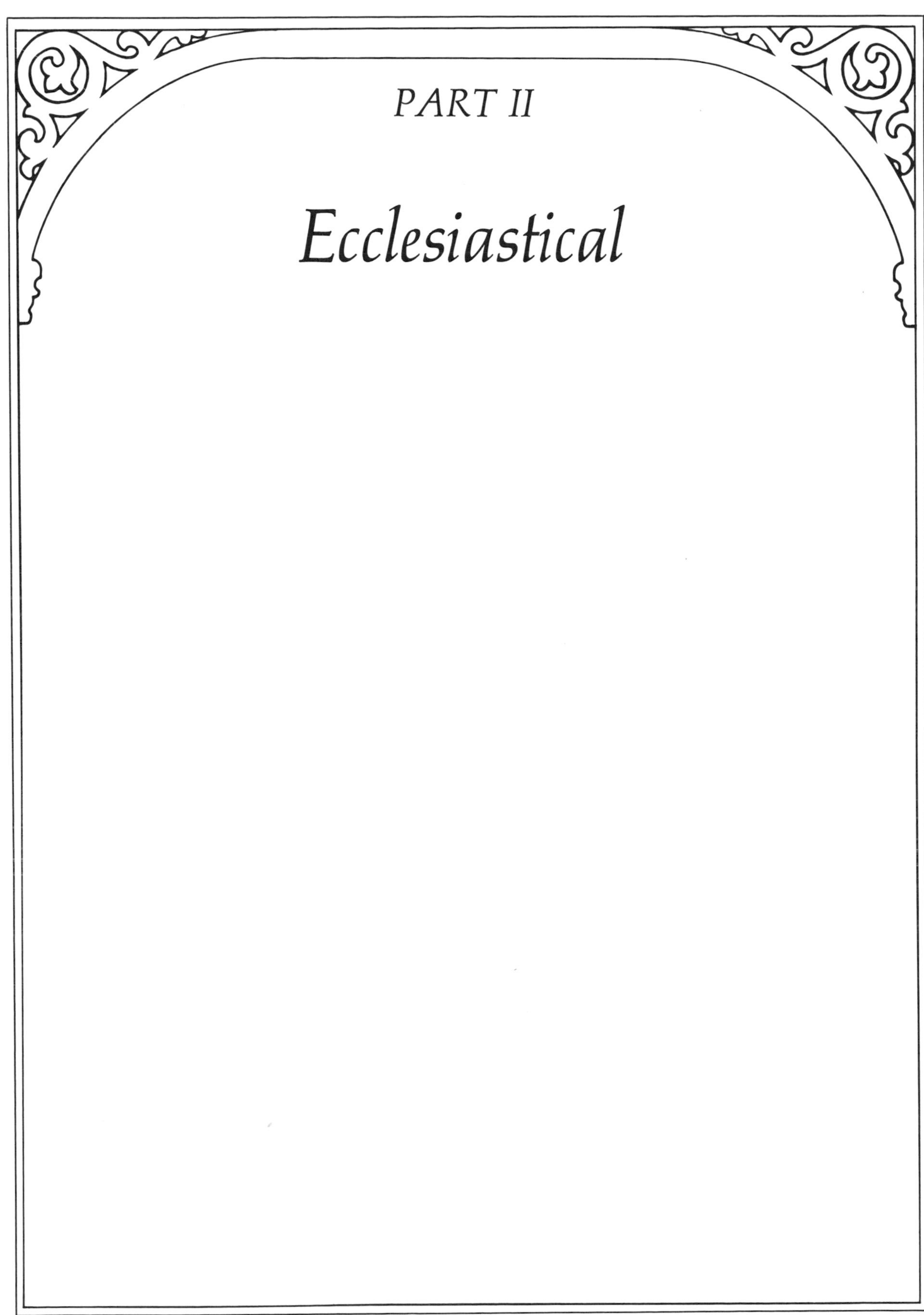

PART II

Ecclesiastical

1680-1790

Colonial

Spanish Colonial • English Colonial, Georgian

THROUGHOUT the colonial era the church was the major edifice in any community. An impressive legacy of these early buildings testifies to the varied cultures, practices, and experiences of the wanderers whose religious beliefs impelled their foray into New World wildernesses.

In the Southwest, religious citadels of a proselytizing Catholicism served as combination church, parish house, novices' residence, military barracks, storehouse, and garden. In the valleys of the Upper Rio Grande surviving missions are distant echoes of Spanish imperial vigor that was infused with the bold primitivism of the Pueblo people. Recalling the opulence of the Spanish Baroque and the Counter Reformation are the richly embellished missions of Texas and Arizona. And testifying to the determination of the Franciscan zealots who evangelized California between 1769 and 1823 are a string of missions that stretch over four hundred miles from San Diego to Sonoma.

In contrast, no single religion and no single church form dominated the Middle Colonies. From Maryland to New York (and also in Rhode Island) there was a heterogeneous population—English Congregational or Anglican, French Huguenot Protestant, Scottish or Scotch-Irish Presbyterian, Reformed Dutch or German, German Baptist, Moravian, Shaker.

Rejecting what was generally the established church in their countries of origin, these groups also tended to reject traditional church hierarchy, liturgy, and physical form. Hence, the traditional basilica-type church—a long rectangle consisting of nave and side aisles, with bell tower and entrance on one short side and sanctuary at the other—was rejected as well.

Emphasizing a central preaching space rather than a sanctuary that climaxed a long axis, the meetinghouse was the favored form for Protestant Dissenters. For Quakers, it was almost domestic in scale and character, resembling the late-medieval English dwelling. For Congregationalist and, later, Baptist as well, it was a squarish structure of imposing proportions, not unlike seventeenth-century Dutch and English town halls and market houses.

For all who sought to purify their religion, the simplicity of their architecture reflected the simplicity of their practice.

In emerging northern cities—notably Philadelphia, New York, Newport, and Boston—Anglicanism had a strong following. Grand in scale and embellishment, the basilica-type church made its colonial-era appearance. Prosperous parishes could afford to follow the high style set by London, familiar to upper-class Americans through travel, imported prints, or English volumes, particularly James Gibbs' *Book of Architecture* (1728).

In the mostly rural South, planters also held to English ways, Anglican faith, and the practices of the Established Church of England. Daughter churches modestly reiterated the form and character of those built in England during the reigns of Queen Anne and the first Georges. Perhaps fifty Virginia churches built before the Revolution and the Disestablishment of the church are extant today, and almost as many in the Carolinas and Maryland.

While differences among various churches in the first century of settlement reflected colonial diversity, the developing similarity among churches after the mid-eighteenth century expressed an emerging American unity. The paradigm was the London church associated with Christopher Wren and Sir James Gibbs—a church of basilica form, with classical portico at one end and tower placed back on the roof.

As the colonies struggled for their political freedom, their religious freedom had long before been won—and it was the bell in the tower of an old Boston church that announced the Revolutionary War.

Materials

A suggestive, though hardly infallible, rule of thumb is that the favored building material is brick or ashlar masonry in the cities and the South, frame sheathed with shingle or clapboard in rural New England, and rubble fieldstone in the Middle Colonies. With advancing taste for Georgian richness, wood may be carved, or stuccoed and scored to resemble stone.

The mission church in New Mexico is built of sun-dried adobe; through frequent repairs and renewals, these have taken on a highly sculptural, undulating quality. Adobe is characteristic of California, too, although rubble stone and kiln-dried brick were also used. Burnt adobe and a soft hewn limestone are the chief materials in Texas and Arizona.

Throughout the Southwest, surfaces are stucco-smoothed, creating characteristically broad and starkly simple wall expanses.

Plan

SPANISH COLONIAL

Common features of the plan of the Spanish mission—from its seventeenth-century appearance in New Mexico to its early-nineteenth-century manifestation in California—are the long narrow rectangle of the basilica church (whose width was generally determined by the length of the available roof timbers); a complex of living and work spaces forming a quadrangle-like configuration; and a relationship to an interior central patio or courtyard and an exterior plaza.

Constructed incrementally with the mission's growth, these complexes gradually deteriorated as they fell into disuse. Today, remains are usually only partial.

ENGLISH COLONIAL, GEORGIAN

The Quaker meetinghouse resembles a dwelling in plan, scale, and proportion. There is an entry at the long side, often with separate doorways for men and women, a covered porch to shelter the entrance, and an interior stairway leading to a second-story balcony.

The Congregational meetinghouse, which also served for town meetings, is considerably larger, nearly squarish in plan, with the pulpit opposite the door and seats arranged for easy hearing.

For Presbyterian, Dutch Reformed, and others, a rectangular church has something of the meetinghouse character when the entrance is on the long wall and the pulpit is opposite it [190].

Large in the cities, small in the rural South, the plan of the Anglican church is generally basilical; there may also be transepts (cross arms) and a deep chancel for the sanctuary [193, 194].

By the last quarter of the eighteenth century, for all denominations except the Quakers, the "church" supplants the meetinghouse. Its plan is of the rectangular, basilical type, with entry at the tower end.

Elevation

SPANISH COLONIAL

The walls of the mission church are heavy and massive, with few and small openings for doors and windows. The main façade may be dramatized by belfry, towers, shaped central gable, and ornament at the portal [185].

Most primitive among them, the New Mexico churches reflect the skill and sensibility of their Indian laborers and lack exterior ornament except for a paneled door or wooden balustrade [186].

California missions are more likely to be enriched by decorative pilasters, pediment, and moldings.

Closest in spirit to the extravagant Spanish Baroque are the mission churches of Texas and Arizona with their richly carved embellishment around the main portal.

ENGLISH COLONIAL, GEORGIAN

Following Nonconformist precepts, the meetinghouse is devoid of ornamentation, although its abstract simplicity and careful proportions achieve a high aesthetic quality [187, 188].

Later-eighteenth-century modifications are a paneled door with pilastered enframement [189], and a bell tower in several stages [190].

Sophisticated taste reflects the aristocratic leanings and Anglophilism shared by Episcopal parishioners, whether in small country churches or in flourishing urban ones. Even in mid-eighteenth-century New England, the Anglican church has such academic elements as Classical cornice, oculus window, and elaborate moldings around arch-headed window openings [195]. In the South, even simple churches [193, 194], display careful refinements, such as a course of molded bricks to define the floorline, cut quoins to mark corners, delicately scaled moldings at the eaves line, and paneling on doors and shutters.

By the time of the Revolution, churches of every denomination carry a full range of Georgian ornament, including pedimented window and door openings, elaborate cornices, and applied orders [192; 196].

Christ Church, Cambridge, Massachusetts; 1759–1761 (see 195, p. 124).

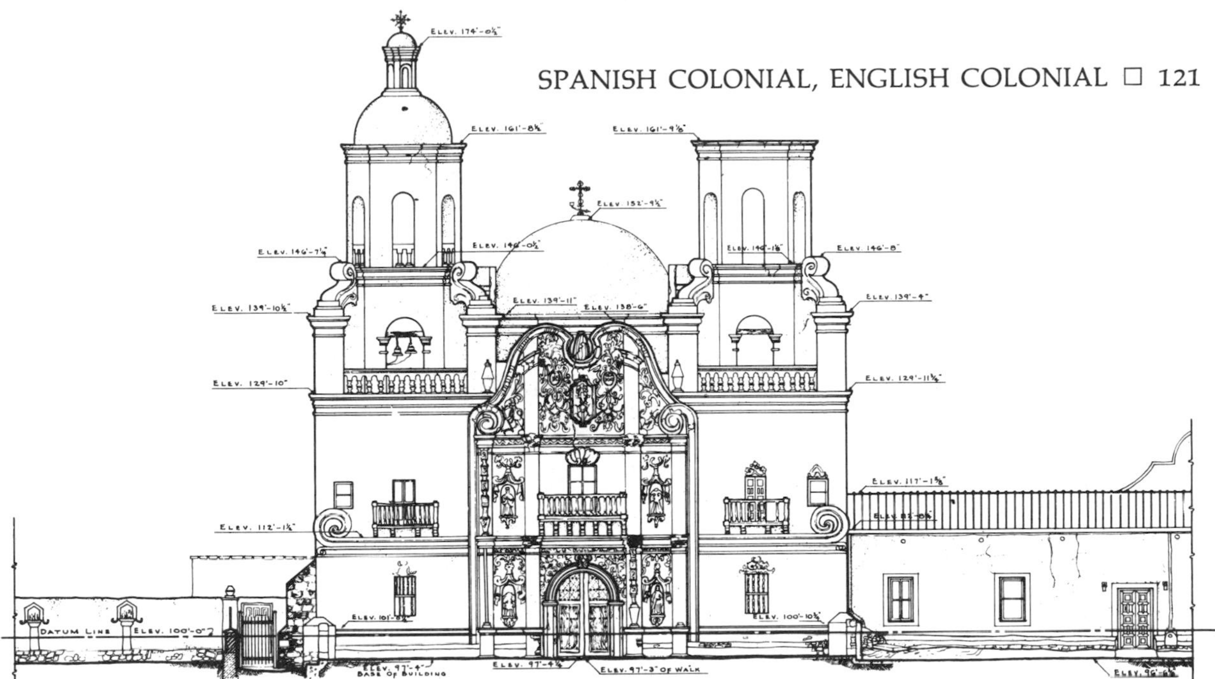

185 Mission San Xavier del Bac. Tucson vicinity, Arizona. 1767–1797, with major early-twentieth-century restoration. Most elaborate of the Spanish Colonial churches, with domed interior spaces and vigorous carved ornament.

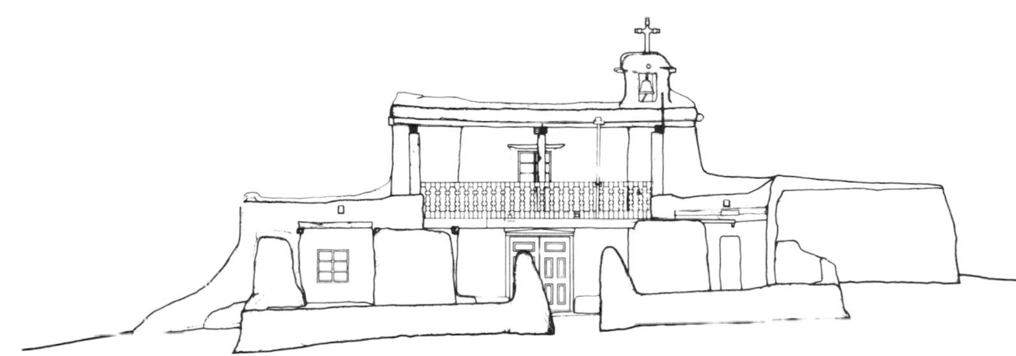

186 Mission church. Santa Ana Pueblo, New Mexico. C.1710–1720. The courtyard is characteristic of the Spanish Mission church plan. The undulating surface of adobe construction is the result of continual repairs of the damage done by wind and rain.

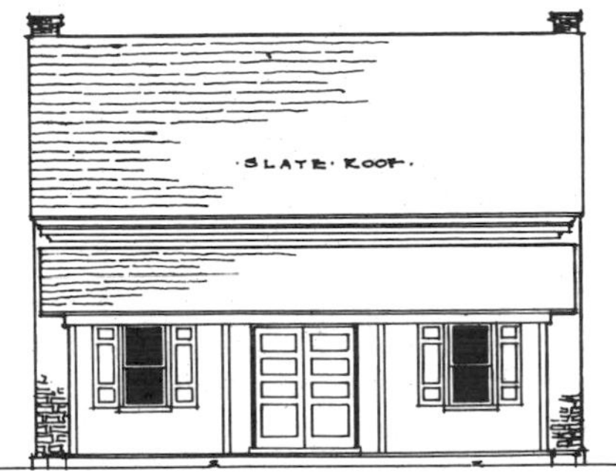

187, 188 Quaker Meetinghouse. Princeton, New Jersey. 1760 rebuilding of 1726 structure. Distinctly without style, this plain house is oblong in shape, entrance on the long side, domestic window type, pitched roof.

189 Rocky Hill Meetinghouse. Amesbury, Massachusetts. 1785. An elaborate entry distinguishes an otherwise plain Congregational meetinghouse.

190 St. Paul's Church, Eastchester. Mount Vernon, New York. Central section, 1765. A hybrid, with characteristics of both church and meetinghouse. The c.1790 tower and later chancel additions confirmed its character as an Episcopal church.

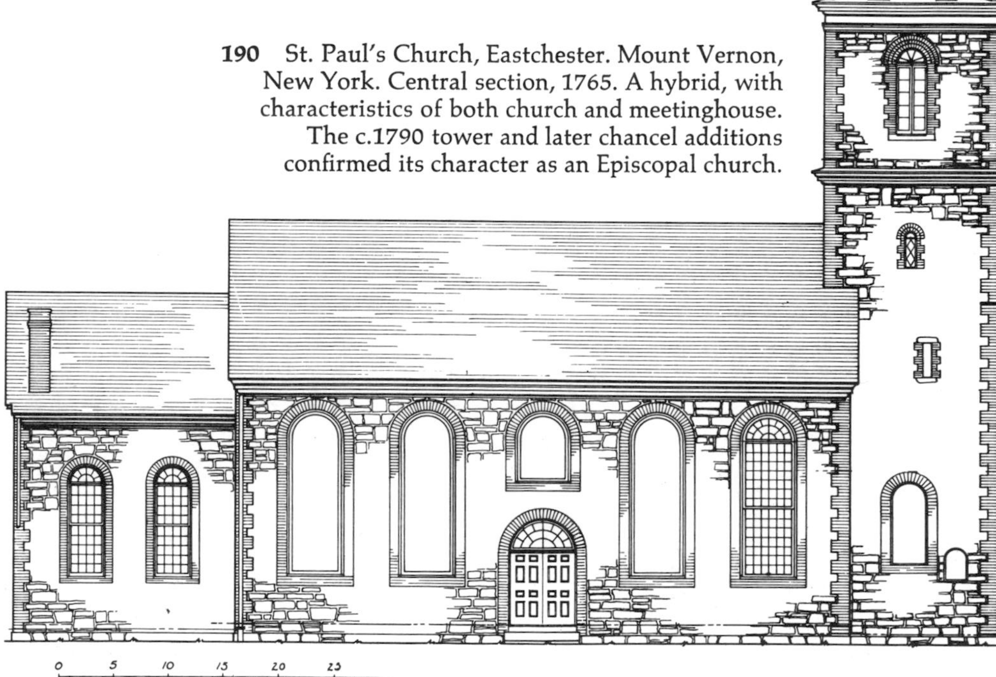

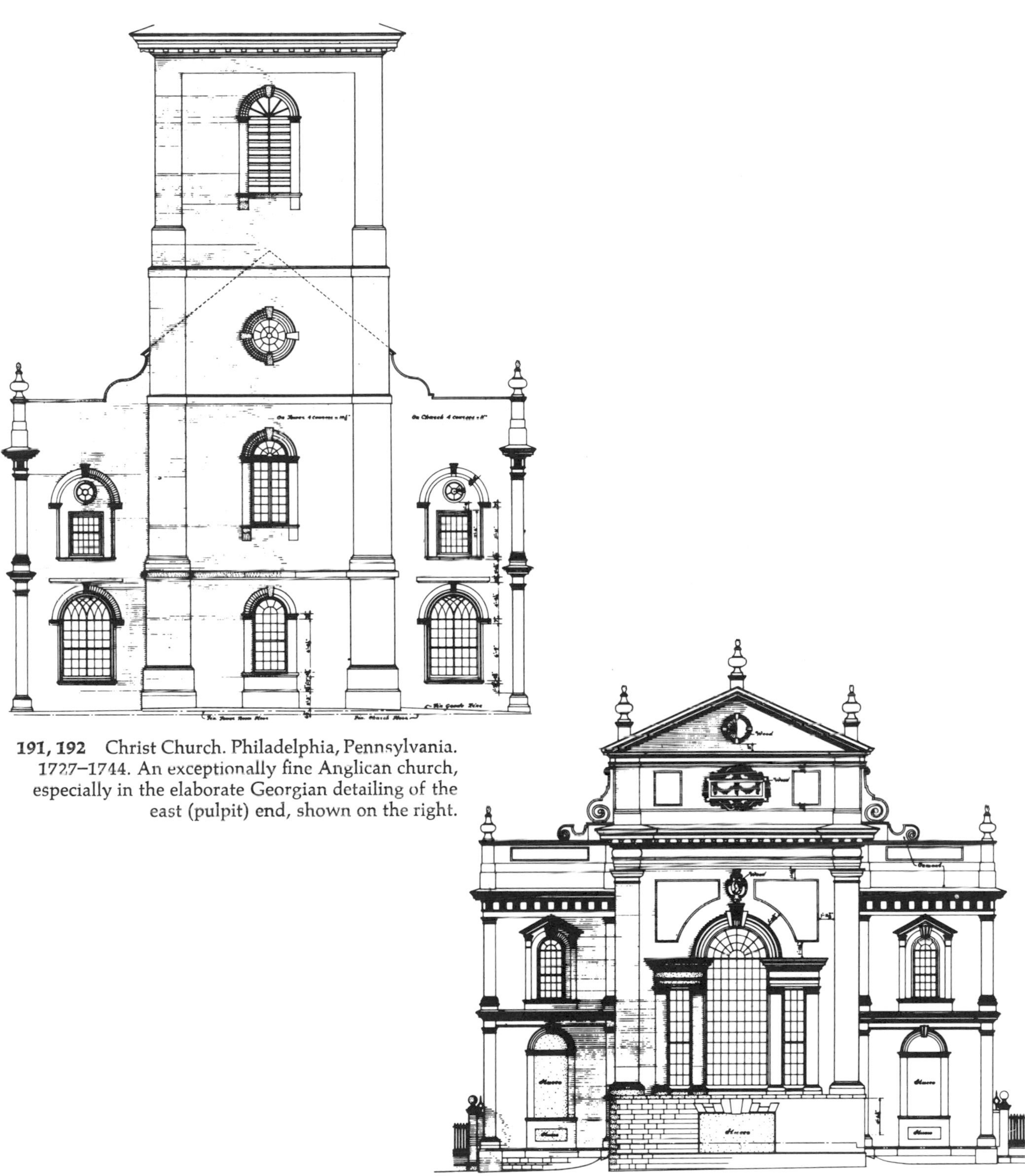

191, 192 Christ Church. Philadelphia, Pennsylvania. 1727–1744. An exceptionally fine Anglican church, especially in the elaborate Georgian detailing of the east (pulpit) end, shown on the right.

193, 194 St. Andrew's Church. Charleston County, South Carolina. 1712–1723. A rural church, lacking tower and belfry. The main entrance is on the short side, shown in the upper view. A transept, shown in the lower view, marks off the chancel end.

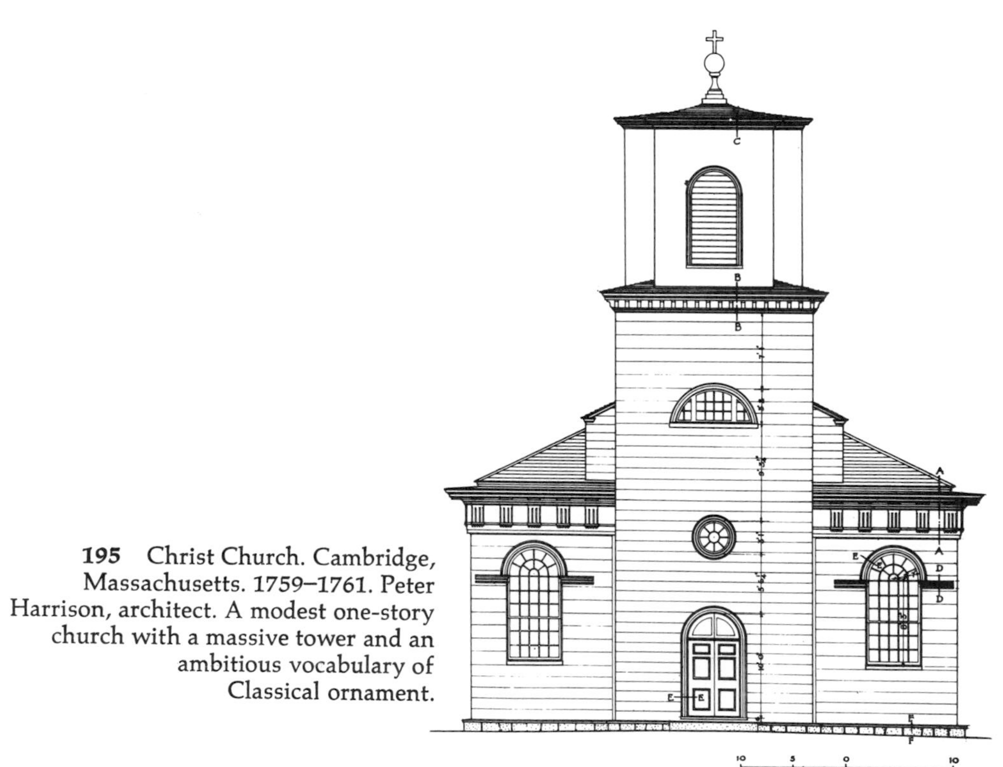

195 Christ Church. Cambridge, Massachusetts. 1759–1761. Peter Harrison, architect. A modest one-story church with a massive tower and an ambitious vocabulary of Classical ornament.

196 First Baptist Church. Providence, Rhode Island. 1774–1775. An outstanding church in Colonial America. The richly decorated five-stage tower derives from a Gibbs design. The tower is not freestanding, but rises directly from the roof of the pedimented central pavilion. The facade lacks a complete classical portico, but exhibits an array of academic ornament, including a pedimented portico at the entry, corner quoins, and Palladian window motif.

1790-1825

Neoclassical

AFTER the War of Independence, taste advanced with the accumulation of wealth even as religion held fast to traditional values. "In this house we discover a just proportion," a Massachusetts minister announced at his church's dedication in 1811. "We see a majestic simplicity; we see a simplicity blended with elegance and beauty."

In prosperous New England, the Wren-Gibbs church introduced into the colonies before the Revolution was translated into American idiom. Reviving Classic forms, this new church refined Georgian vigor by attenuating its proportions, multiplying and lightening its ornament, quickening its rhythms.

While the South experienced a building lull, a growing population in the Northeast and the Middle Atlantic carried this type from the cities to recent wildernesses, where high spirit and carpenter virtuosity produced church buildings with an abstract vigor and naive charm.

New England's accomplishment depended on skilled designers, able craftsmen, and a plentiful supply of good lumber. Even more, it benefited from an effective popularizer—Asher Benjamin, whose architectural handbooks, such as *The Country Builder's Assistant*, first published in Greenfield, Massachusetts, in 1797, were the carpenter's bibles. This was how the brick or clapboard church, with tower and tall spire, and cornice, door, and window modestly embellished with delicate Federal moldings, emanated from the shadows of the tall trees that lined New England's town greens.

Modified by vernacular sensibilities, it spread to the Maine woods and Vermont hills, the Connecticut and Mohawk valleys, eastern Long Island, rural Pennsylvania and New Jersey, and the Ohio frontier. Even as late as the 1830s this church type remained popular, moving west as far as Michigan and Wisconsin.

Materials

The city church may be brick or, occasionally, stone masonry.

Provincial churches, which have survived in the largest numbers, are generally frame, on an above-grade fieldstone, brick, or ashlar masonry foundation.

Plan

A typical church is composed of a rectangular nave, generally three bays wide and five bays long. Most simply, one short side is marked by an entrance tower with spire [202; 203].

On more advanced examples, the tower may be placed back on the roof of the entrance vestibule [200, 201].

The most highly developed examples have a projecting portico and a colonnade [197; 198, 199].

Elevation

The extent of elaboration is consistent with geographical location and the congregation's wealth and denominational preference. In this period, Baptist and Presbyterian churches tend to be spare [202] while Congregational and Episcopal churches are comparatively lavish [197].

An important feature is the steeple, consisting of several stages that make the transition from square base to pointed spire; these may include clock stage, belfry, and cupola.

Federal ornament tends to be delicately defined, dainty in scale, and repetitive. Characteristic motifs include complete Classical orders, arch-headed door and window openings [197], elliptical openings in gable or tower [201, 202] Pointed-arch door or window openings are a Gothicism that is occasionally applied to a Classical form [198, 199].

197 First Church of Christ, Congregational. New Haven, Connecticut. 1814. Ithiel Town, architect. A fully developed Classical Revival church, with triple doorways, pedimented portico, and multistage tower. Federal-style details include delicate moldings, doors and windows set within recessed arches, roof balustrade with urns. A photograph is on the next page.

First Church of Christ, Congregational, New Haven, Connecticut; 1814 (see 197, p. 127).

198, 199 Congregational Church. Atwater, Ohio. 1838–1841. A late, provincial interpretation. The Gothic window treatment on a Classical Revival church is curious, but not uncommon.

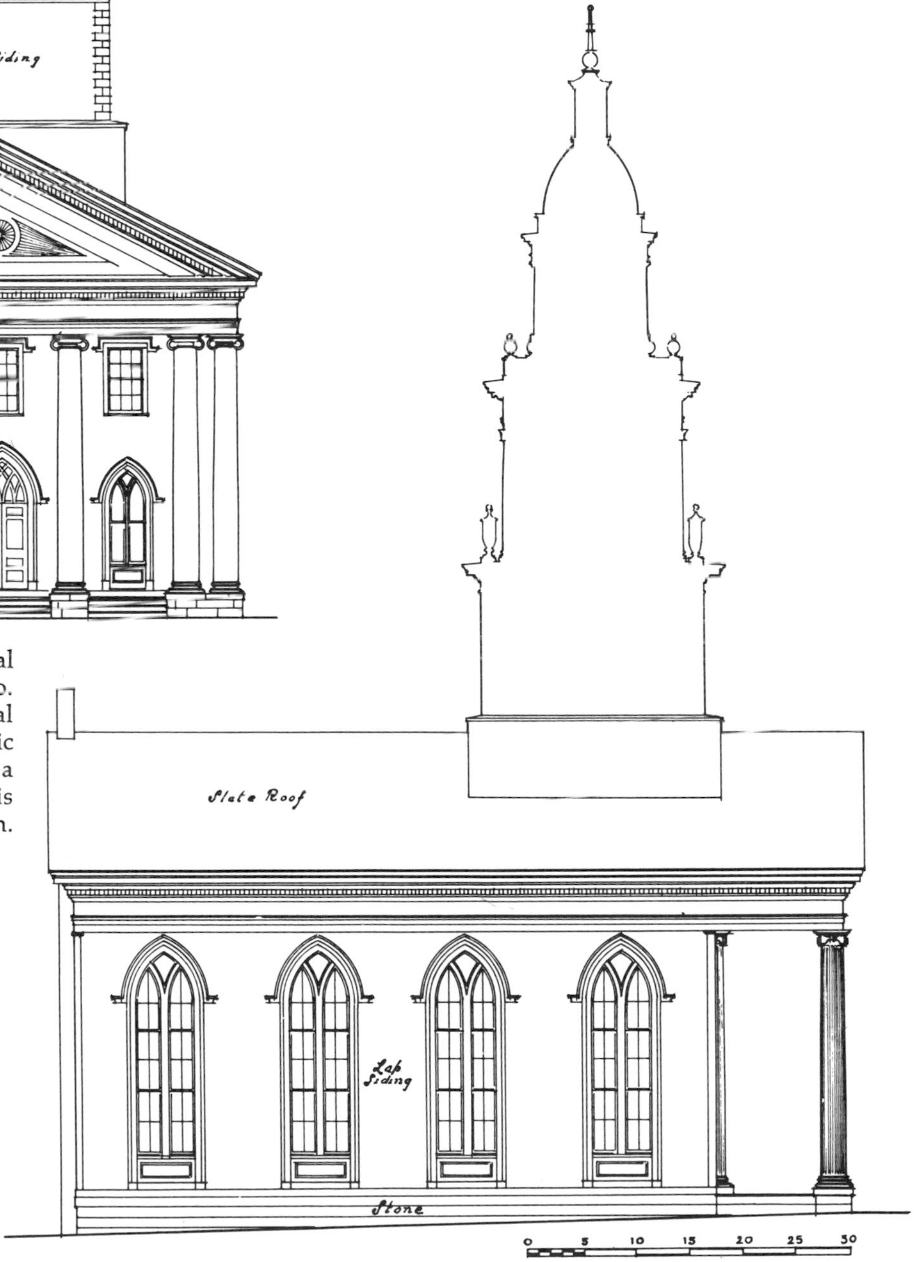

200, 201 First Presbyterian Church. Springfield, New Jersey. 1791. On a modest country church, the belfry, pedimented gable, and ornamental window shapes are ambitious elements.

202 Meetinghouse of the First Baptist Society. Delphi Falls, New York. 1815–1818. A provincial church of great simplicity, distinguished by a belfry and triple doorways.

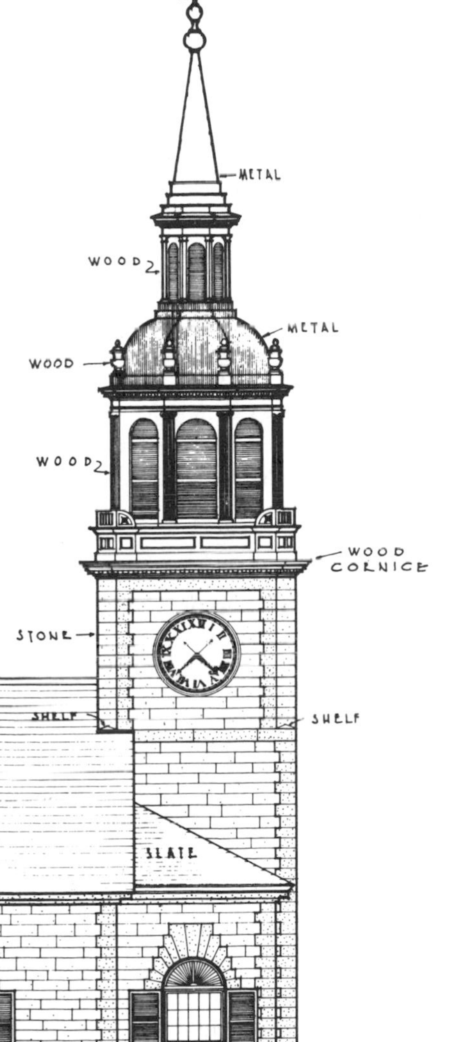

203 First Parish Church. Portland, Maine. 1826. Conservative style, cautious detail in granite and wood.

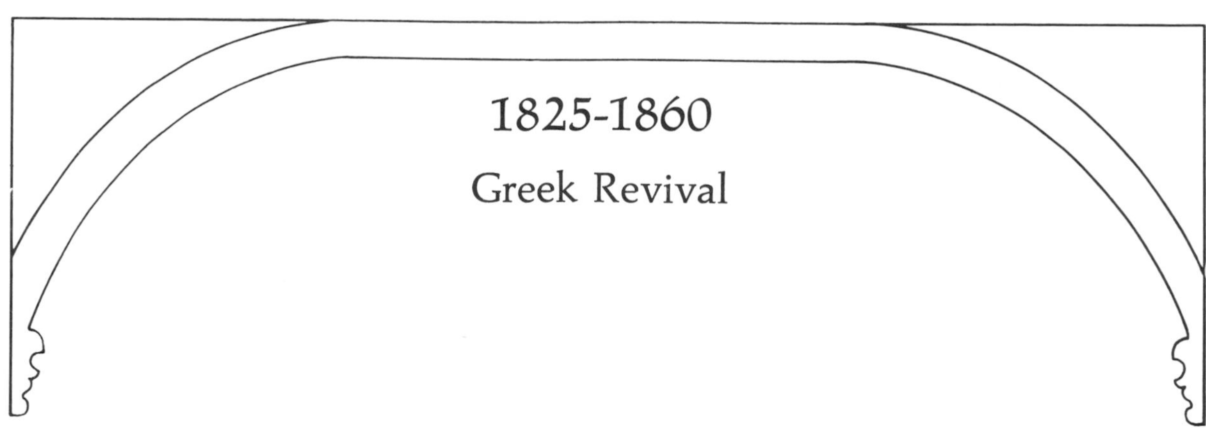

1825-1860

Greek Revival

IN these years, a church-building boom was spurred by a restless human migration—from Europe to America, from farm to city, from east to west. In the 1830s and 1840s in the eastern states, and in the 1850s and 1860s in the western states, amid a general intellectual, emotional, and religious ferment, a single form—the Greek-styled temple-fronted church—served equally the orthodox Congregationalists and the Catholic, the evangelical Methodist and the Baptist, the utopian Mormon and the Oneida Perfectionist, the intellectual Transcendentalist and all who shared a faith in human progress.

"The whole world seems to be looking for a revolution," wrote one contemporary. "Some expect an orthodox millennium; others still, a physiological regeneration of the human race; and not a few are awaiting, in anxious or hopeful suspense, the triumph of the Second Advent and the day of judgment."

The Greek Revival church accommodated the intense religious activism of this era. Ample spaces in basement and vestry welcomed children for education and adults for social activity. The short, wide nave held a large audience in close proximity to the pulpit, encouraging congregational responsiveness and hymn-singing. Offering inviting ambience were central heating, comfortable benches, and tall windows that filled the church interior with sunlight.

From swelling eastern cities to open midwestern farmlands to the wilds of the Pacific Northwest, pagan Greece inspired Christian America. Whether architect-designed or missionary-built, the Greek Revival church was functional in plan, vigorous in style, sturdy in proportions, and honest in its simplicity.

Materials

Ashlar masonry is the Greek Revival paradigm, and wood is often used to mimic stone. Granite is particularly popular, but brownstone and brick are also used, as well as rubble fieldstone in provincial areas. Lesser examples tend to be of complete frame construction. Trim, including columns, is likely to be wood.

Plan

Rectangular in plan, more broadly proportioned than its Classical Revival predecessor, the Greek Revival church is generally three ample bays in width and no more than four in length, without projections for entry, apse, or transepts.

Elevation

Simplicity—from the austere to the majestic—is the hallmark of this era.

A portico may front the entire façade [204], or merely set off the entrance [205; 206]. Vernacular structures may be adorned by no more than a gable front with cornice returns [209]. An occasional feature is an elaborate tower, or paired towers [206]. More common is a squat tower atop the gable, with an open belfry surmounted by turrets [207, 208], or no tower at all.

The Greek orders, a strong entablature, and corner pilasters are the chief embellishments. Molding profiles are bold and simplified. A provincial example may perpetuate Federal motifs, such as a fan-shaped window opening [209], or naively adopt elements of the incipient Gothic Revival, in particular the pointed arch and notched parapets [210].

204 St. Peter's Roman Catholic Church. New York, New York. 1836. With low gable, and lacking a tower, a typical Greek Revival temple-fronted church building. The prominence of unadorned horizontal elements in the entablature is characteristic.

St. Mary's Church, Nashville, Tennessee; 1845–1847.

205 St. Mary's Church. Nashville, Tennessee. 1845–1847, with early-twentieth-century roof and belfry repair. William Strickland, architect. The Greek Revival emphasizes the central entrance, here recessed and set off by pilastered side bays, portico, and belfry.

206 South Park Presbyterian Church. Newark, New Jersey. 1853. A pair of classical tempiettos flank the entry. Note the lively detailing.

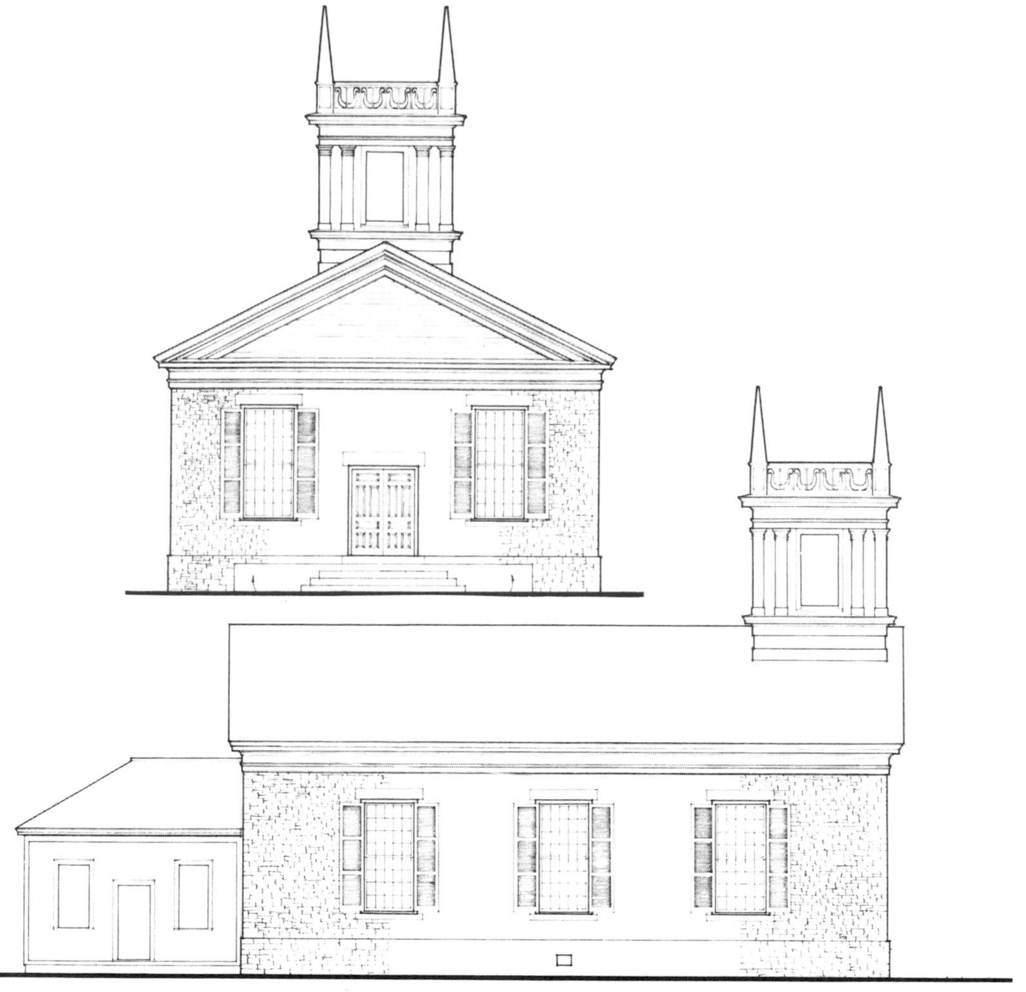

207, 208 Congregational Church. Lisbon, Illinois. 1850.

209 Zions Evangelical Lutheran Church. Middle Smithfield Township, Pennsylvania. 1851.

210 St. Luke's Episcopal Church. Hope, New Jersey. 1832–1839. A curious provincial example, with front tower, the gable masked by notched parapet, Gothic pointed-arch door and windows, quatrefoil and belfry details.

1840-1870

Early Victorian

Gothic Revival
Romanesque and Renaissance Revivals

EVEN as the Greek Revival flourished, the feeling grew that pagan forms were hardly appropriate for Christian worship, that the intensely religious Middle Ages could provide more appropriate models. "The study of medieval art must tend, at least, to revive some of the medieval habits, thoughts, feelings and principles which this age sadly wants," wrote New York lawyer and literary critic George Templeton Strong. And if medieval forms answered to the fervor of mid-nineteenth-century religious beliefs, they responded as well to the contemporary delight in the picturesque.

Thus, in the 1840s and 1850s, the self-contained, horizontal, monumental, static mass of Greek temple-church gave way to the irregular, vertical, picturesque, and lively forms of the Gothic and Romanesque Revival styles.

In England, Gothicist A. W. Pugin hailed the English medieval parish church as "one of the most beautiful and appropriate buildings that the mind of man could conceive." In America, backed by Episcopalian doctrine and led by architects Richard Upjohn and James Renwick, an American version of this thirteenth- and fourteenth-century English mode had tentative beginnings in the 1830s and 1840s, was firmly established in the 1850s, and continued with vigor into the years after the Civil War.

Upjohn was a deeply religious man who can be credited with the design of some 150 churches from Maine to Alabama and Wisconsin, and the authorship of the highly influential *Rural Architecture* (1852). Another popularizer was Minard Lafever, whose *The Architectural Instructor* (1856) showed enthusiastic appreciation for French as well as English models.

While the Gothic Revival was particularly favored by Episcopalian and Catholic parishes, the German or Italian Romanesque or early Renaissance style was generally preferred by Congregationalist, Methodist, Baptist, and other low-church groups. The distinguishing characteristics of the Romanesque was its use of the round arch for door and window openings and its distinctive rounded moldings. In mood, it was less spiritual than the Gothic, but more reasoned; less picturesque, but more serene.

Gothic or Romanesque, the church building embodied a new intensity of religious attitude and a revived orthodoxy in religious practice. As one midcentury observer remarked: "If churches were the expression of the piety of a people then the Americans would be the most pious in the world."

Materials

Brick or ashlar masonry, laid with thin mortar joints, is characteristic of Romanesque and Renaissance Revival churches.

Gothic churches naturally favor a picturesque treatment of materials. Masonry may be fieldstone (in roughly hewn blocks of irregular sizes) or brownstone. Board-and-battens siding is a distinguishing feature of the frame church.

Plan

The Gothic Revival church plan evolves to a complex, irregular, expansive shape by the addition to a rectangular nave of projecting transepts, tower, vestibule, baptistry, vestry room, or organ loft.

211 Grace Church. Georgetown, District of Columbia. 1867.

The Romanesque Revival plan has a long, narrow nave, preceded by a vestibule and a central tower or paired side towers. It is more self-contained in massing.

Elevation

GOTHIC REVIVAL

The Gothic Revival church, echoing its medieval inspiration, creates a picturesque effect by variety, irregularity, and contrasts [212, 213, 214].

The tower with belfry is important as a symbol and as a design element. It may be flat [213], topped by a spire [215], or rise from the roof ridge as a bell cote [211].

Omnipresent pointed-arch window openings may be single or grouped and of various shapes. Other characteristic Gothic devices are the quatrefoil [211], stepped buttresses, deeply recessed openings, and wooden doors with heavy iron strap hinges [214].

For the unpretentious wooden church, steep gables and vertical board-and-batten sheathing are the signature of a medieval spirit [216].

ROMANESQUE AND RENAISSANCE REVIVALS

The Romanesque Revival church, somewhat Germanic in character, is severe and symmetrical, with brisk articulation and strong rhythms established by regular fenestration, projecting buttresses, and surface patterning [217].

Single or paired round-arch door and window openings are most characteristic, although pointed-arch openings may also be observed [218, 219]. The tower is a decisive element; it often has a low or flat roof.

Renaissance elements include Classical orders, elaborately pedimented arch-headed window openings, and rich moldings [222].

Provincial examples, often faithful to Greek Revival forms, adopt superficial Romanesque characteristics, particularly the round-arched opening [220].

Grace Church, Georgetown, District of Columbia; 1867 (see 211).

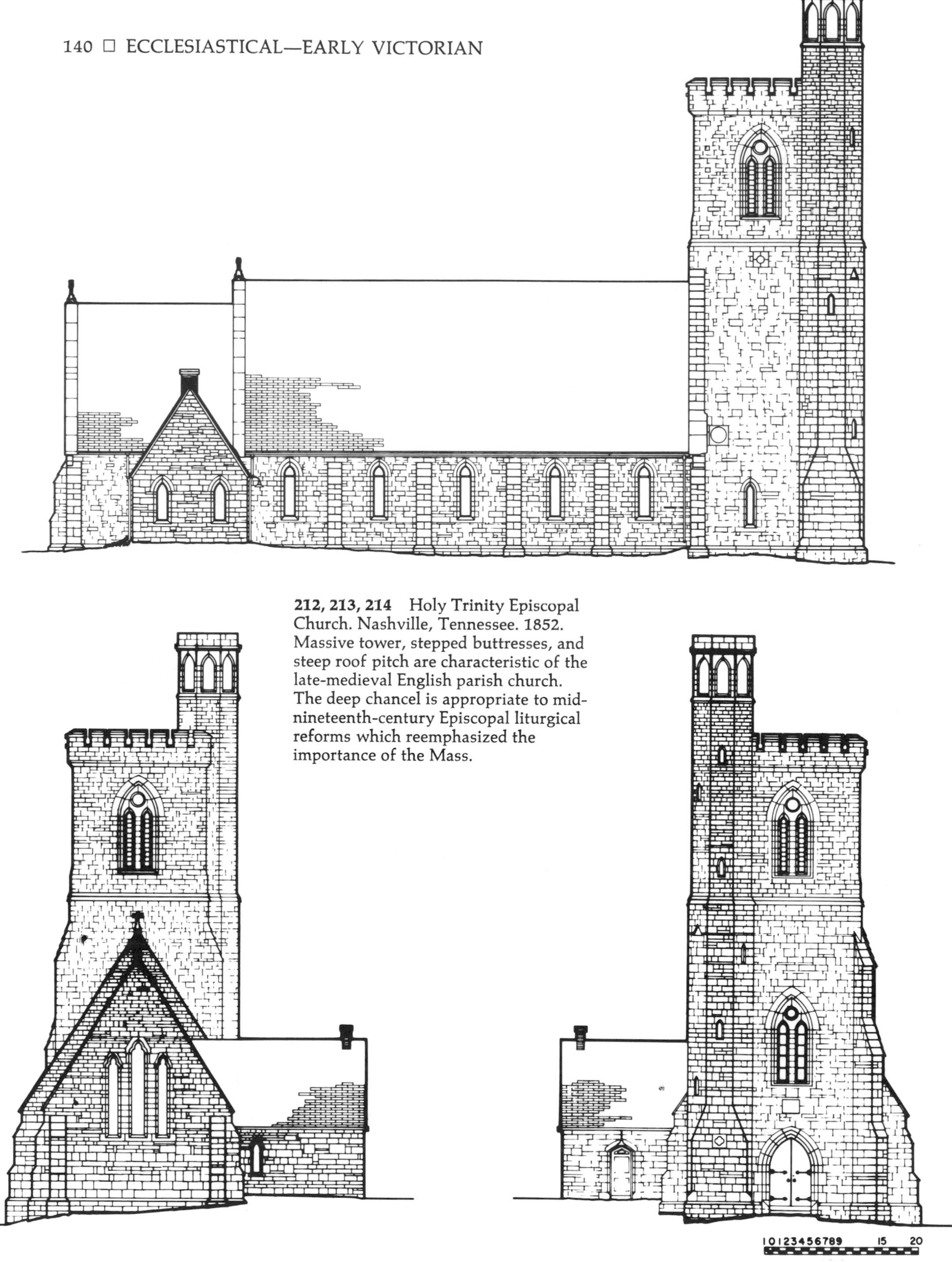

212, 213, 214 Holy Trinity Episcopal Church. Nashville, Tennessee. 1852. Massive tower, stepped buttresses, and steep roof pitch are characteristic of the late-medieval English parish church. The deep chancel is appropriate to mid-nineteenth-century Episcopal liturgical reforms which reemphasized the importance of the Mass.

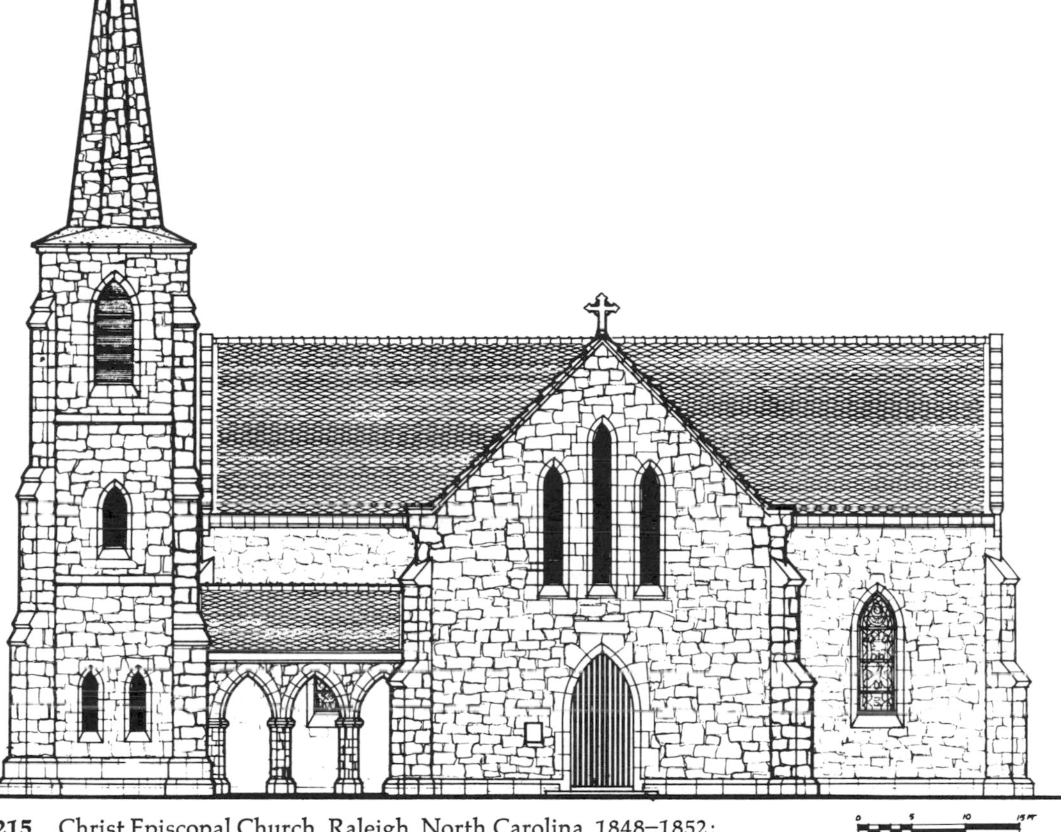

215 Christ Episcopal Church. Raleigh, North Carolina. 1848–1852; Richard Upjohn, architect. Elaborate Gothicisms include the broad transept, porch, stained-glass windows with tracery, and rough stonework.

216 St. Luke's Episcopal Church. Martin's Station, Alabama. C.1860. American carpenter Gothic, with board-and-batten sheathing and hollow wooden buttresses.

217 St. Benedict's Parish Church and School. Nebraska City, Nebraska. 1861. On this unassuming structure, decorative arcading beneath the eaves and round-arched windows are used as signatures of the Romanesque Revival.

218, 219 St. Anne's Catholic Church. Columbia, California. 1856. A provincial Gothic-Romanesque hybrid.

0 1 5 10 15

220, 221 Cape Island Presbyterian Church. Cape May, New Jersey. 1860. Almost domestic in character, with a fanciful belfry. The arch-headed window openings are allusions to Romanesque style.

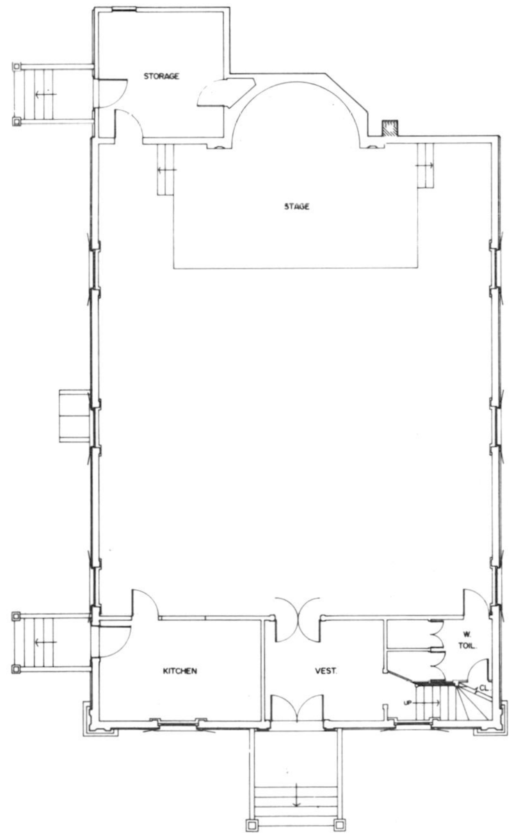

FIRST FLOOR PLAN

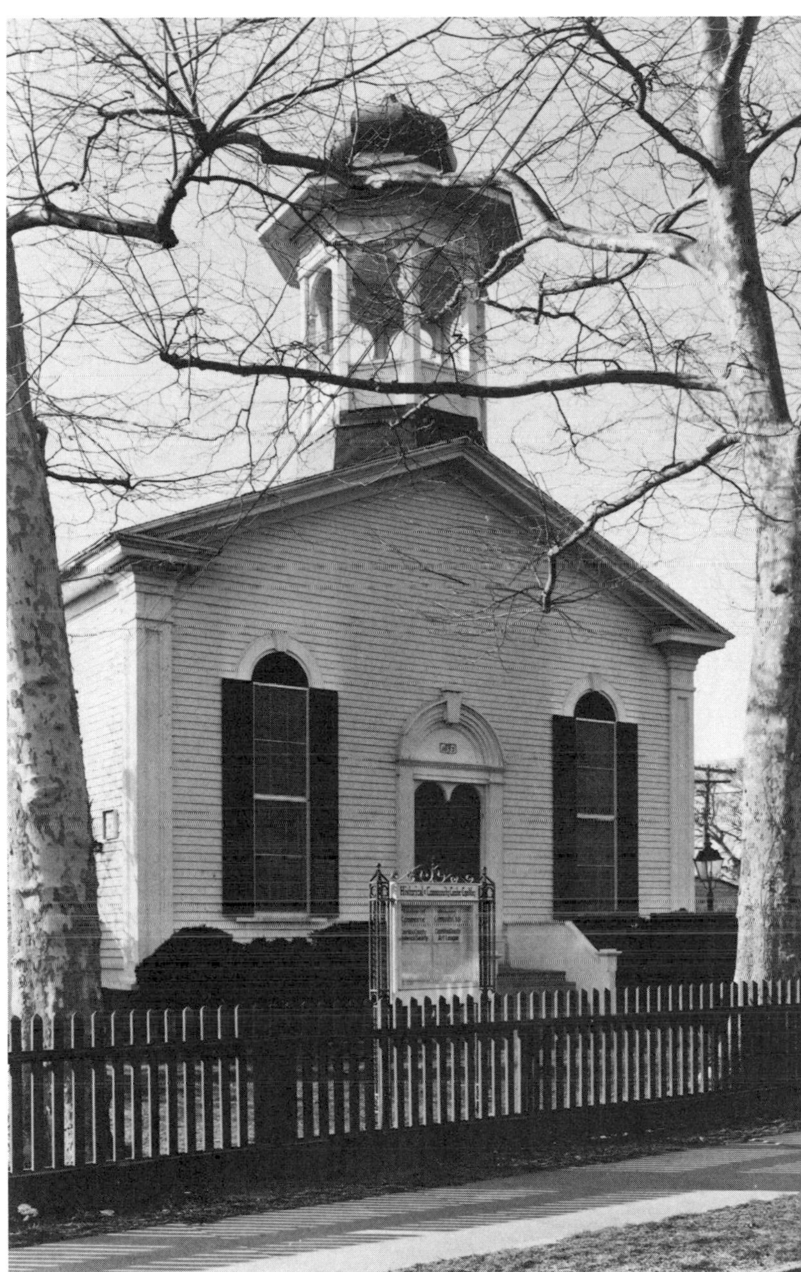

Cape Island Presbyterian Church, Cape May, New Jersey; 1860.

222, 223 First Baptist Church. Chicago, Illinois. 1853. An arresting juxtaposition: Renaissance facade, Gothic spire. Worship is conducted at the second story, with community meeting space below. Note the floor plan on the facing page.

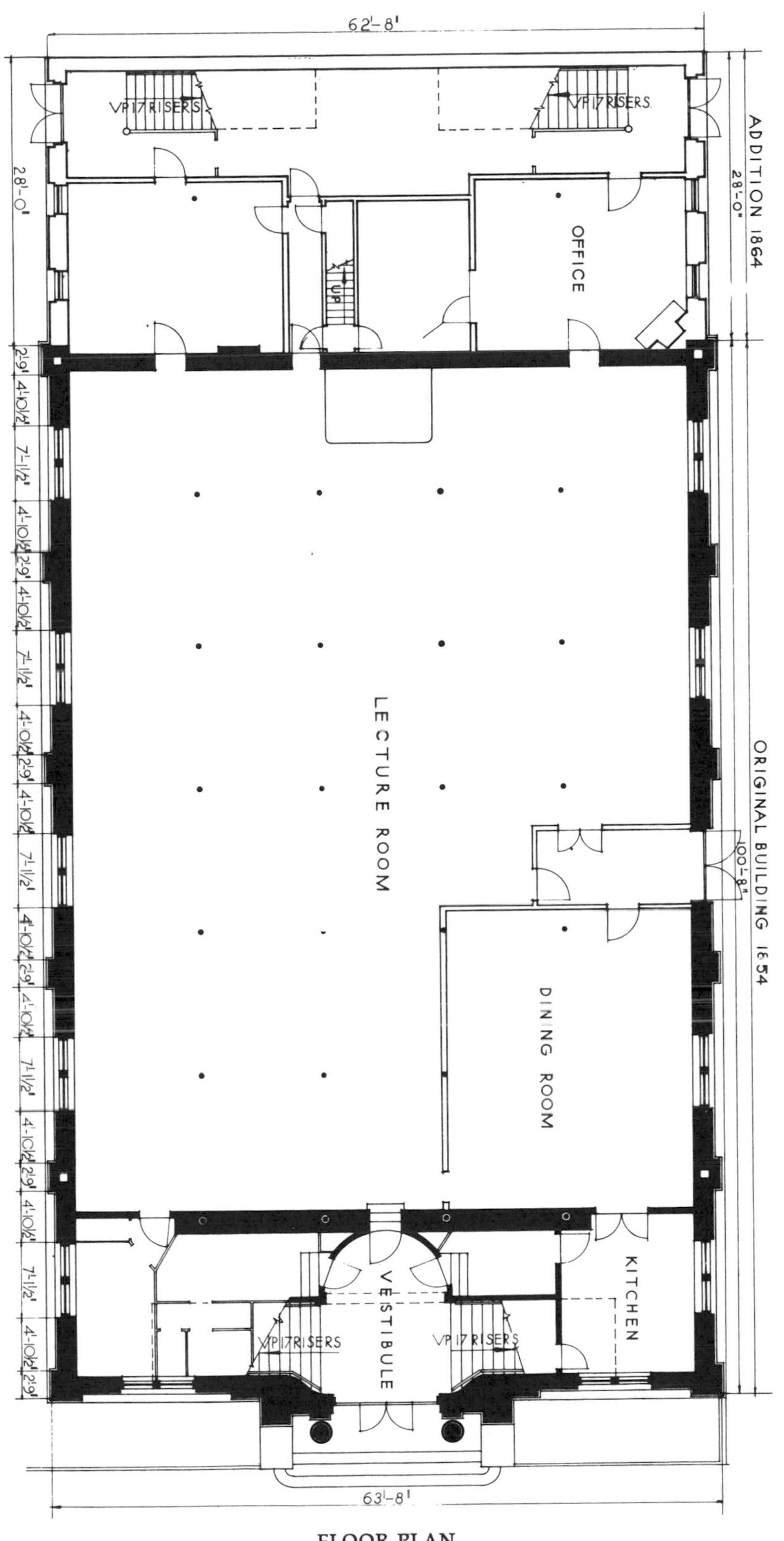
62'-8'
VP 17 RISERS
VP 17 RISERS
ADDITION 1864
28'-0"
28'-0'
OFFICE
UP
LECTURE ROOM
ORIGINAL BUILDING 1654
100'-8"
DINING ROOM
KITCHEN
VESTIBULE
VP 17 RISERS
VP 17 RISERS
63'-8'

FLOOR PLAN

1870-1900

Victorian

Victorian Gothic • Richardsonian Romanesque

IN the last third of the nineteenth century, organized religion was confronted by the social ills resulting from an extraordinarily rapid rate of immigration, urbanization, and industrialization: weakened family and clan ties, rural isolation, public health and education problems, labor exploitation, and slum immorality.

The attempts of the church to extend its ministry to the entire social organism resulted in an expanded church plan. Within a larger configuration that included parish house, lecture room, day-care center, social hall, and gymnasium, the house of worship was but a constituent element.

Internal problems were as severe as those that attacked the church from outside. The popular acceptance of Darwinism, the development of "higher criticism," and efforts to reconcile science and dogma raised serious doubts that historical Christianity could even survive the century.

The era's unabashed materialism was no less threatening to spiritual well-being—although one benign effect was its stimulus to new church construction. "Money printed your Bible, money builds your churches, money sends your missionaries, and money pays your preachers," a cleric baldly reminded his parishioners.

Visually, church architecture expressed the complexity of its era. Thus, the late-nineteenth-century church was characterized by grand scale, intricate and picturesque massing, dynamic contrasts, complicated three-dimensionality, textural richness, and opulent detail. There was a sharp break from convention, a restless originality, an eclectic daring.

Regarding historical styles, "the question is not whether we should use them at all, but how we shall choose among them," wrote the architect Henry Van Brunt in 1877 in the pioneer professional periodical *American Architect and Building News.*

Several trends were seen in rapid succession. In the 1870s and 1880s, Victorian Gothic had its heyday. One version, called Venetian Gothic because of its polychrome masonry, was admired enormously by the popular English critic John Ruskin, for its "Christian aspect." In wood, America's special version of this style was the Stick Style, known as Carpenter Gothic, which fused carpenter tradition with the structural expressiveness that suited popular taste—and, by virtue of its "truthfulness," suited popular standards of morality as well.

Hardly did the Victorian Gothic mature than it was surpassed by a Romanesque reinvigorated by contact with southern Europe and Byzantium. This was an architecture of round arches, solid volumes, weighty masses, and dark hues. This Romanesque Revival, a triumph of primitive strength, monumental concept, and painstaking execution, was the lifework of architect Henry Hobson Richardson, and it survived in the hands of his followers almost to the end of the century.

During these years, vernacular architecture tended to develop at an erratic pace and in an idiosyncratic course, particularly in provincial or bonanza towns where books like Gardner's *Commonsense in Church Building* (1880) transported high style—or rough approximations of it—to the frontier.

The late-nineteenth-century church moved from "downtown" to new neighborhoods, serving and symbolizing the period's religious and ethnic enclaves—Episcopalian or Presbyterian suburban commuters; Irish Catholic workers living near New York or Boston factories and in Colorado or Idaho mining towns; German Catholic, Lutheran, Baptist, and Jewish merchants in Cincinnati, Milwaukee, and St. Louis neighborhoods; Scandinavian Lutheran farmers in Kansas and the shores of the Great Lakes and Puget Sound; Eastern Orthodox laborers in eastern factory towns and the Pacific Northwest.

Materials

In the Victorian Gothic church, materials of contrasting color and texture enliven the building surface. Popular combinations are dense red or brown brick with terra-cotta or light stone; light and dark sandstone (especially in an alternating pattern around windows); and clapboard, laid vertically, horizontally, or diagonally and contrasted to exposed beams, shingle, and stucco.

Distinctive of Stick Style churches are vigorously articulated wooden beams that create the effect of an exterior skeleton.

Like the Victorian Gothic, the Richardsonian Romanesque church uses materials in combination, but handles them to achieve a quieter, though no less expressive, effect. Granite is rough-hewn; dark and light sandstone are contrasted to articulate wall surfaces; boulder-like fieldstone is combined with shingle in deep tones of green, red, brown, and yellow.

Plan

As new tasks are imposed upon the church, its plan grows in size and complexity.

For Protestant worshipers, the auditorium church is wider, its breadth augmented by the placement of children's classrooms which can be opened into it. A similar plan is adopted by a growing number of Jewish congregations.

The narrow-nave plan remains most suitable for Catholic practice; lengthening the nave or adding transepts provides additional space.

Elevation

VICTORIAN GOTHIC

Compared to the earlier, picturesque, phase of the Gothic Revival, the Victorian Gothic is more imposing, daring, and complicated. Exaggerated shapes may include exceptionally tall spires, steep roofs, and broad gables [224].

An insistent verticality is created by thrusting elements such as pointed arch, steep gable, spire, pinnacle, and finial [225; 227; 230]. Board-and-batten siding also creates this effect [228].

To create visual excitement, projecting surfaces show rich shadow patterns, ornament is increased in quantity and originality, and materials are varied in quality and texture.

RICHARDSONIAN ROMANESQUE

Like the Romanesque Revival of the 1850s, the style is distinguished by the round arch, but the Richardsonian Romanesque is more forceful and its originality more impressive.

Massing emphasizes heavy horizontality, set off by emphatically upright gable or tower [232]. Expressing interior spaces and functions, window openings are varied in size, shape, and placement, with an effect at once lively and dignified.

Highly inventive elements are turrets at the base of the steeple; roof, attic, and tower windows of novel shape and capricious placement; windows grouped in bands; an outscaled rose window; or an eccentric chimney beside the entry.

Decorative motifs that refer to historical Romanesque forms include the deeply recessed arched door opening with a band of moldings following the curve of the arch [233; 234], turrets at the corners of the tower and columns that are exaggeratedly tall or short, thin or fat [233].

Incipiently modern, the Prairie School church also grows from the Romanesque—regularizing, reducing, and simplifying its forms [236].

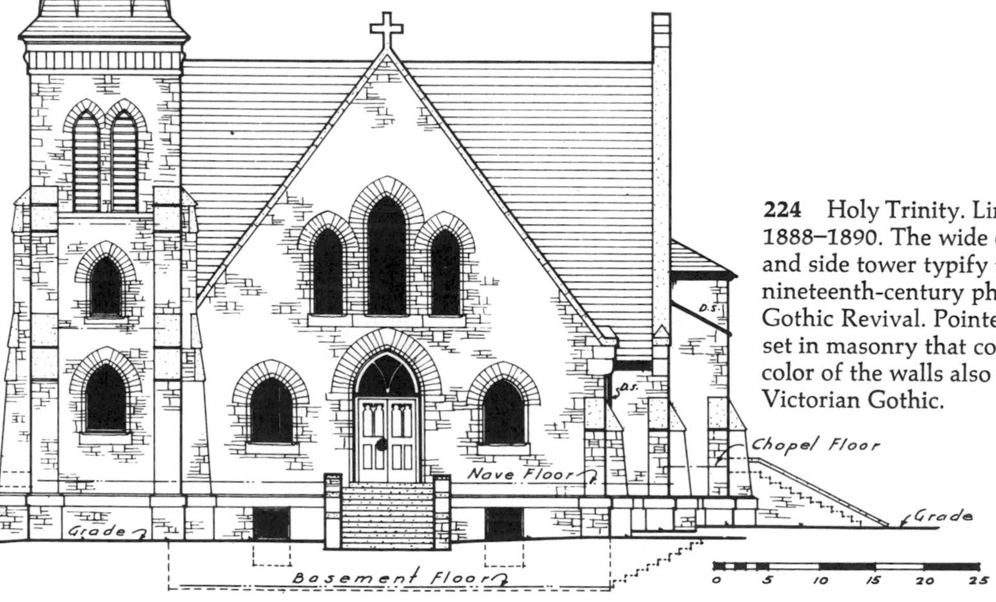

224 Holy Trinity. Lincoln, Nebraska. 1888–1890. The wide entrance front and side tower typify the late-nineteenth-century phase of the Gothic Revival. Pointed-arch openings set in masonry that contrasts with the color of the walls also represent the Victorian Gothic.

Holy Trinity, Lincoln, Nebraska; 1888–1890 (see 224).

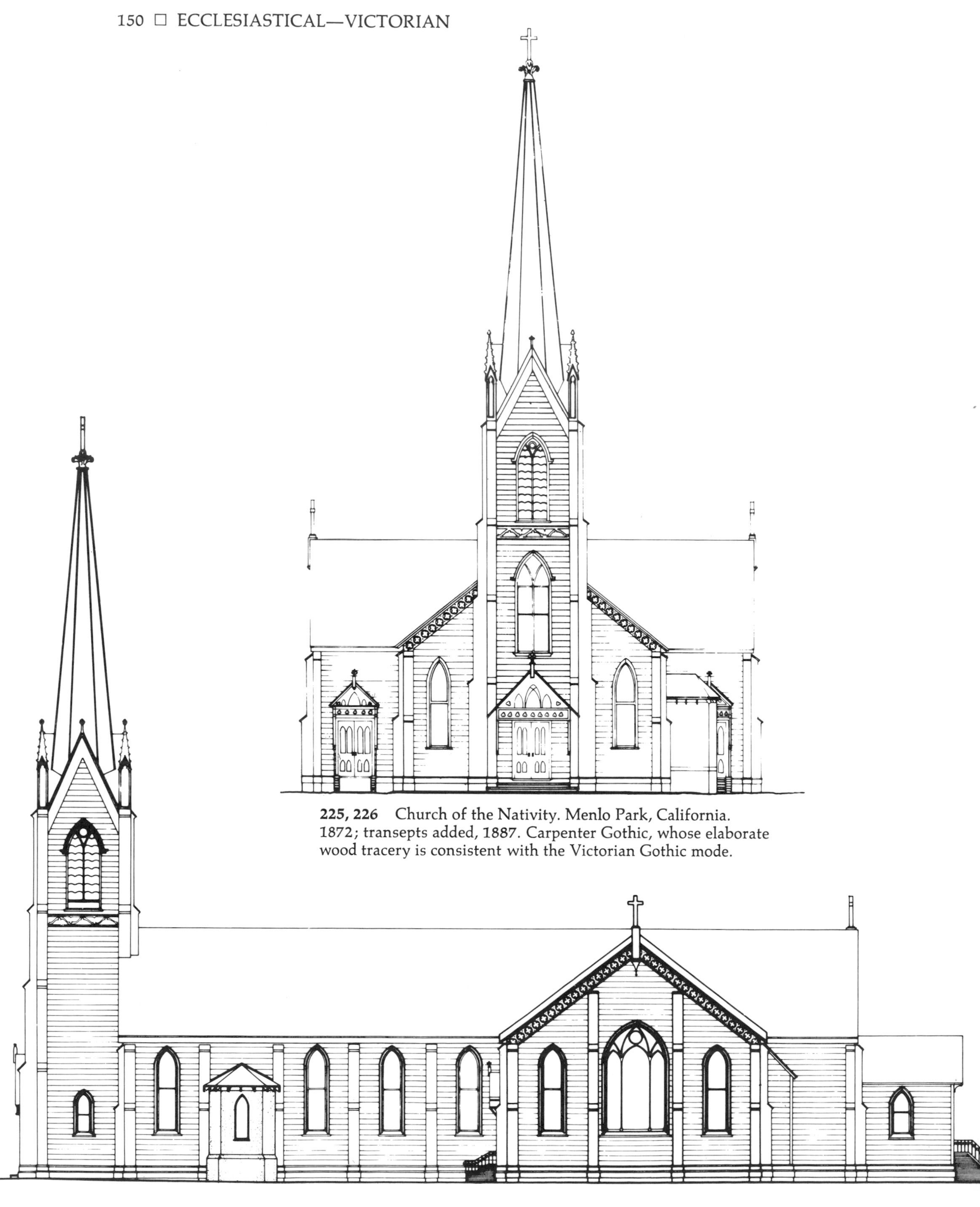

225, 226 Church of the Nativity. Menlo Park, California. 1872; transepts added, 1887. Carpenter Gothic, whose elaborate wood tracery is consistent with the Victorian Gothic mode.

227 St. Peter's Episcopal Church. Fernandina Beach, Florida. 1881–1884. A cruciform plan yields a compact and complicated silhouette.

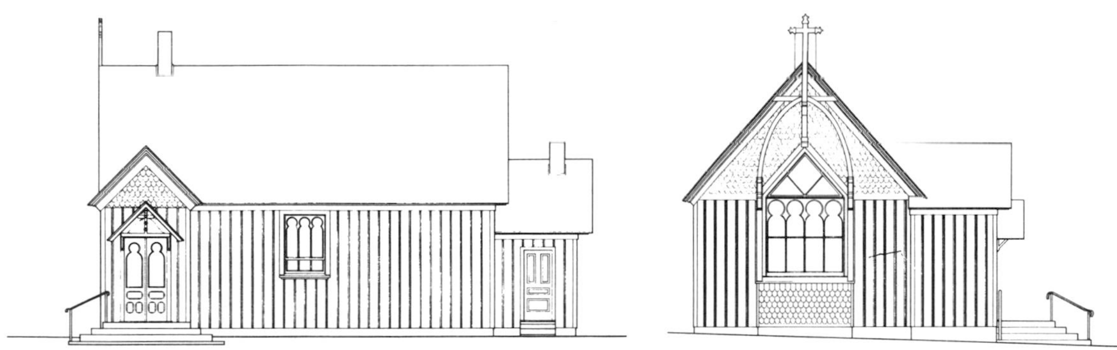

228, 229 St. Katherine's Episcopal Church. Williamstown vicinity, Michigan. 1888.

St. Matthew's Episcopal Church, National City, California; 1887 (see 230, 231).

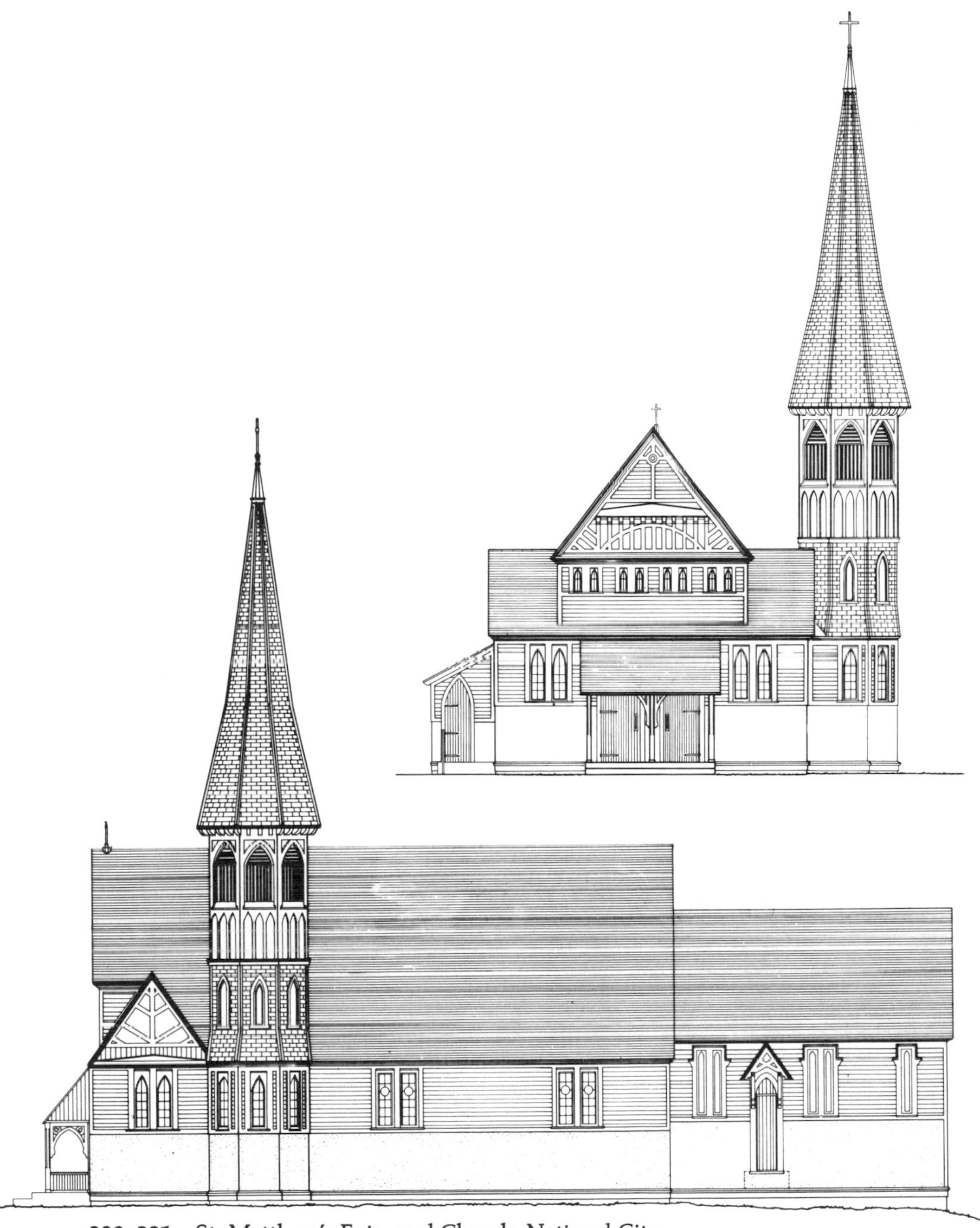

230, 231 St. Matthew's Episcopal Church. National City, California. 1887. Wood framing serves as a reminiscence of medieval half-timbering.

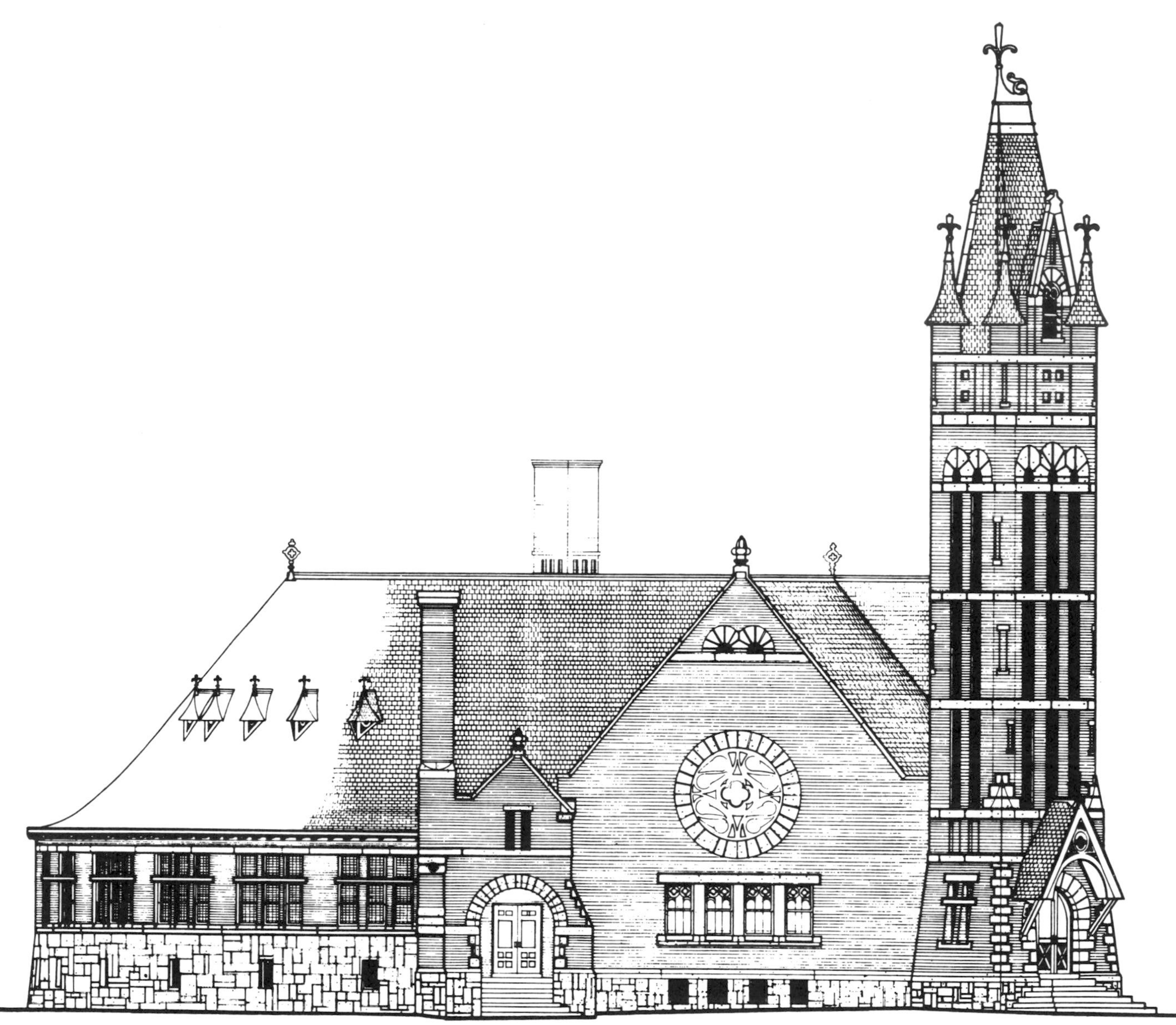

232 First Presbyterian Church. Salisbury, North Carolina. C.1890. Richardsonian Romanesque style uses brick and stone in combination, or masonry in contrasting colors, to emphasize mass and heaviness, rather than to generate liveliness.

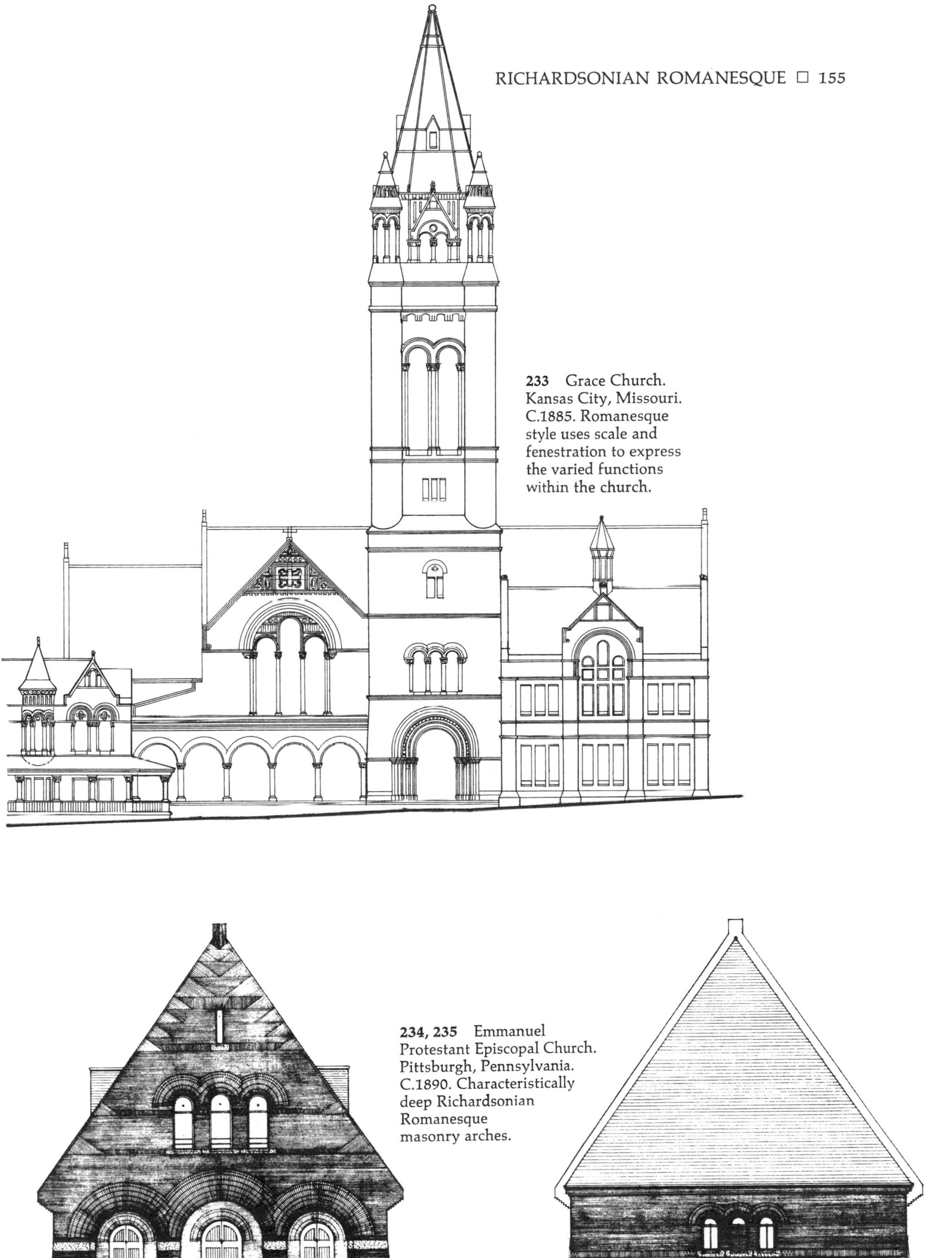

233 Grace Church. Kansas City, Missouri. C.1885. Romanesque style uses scale and fenestration to express the varied functions within the church.

234, 235 Emmanuel Protestant Episcopal Church. Pittsburgh, Pennsylvania. C.1890. Characteristically deep Richardsonian Romanesque masonry arches.

236 Kehilath Anshe Ma'Ariv Synagogue (Pilgrim Baptist Church). Chicago, Illinois. 1890–1891; Adler & Sullivan, architects. The arches and fenestration reflect Richardsonian Romanesque, but the totality expresses Prairie School modernism.

1900-1940

Twentieth Century: Period Revivals and Modern

DISTURBING uncertainties racked the period that began at the height of the Progressive Era and ended in the depths of the Great Depression. The World War was followed by a hedonistic binge; the small town yielded to the city; family and church struggled to adapt to a new social order.

It was a time when money was enshrined as the new American god while the Social Gospel was eloquently proclaimed; when church membership waxed and church attendance waned; when conscientious scholarship sifted the fundamentals of religious doctrine and liturgy grew ever more elaborate. A time of Mencken skepticism and Billy Sunday evangelism.

Through all this, fine churches grew up along grand residential avenues in the nation's great cities, in thriving automobile suburbs, in booming resort towns. Between 1900 and 1927, the annual sum expended for church construction rose from $55 million to $179 million. And while the temper of the times was volatile, flamboyant, and emotional, seen against the eccentricities of the Late Victorian years church architecture was nothing if not careful, correct, and sincere.

Ralph Adams Cram, foremost church architect of the period, best expressed the mood that would dominate the first third of the twentieth century: "Build in stone or brick; plan with rigid simplicity; design both interior and exterior with reserve, formality and self-control; have the mass simple, the composition equally so; imitate no form or detail of larger structures, but work for the dignity and the reverence that are theirs. Above all, let the spirit be that of the unchanging Church, the form alone that of the present day."

Respectful students of historical precedent and quality construction, twentieth-century revivalists conscientiously searched the past for inspiration and symbolism more than for form or content. "We must return for the fire of life to other centuries," said Cram. "We must return, but we may not remain."

All the same, nonhistorical or avowedly modern designs were few. Besieged by science and strife, the early-twentieth-century church sought an "ecclesiastical atmosphere" for its buildings. Religion protected itself within solid walls of familiar shapes: Gothic and Romanesque in their regional variations, English or Spanish Colonial, French or Roman Renaissance, Moorish or Byzantine.

Materials

Brick masonry is popular in buff tones and in a large flat size resembling Roman brick. Light colors are also favored for stone masonry. Plastered and painted poured concrete also comes into use. Smooth surfaces are favored, and carving is likely to be simplified and in low relief.

Plan

The plan of the church complex tends to be functional and clearly organized. Laterally extended, it encompasses parish house, rectory, and educational and social facilities. The Gothic plan is elaborated and enlarged by transepts and additional chapels. The Byzantine plan tends to be compact.

Elevation

Twentieth-century church design is careful and correct in selecting historical details, and inventive in using them to fulfill modern requirements. The contemporary aesthetic prefers simplicity and crisp surfaces. Proportions are generally horizontal, accentuated by tall tower or high dome [237; 238].

Ornament is generally selected from a single historical style, mostly Gothic through the 1920s, Georgian and Colonial thereafter. It is reworked in a new design for a quiet, rather than a blatant, originality. Romanesque or Byzantine is popular for Catholic, Eastern Orthodox, and Jewish parishes. Formal and symmetrical, it may be distinguished by an exotic dome, circular windows, and round arches [242; 243].

Modern church design—attempting contemporaneity—eliminates references to historical precedent, strips away ornament, searches for original forms [246; 247; 249].

237 Calvary Church. Pittsburgh, Pennsylvania. 1907; Cram, Goodhue & Ferguson, architects. The twentieth-century Gothic mode: academic application of Gothic ornament; judicious organization of volumes; audacious use of overscaled forms. The tower, extraordinarily tall and massive, rises from the crossing of nave and transepts.

238, 239 Congregational Church. Naugatuck, Connecticut. 1901–1903; McKim, Mead & White, architects. Historical Georgian motifs assembled in an original way.

240 Plymouth Congregational Church. Minneapolis, Minnesota. 1907; Shepley, Rutan & Coolidge, architects. The expanded function of the modern church is expressed in its lateral extension.

241 Mission Church of St. Giles. Philadelphia, Pennsylvania. 1930. A configuration of modern proportions, with restrained application of late Georgian ornament.

242 Oriental Greek Orthodox Church. Jacksonville, Florida. 1902. A vernacular church, adorned with an embroidery of decorative detail.

243 St. Catharine's Catholic Church. Somerville, Massachusetts. C.1915; Maginnis, Walsh & Sullivan, architects. A careful application of early Christian ornament to add a religious tone.

244, 245 Knowles Memorial Chapel. Winter Park, Florida. 1933; Cram & Ferguson, architects. The details are Spanish in inspiration, but do not attempt authenticity.

246 First Congregational Church of Austin (now Our Lady of Lebanon). Chicago, Illinois. 1908. A Prairie School church whose structure expresses function. Mainly limited to the use of contrasting stone, ornament defines component spaces—the basement-story school and social rooms, second-story sanctuary, side-bay stairways.

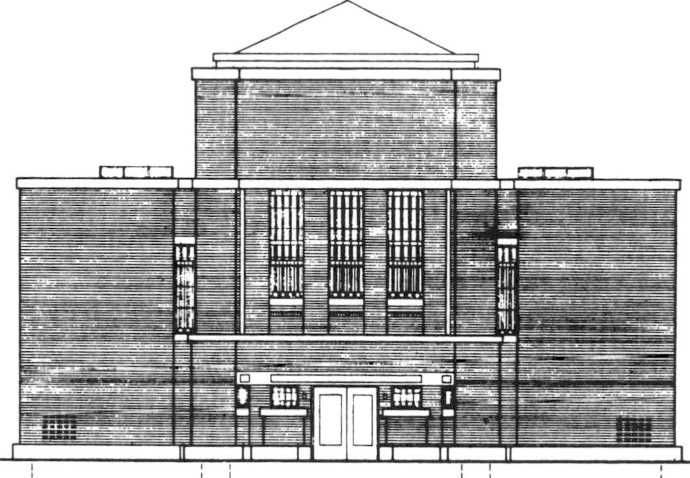

First Congregational Church of Austin (now Our Lady of Lebanon), Chicago, Illinois; 1908.

247, 248 Church of the Most Precious Blood. Astoria, New York. 1936. Traditional form, Moderne style—with chunky silhouette, smooth surfaces, and decoratively patterned door and window shape and spacing.

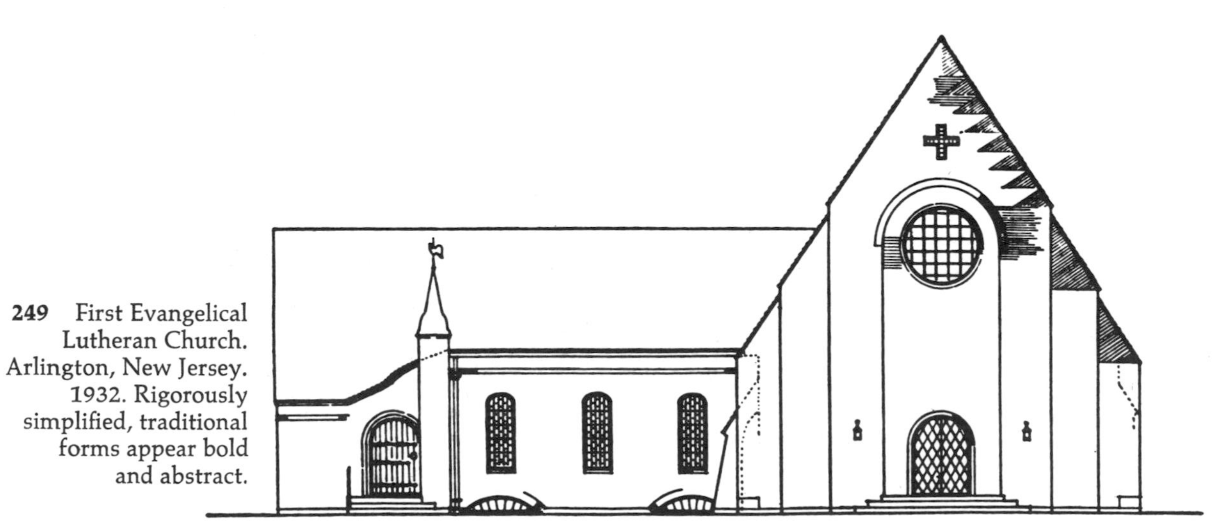

249 First Evangelical Lutheran Church. Arlington, New Jersey. 1932. Rigorously simplified, traditional forms appear bold and abstract.

PART III

Civic and Commercial

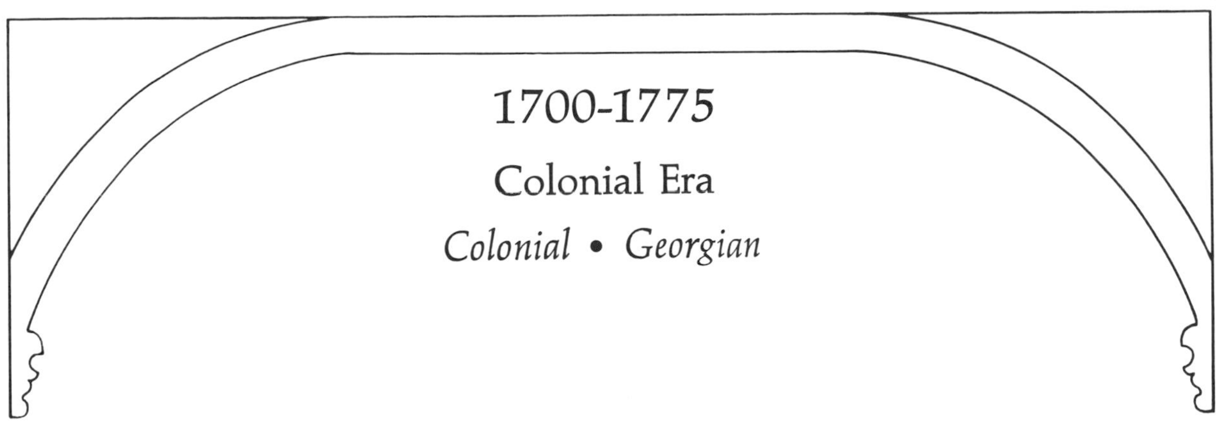

1700-1775

Colonial Era

Colonial • Georgian

IN 1775, two million souls inhabited the English colonies in America. Less than one in twenty lived in cities—yet it was the urban centers that were the proving grounds for self-government. In the cities, American politicians achieved an adequate mastery of the necessary skills to communicate, raise revenue, and aid public thoroughfare, health, education, safety, and welfare. Here were trained cultural and intellectual leaders who supported an outspoken press, theatrical and musical performances, and political, philosophical, literary, and scientific exchange.

And cities flourished as commercial hubs—first as dependent units within the British mercantile network, but increasingly, as the eighteenth century passed its midpoint, as individualistic entities engaged in active intercolonial trade.

Foreign visitors were amazed at the nature and extent of colonial urbanization, except in the South, where the plantation system slowed the development of cities. The first "metropolises" were Philadelphia (the largest, with 40,000 citizens), New York, Boston, Charleston, and Newport. From Portsmouth to Savannah, other thriving seaport cities were Marblehead, Providence, Norwich, New London, New Haven, Baltimore, and Annapolis. First among the populous inland towns were Albany, Middletown, Hartford, and Lancaster. In the Far West, New Orleans was a civilized French outpost and Santa Fe was the seat of the ailing Spanish empire.

Observers were also struck by the remarkable differences among the leading cities. Some, whether once-fortified communities (Manhattan, for example) or agricultural communities (Boston), had grown in an agglutinative manner, as new streets were rather pragmatically laid out. Others (such as Charleston or Philadelphia) followed more advanced Renaissance precepts, with a planned geometry that established a continuous gridiron pattern of streets and public spaces.

No wilderness outposts, American cities were gracious, urbane, and dignified.

Imported architectural handbooks informed both patron and builder of English Georgian style trends. Though political ties to the mother country were straining to the breaking point, in architecture the links remained strong, even including the American publication, in 1775, of Abraham Swann's immensely popular "how-to" book, *The British Architect.* And while the colonies could not yet claim a single professional architect, accomplished amateur architects and ambitious craftsmen-builders were able American interpreters of English practice.

As the American nation was born, her cities expressed the vigor of her civilization; in neatly constructed shops, in capacious brick warehouses, in well-appointed public gathering places, in monumental collegiate halls, in London-inspired governmental edifices—in architecture that was at once evidence and stimulus for a swelling civic pride.

Materials

For public buildings brick is increasingly common as the eighteenth century progresses. Clapboard continues to serve for smaller and less important structures. Fieldstone is also characteristic in the Middle Colonies.

Plan

In the early eighteenth century, church, inn, and market house (whose upper stories also serve for public offices) are the significant public buildings.

The plan of the inn is domestic in character, with first-story rooms reserved for community use and private accommodations above. The plans of multipurpose buildings—such as dwelling-workroom or warehouse-shop—are functional.

The differentiation and specialization of existing building types that accompany the growth of civic and commercial activity involves increased size and number of rooms and variety of plans.

The county courthouse—a well-established type by the middle of the century—typically has a central section (crowned by a tower) and symmetrical side wings.

Elevation

The warehouse remains utilitarian, the shop becomes more elaborate [250; 251, 252]. Civic buildings are modest in scale. From the simplest to the grandest, they echo early Georgian style, the chief differences among them being the extent of their ornamentation. The most ambitious, such as the courthouse of a prospering county seat [253], has impressive embellishments. Other buildings lack many or most of these distinguishing features.

For the high-style building, a hipped roof is characteristic; lesser examples may have a pitched or gambrel roof. In this period, the shape of the gambrel shows regional variations: in the South and the Middle Colonies, the lower slope may be steeper than in New England [compare 255 with 258].

Reynolds' Tavern, Annapolis, Maryland; 1737 (see 257, 258, p. 173).

250 Haven warehouse. Washington, North Carolina. C.1800. For its period, an unusually large structure, reflecting North Carolina's commercial and maritime prominence.

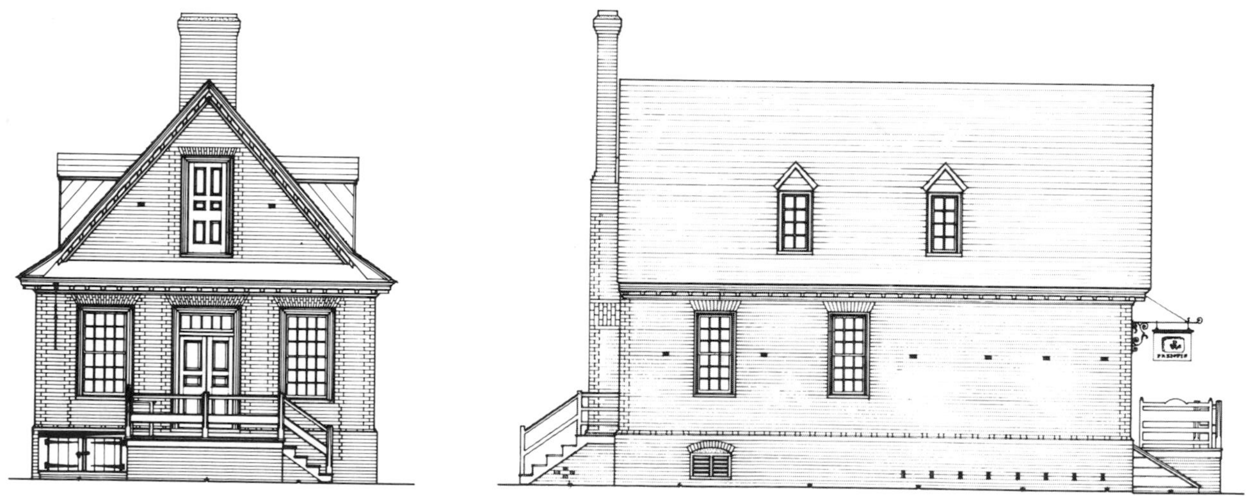

251, 252 Prentis store. Williamsburg, Virginia. 1740.

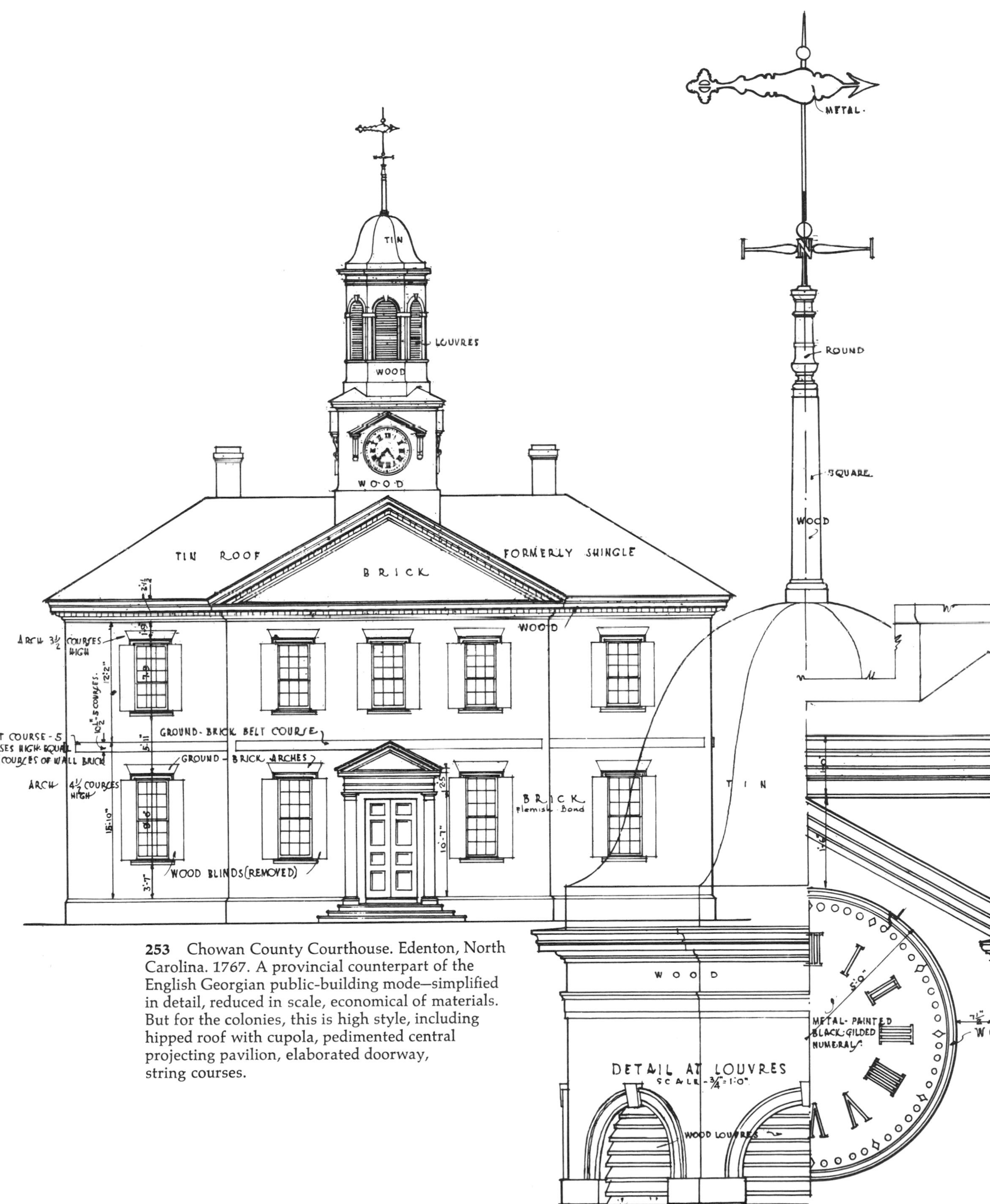

253 Chowan County Courthouse. Edenton, North Carolina. 1767. A provincial counterpart of the English Georgian public-building mode—simplified in detail, reduced in scale, economical of materials. But for the colonies, this is high style, including hipped roof with cupola, pedimented central projecting pavilion, elaborated doorway, string courses.

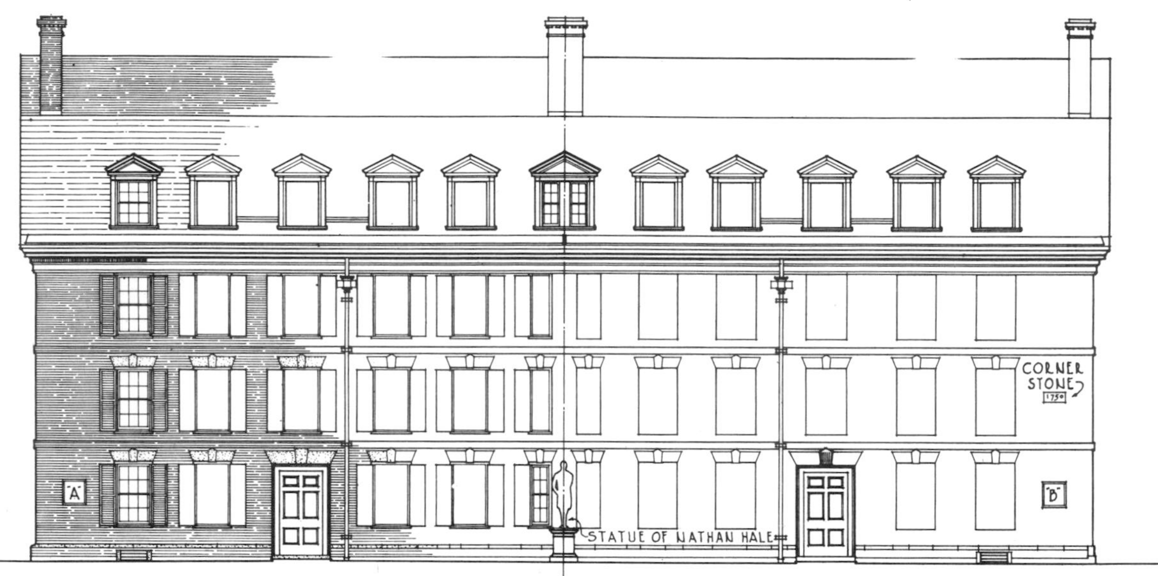

254, 255 Connecticut Hall, Yale University. New Haven, Connecticut. 1750–1757. An early college building, linked to residential design.

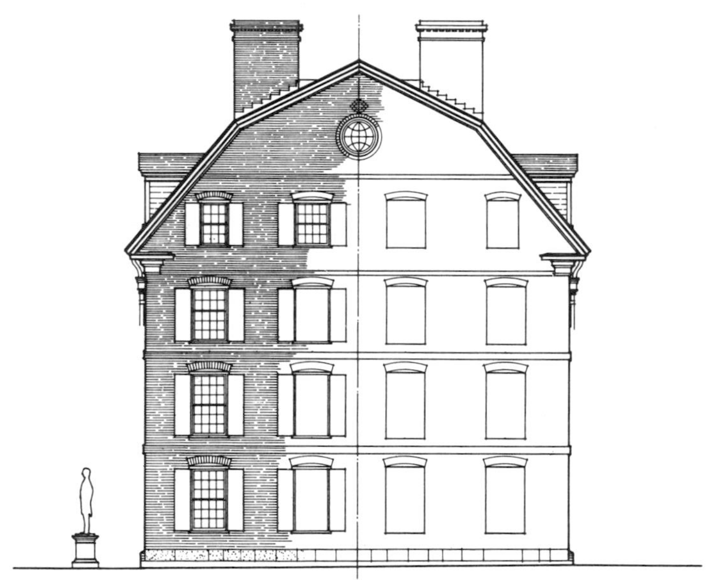

256 Old Masonic Temple. Trenton, New Jersey. 1793.

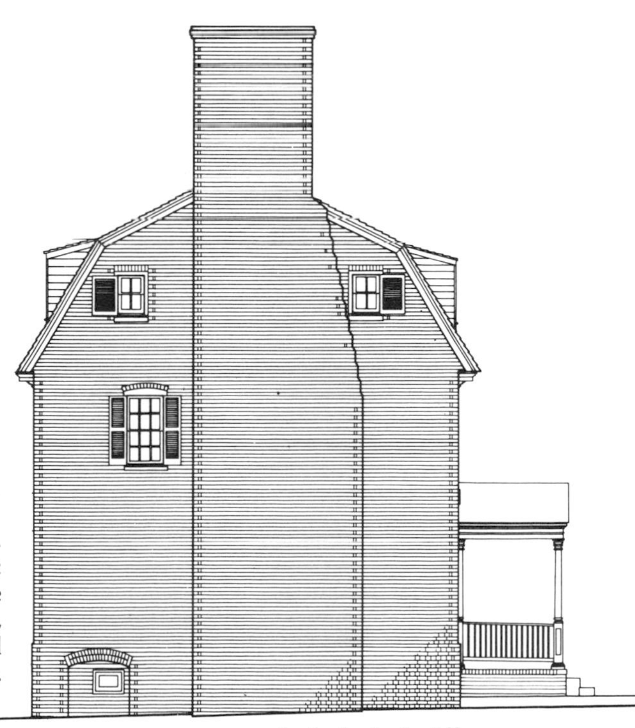

257, 258 Reynolds' Tavern. Annapolis, Maryland. 1737. A significant structure in an important governmental center. At this date, style is more ambitious than consistent, with awkward height, shed-roof dormers, all-header brick bond, and idiosynchratic arched string course.

1780-1830

Classical Revival

"THE eighth wonder of the world!" one contemporary marveled upon the completion of the United States Capitol in 1827. Here was a fitting symbol for the success of the young nation.

America took her place in the community of nations: her population, less than four million in 1790, had swelled to ten million by 1820; her western boundary stretched to the Mississippi. Capitols rose in every state (altogether, seventeen were built between 1783 and 1820), courthouses in every county, town and city halls from Maine to Kentucky.

In a Neoclassical style that looked to ancient Rome, fronted by columned portico and crowned by shallow dome, the grand new public building proclaimed the nation's destiny.

A wave of immigrant architects and engineers infused the late-eighteenth-century Georgian style with fresh ideas from abroad. Benjamin Latrobe, George Hadfield, and William Jay from England; Pierre L'Enfant, Maximilian Godefroy, Joseph Mangin, and Jean-Jacques Ramée from France; and native Americans returning from European travels—Thomas Jefferson, Charles Bulfinch, and Robert Mills—brought to American building a new level of aesthetic sophistication. Immigrant artisans—stonemasons, plasterers, carpenters, and metalworkers—set new standards of craft and competence.

The increasingly differentiated plan of capitol, courthouse, customhouse, record building, hospital, college, and jail accommodated the growing scope and complexity of government and institutional authority, while an impressive appearance lent weight and authority.

A new building type appeared in the commercial block, a row of three or more uniform buildings with shop entries at street level and two stories above for office or dwelling. First of all practical, these buildings achieved an impressive effect from solid construction, good proportion, and careful details, and they were right at home in the grid-plan city, the urban vision of this early Republican era.

As trade and commerce grew, warehouses lined the wharfside and shops ranked the streetfront; the urbanization of America had begun.

Materials

Smooth surfaces are favored; brick laid in Flemish bond in urban centers, frame with clapboard or matchboard cladding or fieldstone in provincial areas.

Surfaces may be plastered and painted. Smoothly dressed sandstone, marble, or granite frequently appears in basement, lintel, or coursing.

Plan

Public buildings are generally rectangular, long side facing the street. More elaborate buildings may have several symmetrically disposed wings and a projecting central pavilion [259; 260; 261].

Commercial buildings are freestanding [264] or in a row, joined by party walls and set short side to the street, usually with the eaves facing the street [262].

A variety of building types evolve for new or

more developed functions, including state capitol, customhouse, courthouse, town and city hall, library and archive, jail, hospital, and retail store.

Elevation

Civic buildings are simple and dignified, notable for their monumentality more than their size, for their restraint more than their exuberance, for their reticence more than their eloquence. Reflecting Jeffersonian Classicism, the southern example may be more impressive, with a monumental portico [261]. A projecting central pavilion, a central pediment, and a cupola with arched openings are other characteristic high-style forms [259; 260, 265].

Federal taste favors an entry with fan-shaped light, attenuated columns at the portico, delicate coursing, a finely detailed cornice at the eaves, and a low hipped roof [260].

Window size, shape, and placement tends to be regular with larger window openings or a Palladian motif to express a major public space.

Provincial examples have minimal ornament and are almost domestic in scale [263; 264; 266].

259 Old Fairfield Academy. Fairfield, Connecticut. 1804, restored in the 1920s. Cupola and doorways are a twentieth-century reinterpretation.

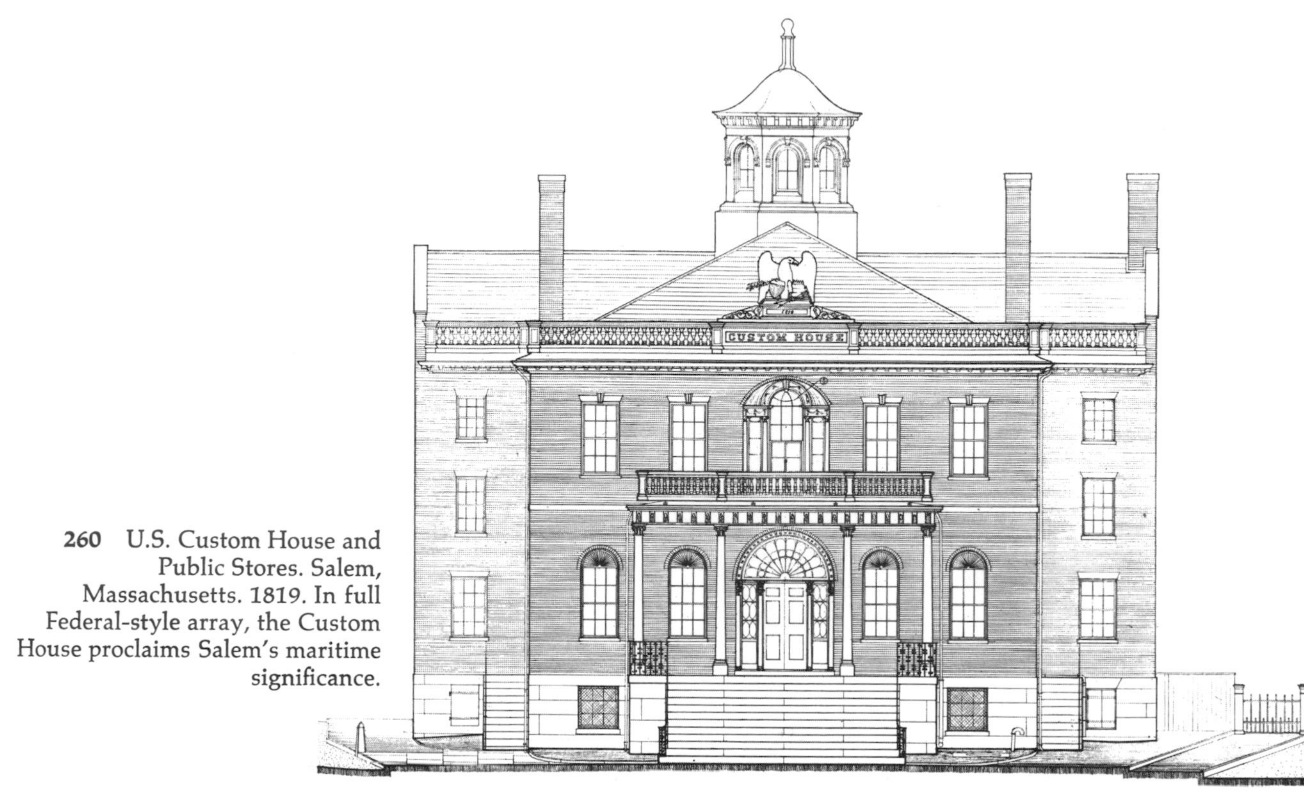

260 U.S. Custom House and Public Stores. Salem, Massachusetts. 1819. In full Federal-style array, the Custom House proclaims Salem's maritime significance.

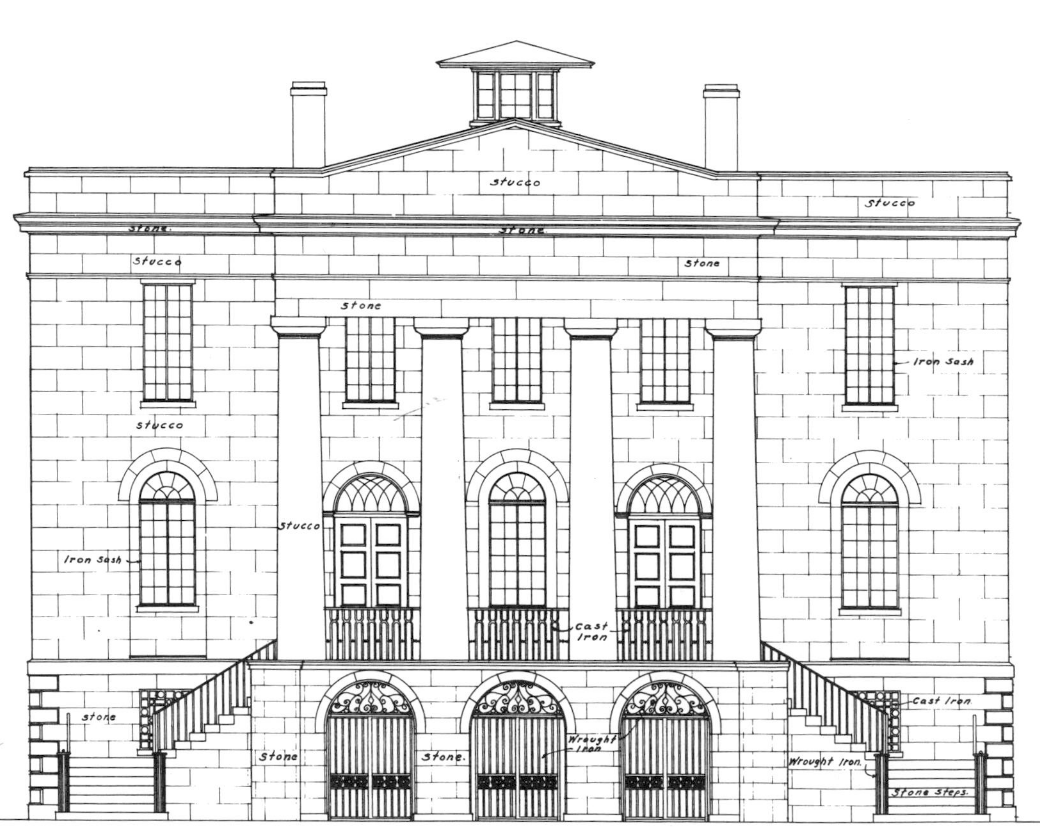

261 County Records Building. Charleston, South Carolina. 1822–1827; Robert Mills, architect. A monumental structure, advanced for its technology (fireproof, all-masonry construction) and its style (a two-story portico that heralds the Greek Revival).

County Records Building, Charleston, South Carolina; 1822–1827 (see 261).

262 John Read's Row. Petersburg, Virginia. C.1815. The developed form of the commercial row, shopfronts below, dwelling or offices above. The shop windows originally would have had glazing bars.

263 Netherland Inn. Kingsport, Tennessee. 1812. Now lacking the original porches and elevated walkway over adjacent stage route.

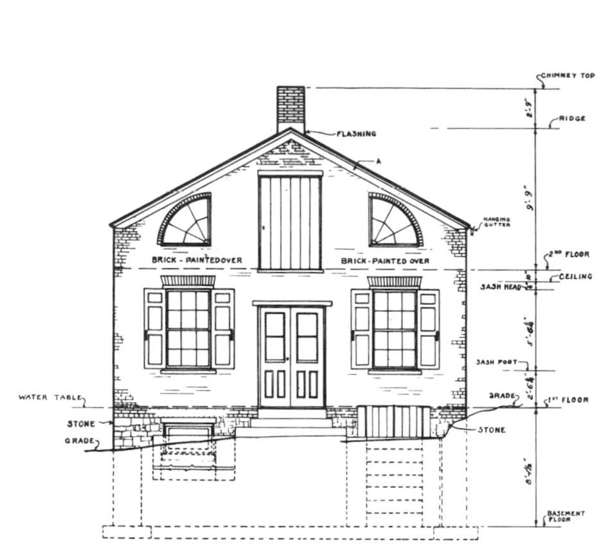

264 Old Stone Store. Pleasant Valley, New York. C.1825. A pragmatic design, to accommodate the dual requirements of storehouse and salesroom.

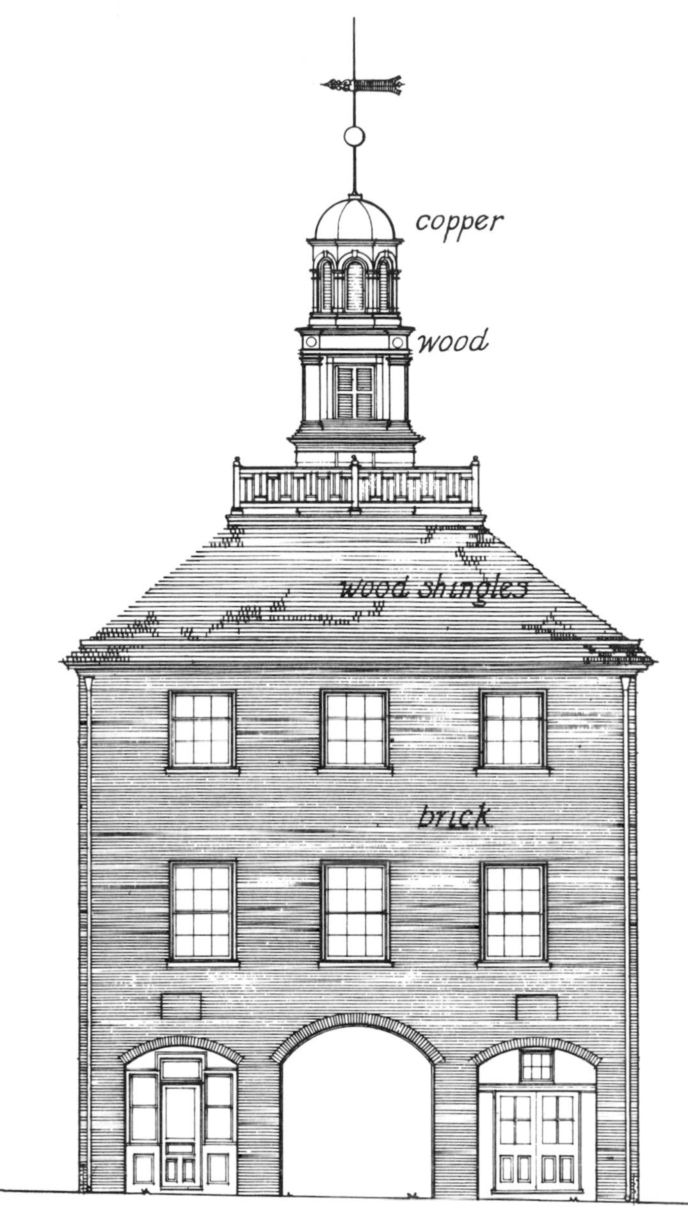

265 Old Town Hall. New Castle, Delaware. 1823. A square-plan building constructed for town offices, with access to a rear market house through the arched passage at its base. Hipped roof with balustraded deck, octagonal cupola, Flemish-bond brickwork on the facade.

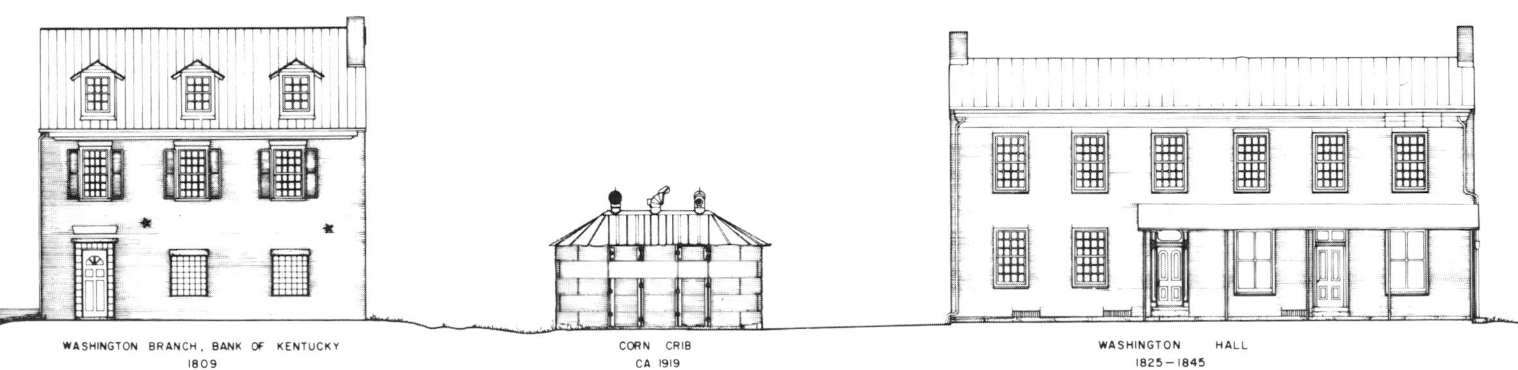

266 Washington Historic District. Washington, Kentucky. 1809, Bank of Kentucky; 1820–1845, Washington Hall. Vernacular commercial buildings, domestic in character.

1820-1860

Early Victorian

Greek Revival
Renaissance and Romanesque Revivals

WHILE the taste for Roman motifs endured, Benjamin Latrobe's temple-fronted Bank of Pennsylvania (designed in 1798) and John Haviland's drawings of Greek orders in *The Builder's Assistant* (1818) proclaimed the imminent ascendancy of the Greek Revival.

After the late 1820s, the first generation of American-born and American-trained professional architects—Robert Mills, William Strickland, Gideon Shryock, and Thomas U. Walter—took this Greek-temple mode as their own. Boston could claim native-born professionally trained and influential architects—Isaiah Rogers, Solomon Willard, Alexander Parris, and Ammi B. Young—and an important innovation, the commercial row of storefronts framed by monolithic stone piers. But New York City—"Athens Revived"—was home to the nation's first professional architectural firm, that of Ithiel Town and Alexander Jackson Davis. Here the freestanding temple-fronted public building and the colonnaded street-front stood as shining examples to the nation.

Urban development progressed rapidly. By 1860, one-sixth of the nation's population lived in cities: customhouses, post offices, state capitols, courthouses, city halls, hospitals, hotels, colleges, banks, exchanges, theaters, clubhouses, market houses, and retail stores filled in the urban grid.

In robust midwestern towns, in the rural South, in villages that grew along western trails and in Gold Rush California, the Greek Revival was a vigorous vernacular expression right up to the Civil War years.

In a young country, the Greek Revival symbolized a past that was missing; more significantly, in an ambitious country, the Greek Revival held the promise of a great future.

But the demands of the age were for structures that could be contained in an urban streetscape, for plans that accommodated complex functions, for construction that incorporated iron and glass, for style that was evidence of material progress.

As early as the 1840s, in the rapidly growing cities of the Northeast and Midwest, the palace of the Italian prince, rather than temple of the Athenian citizen, proved to be a more fitting symbol and a more serviceable form. Aesthetically, this shift was gentle. The architecture of late-medieval and Renaissance Italy—itself an echo of the Classical past—was, in its clarity, balance, rational proportions, and measured rhythms, an apt expression of Greek Revival ideals.

For monuments of culture and commerce, freedom of expression—tempered by well-understood concepts of order—was the principle of the time.

Materials

Stone, brick, and timber are employed to suggest weight and permanence. Ashlar masonry is laid in regular courses with fine mortar joints; granite in New England, limestone in the West, and Tennessee marble in the South are popular.

Wood is frequently used to mimic stone, whether in matchboarding, quoin blocks, columns, or pilasters.

Cast iron is sometimes used for column capitals and in geometric or foliate designs, for balustrade, grille, rail, or fence.

As this period progresses, there is increasing use of cast iron for interior (columns and girders) and exterior framing (shopfronts, window lintels, and eventually complete façades).

Structural concrete is a new material which has a minor vogue during the 1840s and 1850s in New York, New Jersey, and the Midwest, specifically for octagonally shaped structures.

Plan

For public buildings, the freestanding Greek temple type serves equally well—if at radically different scales—for bank, courthouse, market-house, and office.

Typically, the volume is self-contained and horizontal; cupolas or towers may be vertical accents. [271; 274]. Interior spaces are made more flexible by the use of the dome [269]; by basement public space beneath a high pedestal [273]; or by flanking wings [271].

Elevation

GREEK REVIVAL

The building with columned portico—either with triangular pediment or flat entablature—is an imposing monument and an impressive symbol of government power, civic spirit, and commercial enterprise. Major buildings are all-masonry construction with interior vaults for support. On vernacular buildings, where the colonnade serves for porch supports, Classical proportions may be thoroughly distorted [275].

Shopfronts or vernacular examples may lack columned portico, but they too are characterized by broad proportions, regular fenestration, and sparse and boldly simple detail.

In stone, the shopfront is framed by monolithic piers and lintels [276]. Upper-story window openings may also be headed by flat stone lintels, with or without carved end blocks [280—no. 305]. There may be a simple cornice at the eaves, with or without dentil moldings.

Alterations over time alter shopfront, window sash, and roofline [279].

With decorative iron railings, a second-story balcony that forms a covered streetway is a device associated with warmer climes [278, 279].

RENAISSANCE AND ROMANESQUE REVIVALS

With the taste for the Italianate which emerges in the 1840s and continues for two decades and more, Greek Revival forms are recast in a grander mold; massing is more complex, proportions are taller, ornament is richer.

A distinguishing characteristic of the Italian Renaissance is the tall, narrow window opening with pedimented window cap [280—no. 303; 281; 282]. Also typical is the use of strong cornice lines, rusticated masonry, heavy brackets, and richly detailed moldings.

The Romanesque elaborates on the Greek Revival. Characteristically, also it employs round-arch openings, heavy masonry piers, and richly profiled cornices [284, 285; 287].

Provincial structures may demonstrate ingenious hybridization [281; 288].

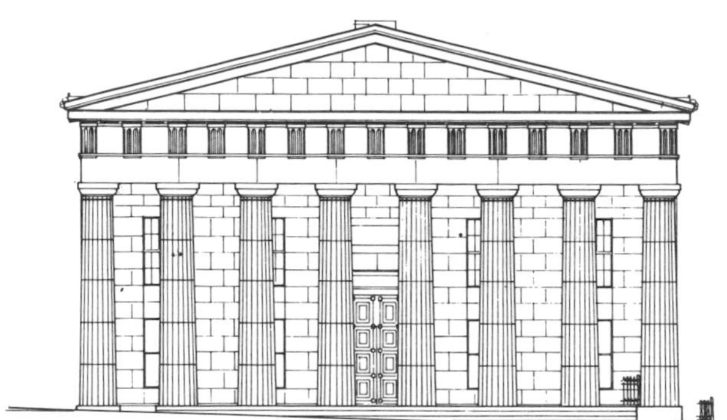

267, 268, 269 United States Sub-Treasury. New York, New York. 1832–1842; Ithiel Town and Alexander Jackson Davis in association with Ross & Frazee. Originally built as a U.S. custom house. The facade has a Greek Doric portico, Parthenon-like in breadth and proportion, while lacking sculptural embellishment. On the side walls, engaged pilasters reflect the post-and-lintel construction, but the great domed interior space is hardly revealed on the exterior.

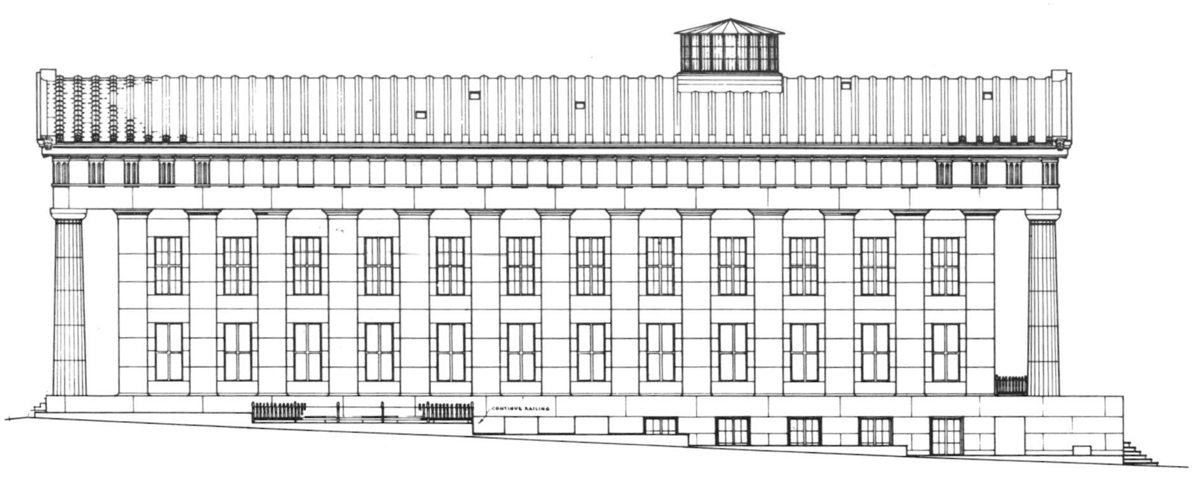

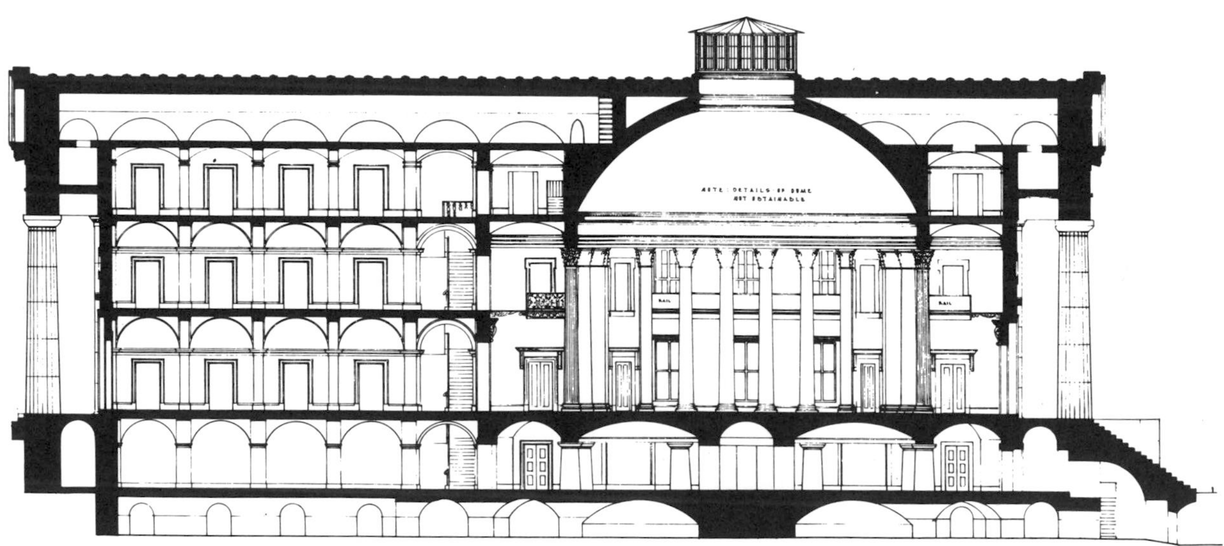

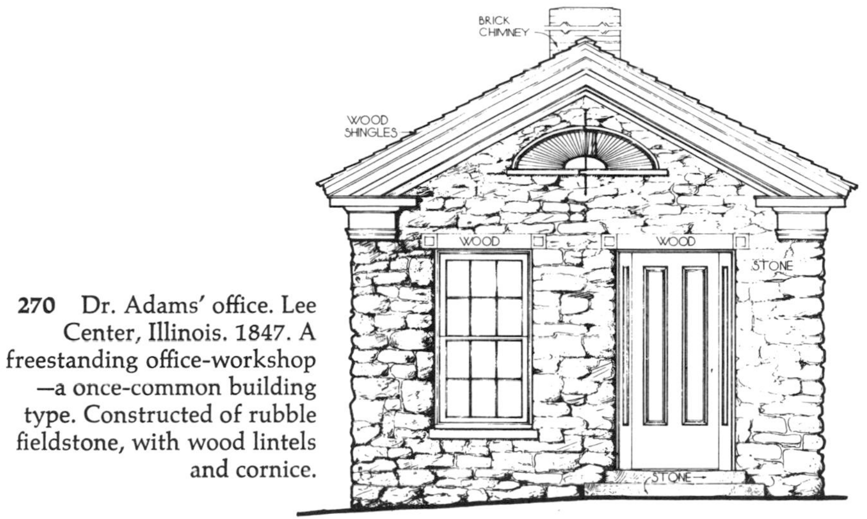

270 Dr. Adams' office. Lee Center, Illinois. 1847. A freestanding office-workshop —a once-common building type. Constructed of rubble fieldstone, with wood lintels and cornice.

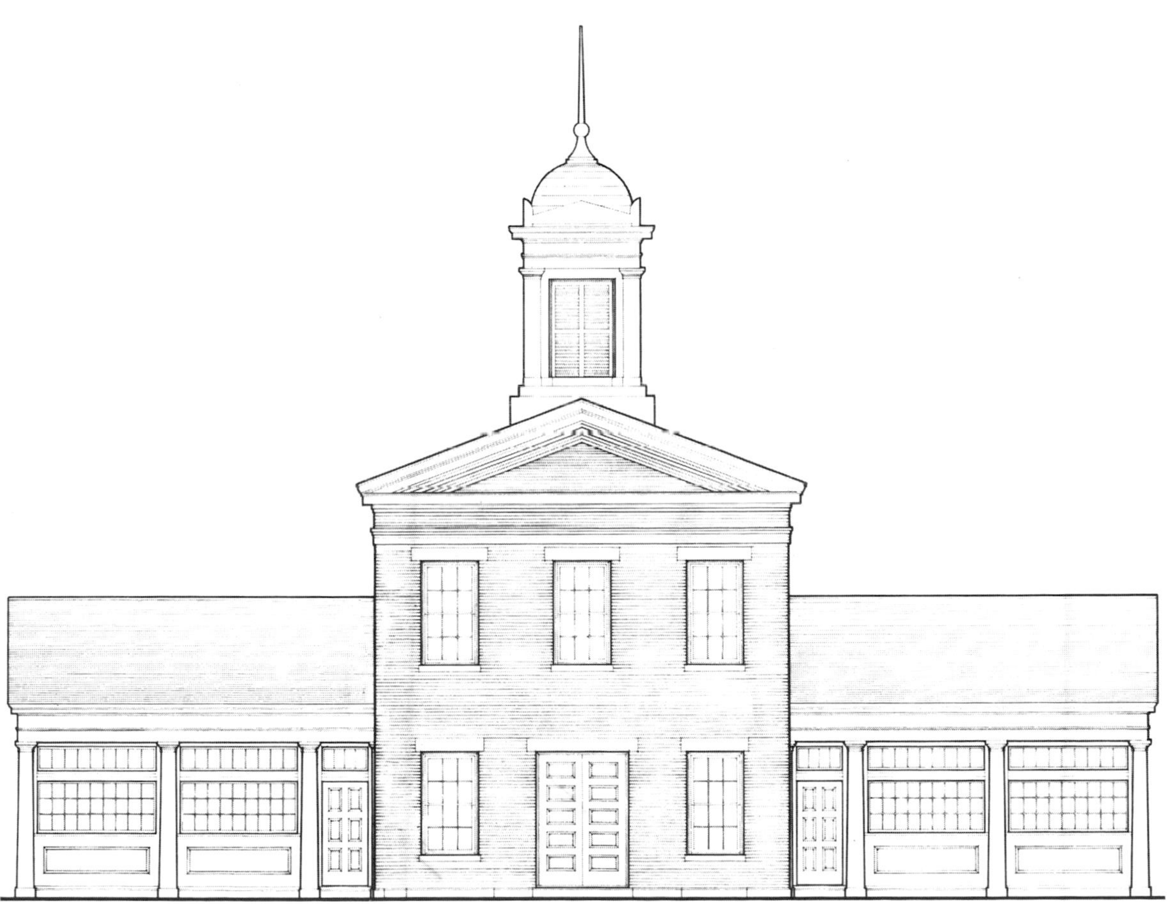

271 Old Market House. Galena, Illinois. 1845. Constructed of brick with limestone trim, and cupola and cornice of wood.

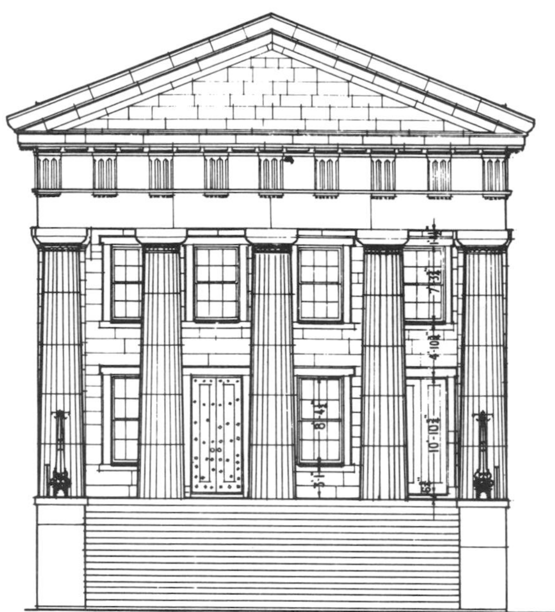

272, 273 Old State Bank. Shawneetown, Illinois. 1839–1840. Greek proportions modified to suit contemporary needs. Stone masonry for basement, facade, and entablature, brick for the side walls.

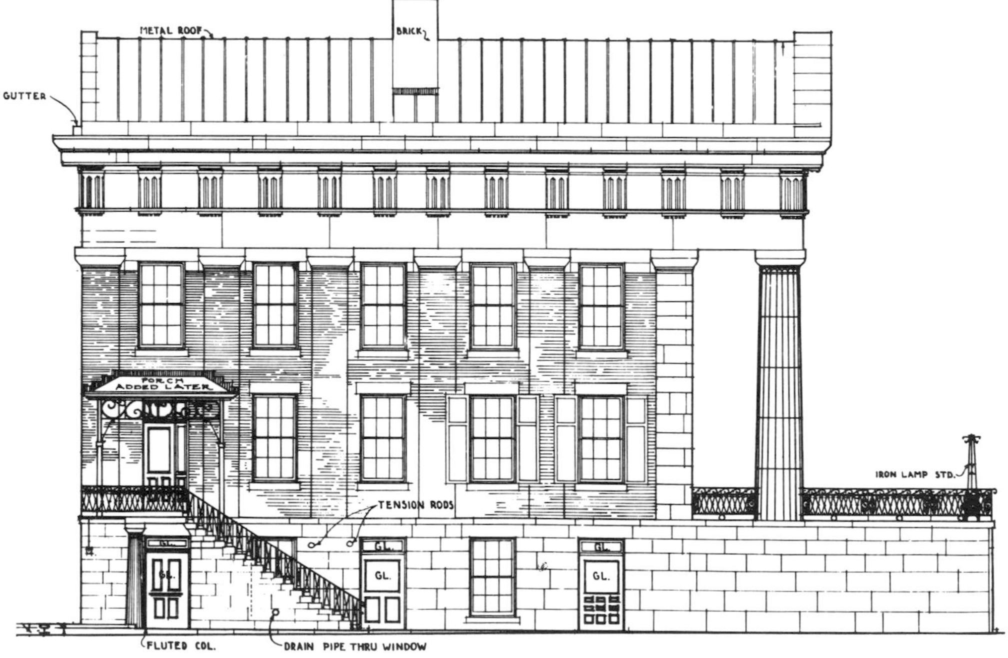

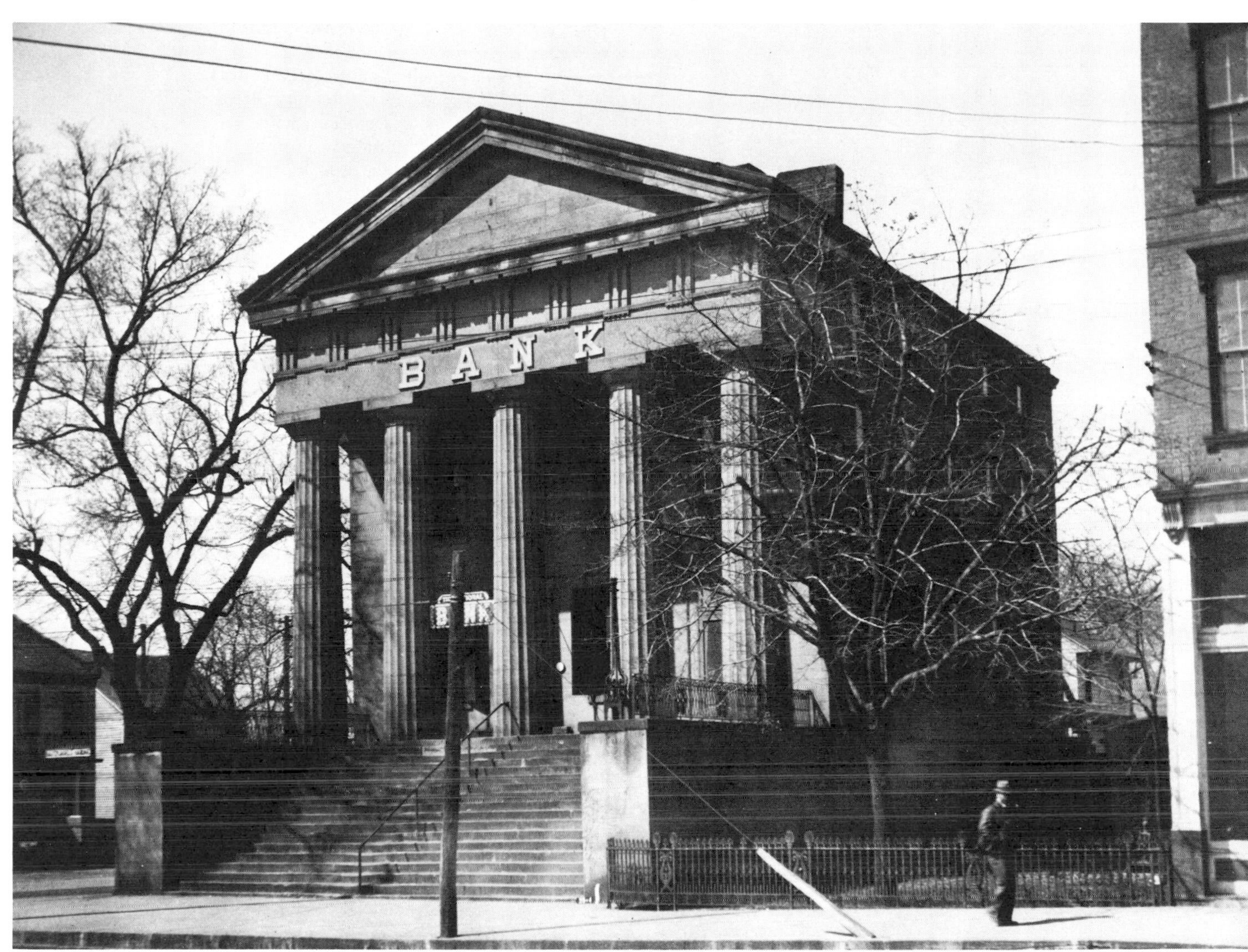

Old State Bank, Shawneetown, Illinois; 1839–1840 (see 272, 273).

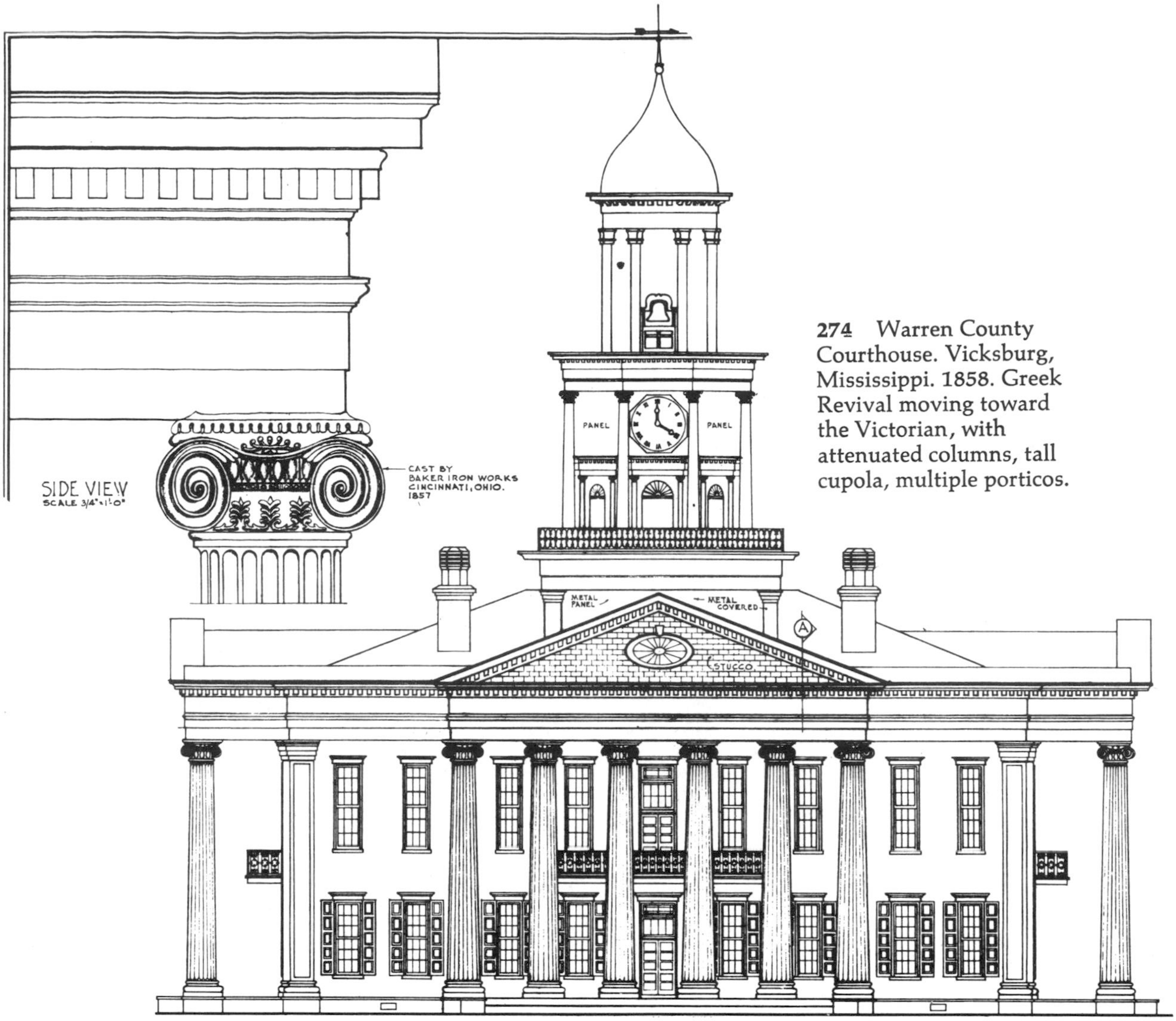
SIDE VIEW
SCALE 3/4"=1'-0"
CAST BY
BAKER IRON WORKS
CINCINNATI, OHIO.
1857
PANEL
PANEL
METAL PANEL
METAL COVERED
STUCCO

274 Warren County Courthouse. Vicksburg, Mississippi. 1858. Greek Revival moving toward the Victorian, with attenuated columns, tall cupola, multiple porticos.

SHINGLES
SEE BALUSTER DETAIL
2'-10"
8" FRIEZE
8'-10"
0
5
10

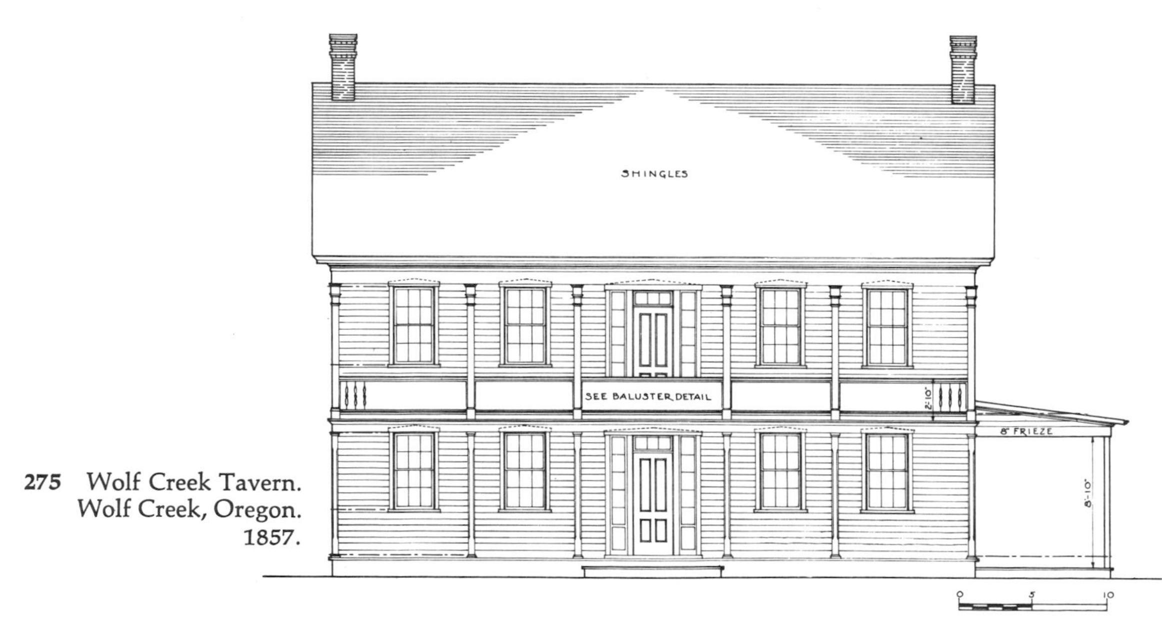

275 Wolf Creek Tavern. Wolf Creek, Oregon. 1857.

276 25–27 State Street. Newburyport, Massachusetts. C.1820. A commercial row with windowed shopfronts framed by granite posts and lintels which support brick masonry above. Eaves treatment is an abbreviated cornice.

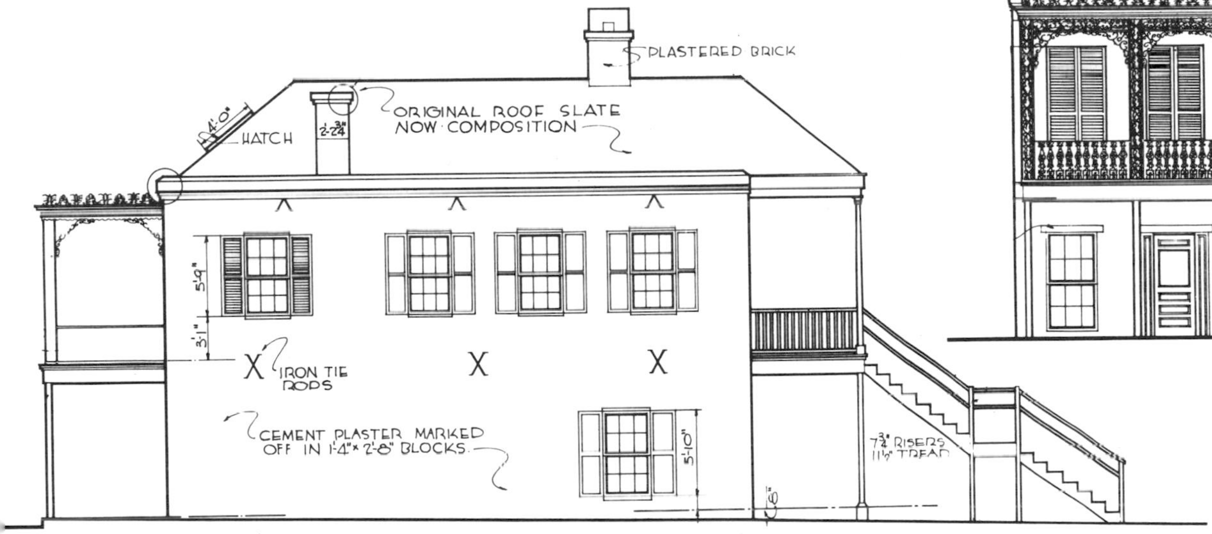

277, 278 Conrad Meuly House and Store. Corpus Christi, Texas. 1852–1853. Unadorned Greek Revival forms are an effective foil for ornate cast-iron embellishment.

279 Schermerhorn Row. New York, New York. C.1830, with later alterations. As originally built, a unified commercial block, strongly defined by its continuous roofline.

280 Mulberry Street Block. Madison County, Indiana. Nos. 307, 305, c.1835; no. 303, c.1865; no. 301, c.1875. From right to left, the transition from Greek Revival to Victorian Italianate.

281 Southport Savings Bank. Southport, Connecticut. 1854. A small-town bank, with emphatically pedimented gable, round- and square-headed windows, brick walls, and brownstone trim.

282 U.S. Custom House. Galveston, Texas. 1859–1861, and later alterations. Tall proportions and flat-pediment window treatment are characteristically Italianate; so too are the superposed colonnades, balustrades, and use of both Ionic and Corinthian capitals.

U.S. Custom House, Galveston, Texas; 1859–1861.

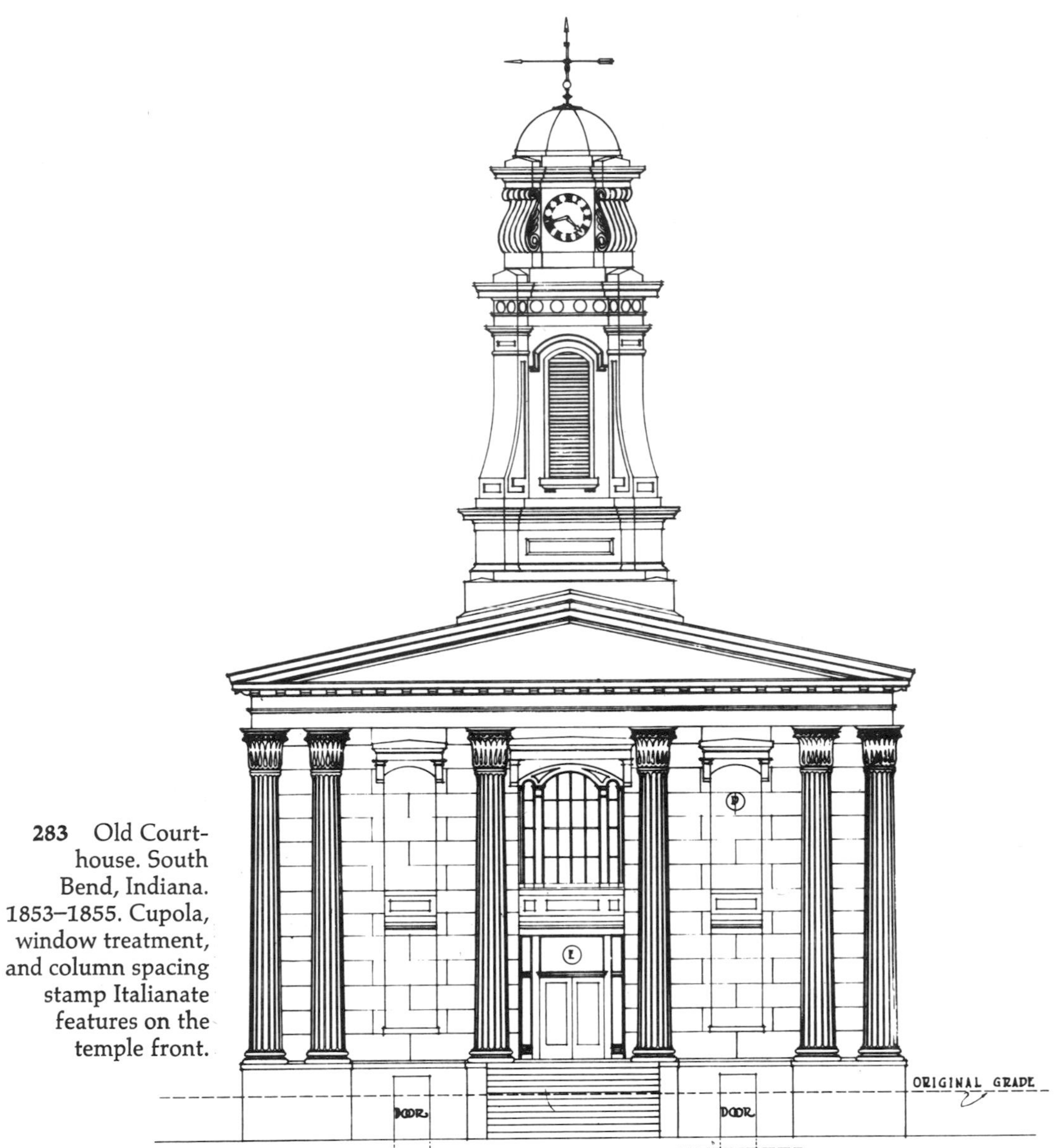

283 Old Courthouse. South Bend, Indiana. 1853–1855. Cupola, window treatment, and column spacing stamp Italianate features on the temple front.

284, 285, 286 Cooper Union for the Advancement of Science. New York, New York. 1853–1859; two stories and attic added above main cornice, 1891. With brownstone facade composed to reduce the structure's apparent height and bulk, a portent of an ever-increasing urban scale after the mid-nineteenth century.

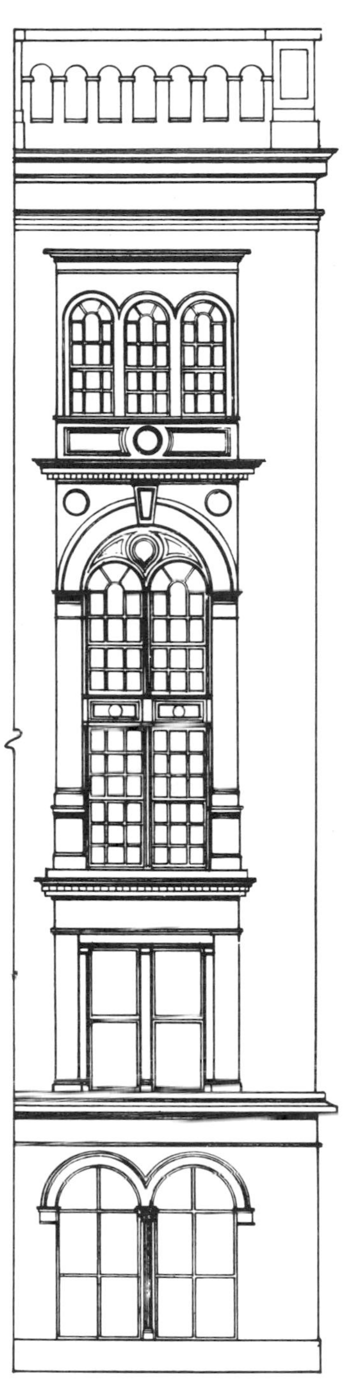

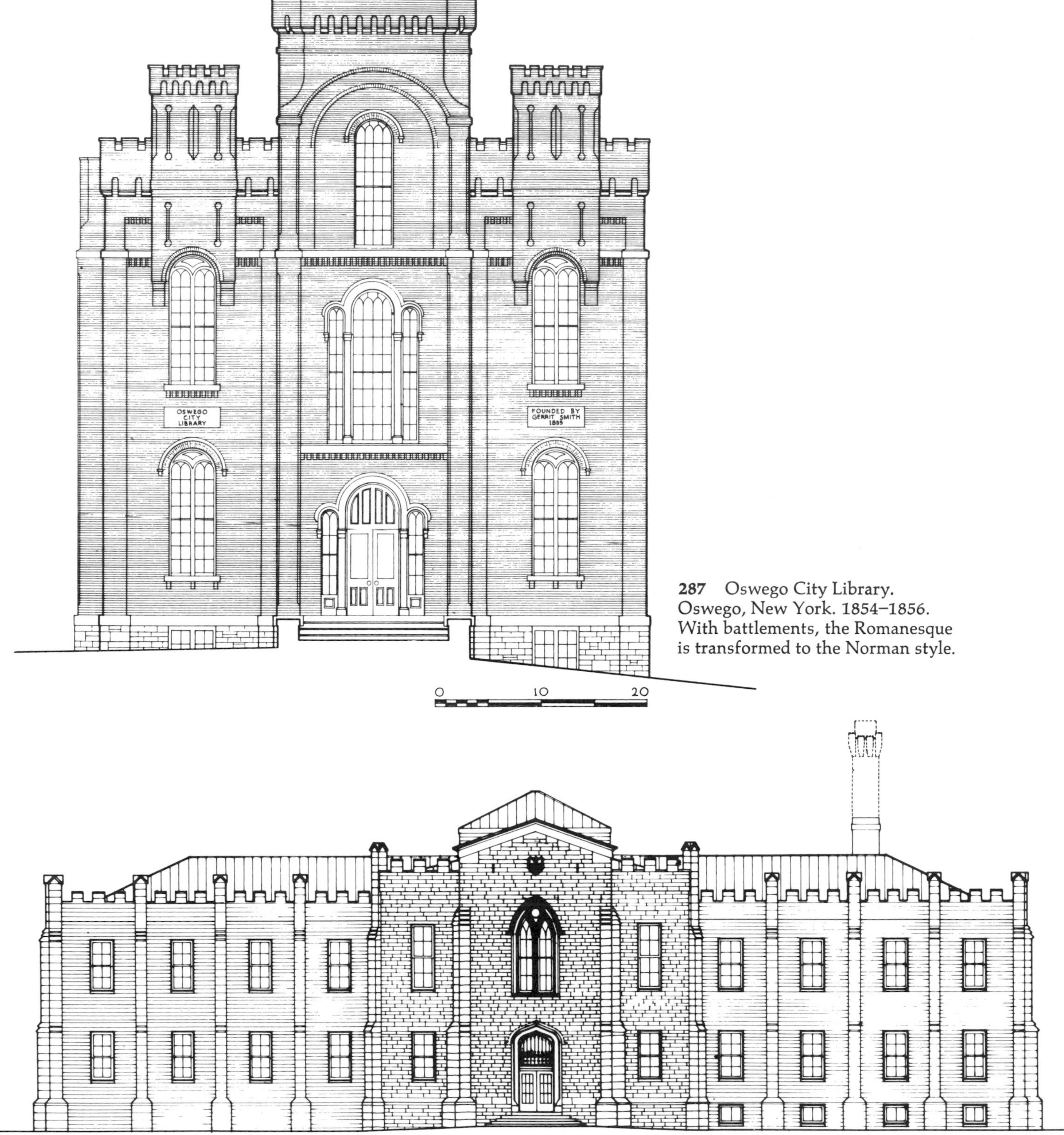

287 Oswego City Library. Oswego, New York. 1854–1856. With battlements, the Romanesque is transformed to the Norman style.

288 University of Nashville. Nashville, Tennessee. 1853–1854. Despite medieval detailing (buttresses, pointed-arch openings, crenellated parapet), the structure is Classical in its horizontality, regularity, and self-contained silhouette.

1860-1895

Victorian

Italianate • Second Empire
(also Eastlake, Queen Anne, Victorian Gothic)
Richardsonian Romanesque
Vernacular Victorian • Tall Building I

IN 1860, thirty-five urban centers had a population exceeding 25,000; thirty years later, there were almost four times that number, and at least two dozen cities claimed more than 100,000 inhabitants each.

As stunning as the rapid rise of the city in size, significance, and influence was its radical transformation in complexity, composition, and character. Ever sharper differences emerged between East and West, village and town, town and city, administrative center and industrial site. Downtown streets, almost exclusively commercial, tended to become specialized according to administrative, retail, wholesale, industrial, or recreational use.

New building types or fundamental reinterpretations of familiar types were the commercial block, office building, town or city hall, courthouse, schoolhouse, opera house, hotel, department store, loft building, and wholesale storage depot.

Styles changed with staccato speed, in time with the rhythm of big-city life. Italianate, Second Empire, Romanesque—all were rich and robust and exuberantly displayed the design "excesses" so beloved by the Gilded Age.

As city borders expanded, there dawned awareness of the need to control urban disorder. In answer to urgent space, transportation, and communication needs, hills were leveled, bridges stretched, rivers channeled, land filled, streets widened and paved. In response to concerns for urban safety and health, fire codes were promulgated and water, sewer, gas, electricity, telegraph, and telephone lines installed. And to satisfy a gradually emerging interest in civic amenity there were built grandiose public buildings and embellishments for park and square.

Yet, it was commercial more than civic consideration that dominated urban mood, and it was commercial need that determined urban form.

In the large cities, as Baedecker author John Muirhead observed, "the prevailing note is that of wealth and commerce, the dominant social impression is one of boundless material luxury, the atmosphere is thick with the emanation of those who hurry to be rich."

Through boom and bust, the shape of the new downtown bulged—with investment and commercial banks, stock and commodity exchanges, industrial and utility headquarters, insurance offices and shipping agencies, hotels and retail shops catering to consumers with ever-greater purchase power.

Possessed of engineering skill, aesthetic sophistication, and financial acumen, the large architectural firm, especially in New York and Chicago, flourished: Adler & Sullivan; Holabird & Roche; Burnham & Root; McKim, Mead & White; Shepley, Rutan & Coolidge.

The most eloquent demonstration of the era's accomplishments, of its ingenuity and its driving energy, was the tall building—a remarkable advance whose development scarcely spanned a generation. By the 1890s, in any number of the nation's cities, the masonry-sheathed, steel-framed office building rose ten, twelve, sixteen stories or more. Louis Sullivan, its prophet and procreator, recalled of these years, " 'Big' was the word. 'Biggest' was preferred, and the 'Biggest in the world' was the braggart phrase on every tongue. . . ."

Materials

A wide variety of traditional and innovative materials are exuberantly employed, often several in combination for visual richness and dramatic effect.

Typical of the juxtapositions that the period favors are smooth, hard dark-red or dark-brown brick with sensuously carved frosty-toned limestone, and densely overlapping smoky-hued slate roof tiles against the brittle silhouette of iron roof cresting.

Cast iron has its heyday in the 1870s; later, zinc, galvanized iron, and pressed tin also come into use.

For fire safety in rapidly growing urban areas, masonry replaces timber. Industrially produced pressed brick is sometimes laid in ornamental patterns. Terra-cotta, cast in panels and as moldings and columns, is also used to enliven and articulate building surfaces.

Brownstone and dark-toned granite are dressed to enhance their visual and tactile appeal: hewn, for a rough rockiness; cut, for an elegant urbanity; polished, for a mirrorlike smoothness; drilled, for a lacy ornamentality.

Plan

Answering the ambitions of city boosters and image makers, a vastly grander scale characterizes the public buildings of the Gilded Age.

The open-plan department store is a spacious symbol of a consumer society. And even when the commercial building is a modest twenty-five to thirty feet wide, its integration into a three- to six-unit block lends an impressive visual effect.

For the partially detached or freestanding structure, a complex plan results from projections and recesses, lateral extensions, cross axes, and asymmetries. For courthouses or state capitols, a laterally extended three-block plan with connecting wings is favored.

Tall buildings are usually L- or U-shaped in plan with large interior spaces that permit a variety of office layouts.

Elevation

With daring and imagination, the architect explores the plastic and three dimensional possibilities of the building façade, seeking splendor, eloquence and drama. Each decade vaunts still another style.

ITALIANATE (after 1855)

On the mercantile palazzo the shopfront has broad expanses of plate-glass windows, framed by columns-in-the-round with rich capitals and cornices [289, 290] or decorated piers [291]. Upper-story windows may be headed by round arches with projecting keystones and richly profiled moldings, and floor levels expressed by elaborate horizontal coursing.

The roofline is flat, emphatically crowned at the eaves by a projecting cornice with modillions [289] or brackets [291]. Alternatively, there may be an elaborately shaped pediment embellished with molding, finial, and inscription [291].

Balustrade, cornice, and other Classical motifs have a florid Italianate character.

SECOND EMPIRE (ALSO EASTLAKE, QUEEN ANNE, VICTORIAN GOTHIC) (1870s on)

The vigorous Second Empire mode—a grandiose elaboration of the Italianate—shares the stage during this decade with such Gothicizing cousins as Eastlake, Queen Anne, and (occasionally) Victorian Gothic styles.

Each can be simply categorized by a single feature, as follows: Second Empire, a highly sculptural mansard roof [292; 293; 294]; Eastlake, a "tooled" quality resulting from chamfering, embossing, and linear embellishments of the surface [295]; Queen Anne, a picturesque roofline, broken by gable, pediment, and chimney stack [296; 298]; Victorian Gothic, pointed arch window openings with masonry of contrasting colors in alternating bands [299, 300; 301].

Common to all is bravura boldness and willfulness in manipulating and distorting familiar elements. Arches are flattened (except for the Gothic); windows are clustered; ornament is piled on in profusion; cornice and column are reinterpreted for richer decorative effect.

In florid Italian Renaissance or imaginative and picturesque Gothic, the legacy of the post–Civil War parks movement includes gates, statuary, and shelters [302, 303, 304].

RICHARDSONIAN ROMANESQUE (1880s on)

Monumental and stately, grave, yet not without its lighter side, this mode depends on the heaviness, solidity, and ruggedness of brick and stone masonry, massive low arches, and imaginative towers, turrets, and dormers. It also employs novel treatment of terra-cotta, particularly in cast panels and in column capitals.

Window openings, variously shaped and sized, activate the façade [305; 306; 307; 309; 310; 311]. Although five or six stories tall, a structure's apparent height is diminished when several stories are grouped within a single motif [309; 311].

This style bloomed most impressively in the West, where cities achieved their first maturity in its heyday.

VERNACULAR

The freestanding narrow and deep retail store is an Americanism that dots rural hamlets across the country, although it is particularly associated with the frontier. Typically, the structure is one or two stories, clapboard-sheathed, and porch-fronted. Facing the street, the gable end may be exposed [313] or concealed by a flat-roofed "false front" [314].

Faint echoes of high-style sources are abstractly simple ornamental details: door paneling [313], shaped lintel [312], or balustrade [316]. Often only minor features such as brick patterning at the eaves or carved porch supports [315] are indicative of the particular period.

A provincial version of the Shingle Style is a commonplace sight at resorts [320].

Periodic renovation keeps the commercial row in style [317, 318, 319].

TALL BUILDING I (after 1885)

Soaring higher each decade, the tall building is an impressive sculpture in its own right, demanding audacious innovation from the architect who would master the form. One solution is to band ascending stories at intervals by horizontal courses, changes in materials, and a rich vocabulary of Classical or Romanesque ornament, hence obliterating the cell-like monotony of repeating units [321]. Another, a Chicago achievement, is to suppress ornament, but to express the cage-like reality of steel-skeleton construction in the balanced treatment of horizontal spandrel and vertical pier elements [323]. The three-part window, with a wide fixed pane flanked by narrow double-hung sash windows, is also closely associated with Chicago.

After 1890, the synthesis achieved by architect Louis Sullivan is the model to emulate: lower stories (public or semipublic) function as a heavy base; attic stories (service) as a rich and emphatic crown; intermediate stories (office) as a tall shaft, with soaring piers that express verticality, and decorated spandrels that recall the horizontal dimension [323]. A lush interweaving of foliate and geometric motifs, Sullivanesque ornament expresses the function of structure and enhances the richness of form [322].

Detail of Haughwout Store.

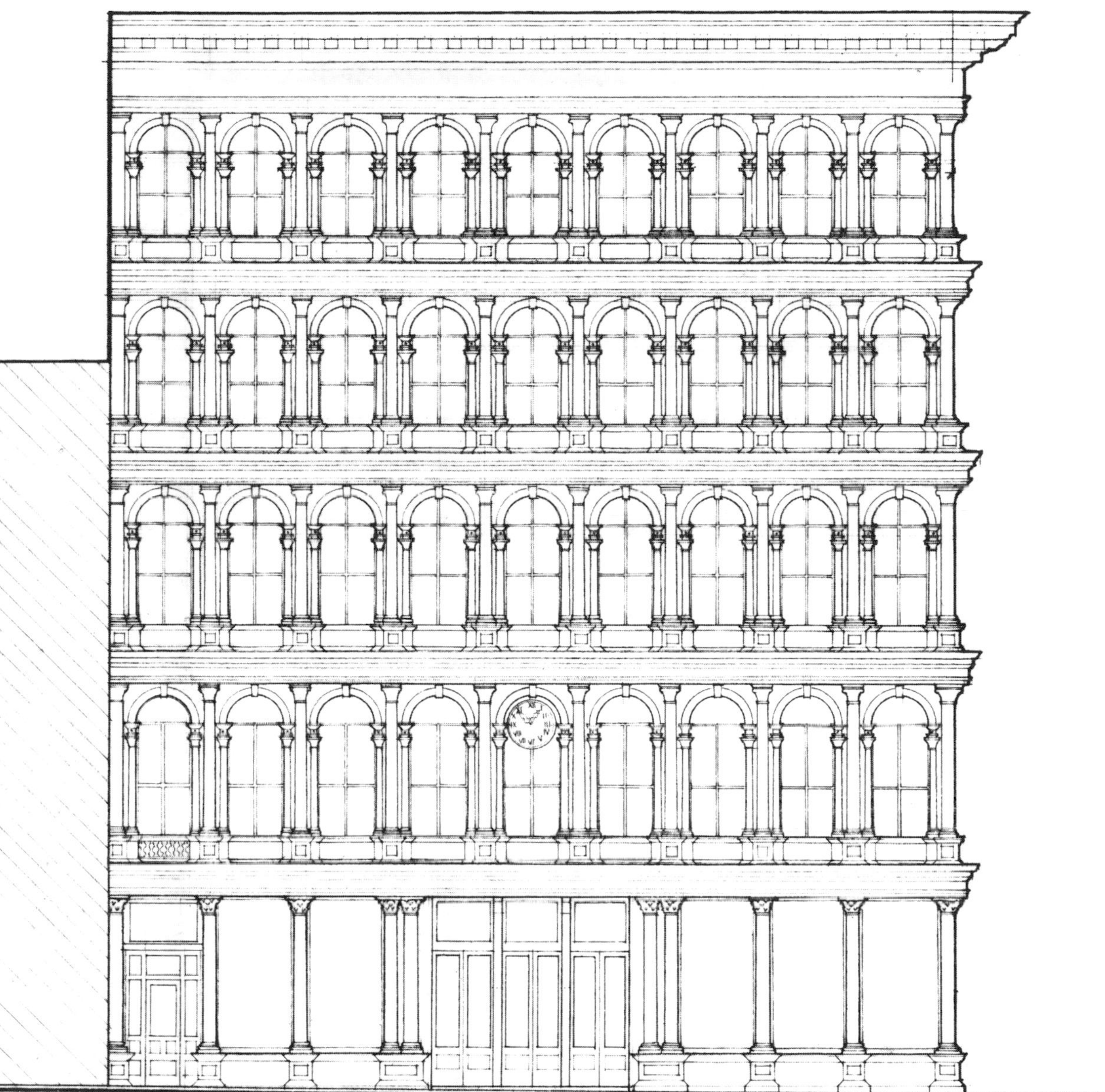

289, 290 Haughwout Store. Manhattan, New York. 1857; John Gaynor, architect; foundry of Daniel Badger. A complete cast-iron front, in the Venetian mode, with superposed arched openings, and stories of successively diminished heights. The detail reveals the visual richness achieved by the use of cast iron, an industrially produced building component.

Public Square, Nashville, Tennessee; 1856–1878.

291 Public Square. Nashville, Tennessee. Right to left: 1856; 1865; c.1878—increasingly elaborate Italianate ornament.

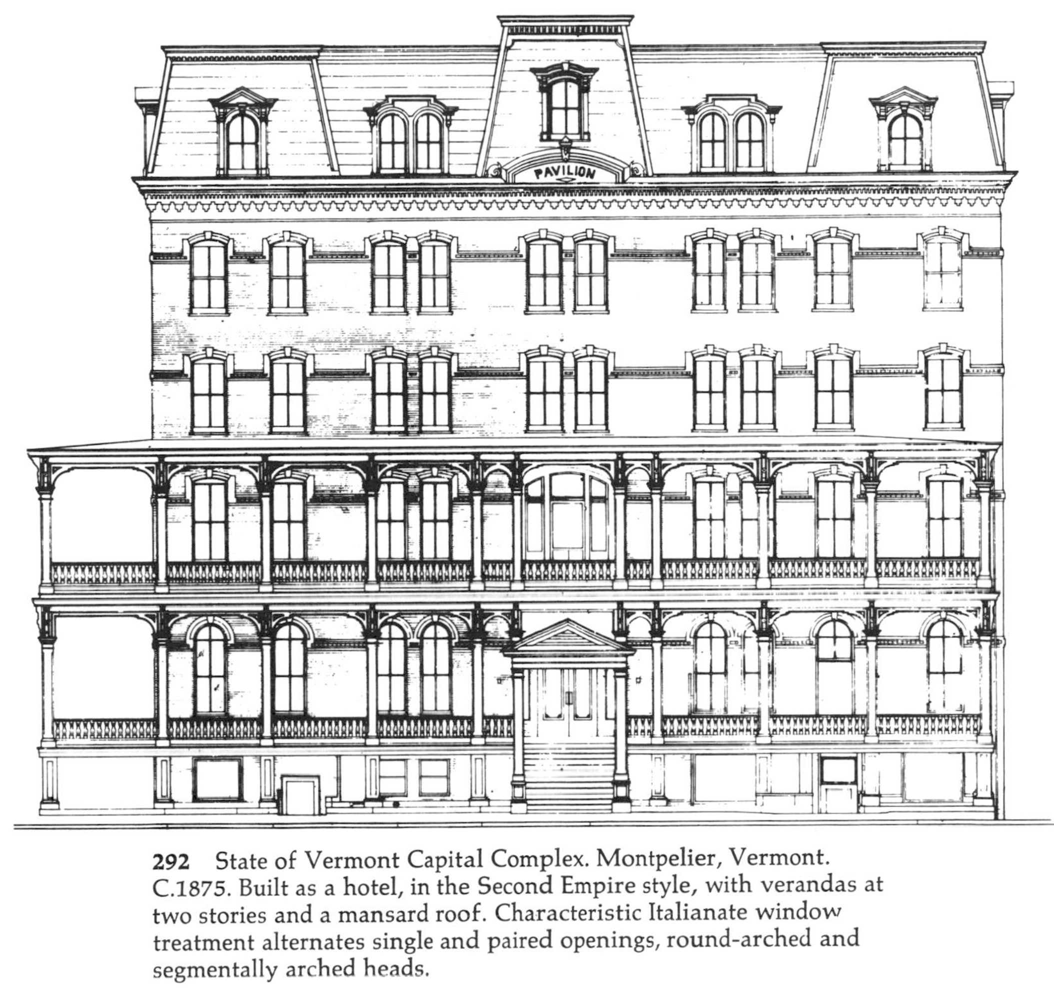

292 State of Vermont Capital Complex. Montpelier, Vermont. C.1875. Built as a hotel, in the Second Empire style, with verandas at two stories and a mansard roof. Characteristic Italianate window treatment alternates single and paired openings, round-arched and segmentally arched heads.

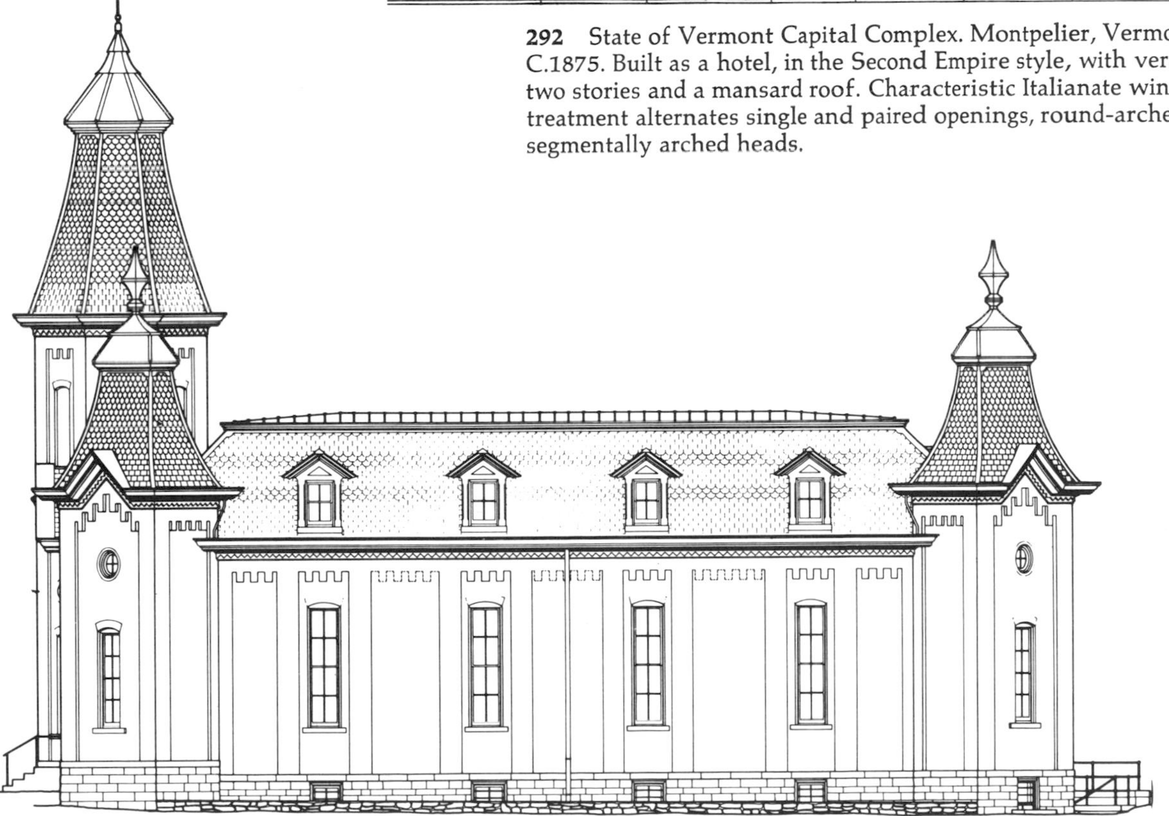

293 Vanderbilt University. Nashville, Tennessee. 1880. Mansard roof and towers with ornate crests activate an otherwise self-contained composition.

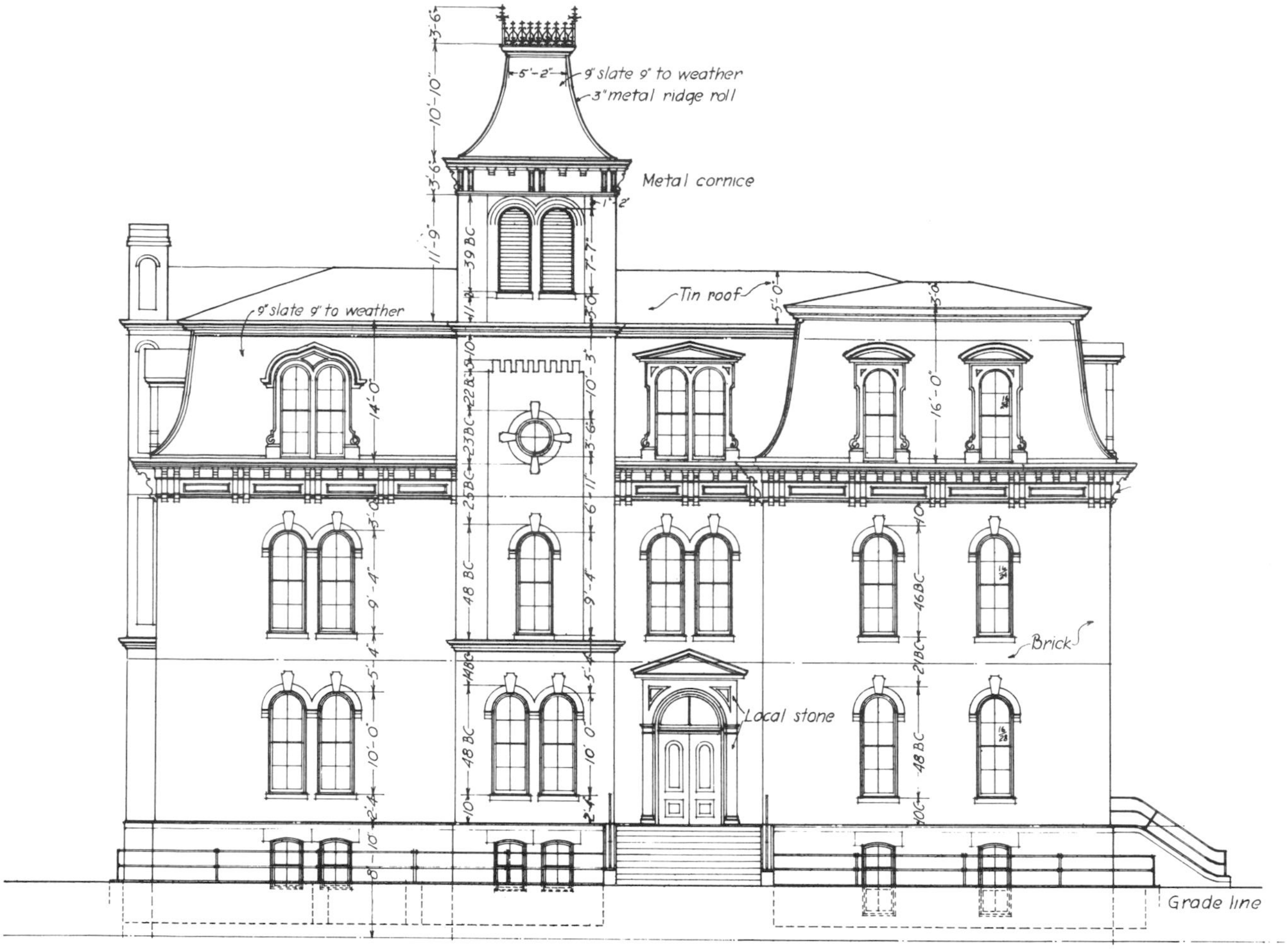

9" slate 9" to weather
3" metal ridge roll
Metal cornice
Tin roof
9" slate 9" to weather
Brick
Local stone
Grade line

294 McKinley High School. Lincoln, Nebraska. 1872. The tall mansard roof has an elegant flare, and dormers with impressive pediments.

Hotel Florence, Pullman, Chicago, Illinois; 1881 (see 298, p. 203).

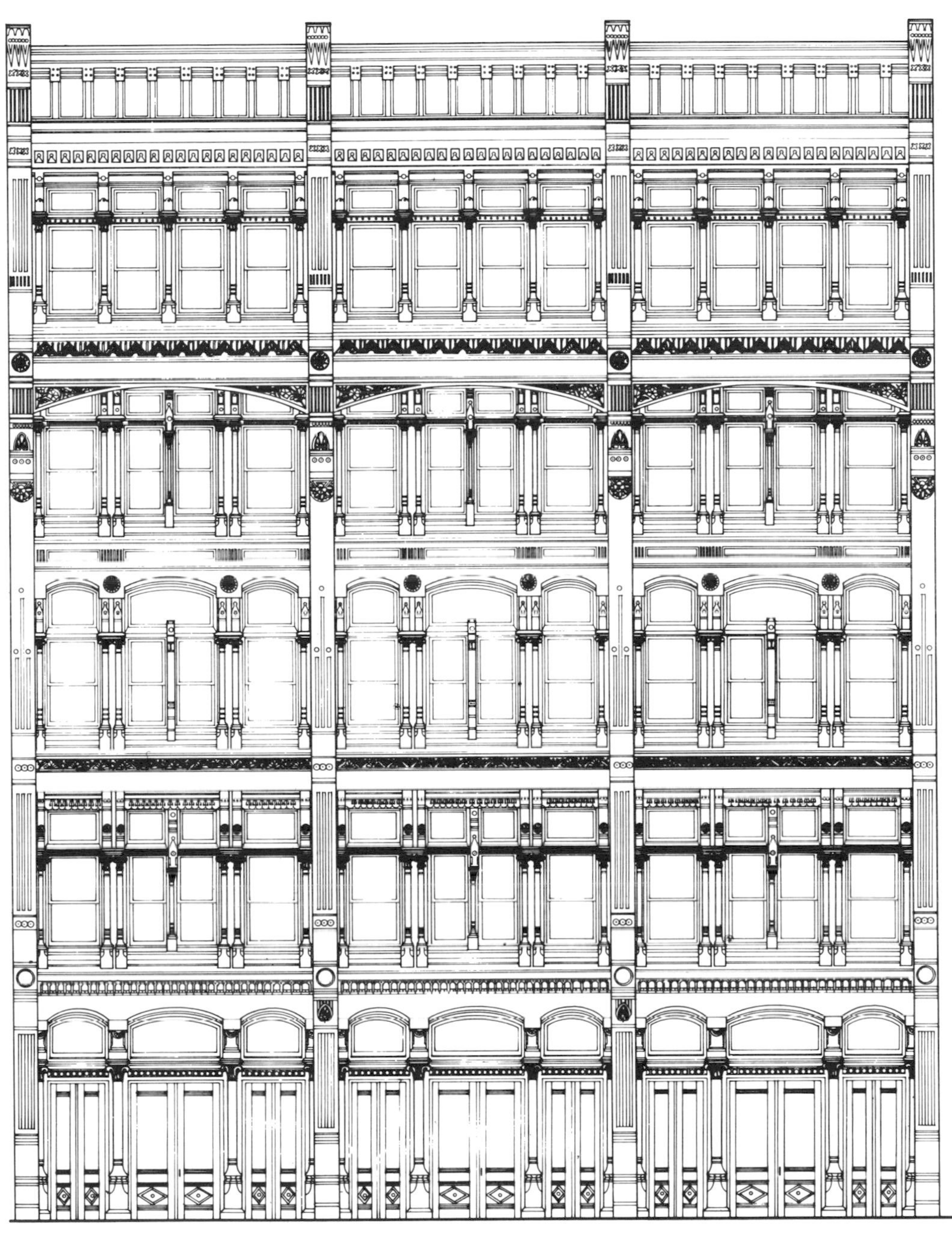

295 Hart Block. Louisville, Kentucky. 1884. A technical tour-de-force: the intricate Eastlake ornament—which gives the appearance of hand tooling—is actually cast in iron.

296 Bank of Commerce. San Diego, California. 1888. The Queen Anne, essentially a domestic style, is here seen in a commercial adaptation.

297 Scoville Building. Chicago, Illinois. 1884 remodeling of center four bays and addition of fifth story; Sullivan & Adler architects. Restrained, but notable for its originality: a design for the upper stories of a commercial building, emphasizing horizontal and vertical structural members, that opens the solid wall to light and air.

298 Hotel Florence. Chicago, Illinois. 1881; Solon Beman, architect. The photograph of this building is on page 200.

299, 300 Public library—design. C.1877. Pointed-arch window openings set off by masonry of contrasting color, shifting scale, dynamic silhouette—Victorian Gothic at its most audacious and optimistic.

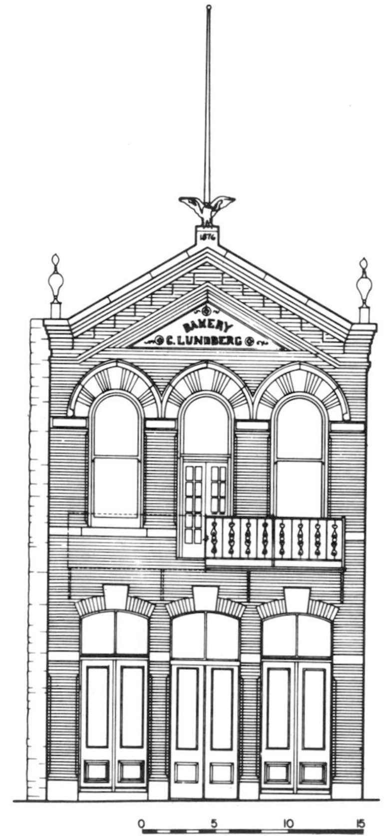

301 Lundberg Bakery. Austin, Texas. 1875–1876.

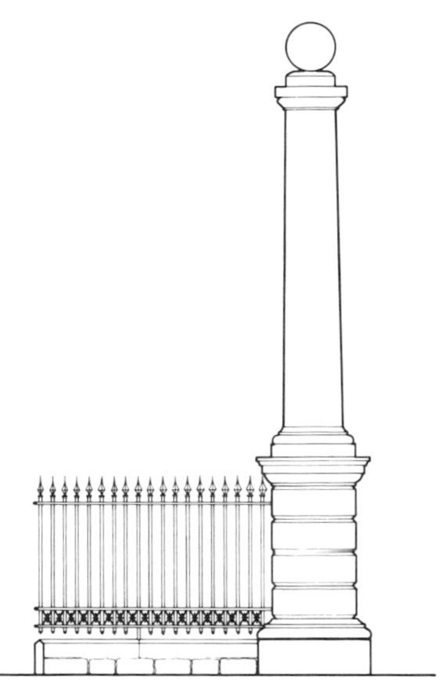

302, 303, 304 Tower Grove Park structures. St. Louis, Missouri. 1870–1873. For a Victorian driving park, horse shelter, summerhouse, pillar, pedestrian gate.

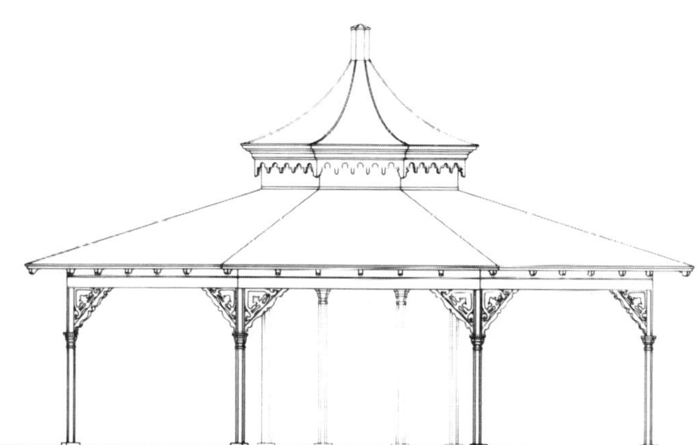

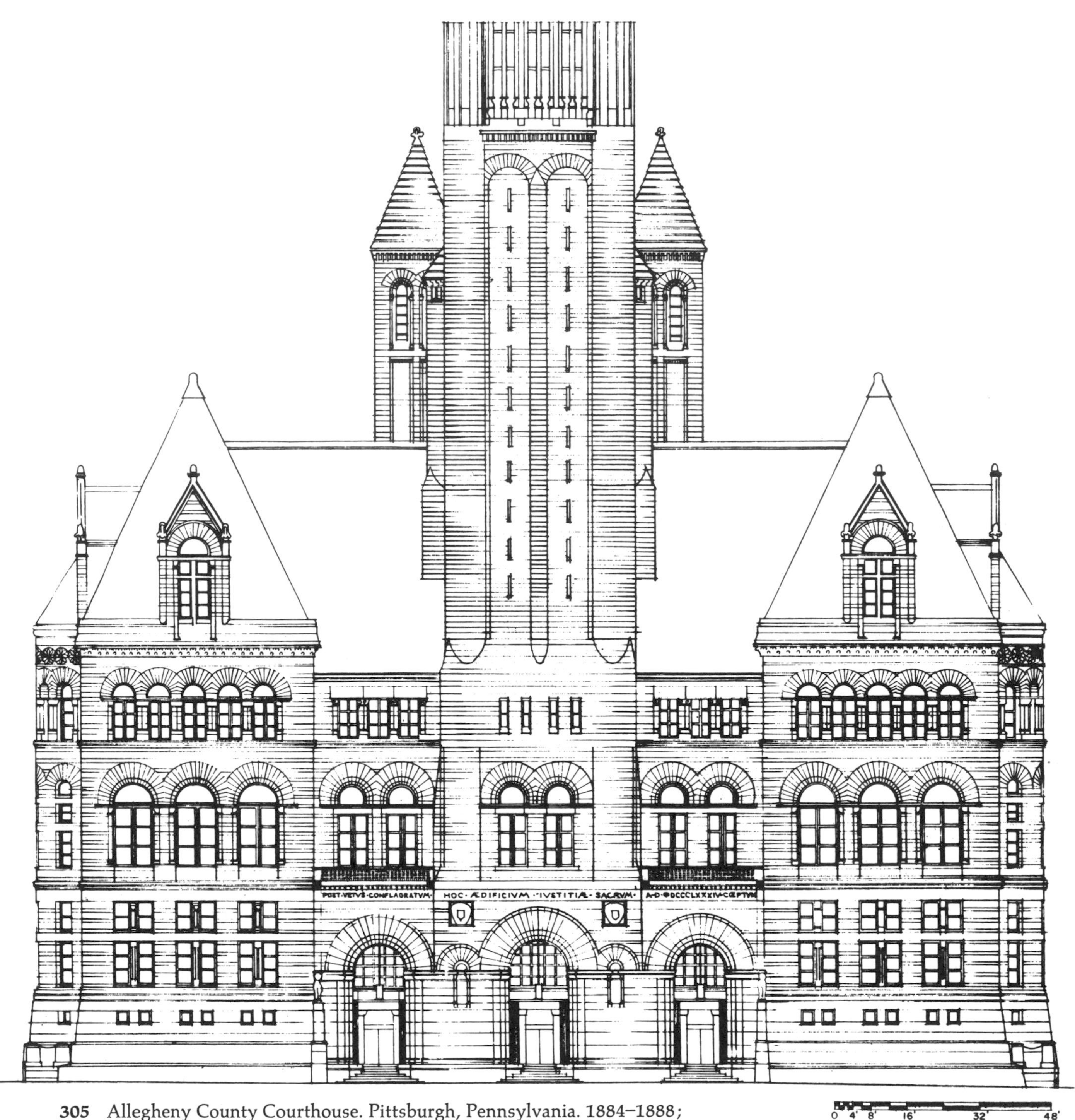

305 Allegheny County Courthouse. Pittsburgh, Pennsylvania. 1884–1888; Henry Hobson Richardson, architect. A strong and scuptural composition, with an enormously tall tower rising from the massive triple-arch entry at its base.

306 McCormick Hall, Tusculum College. Greeneville vicinity, Tennessee. C.1885. The Romanesque, placidly composed.

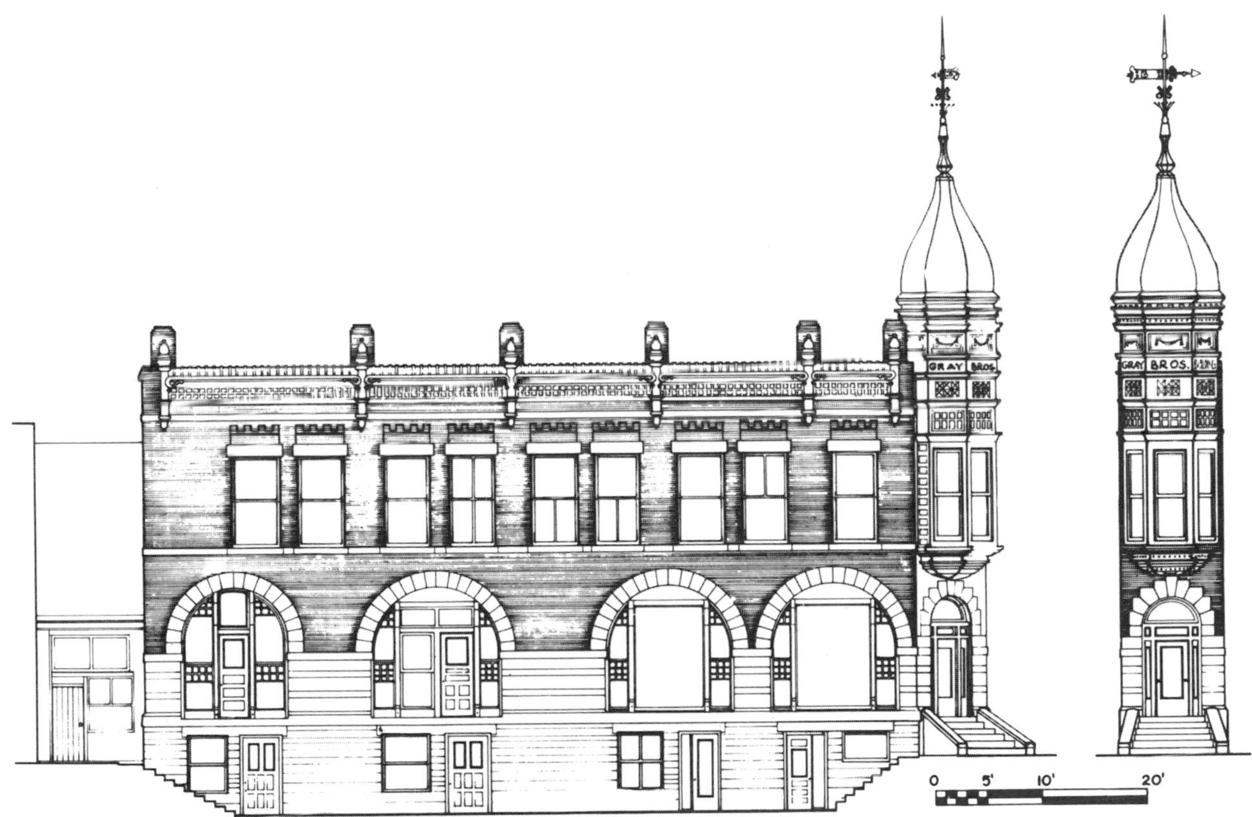

307, 308 Gray Brothers Block. Guthrie, Oklahoma. 1890. Corner storefront vernacular in the Richardsonian mode; the turret is a hallmark of this decade.

309 Times Building. Chattanooga, Tennessee. 1888–1892. Characteristically Richardsonian is the arcade which organizes several upper stories so they appear as one.

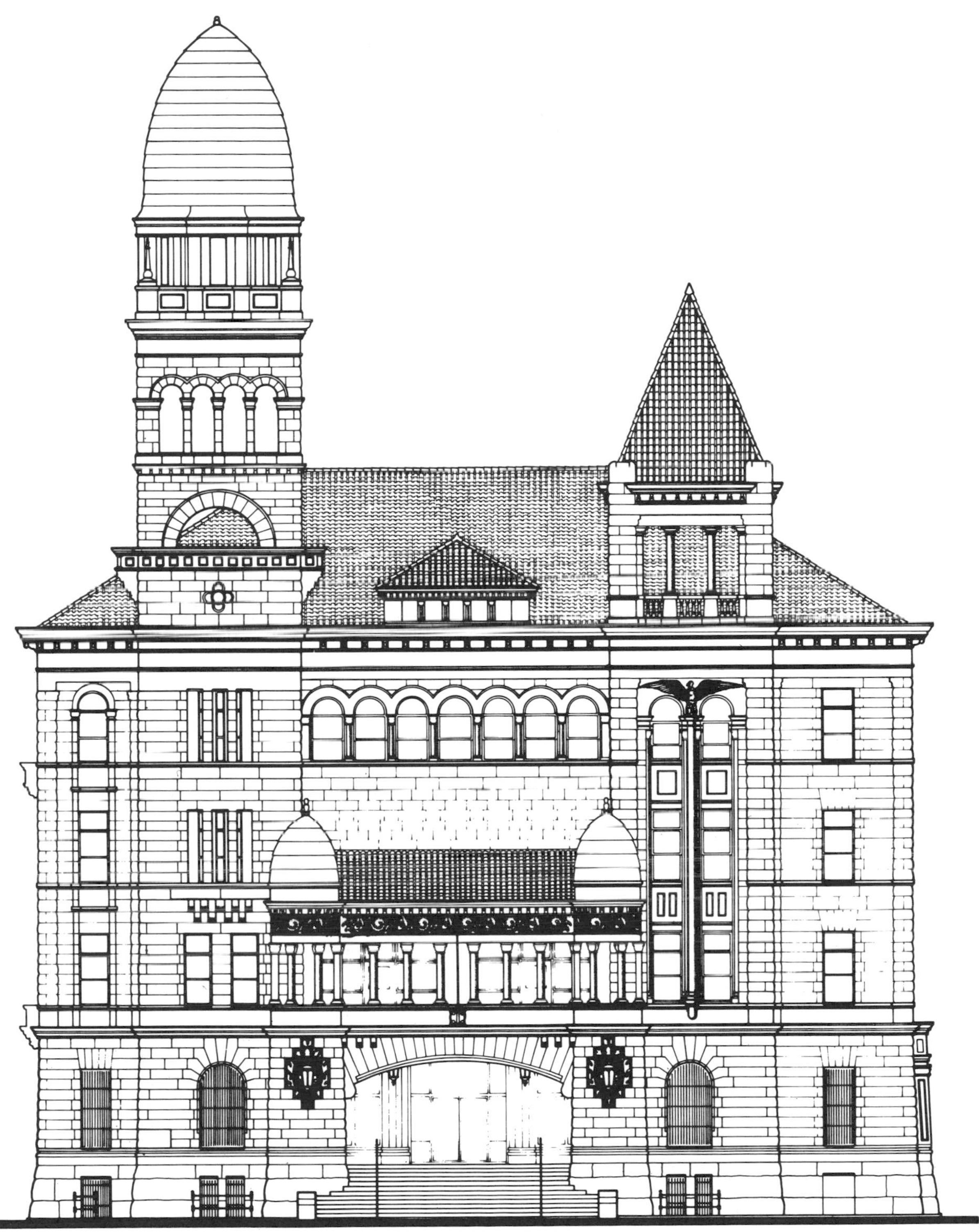

310 Bexar County Courthouse. San Antonio, Texas. 1892–1894. An individualistic interpretation of Richardsonian Romanesque.

311 Bradbury Building. Los Angeles, California. 1893. The office building in its Late Victorian phase: steel frame, wide-windowed first story.

Bradbury Building, Los Angeles, California; 1893.

313 412 Hurt Street. Petersburg, Virginia. Mid-nineteenth century vernacular expression.

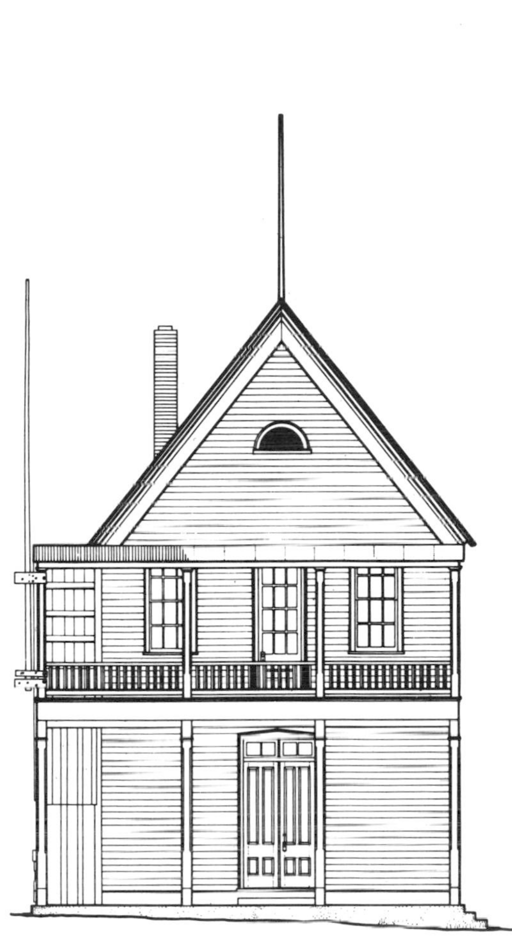

312 Pioneer Lodge No. 1, International Order of Odd Fellows Hall. Idaho City, Idaho. 1875. Vernacular, with a taste of the Victorian in the door design.

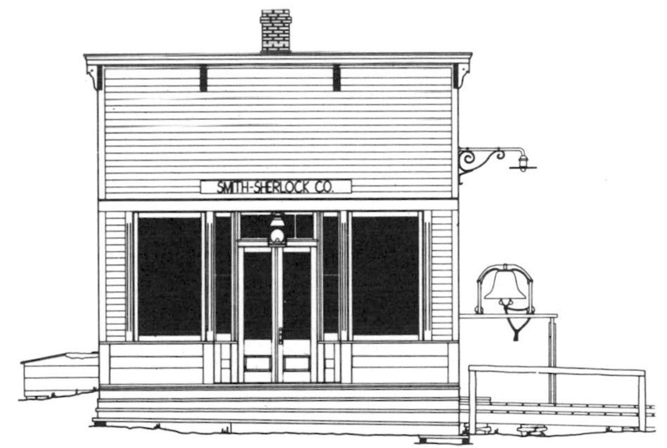

314 Smith-Sherlock store. South Pass City, Wyoming. C.1898.

315 Lawyer's Row. Winchester, Virginia. 1874.

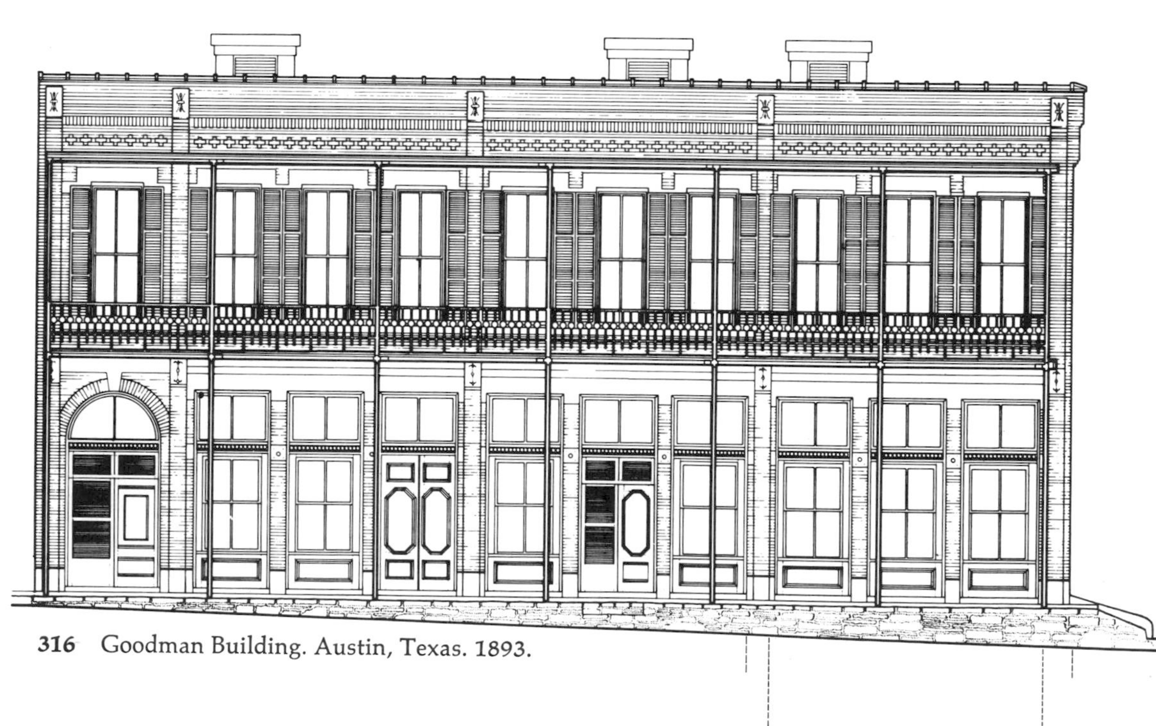

316 Goodman Building. Austin, Texas. 1893.

317, 318, 319 State Street. Newburyport, Massachusetts. The same building over the course of time. Left to right: c.1820; c.1880; c.1950. Typical storefront history.

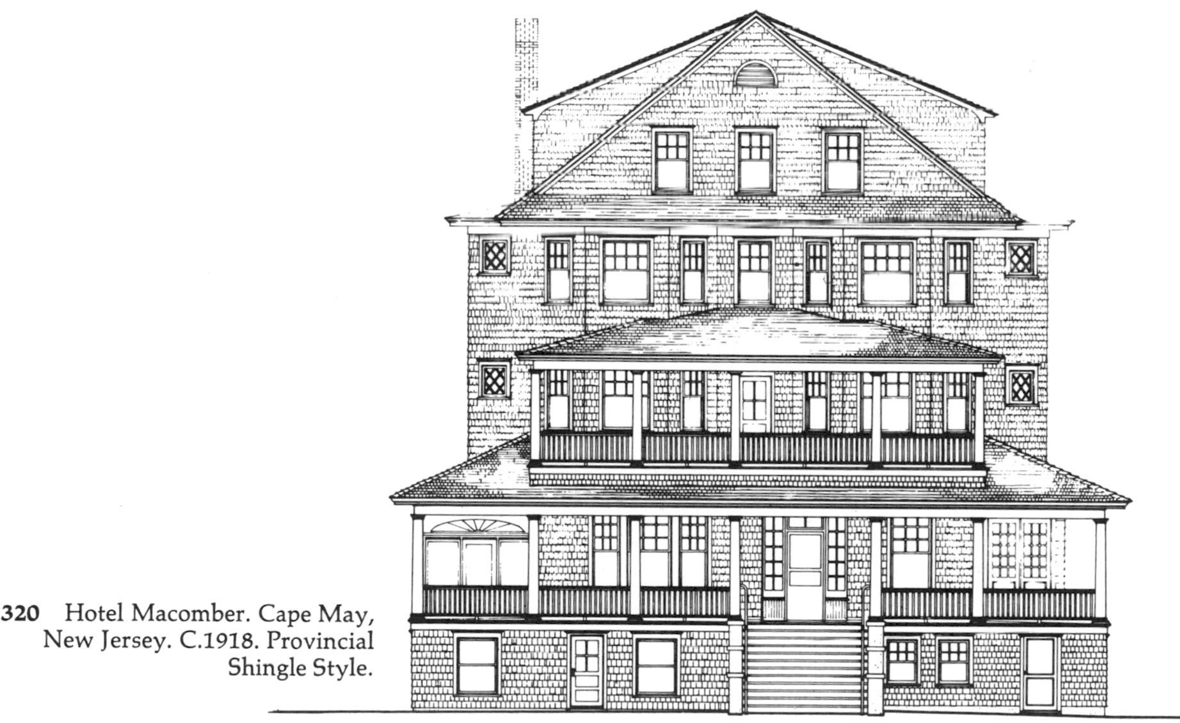

320 Hotel Macomber. Cape May, New Jersey. C.1918. Provincial Shingle Style.

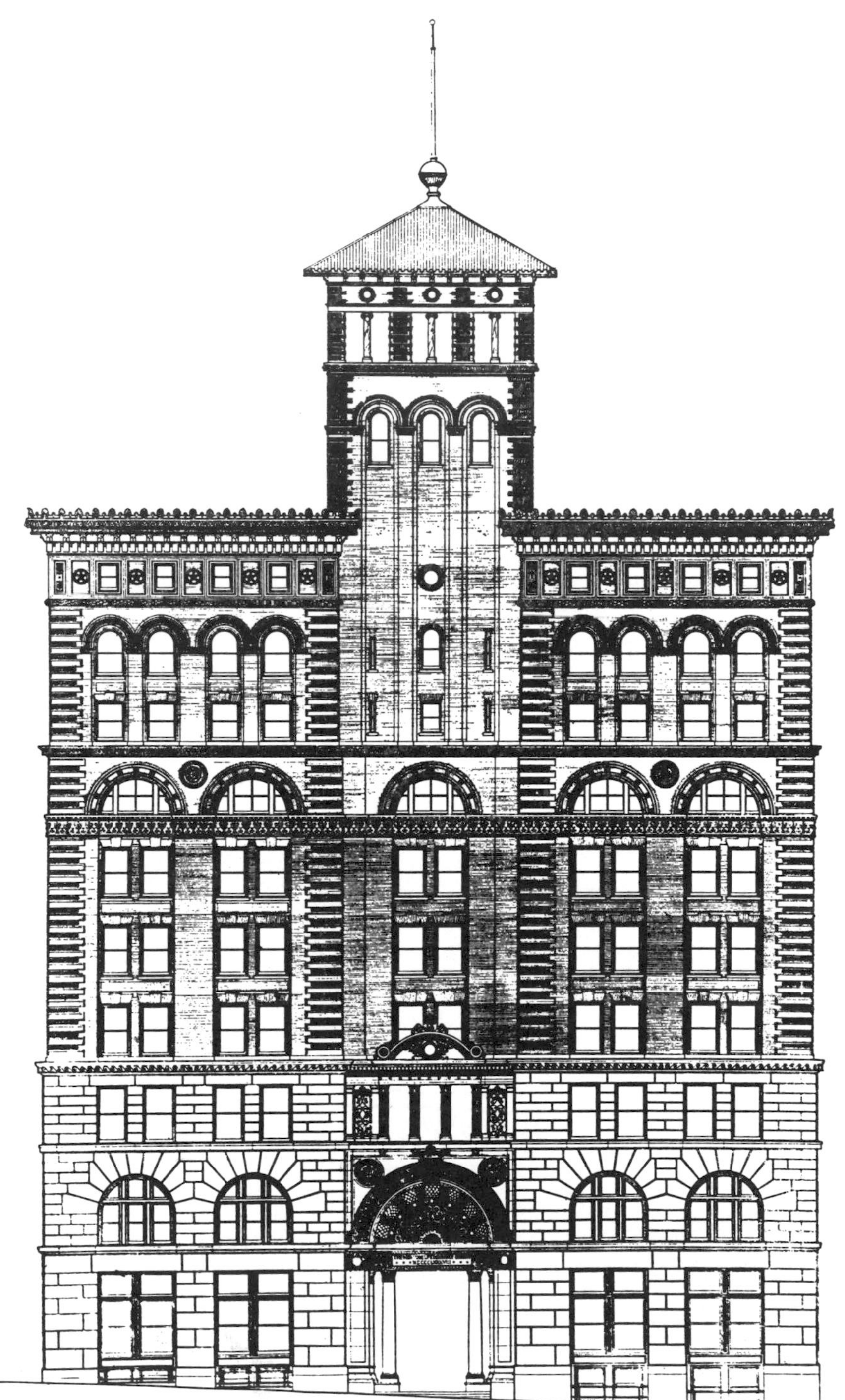

321 New York Life Insurance Company. Kansas City, Missouri. 1888–1890. A nineteenth-century skyscraper—dressed as a palazzo.

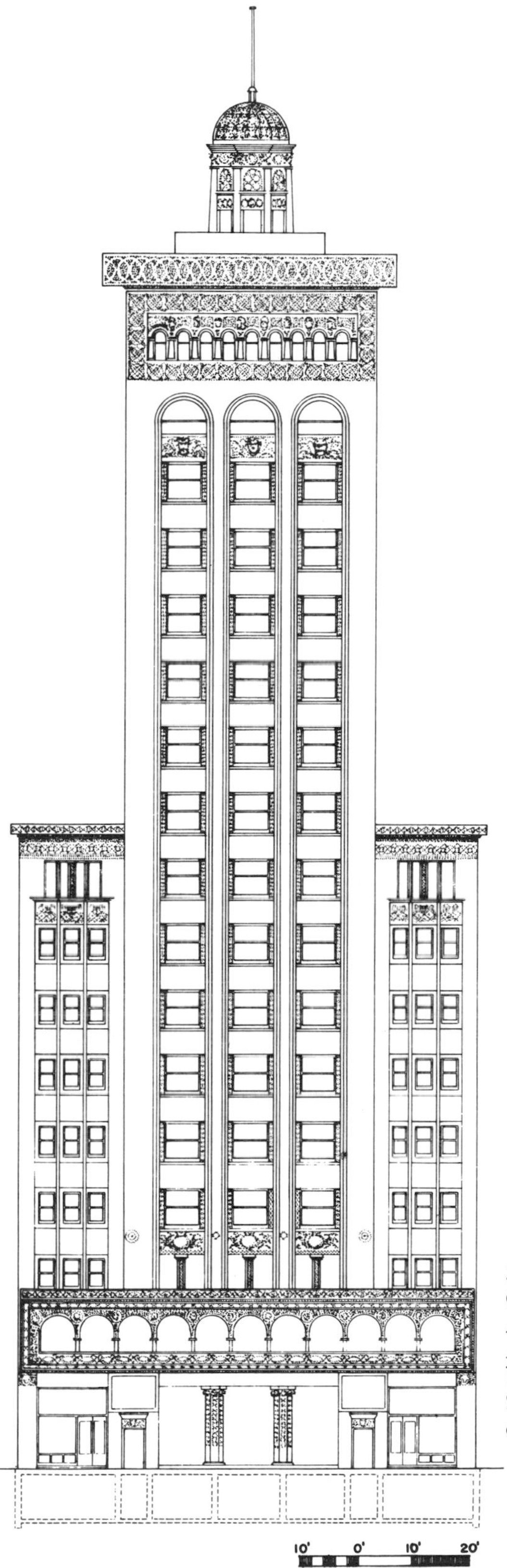

322 Schiller Building. Chicago, Illinois. 1891–1893; Adler & Sullivan, architects. A three-part composition: base, shaft, and crown. Slender piers create a ribbed effect on the shaft.

Reliance Building, Chicago, Illinois; 1895.

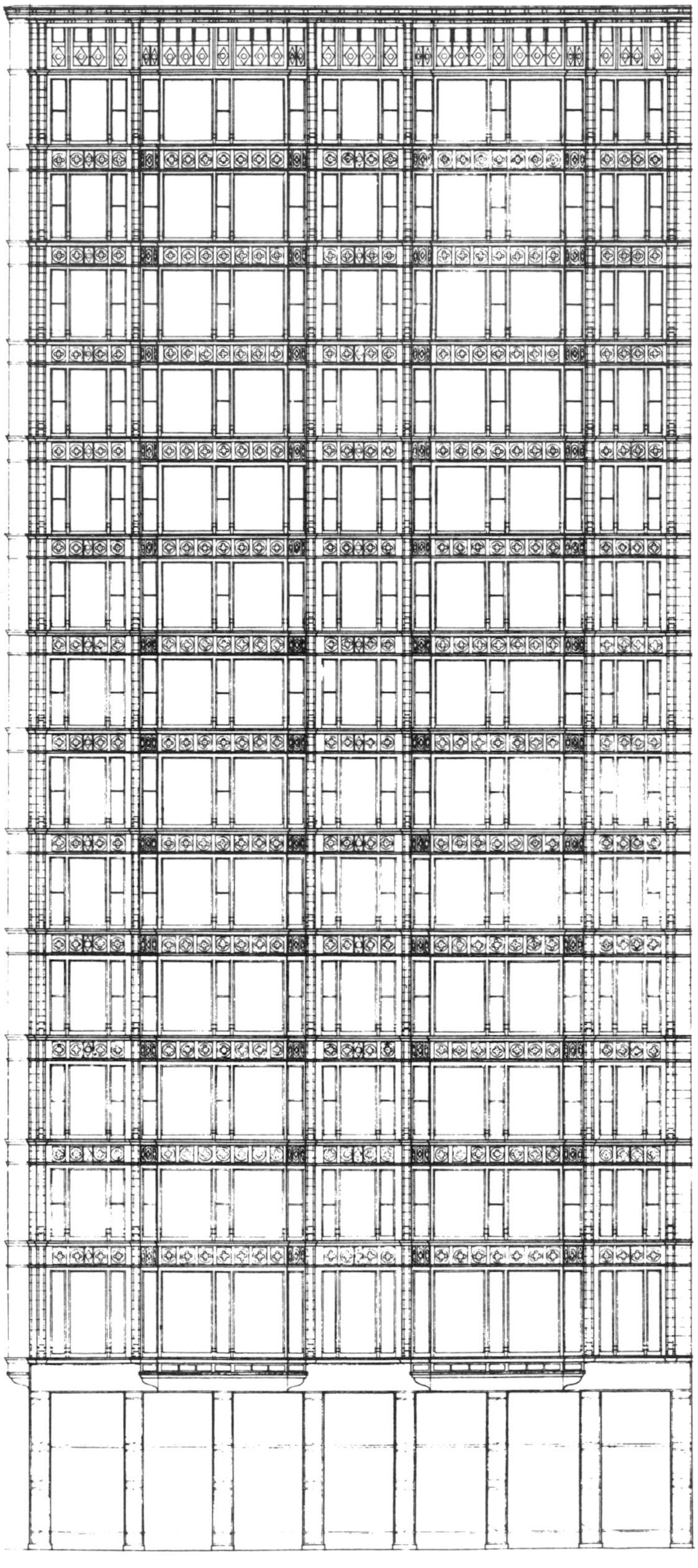

323 Reliance Building. Chicago, Illinois. 1895. The Chicago skyscraper—excluding historical ornament, except for a modified cornice; large expanses of glass; slender piers; thin spandrels sheathed with terra-cotta in foliate or geometric designs.

1895-1940

Twentieth Century

Tall Building II • Tall Building III
Beaux-Arts Classicism • Renaissance and Classical Revivals
Sullivanesque • Period Revivals
Art Deco and Moderne

"MAKE no little plans; they have no magic to stir men's blood and probably will not be realized. Make big plans; aim high in work and in hope. . . . Let your watchword be order and your beacon beauty." These are the words of architect Daniel Burnham, whose magnificent scheme for the Columbian Exposition at Chicago in 1893 inflamed the nation with passion for the City Beautiful.

The Chicago Fair heralded America's expanding international presence—and for this new Imperial Age nothing less would do than the style of Imperial Rome, brought forward in time by academicians of the French Ecole des Beaux-Arts, and practiced in American architectural offices and schools by a Paris-trained generation. This was to be architecture for all time—grand in scale, monumental, symmetrical, luxuriously appointed, with a broad and richly pictorial vocabulary of Classical ornament. Its mode was noble, for it was the architecture of a society that sought reform, progress—perfection.

Civic monuments were customhouse and courthouse, state capitol, symphony hall, museum, (Carnegie) library, university, home of scientific or learned society, memorial building, and commemorative statue—even fire and police stations were decked in Classical garb. Commercial monuments—the Federal Reserve bank, the grand hotel, the tall building, the columned corner bank—were hardly less impressive.

Imagination saw urban ensembles sited along grand axes: the federal buildings of Washington, D.C.; the civic centers of Chicago, Philadelphia, San Francisco, St. Paul, Denver, and Springfield; college campuses from New York's Columbia to California's Berkeley. Planners and philanthropists envisioned neighborhood playgrounds and extended park systems that included museums, zoos, aquariums, and arboretums.

The city planner achieved professional status and held up lofty standards. "The city that would make itself magnificent," said the pioneer urbanist Charles Mulford Robinson, "has the whole world to draw upon."

But the Great War blurred the visions of the City Beautiful. Vaulting civic ambition yielded to nostalgia. America should seek "not heroism, but healing," President Harding advised in 1920. "Not nostrums, but normalcy." When prosperity returned, practical considerations, not an image of grandeur, guided city planning and new construction.

In the boom decade that followed, the tall building rose taller as commercial users scrambled for downtown space. Aghast at the darkening and crowding of city streets, some municipalities restricted building height. In the 1920s, others followed New York City's example and stipulated that building mass must progressively decrease at upper stories. This resulted in the stepped-back skyscraper silhouette that came to be viewed as the very symbol of the energy and power of twentieth-century America.

For a structure of twenty, thirty, forty stories or more, the historical language of ornament was not adequate. Experiments with Period Revival detailing produced vertical ribs to suggest the Gothic, a Georgian cupola for a twentieth-story crown, a Tudor arched doorway at the base of a college library tower, or a Renaissance elevation to distinguish a bank building. The results were all too often unconvincing, although architects continued to draw upon historical motifs for a generation longer.

As the 1920s drew to a close, enthusiasts hailed the creation at last of Art Deco—a style that avoided past styles, yet was more modish than any: with bold vertical ribs, dramatically modern; with intricate crystalline or curvilinear ornament and materials from crafted terra-cotta to machine-age metal alloys, impressively opulent. Its patrons were electric power and light companies, the communications industry (publishing, motion pictures, and radio), the automobile industry, bus terminals, luxury hotels, and chain stores.

Almost every Main Street had at least one modest Art Deco example, but the greatest concentration and extravagance was in the great twentieth-century skyscraper metropolises—New York, Chicago, Cincinnati, Los Angeles, Detroit, and Miami.

The Depression sobered the architect's imagination. And in any case, Europe's stark, cubistic International Style made Art Deco seem fussy and tawdry. In America the Moderne style of the 1930s was stripped of all but a modicum of ornament. It emphasized heavy cubic and cylindrical volumes, horizontality, smooth surfaces, and curving shapes to symbolize Automobile Age streamlining.

In putting hundreds of unemployed architects to work on dams, bridges, post offices, schools, city halls, and fire stations, the Depression-years Works Progress Administration spread modernism from metropolis to backwater hamlet.

But the nation was not really comfortable with modernism or with internationalism. Industrial technology advanced, European war clouds loomed larger. America searched her past for security. For a public image Neo-Georgian or Colonial was a reassuring symbol of stability.

Materials

The palette of the City Beautiful is light and bright: white or light-gray marble, limestone, or cast stone; buff-toned brick; white vitreous-glazed brick. Speciality metals such as bronze, steel alloys, copper, and brass are used for ornament.

Following the First World War, pastel-colored terra-cotta and unglazed bricks in soft yellow and russet tones are used for a rich tapestrylike effect. Also popular is limestone, used as facing.

Favored by the Art Deco are formica, black glass and marble, neon tubes, and bronze and terra-cotta in decorative grilles and panels.

The Moderne style uses large expanses of glass, glass brick, chrome, and stainless steel. Poured-concrete construction and cast-concrete ornament are frequent in 1930s construction.

Plan

Occupying an increasingly larger lot, the tall commercial building necessarily gives up some of its mass to permit adequate illumination and ventilation for interior spaces. The resulting plans are L-, U-, H-, or E-shaped. Alternatively, the building has a sharp stepdown at the rear or side of its lot, or rises as a narrow tower from a wide multistory base.

The plan of the low civic building, axially arranged and relatively self-contained, capitalizes on a grand approach. Designed by Beaux-Arts-trained architects, the plans of Period Revival and modern buildings tend to be similar.

Elevation

TALL BUILDING II (1895–1920)

In this phase, the tall building is composed of a "base," "shaft," and "capital." The base frames wide-windowed retail and/or office space between piers or columns and is itself set off from upper stories by a strong horizontal motif [324; 326]. The shaft, consisting of identical superimposed stories, is "fluted" by the expression of vertical framing members. A Gothic spirit is sometimes achieved by emphasizing the riblike quality of these elements. Like the base, the capital may rise from one to four stories. The roofline may be simple, but may equally well have a crown with colonnade, cornice, or cupola.

Looking toward modernity, the Chicago school suppresses historicizing ornament while using materials so as to express their inherent character and the nature of the building's structure [325]

More common is the use of Classical and Renaissance motifs at base and capital to enliven the building surface and provide human scale [326].

TALL BUILDING III (1920–1940)

The "ziggurat" shape is typical of tall-building construction between the wars. Setbacks may step from front to back as well as from side to side [327; 330]. Rooflines also have a notched or faceted effect.

Historical detailing, reducing and simplified, is likely to be Gothic or Neoclassical in character [327—note first-story arched openings and the use of urns, pediments, and balustrades].

Art Deco invents a Jazz Age array of novel ornament to enrich the building surface, including profuse curvilinear and floral intertwinings, dense crystalline and mechanistic patterns, and carved figures in motion. The dramatic proscenium-like entrance is often two or three stories high and richly ornamented [328, 329]. Intricately decorated window spandrels, recessed from the wall surface, are set off by bold vertical piers which accentuate the sense of upward motion [331].

The Depression-era Moderne, basically similar in form to Art Deco, shears away ornament and dramatizes flat surfaces and bold shadows [332].

BEAUX-ARTS CLASSICISM (1895–1920)

In the Baroque tradition, Beaux-Arts architects admire the drama of motion: the building's domed central section climaxes the composition; planes advance and recede; corners are cut away by multiple angles [333].

The façade is enlivened by dynamic shifts in scale and form: orders may be reiterated; larger motifs enclose small ones; windows receive a variety of treatments [334].

Classical ornament applied for theatrical effect includes paired columns or pilasters, wreaths, festoons, cartouches, and figure sculpture. The skyline may also be enriched by architectural or sculptural elements [335] although provincial versions may tend toward timidity [336].

In theater design, the Baroque tradition continues through the 1920s, in increasingly imaginative and lavish interpretations [337; 338; 339].

RENAISSANCE AND CLASSICAL REVIVALS (1895–1920)

Late-nineteenth-century revivals are larger, grander, and more elaborate than earlier nineteenth-century style revivals. They tend to be stately rather than exciting, "correct" rather than daring.

Characteristic of the Renaissance are arched openings, rusticated masonry laid with deep joints to give the appearance of massiveness, and strong horizontal lines. Cornices are finely detailed and moldings are crisply drawn [340; 341].

Buildings or monuments which revive Classical Greek or Roman styles are notable for their weightiness, solidity, and pretentious figural and ornamental motifs [342].

Compared to eighteenth-century Georgian, buildings in the Neo-Georgian style also tend toward larger scale, elaboration, and enriched ornament [343].

SULLIVANESQUE (1905–1920)

A minor mode, but a distinct one on downtown business streets after the First World War, is the three- or four-story shopfronted building reflecting the inspiration of Louis Sullivan. While the highly individualistic solutions to design problems achieved by the architect were inimitable, followers borrowed freely in attempts to achieve fresh and modern effects. Characteristic features are rejection of formal design in favor of the expression of horizontal and vertical structural relationships, rigorous simplification in door and window enframements, wall surface, and cornice design, and intricate applied ornament incorporating both geometric and plant motifs avoiding reference to historical precedent [344].

PERIOD REVIVALS (1900–1940)

On the neighborhood commercial row, schoolhouse, club building, or the like, motifs associated with various historical styles are interpreted to suggest local idiom or quaint effect.

Associated with an "Old English" style are leaded windowpanes and exposed timbers; with the Colonial, red brick, white wood trim, and bowed display windows [345]; with the Spanish Colonial, shaped gables, tiled roof, and delicately scaled Classical motifs [346]. Glazed tiles, wrought-iron lighting fixtures, and other ornament frequently have a crafted quality.

Vernacular examples perpetuate Late Victorian design, but are simpler and sparer [347].

The Mission style shows itself to have a curious affinity to early-twentieth-century abstract modernism [348, 349].

ART DECO AND MODERNE (1925–1940)

Simple cubic forms and flat surfaces are emphasized for their modernity. Art Deco (1925–1933) ornament has a pronounced verticality and is mechanistic and linear in quality. Favored motifs are faceted surfaces, zigzags, chevron patterns, and octagon shapes [352].

Moderne buildings (after 1930) are drastically stripped of surface ornament. Windows are grouped in bands, and spandrels are expressed as continuous horizontals.

The shopfront is modishly streamlined, using smooth and shiny surfaces with minimal joints, graphics, tinted glass, and neon-light illumination as design elements [350; 351].

Moderne public buildings tend to be low and chunky in proportions; a tall element is carefully balanced by lower sections [353]. Ornament is spare and abstract and, though self-consciously "modernistic," sometimes alludes to precedents in Classical or indigenous architecture.

Richfield Oil Building,
Los Angeles, California; 1929
(see 328, 329, 330, pp. 226–228).

Richfield Oil Building, detail (see 328, 329, 330, pp. 226–228).

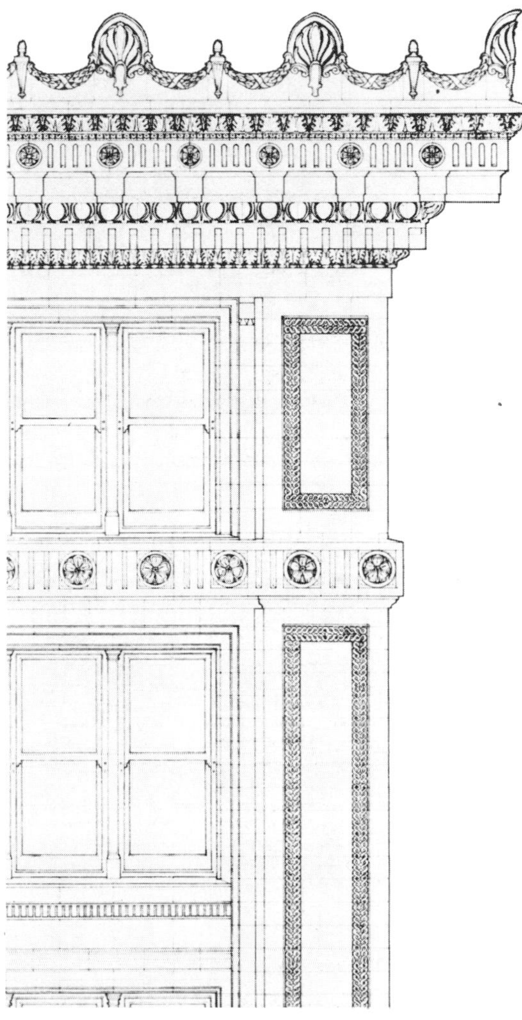

324, 325 Republic Building. Chicago, Illinois. 1903–1905; six-story addition, 1909. The tall building in its Chicago form, with light piers and wide windows.

326 Columbia Trust Downtown Building. New York City. 1908–1912; McKim, Mead, & White, architects. The tall building designed with Beaux-Arts detail, colossal orders defining the base, arches and repetitive cornices marking the skyline.

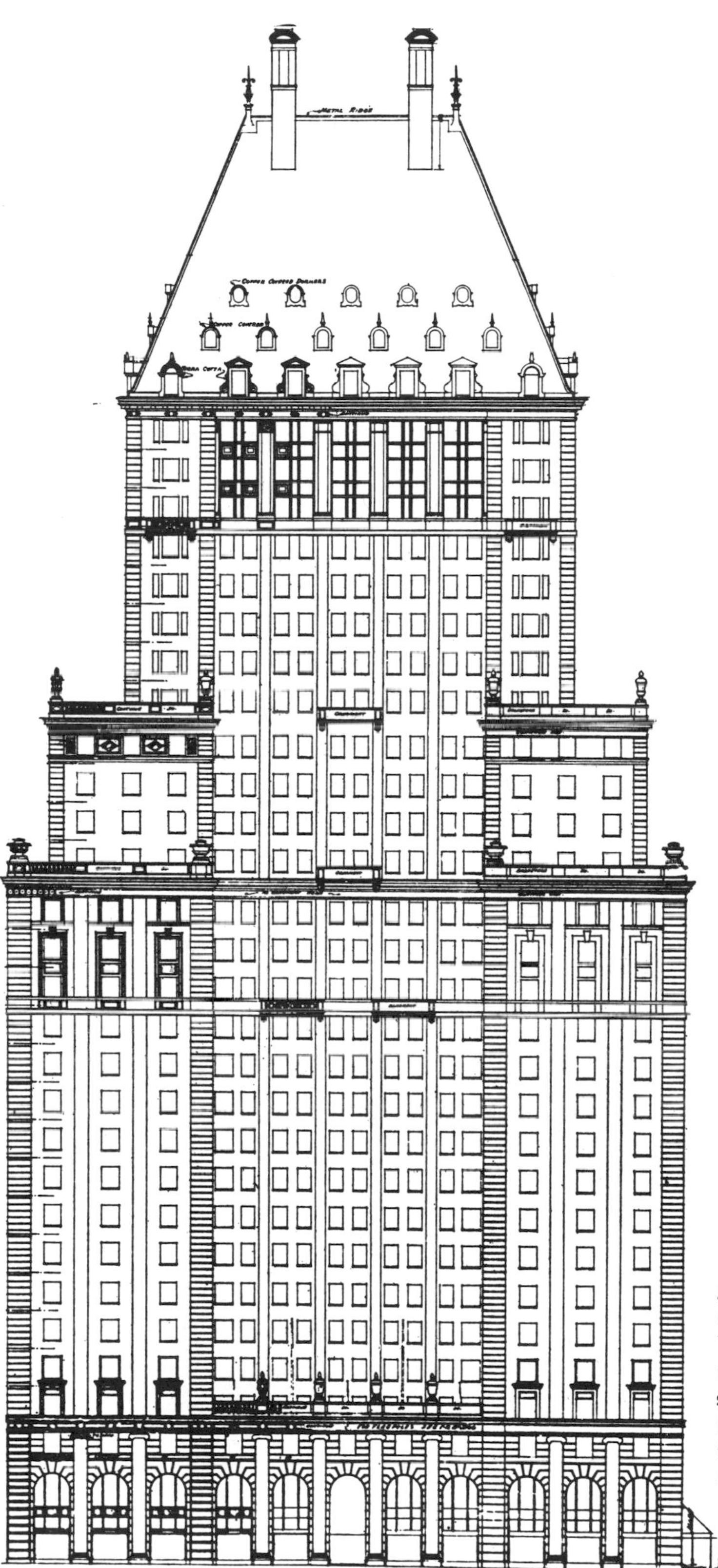

327 Savoy Plaza Hotel. New York City. C.1928; McKim, Mead & White, architects. In this phase, the tall building has a stepped-back silhouette. Decidedly modern is this thirty-two-story example, despite the Chateauesque roof and application of Federal ornament.

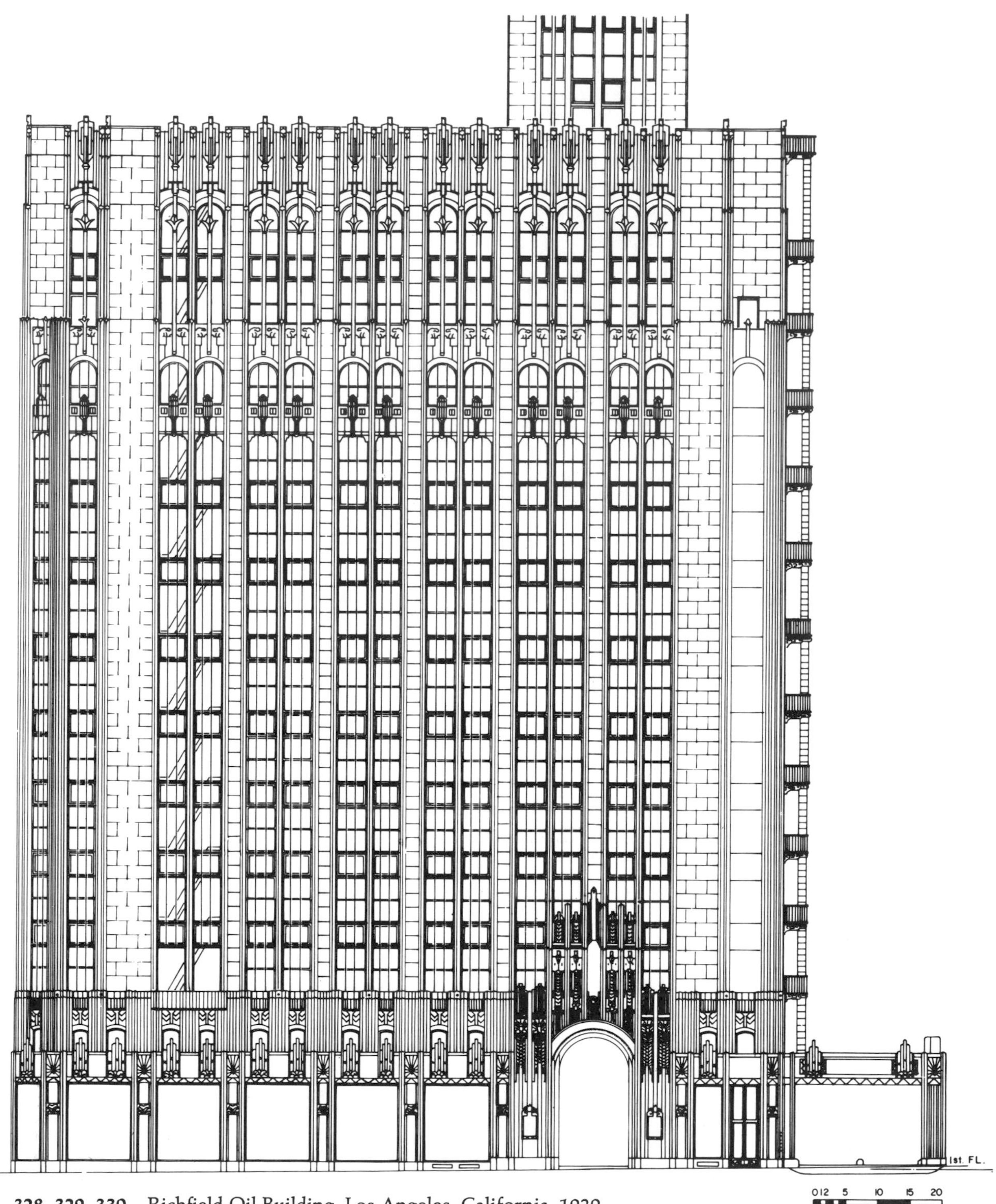

328, 329, 330 Richfield Oil Building. Los Angeles, California. 1929. Black terra-cotta facing and polished glass spandrel panels impart a jewel-like opulence to this Art Deco design. A full view of the building is on page 228.

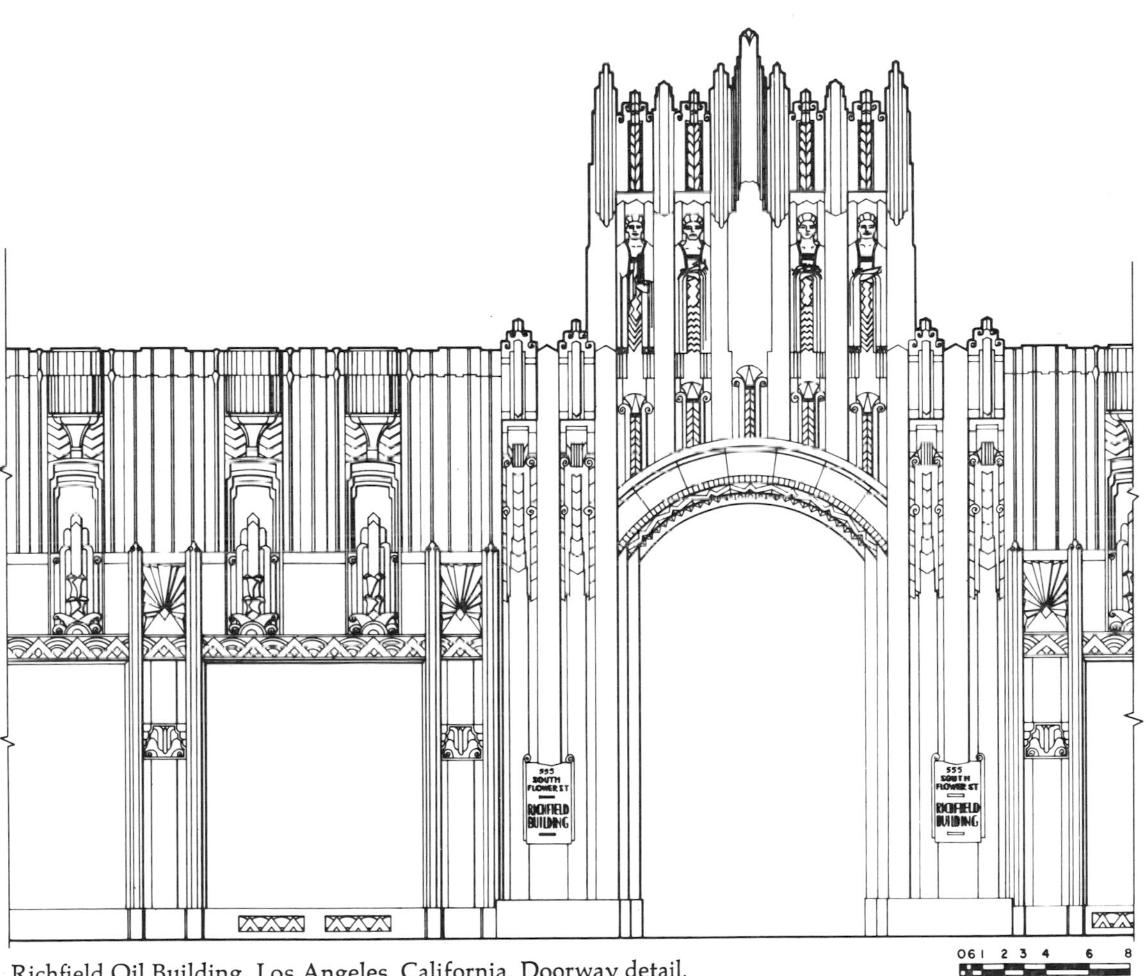

Richfield Oil Building. Los Angeles, California. Doorway detail.

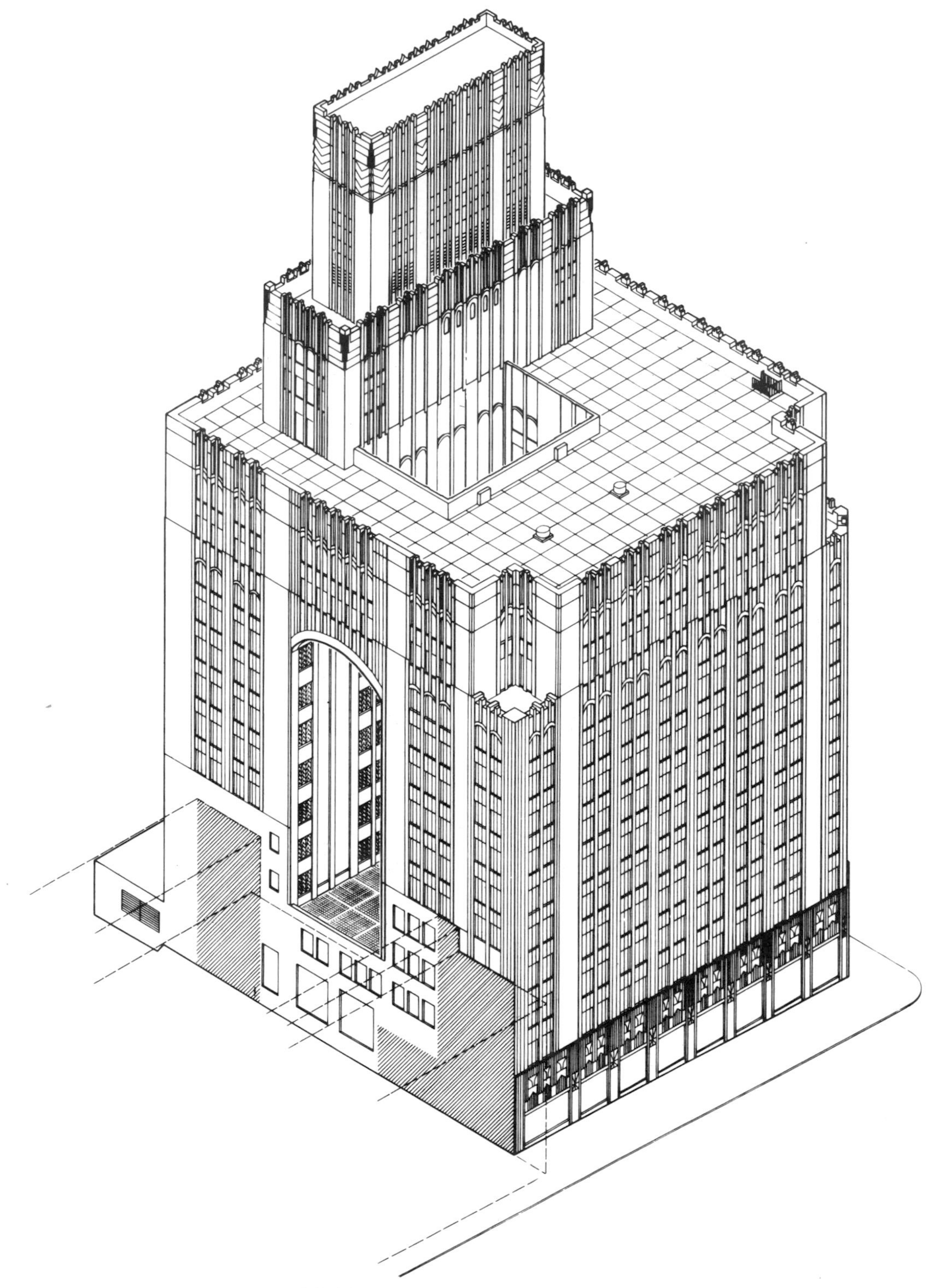

Richfield Oil Building. Los Angeles, California.

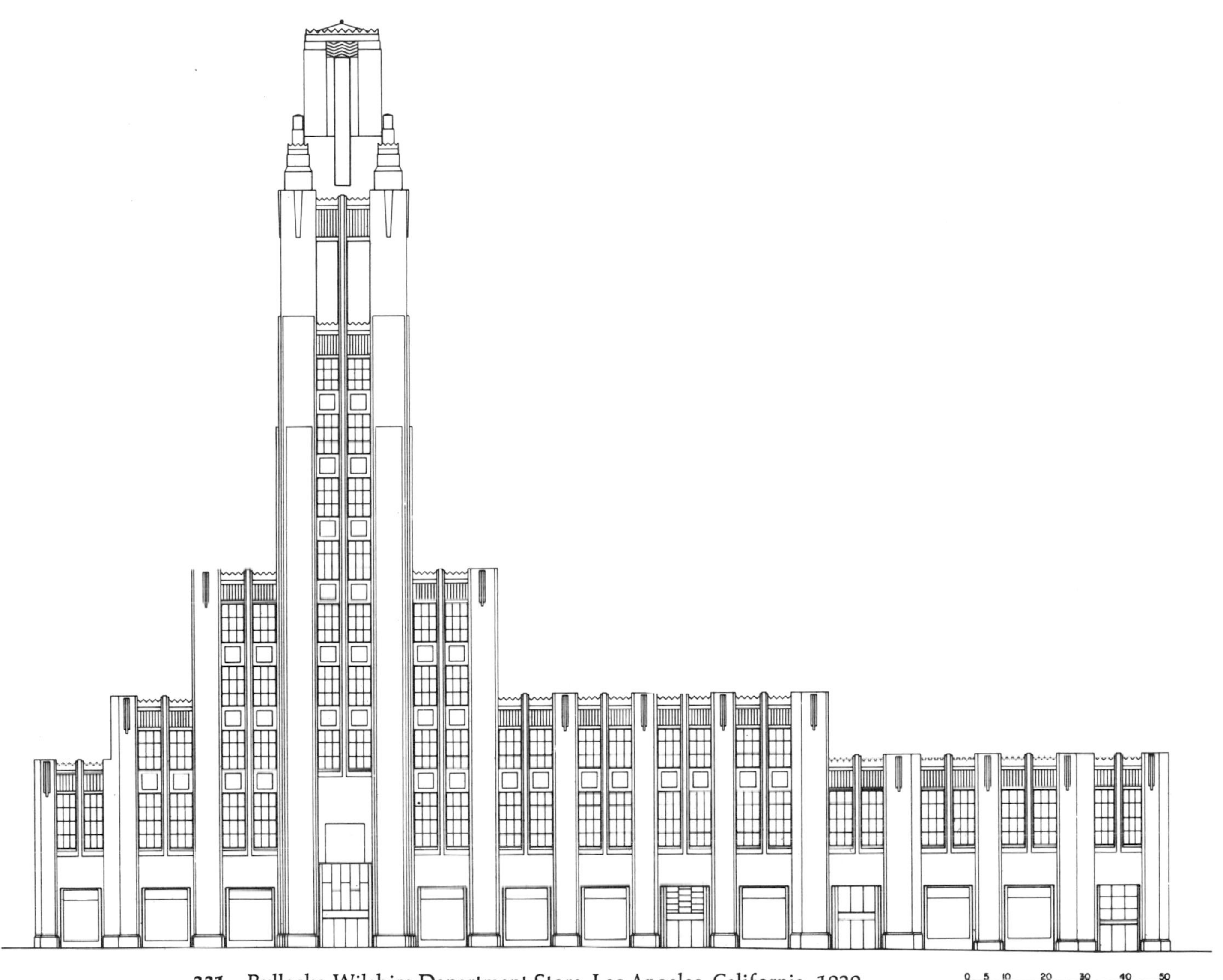

331 Bullocks-Wilshire Department Store. Los Angeles, California. 1929. Art Deco department store *par excellence.*

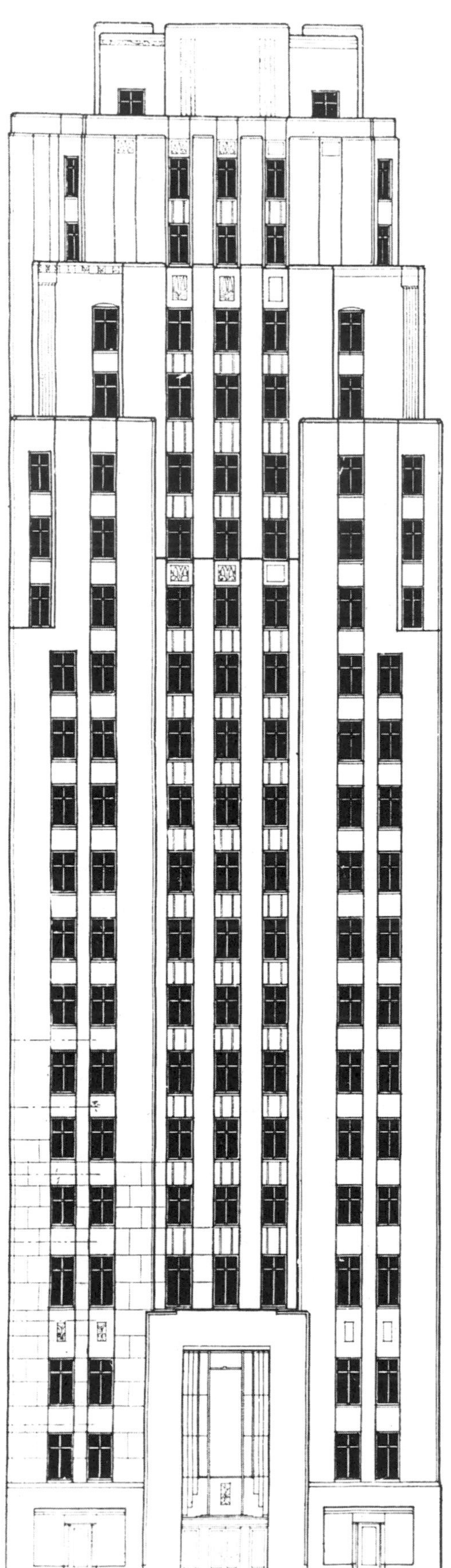

332 Central National Bank. Battle Creek, Michigan. 1933; Holabird & Roche, architects. The Moderne style—simplification of ornament and surfaces are distinguishing characteristics.

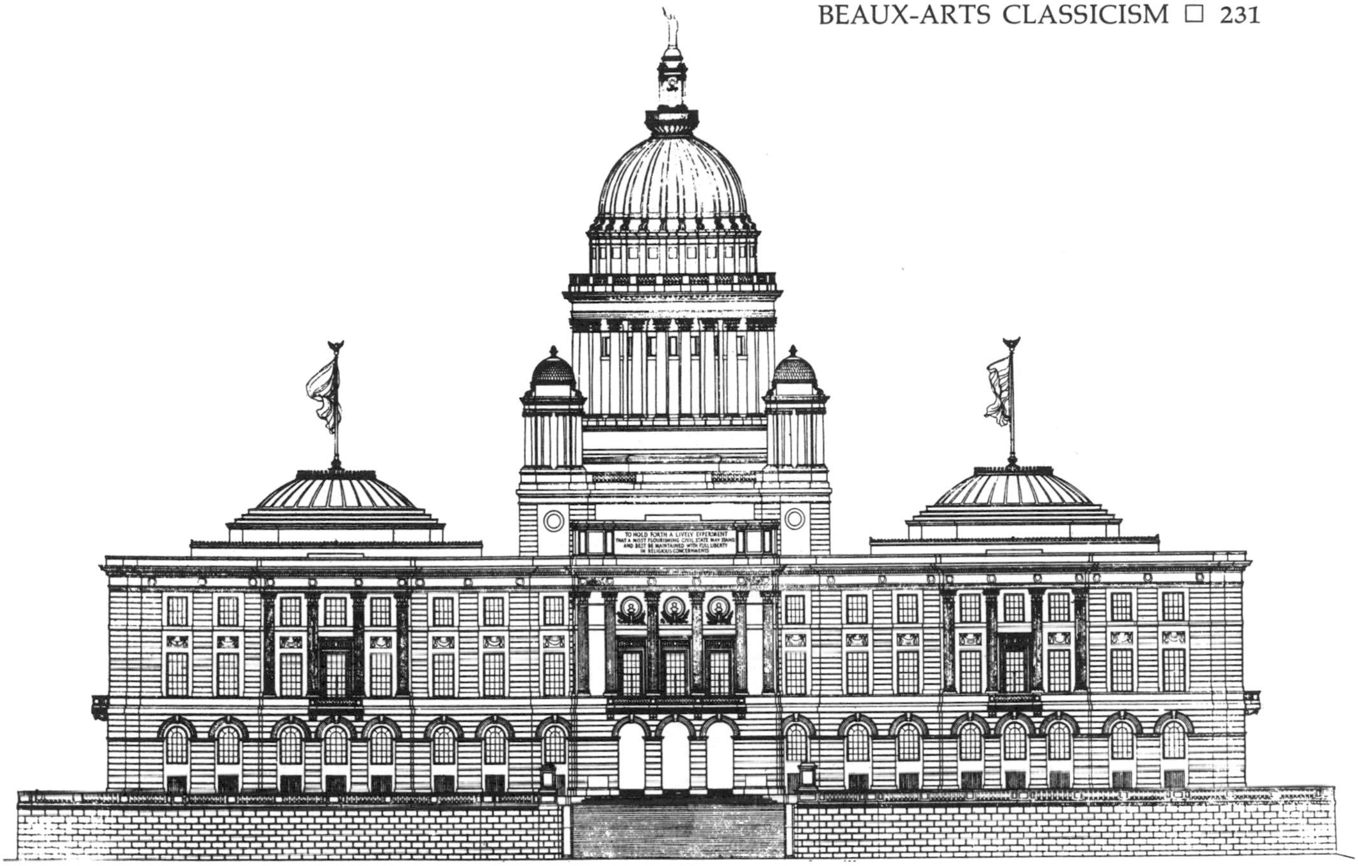

333 Rhode Island State Capitol. Providence, Rhode Island. 1895–1904; McKim, Mead & White, architects. A Beaux-Arts restatement of Imperial Roman grandeur.

334 Bank of San Mateo County. Redwood City, California. 1900; 1909 addition of a new entrance at left. A familiar type: the turn-of-the-century, small-town, corner bank building, a provincial echo of the Beaux-Arts.

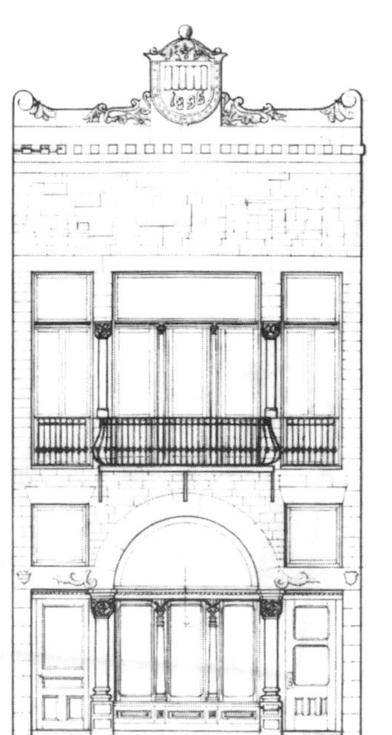

335 Planters and Merchants Insurance Company. Mobile, Alabama. 1896.

Carnegie Library, Guthrie, Oklahoma; 1902–1903.

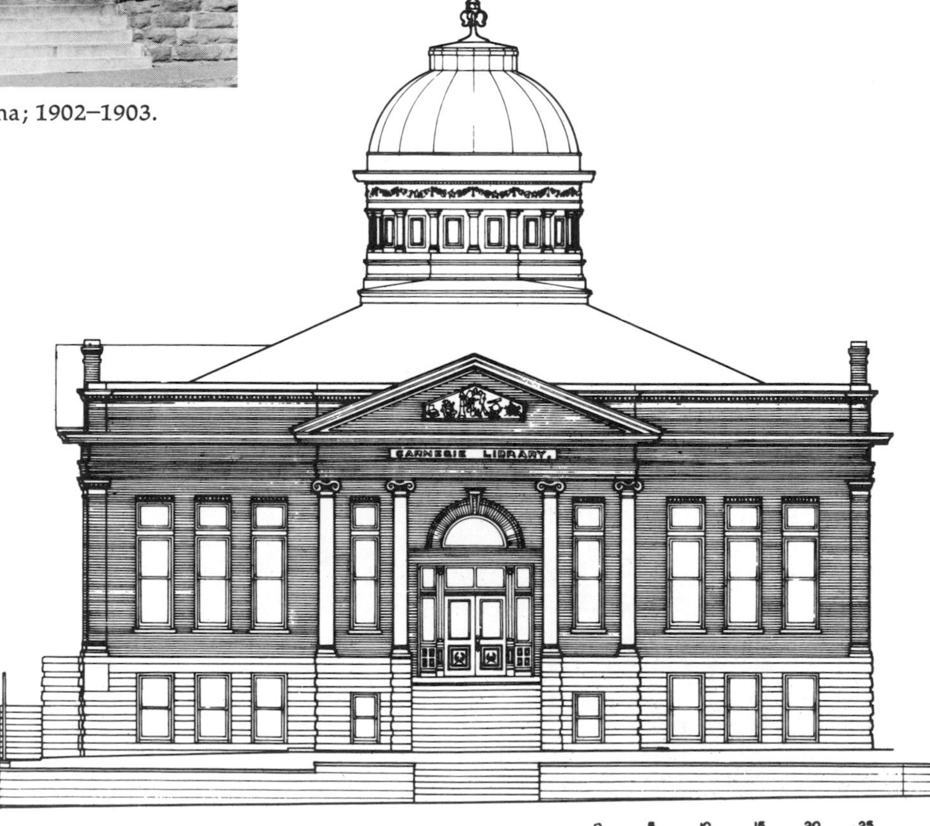

336 Carnegie Library. Guthrie, Oklahoma. 1902–1903.

0 5 10 15 20 25

337 Fulton Theatre. Pittsburgh, Pennsylvania. 1903.

338 Garden Theatre. Pittsburgh, Pennsylvania. 1914.

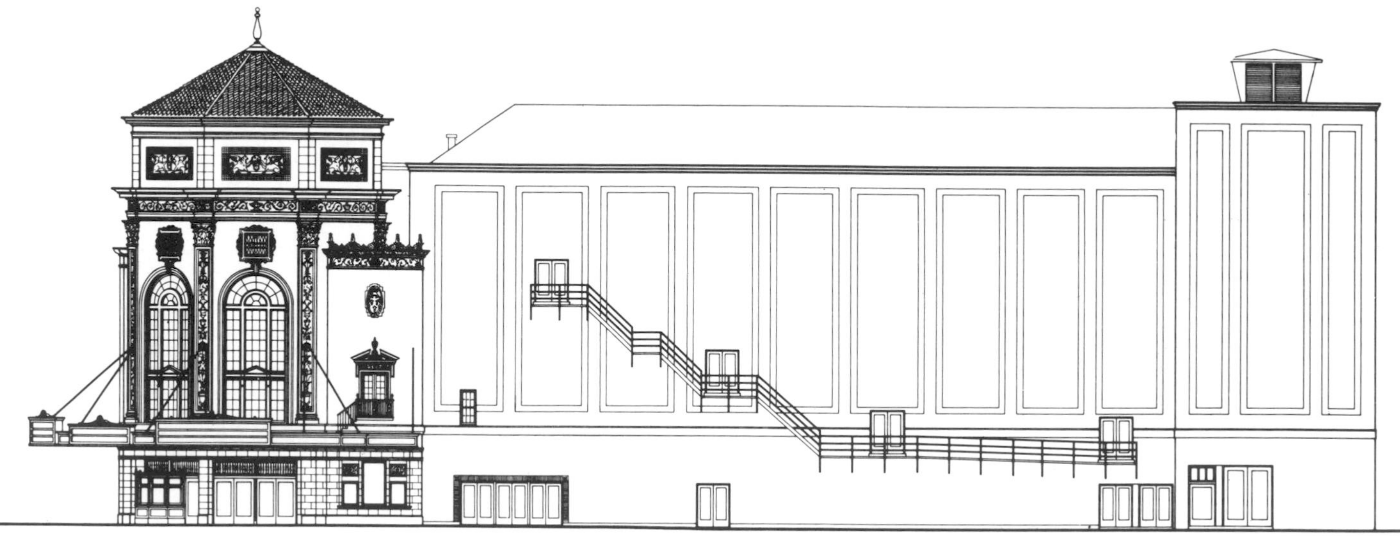

339 Grand Riviera Theatre. Detroit, Michigan. 1924; John Ebersole, architect.

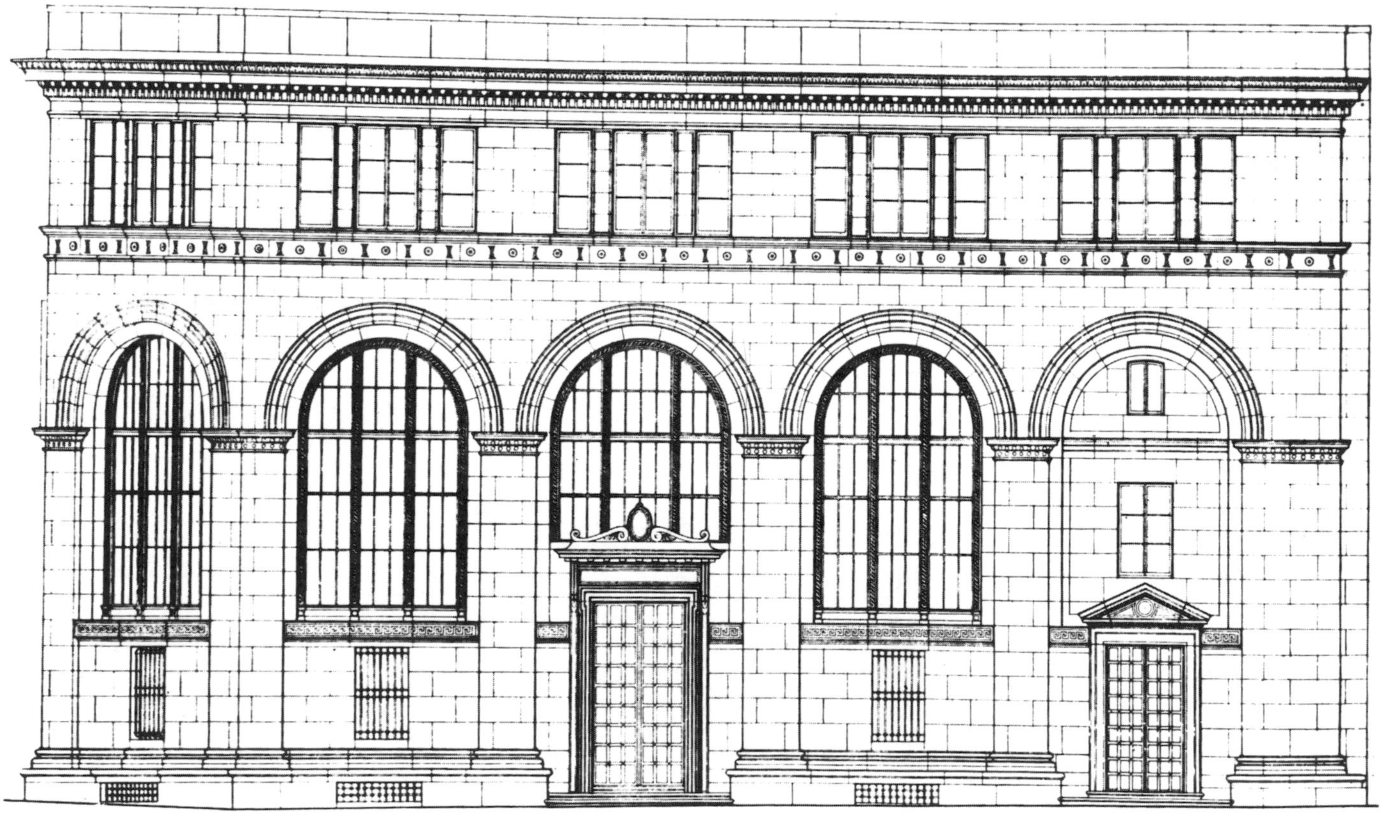

340 New England Trust Company. Boston, Massachusetts. 1905–1907; McKim, Mead & White, architects. Assuredly Renaissance in style, but with large window openings that satisfy early-twentieth-century standards for illumination.

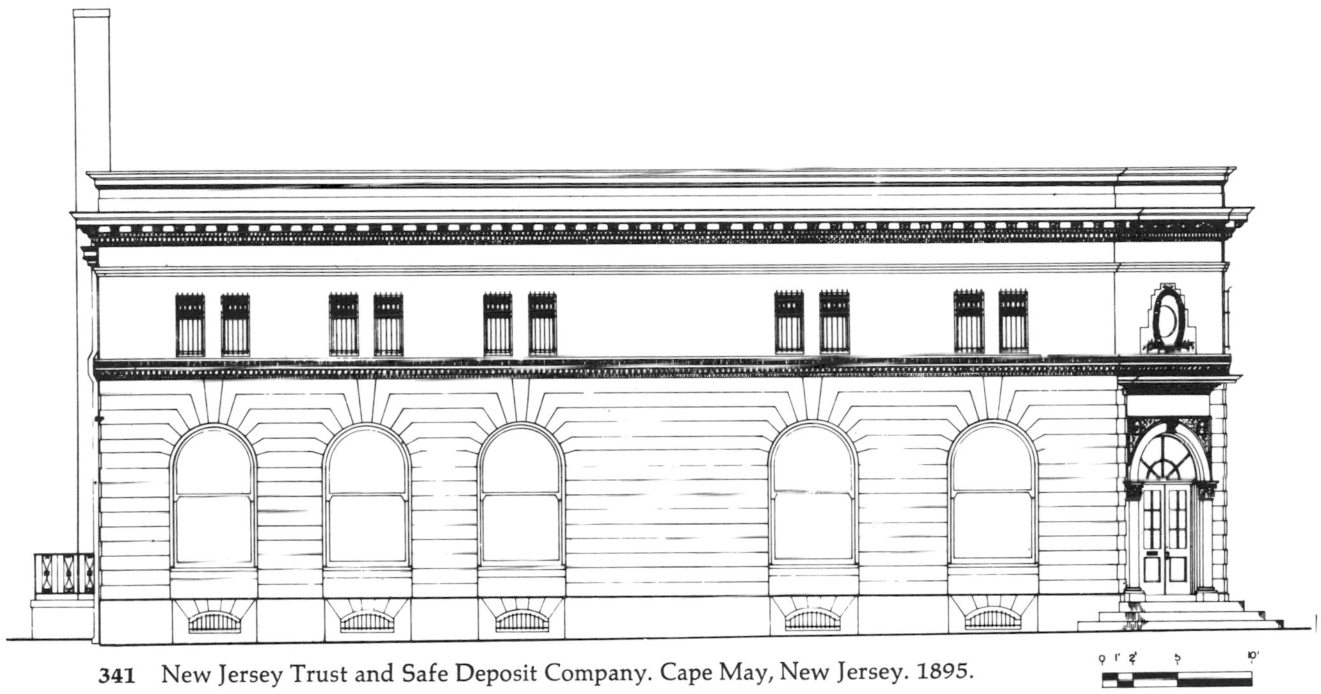

341 New Jersey Trust and Safe Deposit Company. Cape May, New Jersey. 1895.

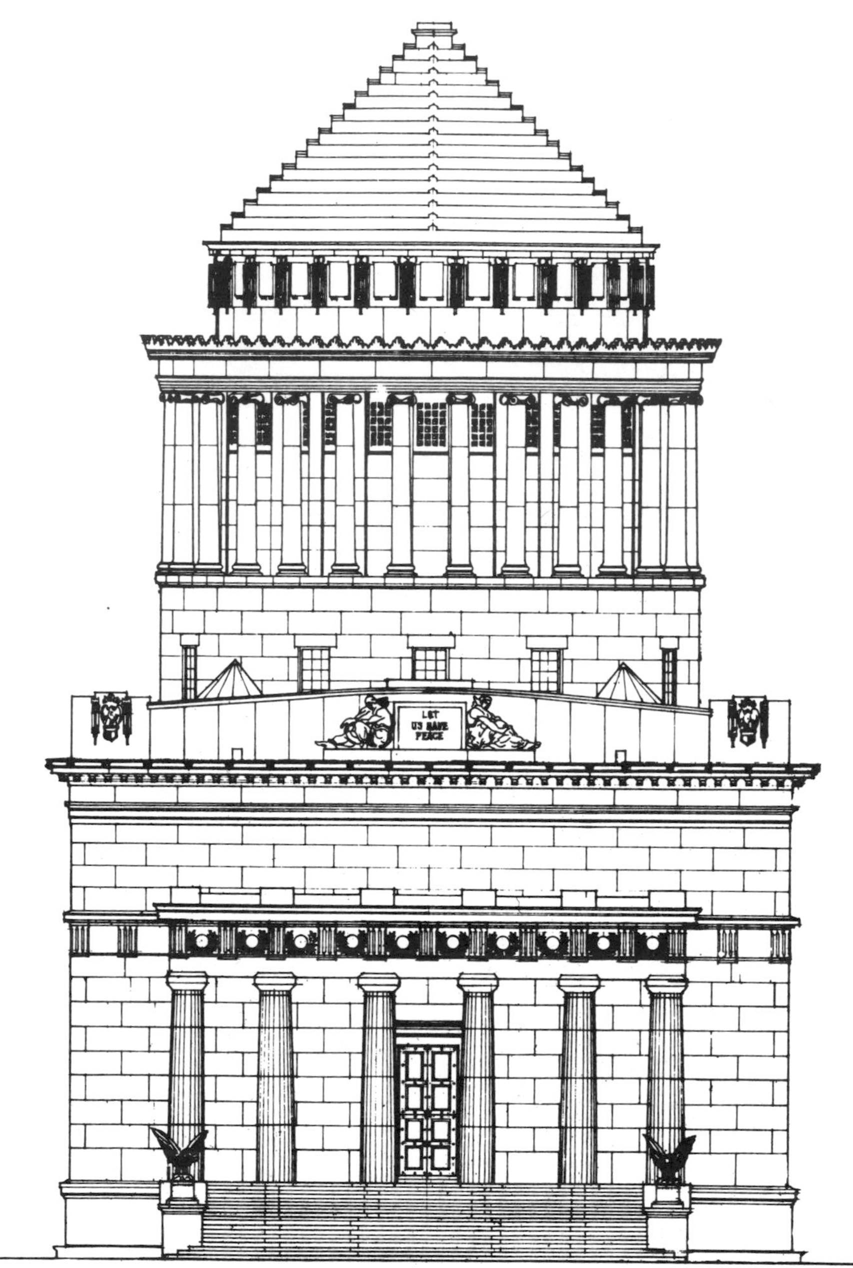

342 Grant's Tomb. New York City. 1897. Eclectic Neoclassicism: grand scale, mix of Greek and Roman motifs, willful distortion of Classical proportions.

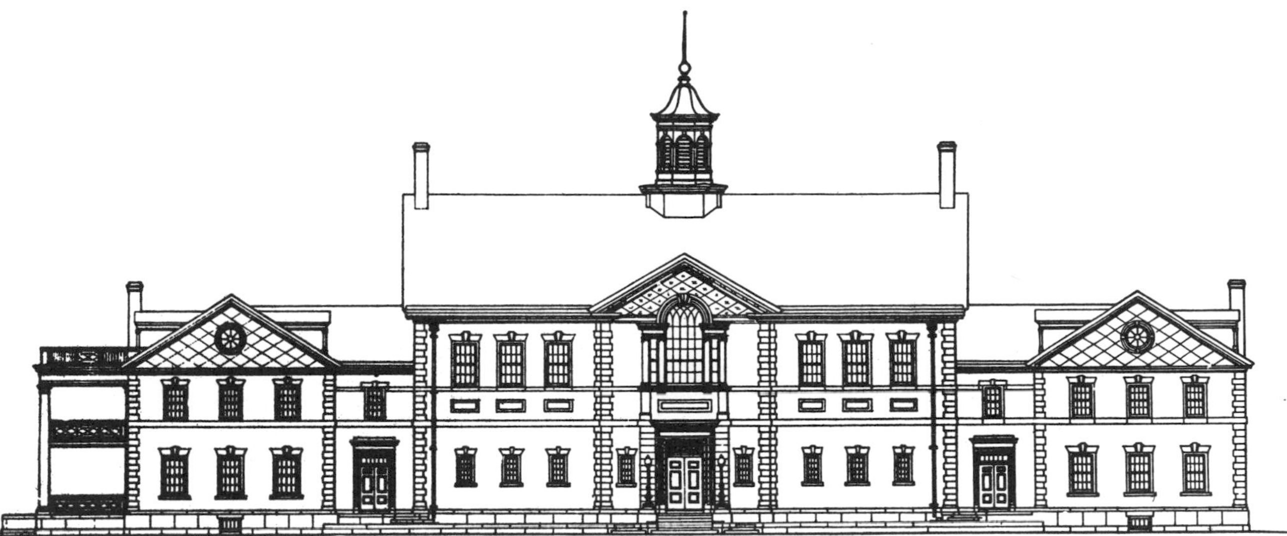

343 Women's Building, University of Illinois. Urbana, Illinois. 1905; McKim, Mead & White, architects. Neo-Georgian design elements freely combined to answer modern taste and needs.

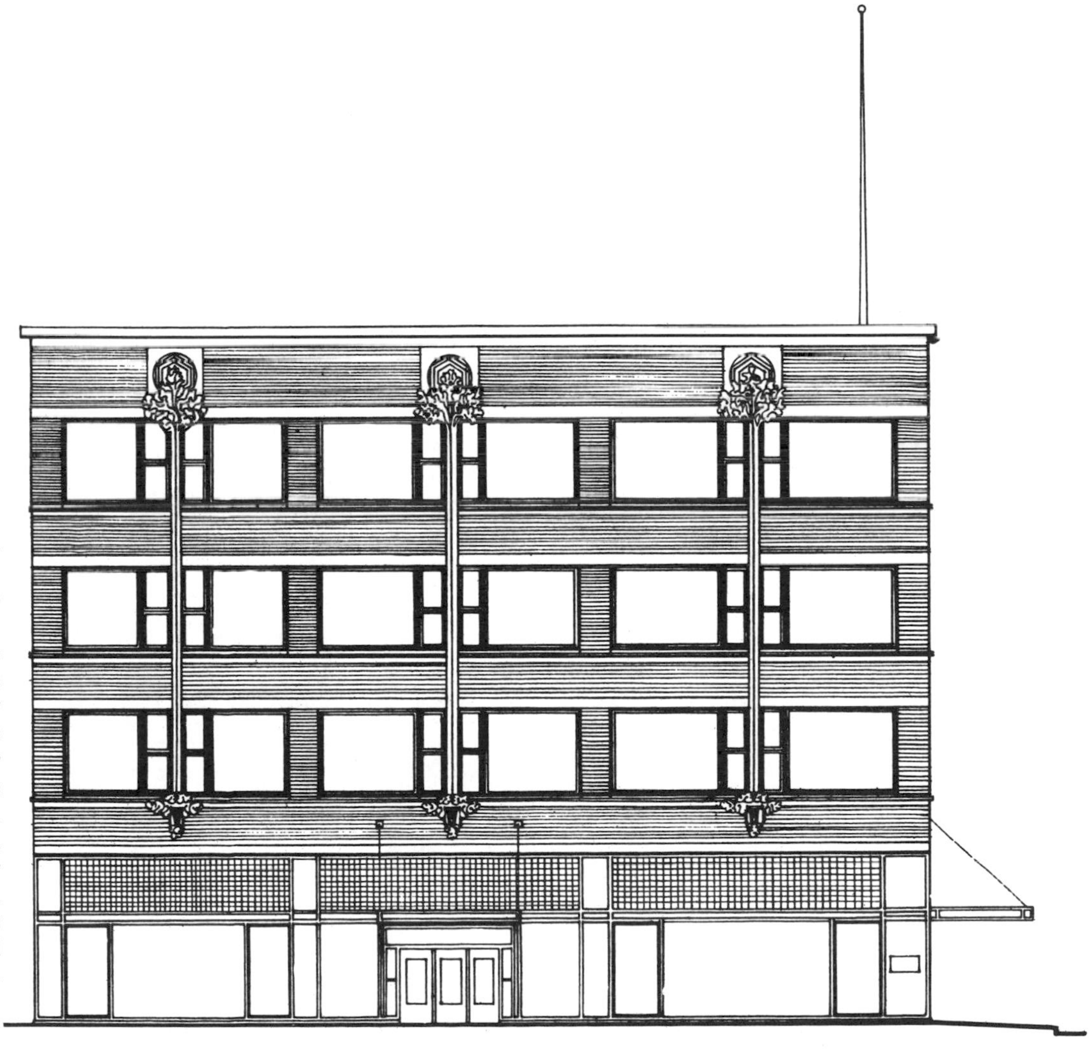

344 Van Allen & Son Store. Clinton, Iowa. 1913–1915; Louis Sullivan, architect. Sullivanesque hallmarks include the use of large, simply framed plate glass windows, clear expression of the horizontal and vertical relationships of steel construction, a veneer of long, thin bricks and elongated mullions capped by florid medallions.

345 Store group. Westhampton, New York. 1933; Peabody, Wilson & Brown, architects.

346 Portola Valley School. Portola Valley, California. C.1900.

347 M. Leibovitz Building. Tampa, Florida. 1917.

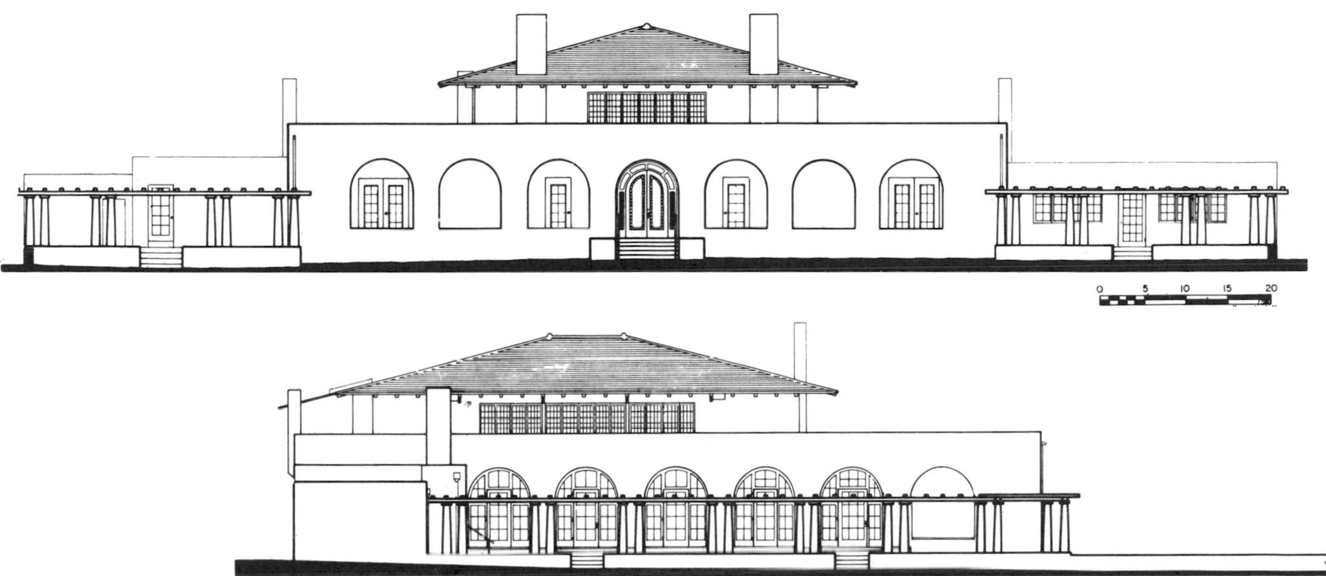

348, 349 La Jolla Women's Club. La Jolla, California. 1913; Irving Gill, architect. The Spanish Mission style, sympathetic to modern construction technology and the modern taste for abstract forms.

350 Fowle's Soda Shop. Newburyport, Massachusetts. An early nineteenth-century structure is given an Art Moderne appearance by a 1940 renovation. (Restored, 1978)

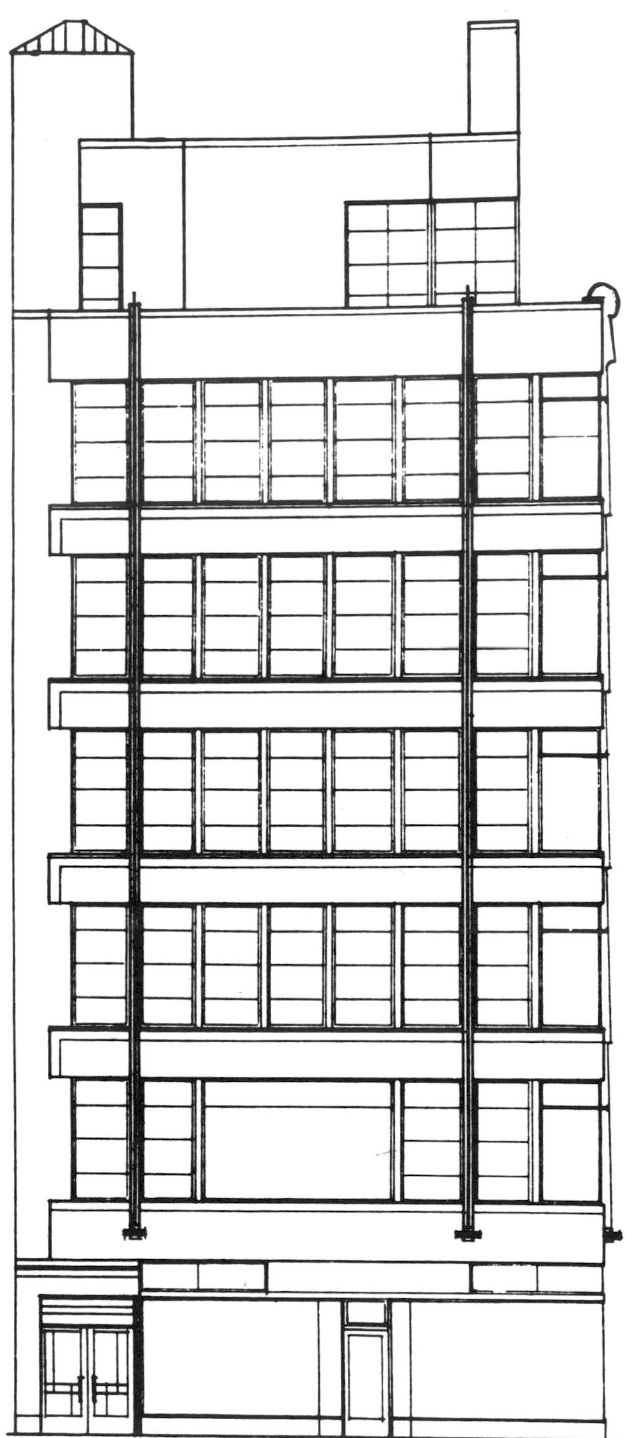

351 Lexington Avenue Office Building. New York, New York. 1931. The window bands and horizontal emphasis are characteristic of Moderne style.

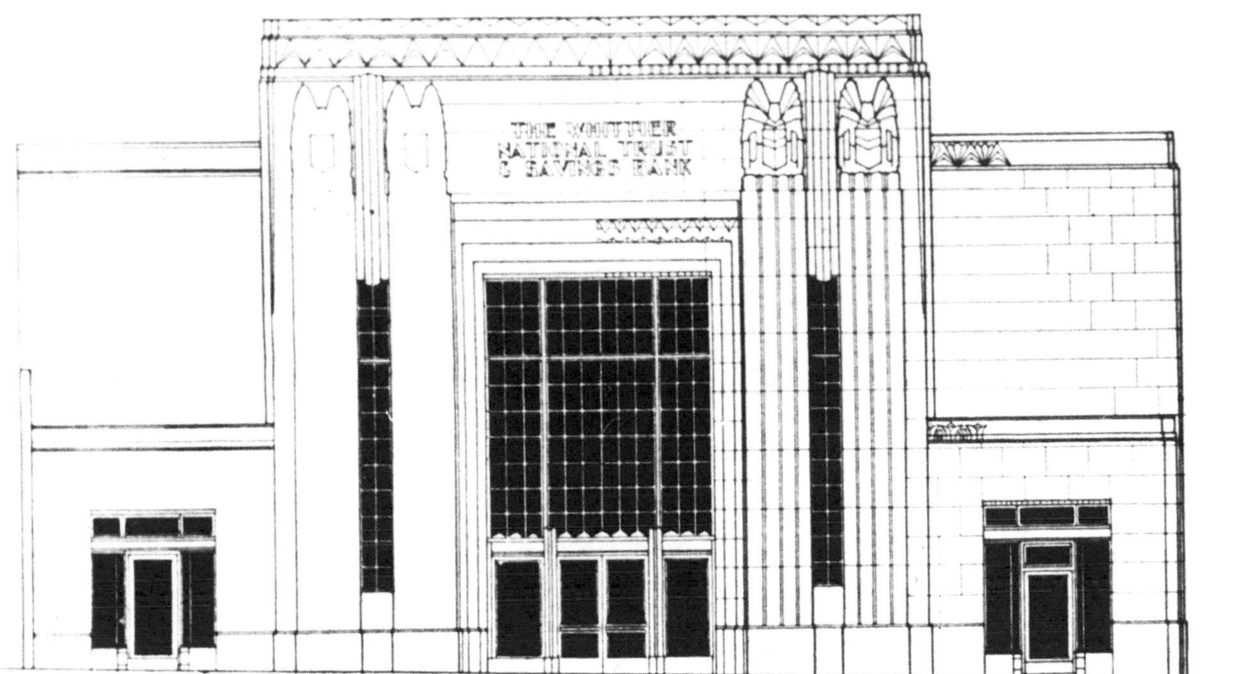

352 Whittier National Trust and Savings Bank. Whittier, California. 1933. William H. Harrison, architect. The stagelike character of the main section is notable.

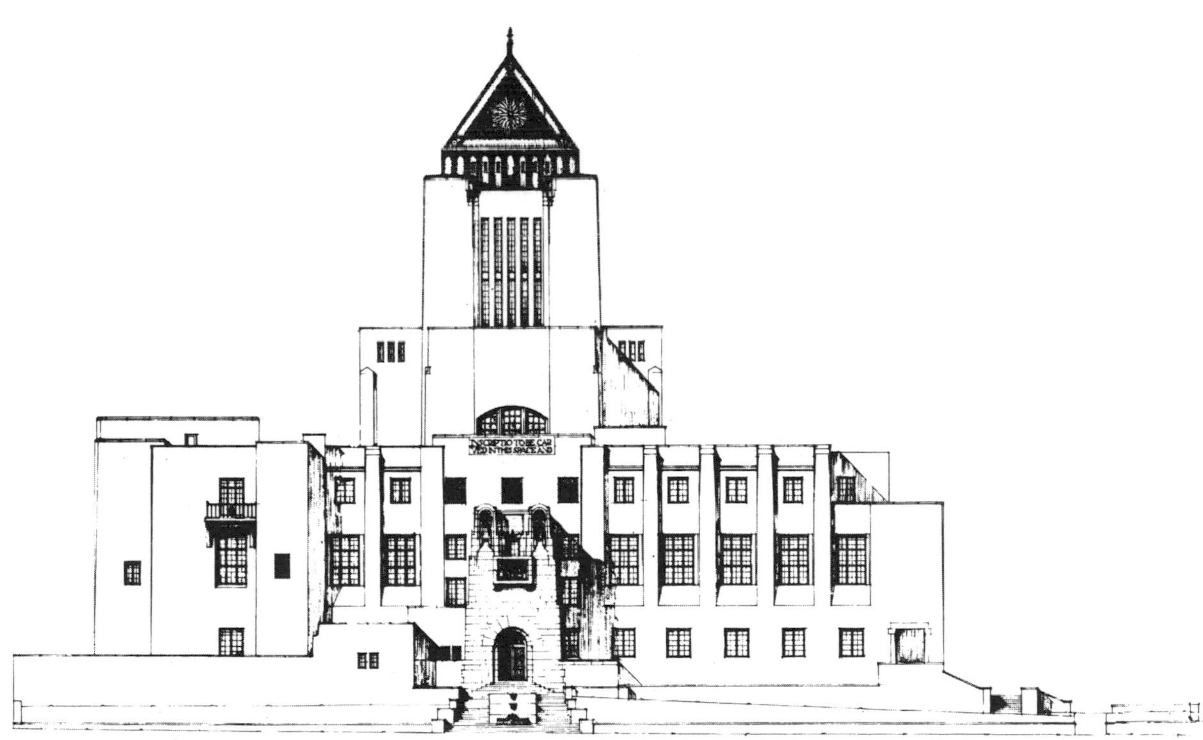

353 Los Angeles Public Library. Los Angeles, California. 1925; Bertram Goodhue, architect. Beaux Arts in its formal composition, Moderne in its plain surfaces, severe detailing, and vigorous articulation of geometrical volumes.

PART IV

Utilitarian

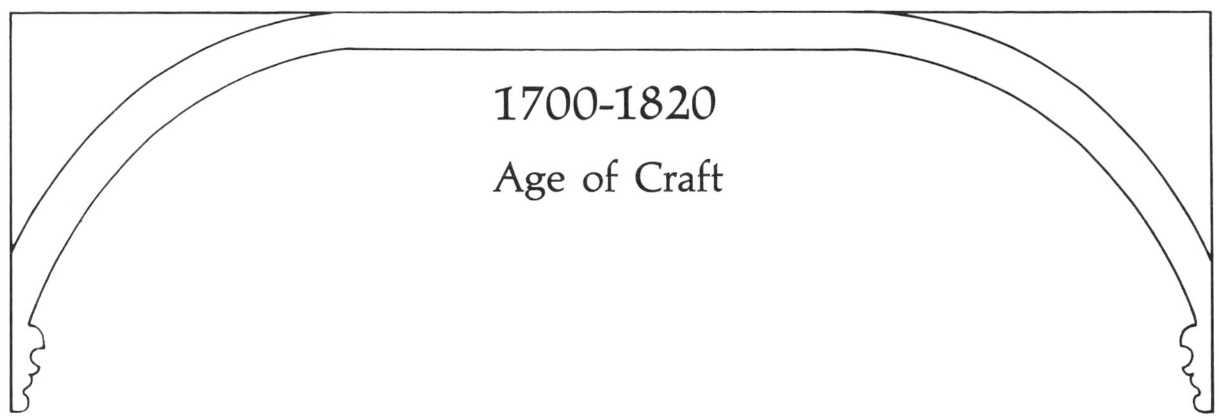

1700-1820

Age of Craft

NOTE: In this part, while the drawings complement the text, they are not referred to directly. For these utilitarian buildings, the emphasis is on construction material and technology, rather than style, and on how buildings and land-use patterns can be clues to agricultural, technological, and economic change and development.

Materials

Through the first half of the eighteenth century, natural materials were used in a relatively simple state.

Fieldstone was dry-laid or bound with lime mortar.

Timber was hewed or sawed into boards and planks (for English and Dutch settlers), or used as round logs (by Germans) or squared logs (first by the Swedes, and then by other wilderness settlers).

Construction in the Southwest utilized cut stone and adobe bricks (under Spanish influence) or sun-baked adobe clay (an indigenous American technique).

Brick—using centuries-old craft technology—was produced throughout the colonies. Special firing techniques produced glazed bricks and bricks of various colors.

Quarried stone was generally used near its source; an exception was a fine material such as marble or granite, which may have been transported some distance to an important building.

Roofing was ceramic tile, wood shingle, slate, or tin. Iron was wrought for use as nails, hinges, braces, and latches. Blown glass, locally made or imported, was used sparingly.

Construction Technology

In the first century of settlement, and longer in isolated areas, medieval technology persisted. Typically, this used heavy frame construction, with an infill of materials like straw or clay. Typical timber construction used heavy framing elements with dovetail or pegged mortise-and-tenon joints.

After the middle of the eighteenth century, the use of more elaborate joints and braces facilitated the construction of larger structures—church, windmill, watermill, bridge, or barn. Hand-wrought iron connecting devices—nails, bars, angles, and straps—were also in general use.

Brick was favored in the South, especially in Virginia and Maryland, and also in larger urban centers in the middle states and New England. In walls that were several feet thick, fieldstone appeared in the Hudson River Valley, eastern Pennsylvania, and elsewhere. Masonry was also used to support beam-and-plank bridges.

Except in the Spanish colonies, where structural vaults were sometimes used, arched forms were limited to door and window heads.

After the Revolution, building crafts became more specialized and higher-quality workmanship resulted from better-trained quarriers, masons, carpenters, woodcarvers, and plasterers.

Agriculture

In a curious way, even the oldest American land-use patterns—patterns that evolved from ways of land acquisition and tenure, agricultural use, climate, and natural resources—remain to this very day.

Urban expansion, suburban growth, corporate colonization, and roadside commercialization have created a palimpsest of spatial designs. Yet earlier patterns have left revealing clues everywhere—in plot size and shape; in street, town, and neighborhood name; in the character of roadways; in stone walls and wood fences; in the size and location of shade, fruit, and forest trees; in the farmhouse itself and its farmyard complex.

In eastern New England and the Connecticut River Valley, older towns have preserved the common—the center of an urban-rural configuration made up of in-town dwellings and outlying fields and pastures. In western New England, New York, New Jersey, and Pennsylvania—mostly settled by Dutch, English Quakers, Scotch-Irish Presbyterians, and Germans—the pattern of open-country farmsteads, widely dispersed along rural roads, predominated. Here towns are geometric in plan and farther apart.

Surviving elements of the typical farm complex, virtually a village itself—and, in colder climes, often so closely built as to be contiguous—are the cow or sheep barn, pig or chicken shed, corn crib or granary, springhouse or wellhouse, and smokehouse. Sited and planned for efficient function, these structures were differentiated in form, size, and construction.

The isolated farmstead moved west with the American farmer-pioneer in the first two decades of the nineteenth century. Ohio, Indiana, and Illinois were joined to the Union, surveyed in mile-square sections, and put up for sale in eighth-, quarter-, or half-section parcels.

In the South, too, there were small farms, but the agricultural pattern tended to be aristocratic in scale. Rural landholdings, domains of hundreds or thousands of acres crowned by venerable manor houses and formally sited outbuildings, originated as riverfront plantations that thrived on the export of cotton, rice, tobacco, and indigo. On the frontier beyond the Alleghenies, primitive structures on small, oddly shaped landholdings were bequeathed by dauntless squatters and intrepid woodsmen—the vanguard of an impatient democracy.

Other configurations reflect different methods of settlement. In the Mississippi Delta, long, narrow field divisions in parishes that ring New Orleans are evidence of the French presence in the New World. And as far west as the Spanish settlements in New Mexico and California, patterns of property division and irrigation contours tell of long-ago efforts by missionary and Indian.

Transportation

The sea was America's first highway. By the early eighteenth century, considerable trade and travel were carried on by numerous small boats plying seacoast and tidewater river.

Fishing and, later, shipbuilding, whaling, and sealing were the natural industries of port towns.

These growing centers—urbane communities such as Salem and Nantucket—acquired a special configuration: a tight web of narrow streets and small lots, later enlarged by grid-plan additions; docks, warehouses, ships' chandleries, inns, and customhouse crowding the waterfront; a lighthouse guarding the harbor.

Only after the mid-eighteenth century did a developing network of intertown and intercolonial roadways begin to bind together once-isolated inland communities. The first roads paralleled older river routes or followed Indian trails.

By the end of the century, a through route linked Charleston and Boston, roads proliferated to the hinterlands, and the Wilderness Road conquered the Appalachian barrier. By the 1830s, turnpikes linked every major town and stretched as far west as Illinois.

Although those roads now appear modern in character, historic names document their early origins: Kings Highway, Albany Post Road, Farmington Road, Lancaster Turnpike, Old Cumberland Road. Also extant are a remarkable number of structures generated by these roads, ranging from embankments and stone bridges to milestone markers, toll houses, smithies, and stage inns.

Industry

Colonial industry was limited to the production of necessities. The dwelling could also serve as workshop for handcrafting products like shoes, tableware, and wood cabinets.

Specialized structures—still domestic in scale—were foundries for the manufacture of horseshoes, building elements, and tools and mills or breweries to process grains, cotton seed, or tobacco.

By the end of the first quarter of the nineteenth century, the first stages of the industrial revolution were manifest: in the multistory factories which contained under one roof all the operations necessary to process cotton from raw fiber to finished product; in the clock and gun manufactories of Connecticut where the system of interchangeable parts was first worked out; in manufactories in Pennsylvania towns where forges yielded iron of better quality and greater quantity.

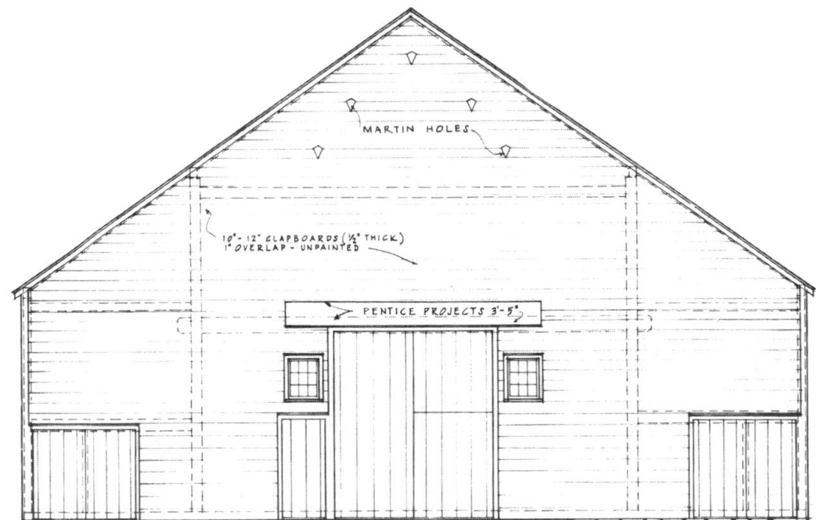

354 Johannes Decker Barn. Shawangunk, New York. Before 1775. A typical Dutch barn, with an entrance in the broad gable end and low eaves at the sides.

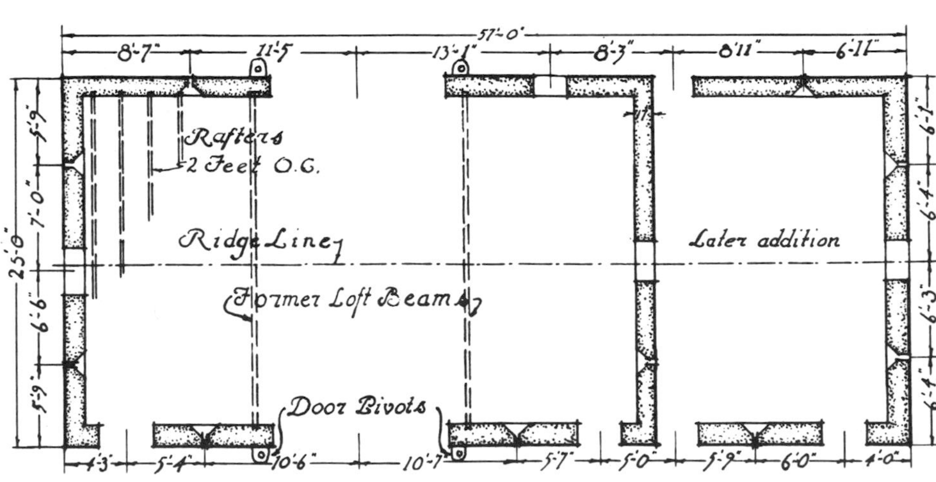

FIRST FLOOR PLAN

355, 356, 357 Glen Fern Barn and Springhouse. Fairmont Park, Philadelphia, Pennsylvania. 1733 and later. The English barn has entrances on both long sides, permitting a wagon to enter and exit without turning around.

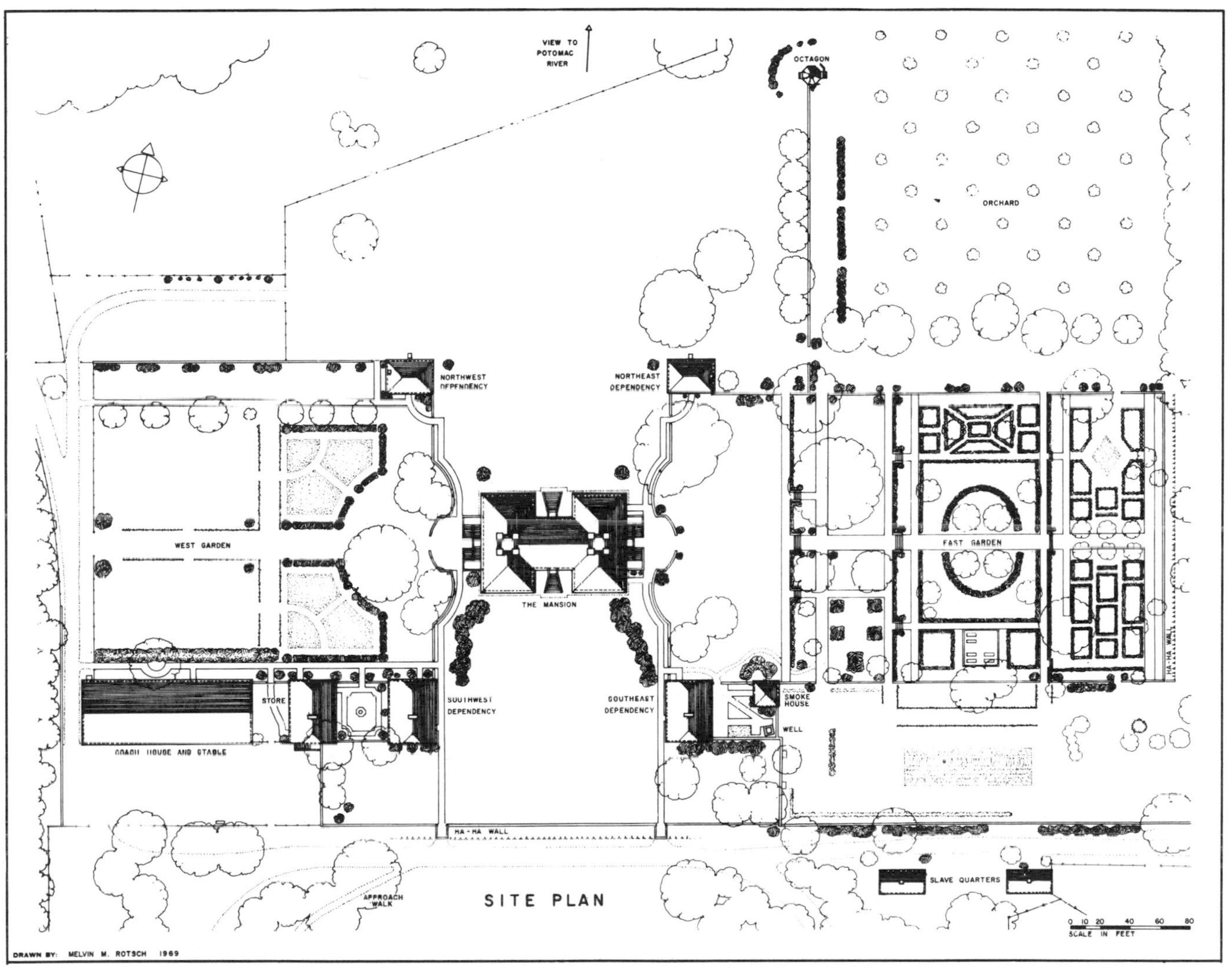

358 Stratford Hall site plan. Stratford, Virginia. 1725–1730. Ornamental gardens and formally sited outbuildings are the immediate setting for the southern plantation house. Orchards and planting fields are beyond.

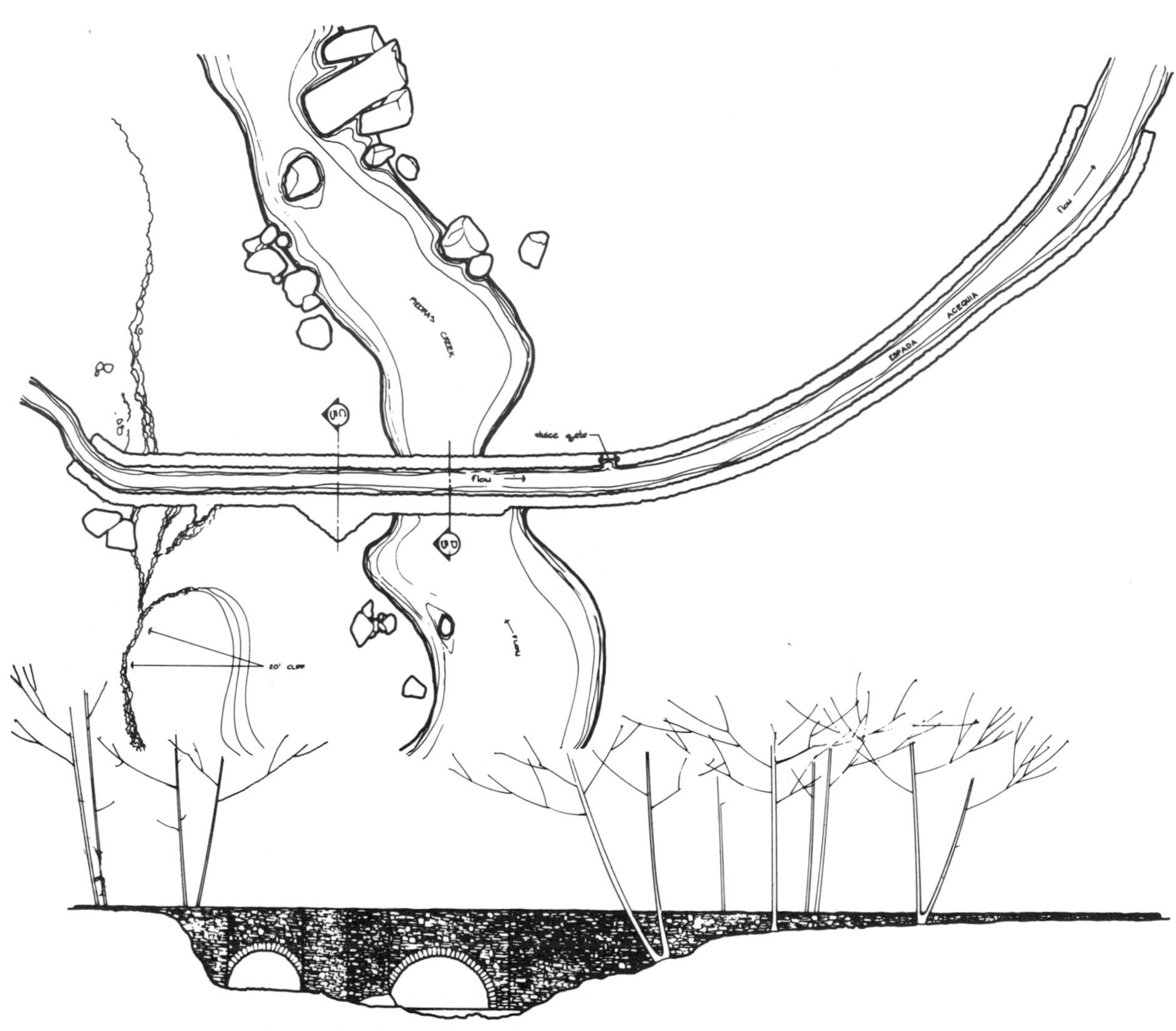

359 Espada Acequia, Pedras Creek Aqueduct. San Antonio, Texas. C.1731. This barrel-arched aqueduct was part of an extensive irrigation system along the San Antonio River.

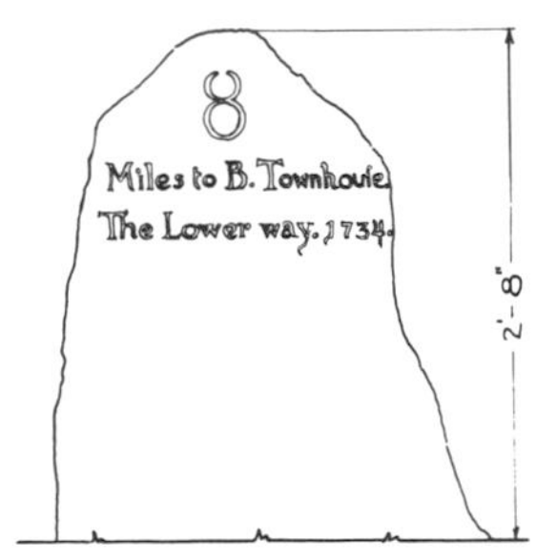

360 Mile Stone,
Plymouth Route.
Dorchester, Massachusetts.
1734.

Milestone. 1763.

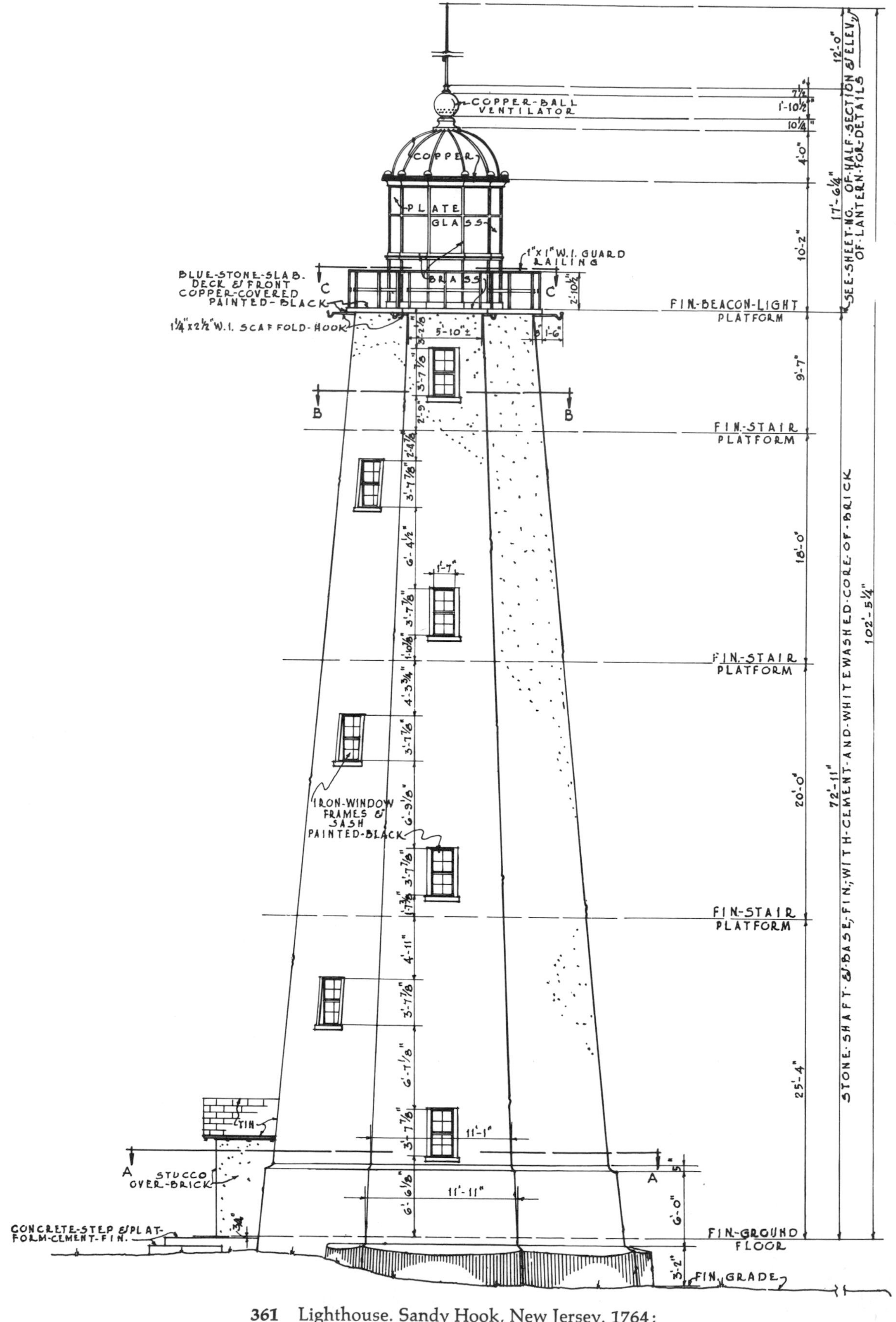

361 Lighthouse. Sandy Hook, New Jersey. 1764; major repairs, 1857.

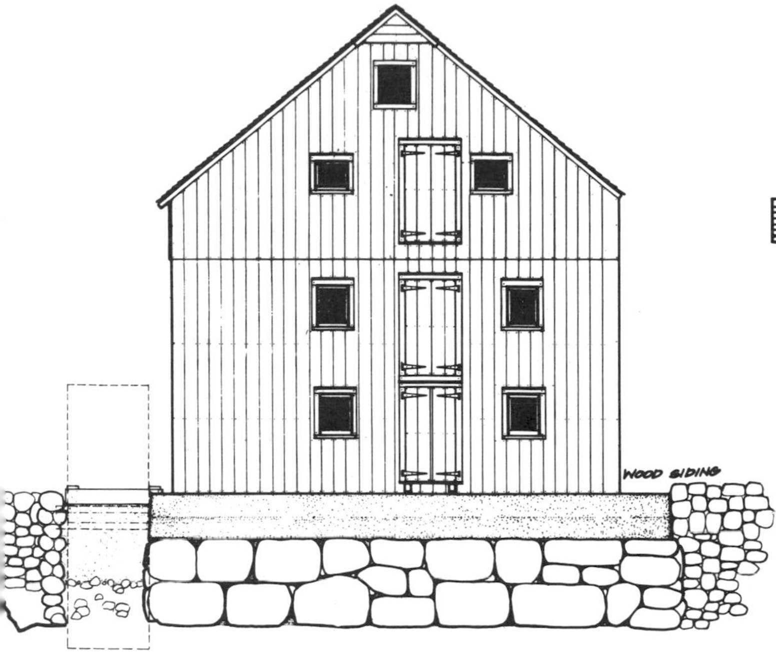

WOOD SIDING

362, 363 Van Wyck–Lefferts Tide Mill. Huntington, New York. C.1793–1797. The mill is on a damned tidal pond; its undershot water wheel was powered by the release of water impounded during high tide.

Van Wyck–Lefferts Tide Mill, Huntington, New York; c. 1793–1797.

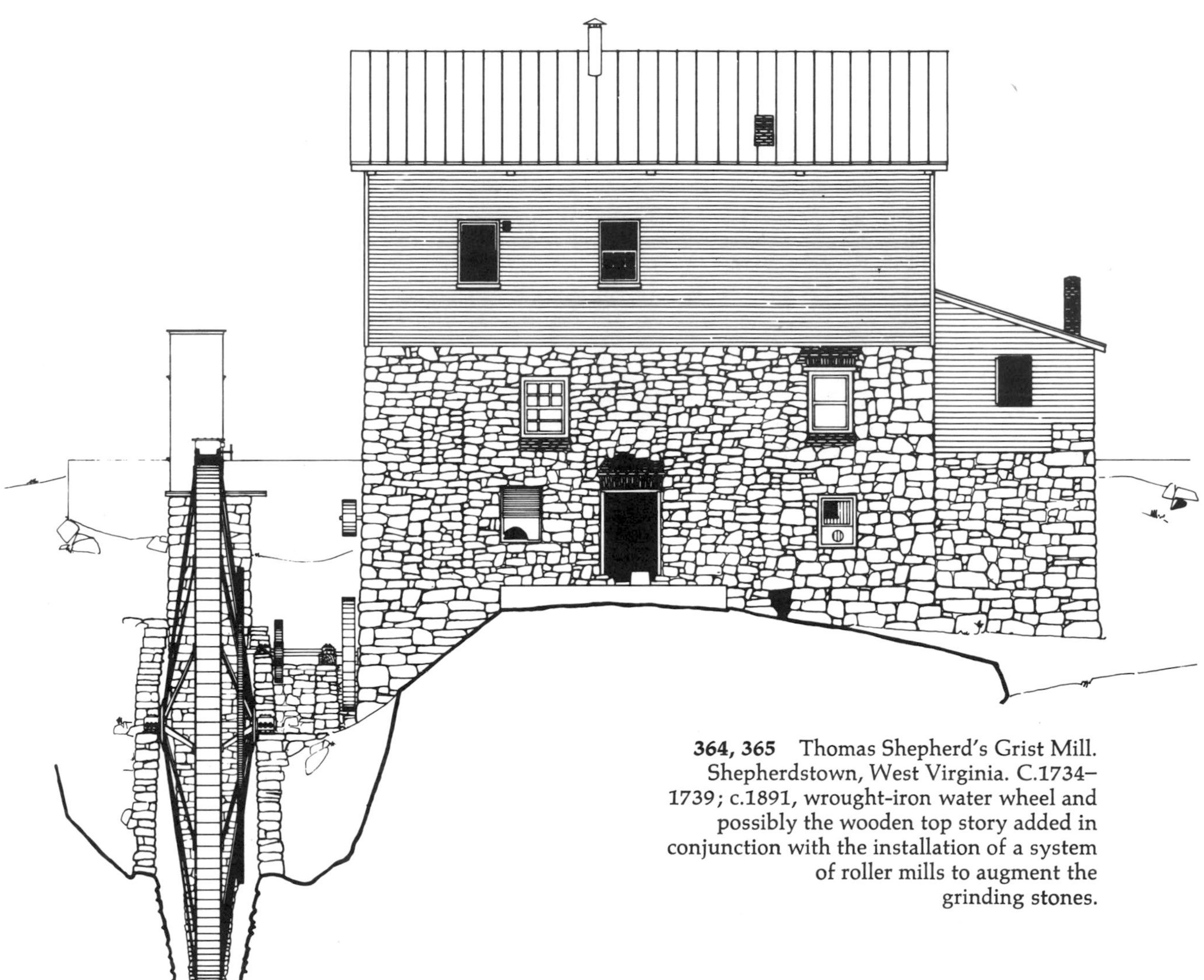

364, 365 Thomas Shepherd's Grist Mill. Shepherdstown, West Virginia. C.1734–1739; c.1891, wrought-iron water wheel and possibly the wooden top story added in conjunction with the installation of a system of roller mills to augment the grinding stones.

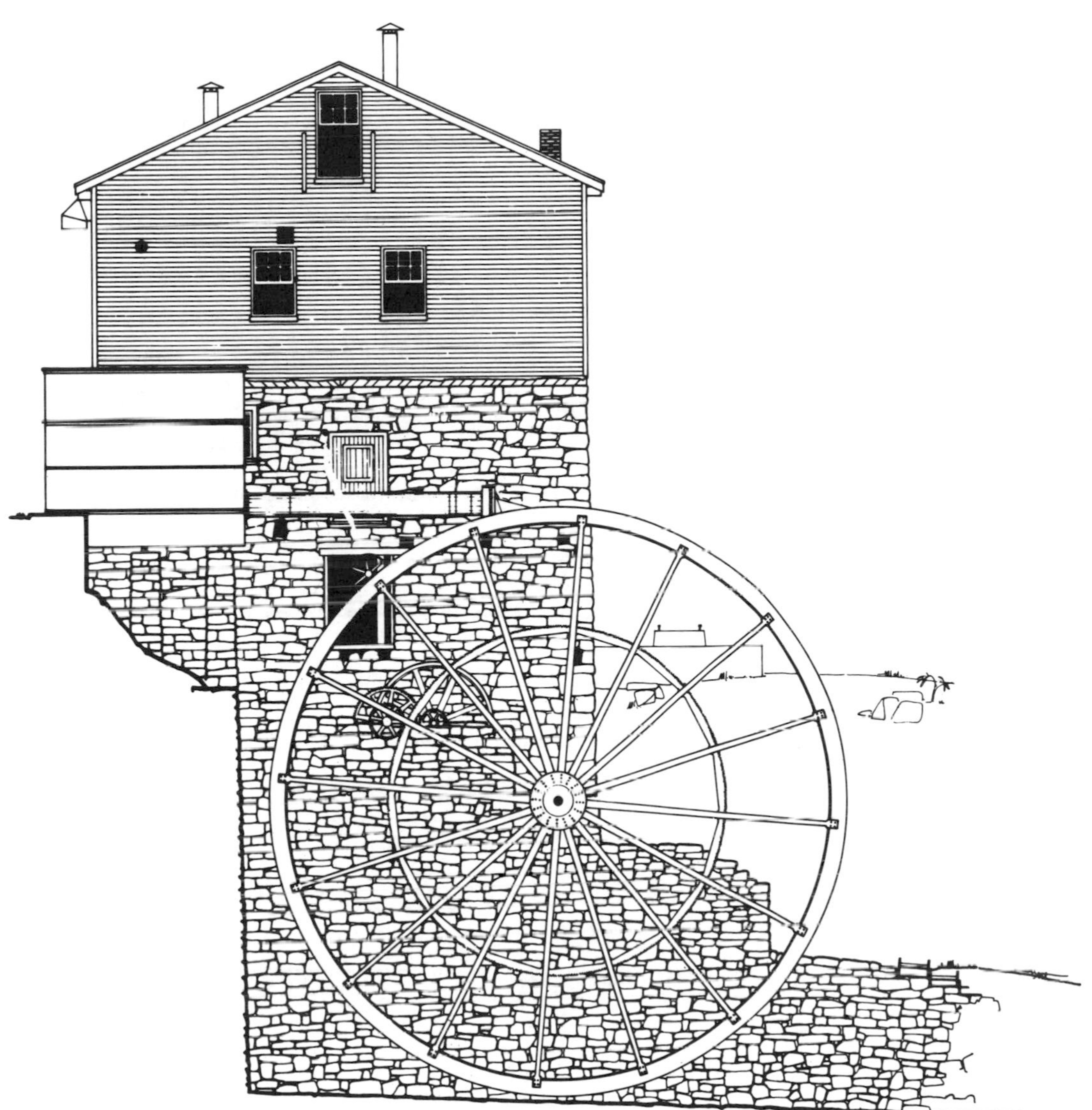

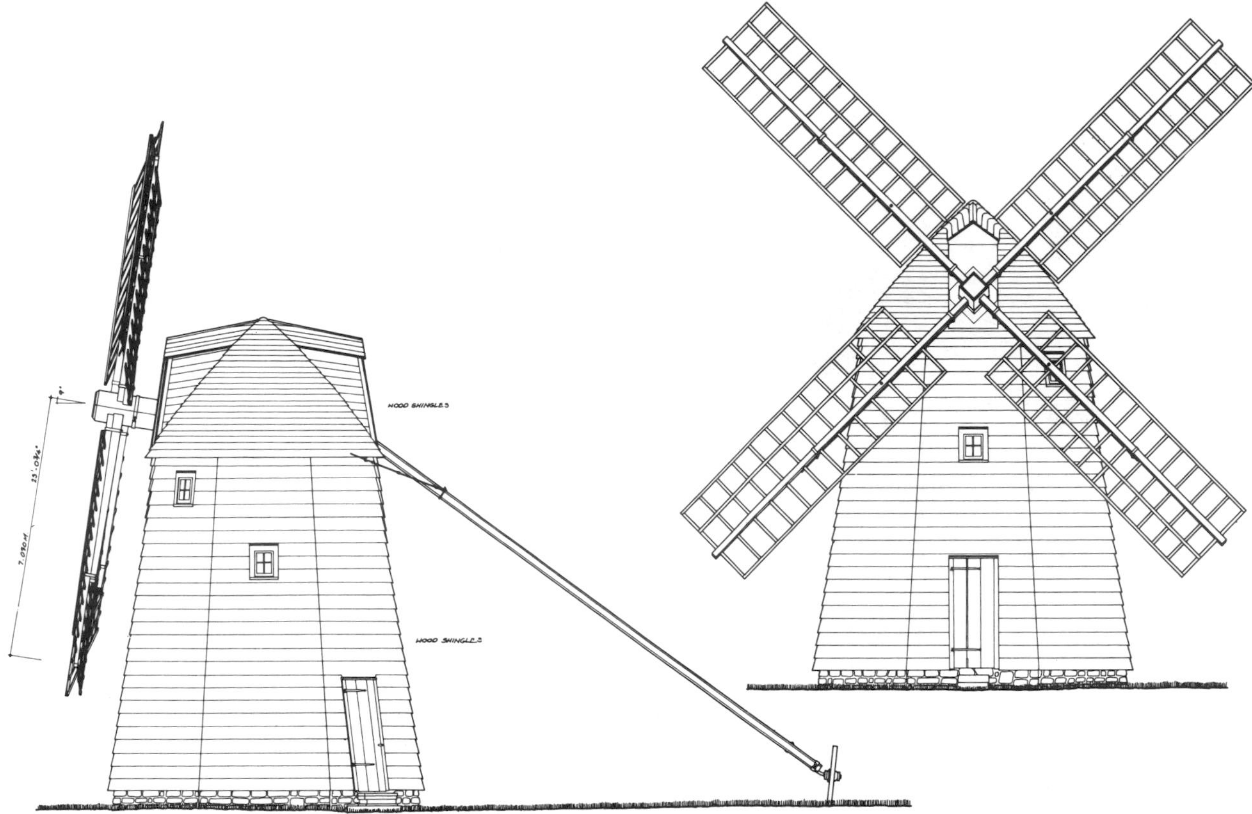

366, 367 Windmill. Watermill, Long Island, New York. 1800. The long tailpole extending from the rear of the cap was a device used to push the sails into the wind. The conical gabled cap is of a type unique to Long Island.

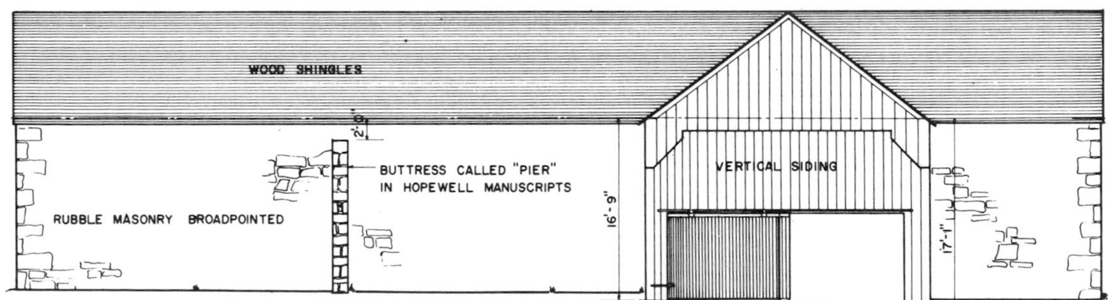

368 Charcoal House. Hopewell Village National Historic Site, Berks County, Pennsylvania. 1810; wooden addition, c.1880. Other structures in this early ironmaking community were the furnace, casting house, blacksmith shop, offices, and boardinghouse.

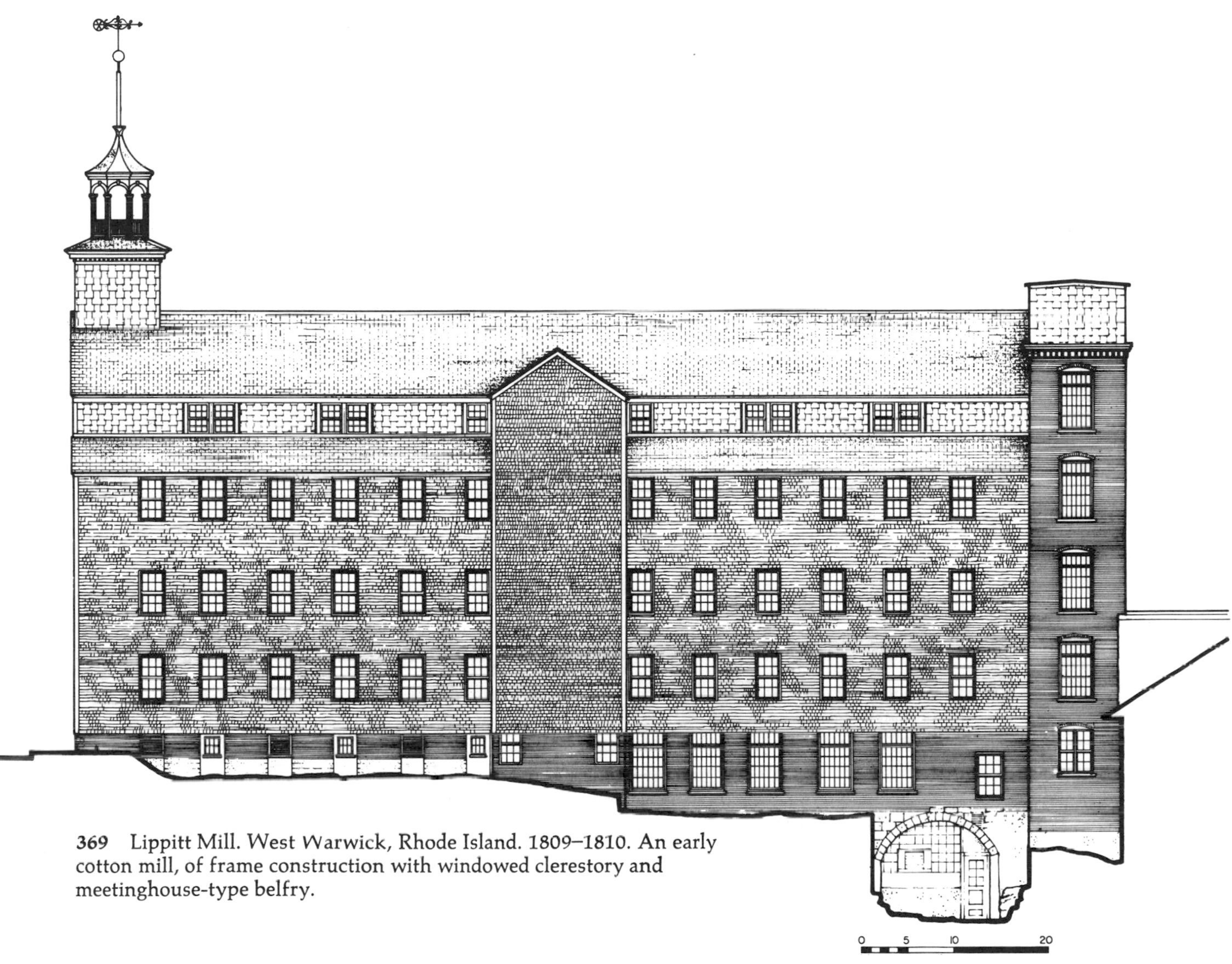

369 Lippitt Mill. West Warwick, Rhode Island. 1809–1810. An early cotton mill, of frame construction with windowed clerestory and meetinghouse-type belfry.

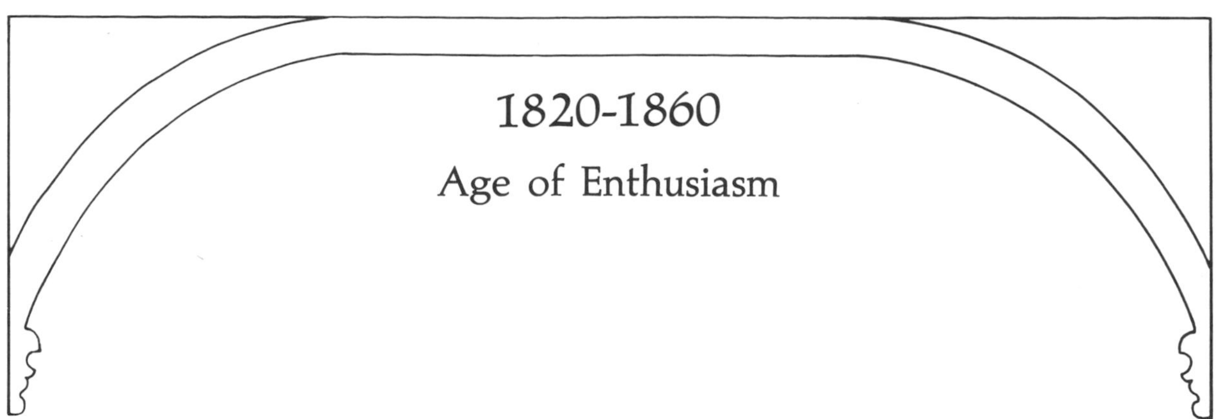

1820-1860

Age of Enthusiasm

Materials

Timber continued to be a favored building material. The development of the power-driven circular saw permitted the fabrication of thinner wooden elements. These could be joined by machine-cut nails, which were in general use after 1830. In mill and warehouse, masonry support for timber framing enhanced strength and fire resistance.

Ashlar masonry was usually used for important public buildings, and coursed or uncoursed cobblestone for vernacular or provincial ones. Masonry was also most suitable for aqueducts and early railroad viaducts and bridges.

The use of glass increased with the availability of plate after the 1830s; sizes three feet by four feet and larger were not unusual for display windows.

Introduced as early as the 1820s, but only common in the 1850s (and later in the West), cast and wrought iron were used as structural elements in train shed, fire tower, lighthouse, and bridge.

After the 1850s, waterproof composition roof materials, with coal tar as the cementing substance, permitted roofs of lower pitch.

Construction Technology

As late as the 1850s, and even later for loft and industrial structures, traditional handcraft techniques were employed for the assembly of wood post, beam, girder, and joist.

First introduced in rapidly growing Chicago, the system of balloon framing (an assembly of lightweight wooden framing elements joined by factory-made nails) proved to be a dramatic innovation in its economy of time, labor, and materials.

Prefabricated wall, window, and roofing units for dwelling, commercial building, and farm outbuilding could be transported over considerable distances.

Improved truss designs in wood and iron permitted the enclosure of larger interior spaces and the erection of longer bridge spans.

The production of high-quality brick and stone masonry—achieved through the use of machinery for brick production and stone dressing—assisted the development of masonry construction techniques, including stone vaults and domes.

Agriculture

In rural New England, agricultural prosperity in the 1830s produced a treasure of Greek Revival farmsteads. But the agricultural frontier moved west to the wheat region of western New York, the limestone valleys of southeastern Pennsylvania, the bluegrass region of Kentucky, and the bottomlands of Ohio. Abandoned dwellings fell to ruin; pasture returned to forest. In the South, too, farm economy was risky, although cotton culture and the slave system built enormous plantations.

The 1840s opened to settlement the vast prairie lands of Illinois, Indiana, Missouri, and Kansas. Shawnee, Delaware, Wyandot, Sauk, and Fox were pushed farther west. The Preemption Act marketed new public lands in small, cheap parcels, and the newly invented steel plow broke the tough prairie sod.

"All the enjoyments of heaven would not suffice to keep an American in one place if he were sure of finding another farther west," one observer marveled. "He never stops. His work and will is to be always working, building, starting fresh or beginning something new." An agricultural golden age reigned in the 1850s. Farm prices were sent soaring by the demand for cotton for manufacture and for market produce, dairy products, and grain to feed the hungry cities.

Zigzag rail fenced square farm fields, and pickets enframed painted wooden houses. Ample barns punctuated the open spaces of Iowa, Wisconsin, and Minnesota. Cyrus McCormick set up his reaper business in Chicago in 1847—and within a decade his annual volume exceeded 23,000 units. The mechanized reaper replaced the swinging blade of the scythe. American farming was more profitable than ever before.

Transportation

"We live in the excitement of a rapid and constantly progressive condition," James Fenimore Cooper wrote of his America, ". . . and we advance because we are not accustomed to stand still."

In the years that followed, the advance was indeed a remarkable phenomenon to behold as moving Americans swelled city boundaries, stretched the western frontier, and roamed the seas from Argentina to Zanzibar. Stout and sturdy square-rigged packet ships and fleet and streamlined Yankee clippers filled the harbors of Portland, Boston, New York, and Baltimore—thriving seaport cities as America began her growth as a great commercial nation.

River and canal ports, too, prospered in the steamboat decades of the 1830s and 1840s, when new-built canals opened to farm settlement and to city building the eastern hinterlands, the Ohio and Mississippi valleys, and the Great Lakes plains. Engineering skill, financial daring, and sheer determination dug navigation canals three hundred miles and more in length. So too, they built water-supply systems that quenched and cleansed rapidly expanding city populations and protected them from fire. Land routes also expanded beyond all expectations. New wood-truss bridges made roadways safer and more reliable; coaches of improved design and macadamized roadways made distances shorter; fine, column-fronted hotels made travel pleasant and convenient.

By midcentury, the horse-drawn omnibus stretched the pedestrian city to many times its former limits. The railroad planted new cities as far west as the Mississippi. By 1860, superimposed over river and canal routes, more than 60,000 miles of track laced the nation. The steam engine sounded on the Kansas prairie.

To today's observer, a host of constructions—solid wharfside warehouses, masonry embankments and bridges, canal locks, toll houses, culverts, ventilators, and railroad rights-of-way—show the efforts of those dynamic years.

Industry

Obsolescence never completely overcame the wooden mill by the side of stream or tide pool until almost the end of the nineteenth century. But the nation's riverfronts were transfigured by incomparably larger fieldstone, brick, and granite factory complexes.

Raceways and waterwheels harnessed the power of the Merrimack, Hudson, Mohawk, Passaic, and James rivers to belt-driven factories which produced—in heretofore unimaginable quantities—cotton textiles, agricultural implements, prefabricated housing components, steam engines, locomotives, machines, and machine tools.

On the banks of the Allegheny, Monongahela, and Ohio, new industry exploited abundant iron and coal deposits and developed new processes for iron refining and rolling. Mill villages, rows of workers' homes, and pediment-fronted boardinghouses are yet another legacy of this early industrial development.

Iron rails and locomotives, exchanging factory products for farm produce, were the surging arteries of a young, healthy, and vigorous nation. The industrial vision was grand; the mood optimistic.

"We have entered a new era in this history of the world," wrote architect Robert Mills. "Our vast country is before us and our motto, Excelsior."

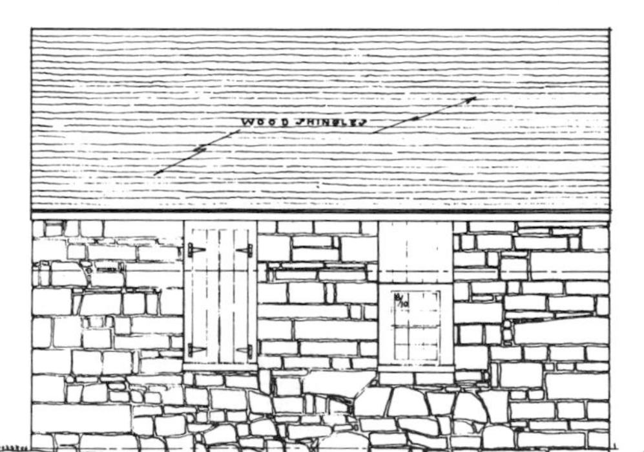

370, 371 Stone barn. Johnsonburg, New Jersey. Before 1819. Built as a storehouse; the windows were at wagon height.

Stone barn, Johnsonburg, New Jersey; before 1819 (see 370, 371).

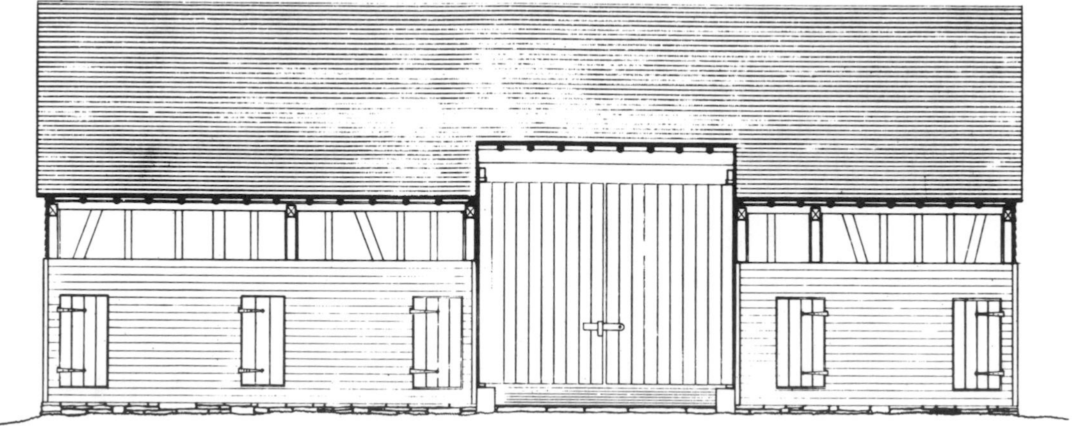

372 Livestock barn, Jones plantation. Bethania vicinity, North Carolina. C.1840. Built of hewn timbers, shown as only partially preserved. Plan provided a two-story workspace, with feeding runs and lofts on either side.

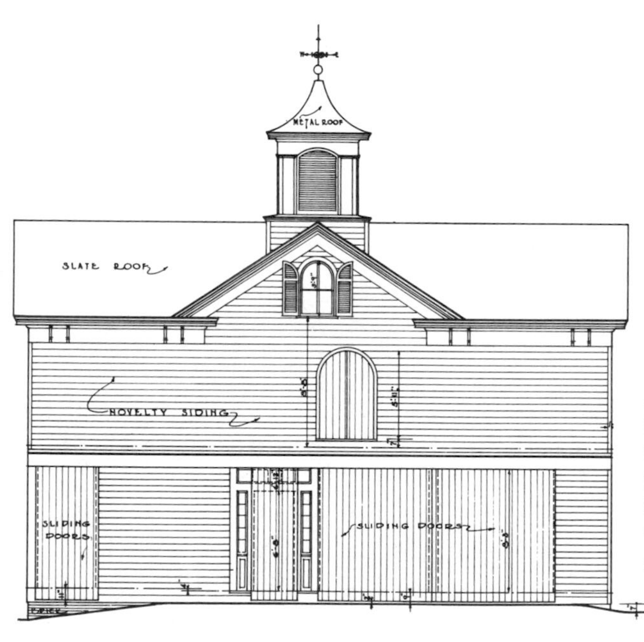

373 John Lindsley Barn. Somerville, New Jersey. C.1850. Italianate in style, the barn was illuminated through the arch-headed windows, and ventilated by means of the louvered cupola.

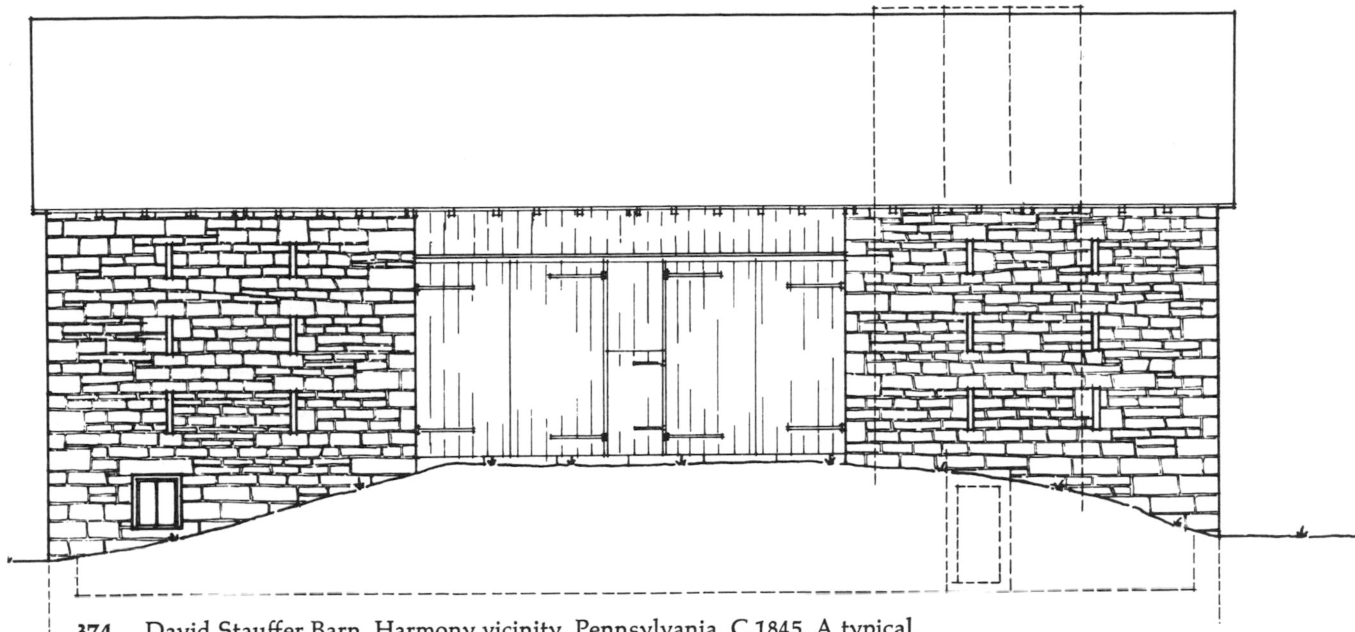

374 David Stauffer Barn. Harmony vicinity, Pennsylvania. C.1845. A typical Pennsylvania stone barn, three bays, and built into a bank with entrances on two levels. Hay unloaded at the first-floor level can be pitched down to feeding stalls below.

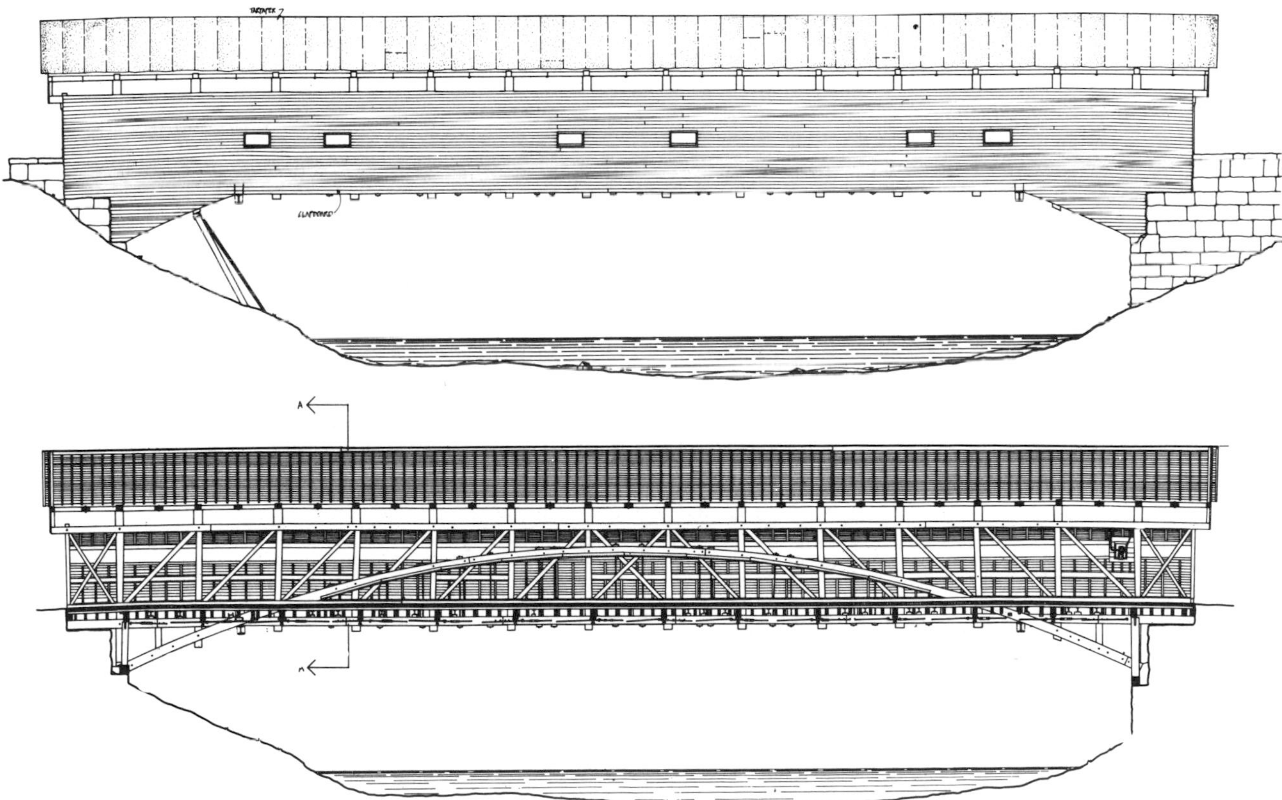

375, 376 Barrackville covered bridge. Barrackville, West Virginia. 1853. Burr arch truss bridge. An example of a type of wooden bridge patented in 1817, it combines the structural properties of the arch and the truss.

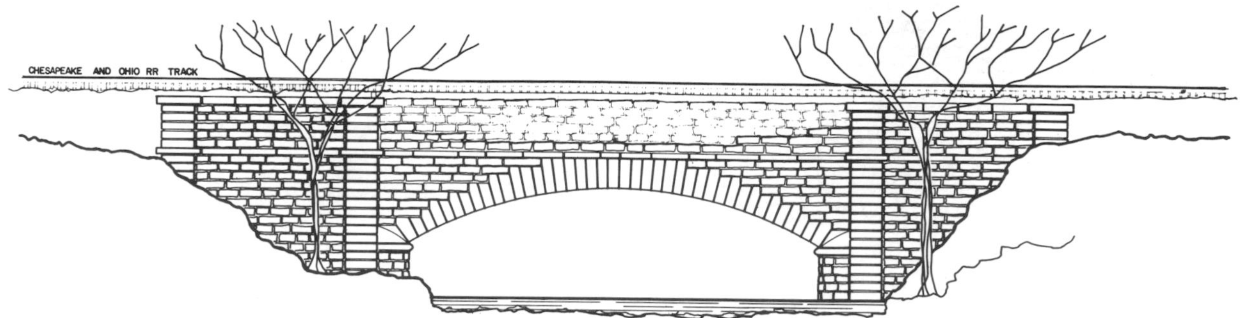

377 Lickinghole Creek Aqueduct, James River and Kanawha Canal. Goochland County, Virginia. C.1827. A single-span stone arch built to carry canal boats across a creek. A railroad line was subsequently installed.

378 Skew-arch bridge, Allegheny Portage Railroad. Johnstown vicinity, Pennsylvania. 1831–1834. Part of a thirty-seven mile portage railroad which carried canal boats across Allegheny Mountain by means of inclined planes, tow ropes, and steam engines.

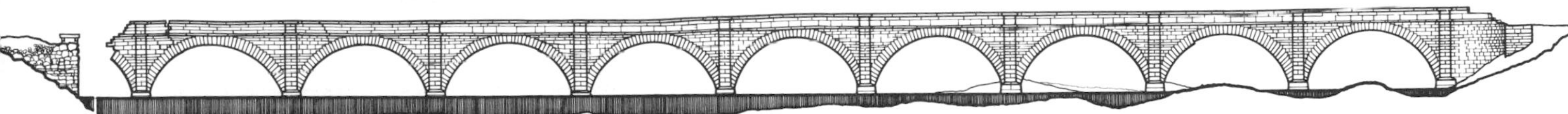

379 Schoharie Creek Aqueduct, Erie Canal. Fort Hunter, New York. 1839–1841. A 630-foot aqueduct carrying the Erie Canal over Schoharie Creek. Originally consisted of a towpath supported by stone arches and a wooden canal trunk carried on stone piers.

Schoharie Creek Aqueduct, Erie Canal, Fort Hunter, New York: 1839–1841.

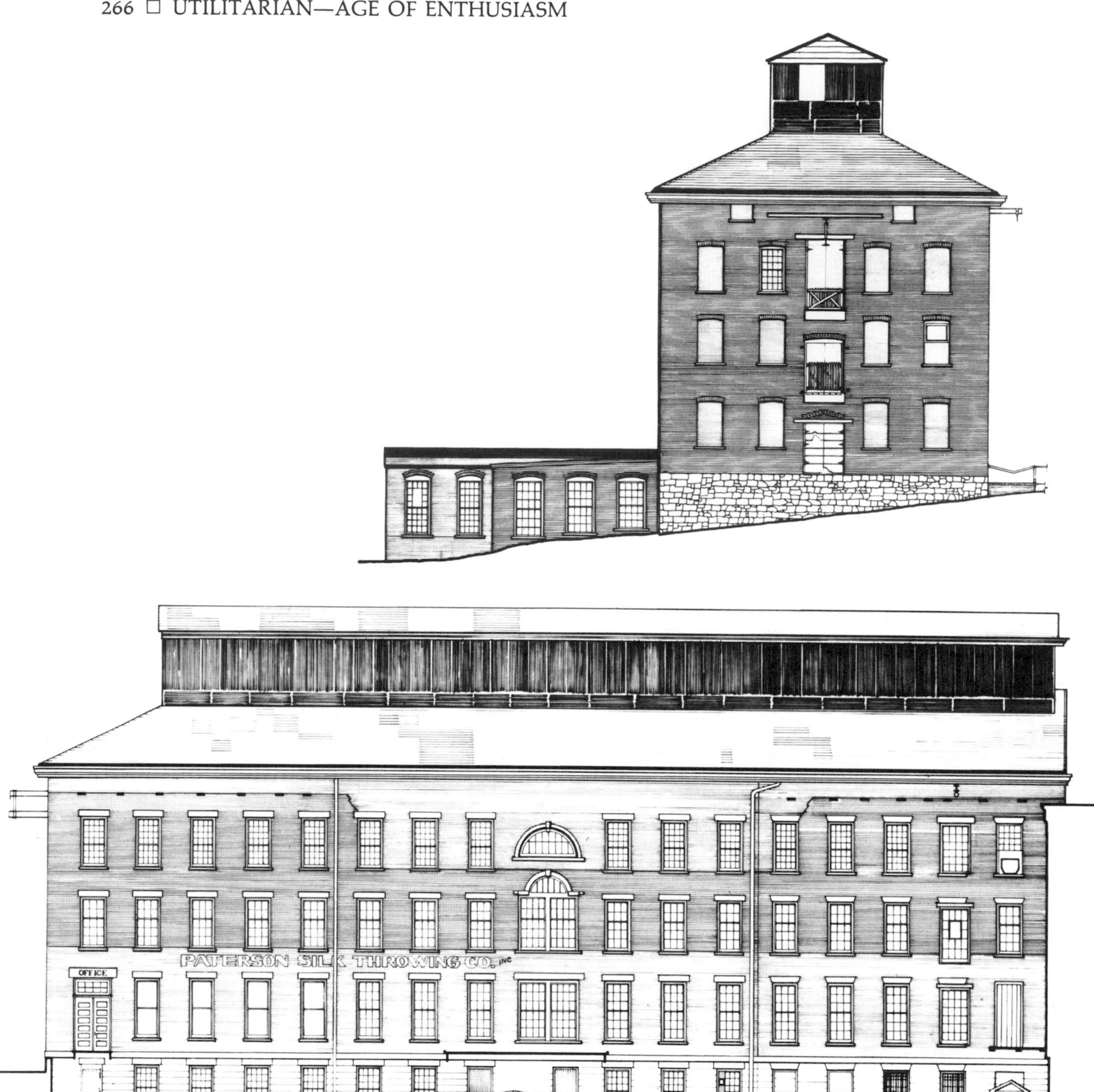

380, 381 Phoenix Mill. Paterson, New Jersey. Five bays at right; c.1813; remainder completed. c.1827. Built as a cotton mill, and converted to silk processing by 1870, this four-story stone mill has a high clerestory and tall windows. The original section was built with a wooden end wall which facilitated the 1827 expansion.

Phoenix Mill, Paterson, New Jersey; c. 1813–c. 1827 (see 381).

Newport Steam factory, Newport, Rhode Island; 1831 (see 382).

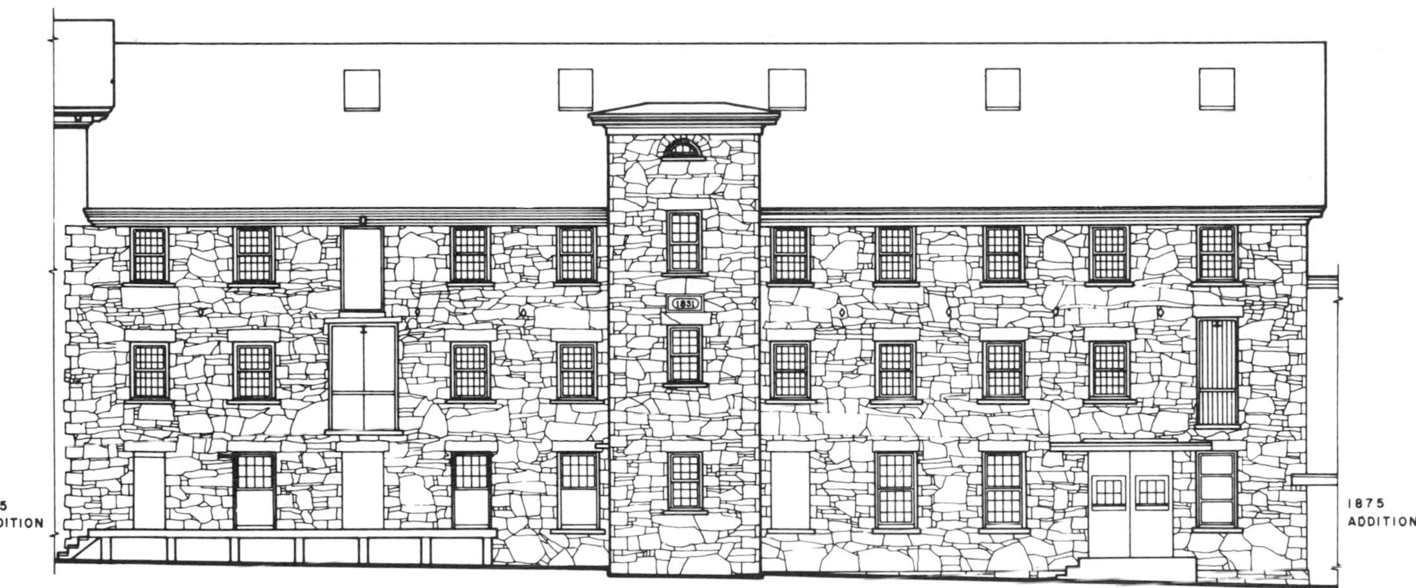

382 Newport Steam Factory, Newport, Rhode Island. 1831. Constructed of heavy timbers and granite masonry. The stair tower originally carried a square wooden belfry. Used until 1851 for cotton manufacture.

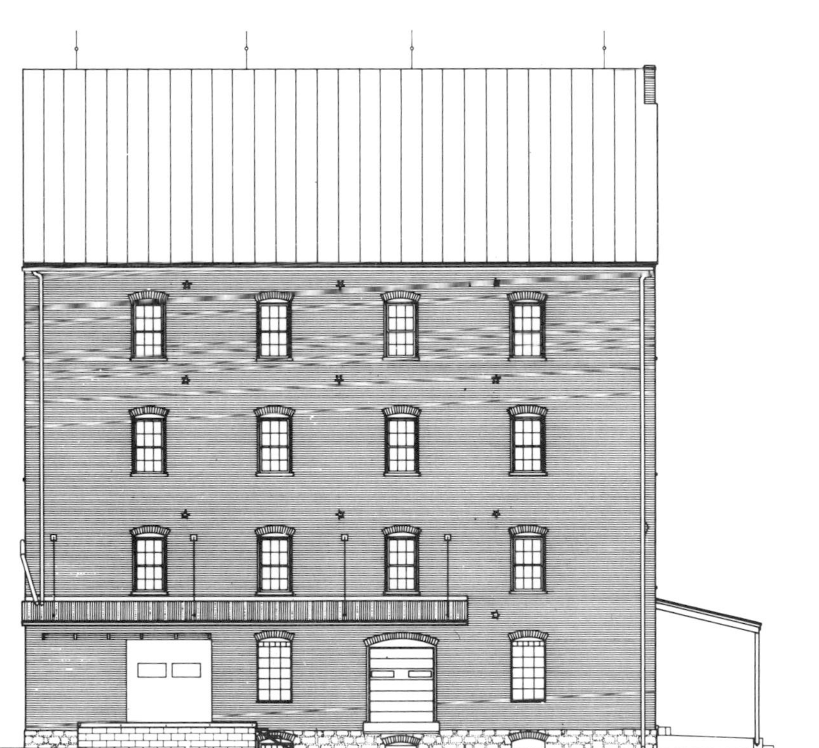

383 Hermann Star Mills. Hermann, Missouri. 1867. A typical steam-powered gristmill. The basement was used for wheat scouring and polishing, the next three stories for milling and flour packing, the attic for dust collection. The concrete loading platform with corrugated metal roof and the garage door are recent additions.

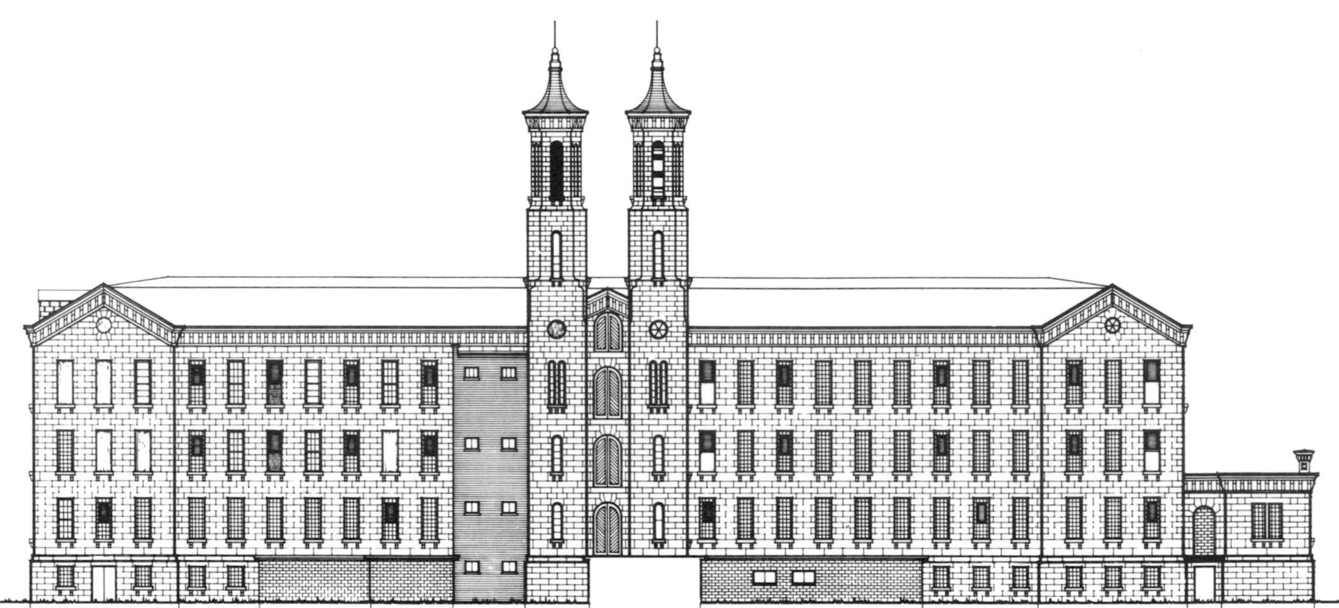

384 Cannelton Cotton Mills. Cannelton, Indiana. 1849–1851. Located in the towers are stairways, built extra-wide as a safety feature. Arched doorways give loading access. Coal was used to manufacture steam power; a massive chimney stands nearby. Of textured sandstone ashlar, the mill has particularly fine architectural details.

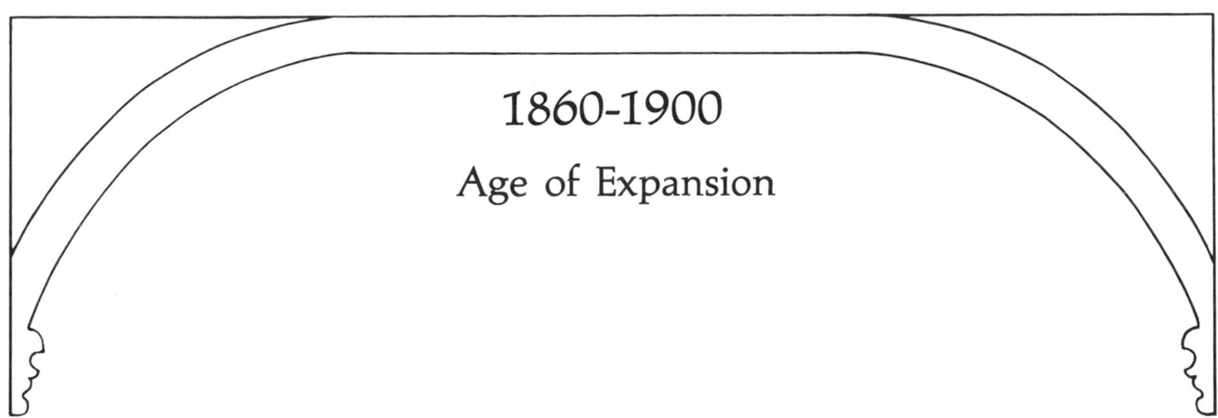

Materials

The industrialized production techniques of the second half of the nineteenth century produced building materials of unprecedented quantity, quality, and variety.

For house frames, timber was, as it had always been, the first material at hand. Wooden embellishments, shaped by band saw or jigsaw, could be imaginative, individualistic, even eccentric. And when the contemporary aesthetic asked for a substitute to the naked white that had covered wooden buildings for several generations, technology answered with a vastly wider range of paint hues—romantic earth tones such a gray, rust, and brown, and modish blue, lavender, yellow, and pink tints.

In masonry construction, modern techniques for quarrying, finishing, and transporting stone improved both its appearance and its availability; industrialized methods of producing pressed brick and cast terra-cotta improved its performance; better ways of making hydraulic mortar enhanced its permanence. Structural concrete slowly gained in popularity; by the 1880s and 1890s, it achieved a significant role in foundations, in footings, and especially in the construction of dams for irrigation, industry, and urban water supply.

The greatest strides during this period were in the fabrication of metal building components. In the third quarter of the nineteenth century, cast iron came into its own, effective as interior framing and attractive in such virtuoso displays as complete iron building fronts, in elaborate roof cresting, and in ornate rails and fences.

In the last quarter of the century, iron gave way to steel, which, by virtue of improved refining techniques, was now available at reasonable cost for tools, wire rope, rails, and structural members.

Construction Technology

The voracious demand for new construction in post–Civil War America was satisfied only by the industrialization of building itself. Steam power was applied to quarry, cut, and polish stone, to hoist loads, to hammer, to excavate, and to drill. Hydraulic lifts, cranes, and elevators performed extraordinary construction feats. Also remarkable were the advances in metal fabrication that permitted mass production of high-quality metal machines and tools.

The science of designing and fabricating iron and steel as construction components further transformed the building art. By the 1860s, foundry-made bridge and building elements included cast-iron columns, spandrels, and lintels and wrought-iron trusses, beams, and girders.

As steel succeeded iron in the 1880s and 1890s, speed, strength, economy, durability, and fire resistance were achieved by the development of "skeleton" construction, a method of steel framing that eliminated timber completely and reduced masonry to little more than an exterior cladding.

While traditional building methods long persisted in smaller urban centers, the braced and riveted steel frame was enthusiastically employed and extravagantly praised in rapidly expanding metropolises such as Chicago and New York. Concurrent advances that made tall buildings

385 Right: Kotthoff-Weeks Barn. Gasconade vicinity, Missouri. 1860–1864. Upper Bavarian-type barn construction, the first level built of stone, the upper of wood frame with weatherboarding. Sliding doors have replaced the original double-panel hinged doors, and a corrugated metal roof covers the original wood shingles. The first level contains a threshing floor, horse and cattle stalls, and a storage room; the second level, a granary and space for hay storage; above, a hayloft.

comfortable, convenient, and efficient for American businessmen included the high-speed elevator, electric lighting, and advanced heating and plumbing systems.

As a new century was in sight, the steel skyscraper rose as tall as thirty stories, and the scientifically designed steel bridge spanned 1,500 feet or more. In the community of nations, America's power was plain to see.

Agriculture

In the years after the Civil War, specialization characterized farm as well as factory production. In the East and in the old West, farm size increased with the use of mechanical farm equipment.

Less fertile or less easily farmed lands were abandoned, leaving the stone walls that marked field divisions to remain amid second-growth forest. When the self-sufficient farmer, bowing to competitive pressures, specialized his production —in dairying in New York or Wisconsin, sheep-raising in Vermont, or corn and hog production in Illinois, for example—the configuration of agricultural outbuildings reflected this development.

The new and larger scale of operation was even more dramatic in the West. In Texas, Wyoming, and Montana, cattle roamed the range; here, far-distant roads marked property divisions. In Nebraska, Dakota, and California, huge barbed-wire-fenced agricultural spreads could be five or ten times the size of old-time farms. In the 1870s or 1880s, "bonanza farms" purchased from distressed railroad companies for as little as fifty cents an acre, were many thousands of acres in size.

Commercial centers as well as dwelling places, the western farmsteads' special features were ample kitchen areas, wings for extra bedrooms, spreading dormitories for farm crews. Fewer and larger outbuildings were adapted to mechanized agricultural practices—among them, the two-story barn with mechanical hay loader, the silo for grain storage, and the dairy barn designed for stall feeding.

Largeness of scale similarly characterized the grain elevators and packing plants at the urban railheads where grain was stored and milled and made into bread, and cattle were herded, slaughtered, and processed.

In the Spanish Southwest, old estates crumbled slowly, while in the South the change from large scale to small scale was precipitous. Generally lacking the capital for mechanization, the agricultural economy remained backward. Once-grand plantations were divided among sharecroppers; great manor houses crumbled and frame shacks sprang up beside them.

Transportation

Even as the battle for the Union raged, Congress authorized rail construction and land grants that would ultimately both spur and symbolize the nation's drive to command the continent. Striking out from the finely drawn eastern rail network were four coast-to-coast rail lines that

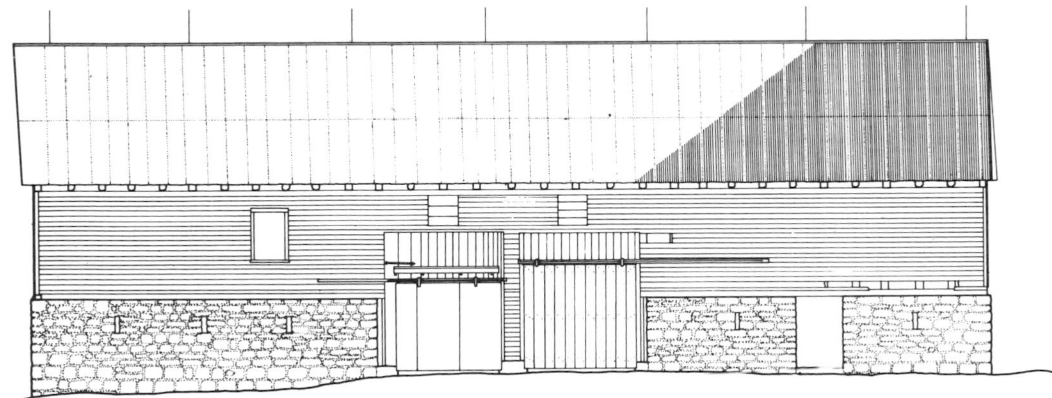

boldly tied the Atlantic to the Pacific. Their completion in the mid-1880s marked the landscape with a vastly larger scale.

By 1860, tracks reached Wisconsin, Iowa, Missouri, Arkansas, and Texas. Railroad towns grew as fast as rails stretched. Platted by speculator or entrepreneur, they reflected the transcendent importance of the rail line: the gridiron town plan deferred to the track's demands; the depot captured center stage; telegraph pole, signal station, tunnel, bridge, watchtower, and freight station stood as trackside sentries.

Served by rail, the farmer on remote prairies achieved a purchase power and an independence unknown to the European peasant. "There is a rush of trade to the small towns," a French journalist remarked. "A few stores spring up close to the station, between the track and the hotel; a wide road is marked out on the prairie, is dignified with the name of Main Street, and the United States is reckoned one city more."

The forested regions of Michigan, Minnesota, Wisconsin, West Virginia, the Gulf states, and the Pacific Northwest supplied prefabricated wooden elements that built the farmhouse on prairie and plain. As rail terminals, even in the far-flung West, great cities grew—Chicago, Wichita, Denver, Salt Lake City, Omaha, and San Francisco. Mineral strikes drew the rail network into rugged mountains and empty deserts.

The railroad encouraged the development of new cities in the West, and after the 1880s, together with the electric streetcar, it also stimulated expansion and suburban development around older cities. Tracks carried gold and silver to bank vaults and supplied eastern and midwestern factories with iron from Michigan's Upper Peninsula, with coal from Appalachia and southern Colorado, with oil from Ohio and Pennsylvania. Tracks transported the worker from tenement to factory, the housewife from row house to drygoods store, the clerk from cottage to ever-taller office building. The telegraph, the telephone, and mass-circulation newspapers also fostered dense urban growth.

By the time the century was over, the city or town, not the farm, was home to most Americans.

Industry

With the expansion of rail transportation, industrialization rapidly intensified. Spurred by wartime demands, the nation shifted from animal or water power to steam to drive the machines that fabricated ever-larger quantities of cotton and wool textiles, shoes and boots, clay products, and transportation equipment.

By the 1870s, city dwellers were large-scale consumers. Factory-made furniture, for example, was so cheap that even families of modest means could afford its purchase.

In the next decade, the proliferation of three-, four-, and five-story red-brick factory buildings measured the nation's progress. Western farmers, greater in numbers and prosperity, demonstrated a seemingly insatiable demand for eastern goods, while mechanized western farms supplied the grain and meat to feed the swelling populations of eastern cities.

Massive factory complexes with tall chimneys clustered along rail lines and river fronts. An early by-product of industrial capitalism was the single-industry town, but the imprint of industrialization was also marked on transport and market centers. Thus, Yonkers grew as a leader in wool-carpet production, Manchester in metal wire, Troy in locomotives, Holyoke in paper products—one city in cotton goods, another in machine tools and machinery.

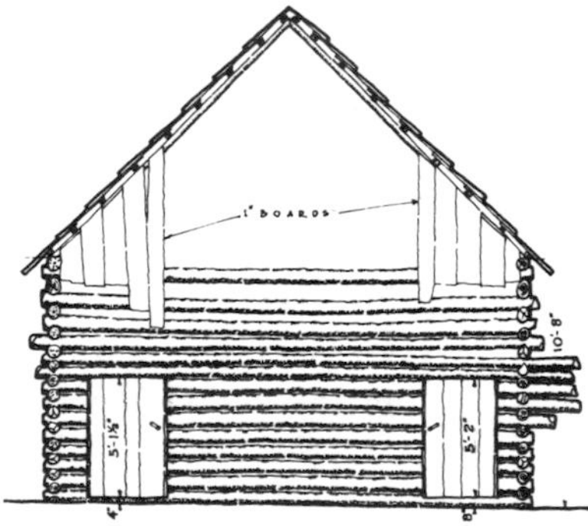

386, 387 Clugston Barn. Colville vicinity, Washington. 1860. Built in a wilderness area, of tamarack logs, sapling rafters, and shingle roof.

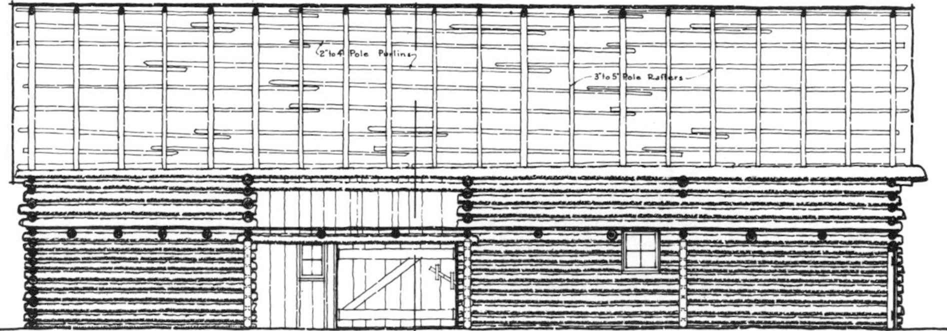

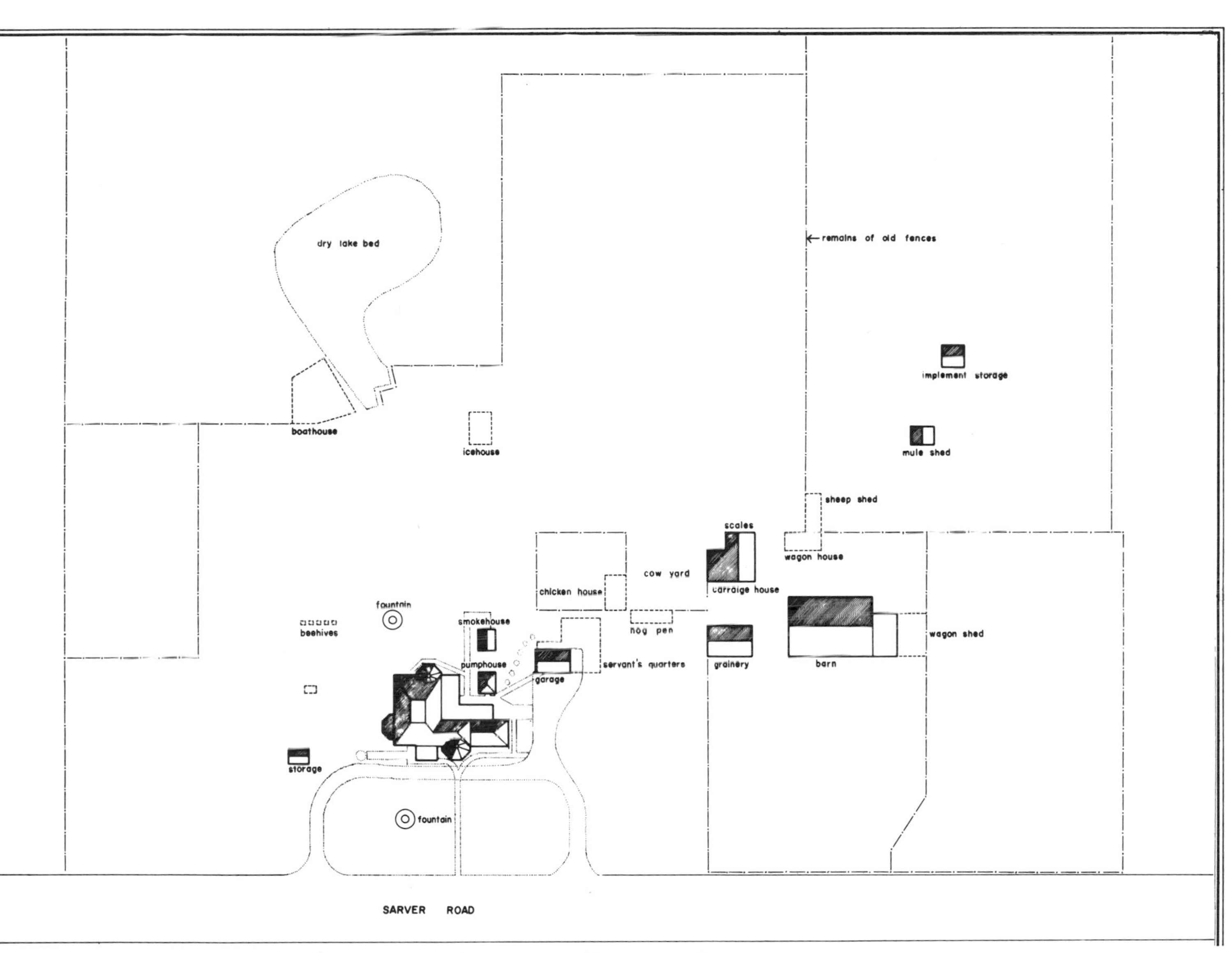

388 Isaac Kinsey Farm. Milton vicinity, Indiana. 1871 and later; part of a prosperous six-hundred-acre farm whose owner was known for his efforts in scientific farming.

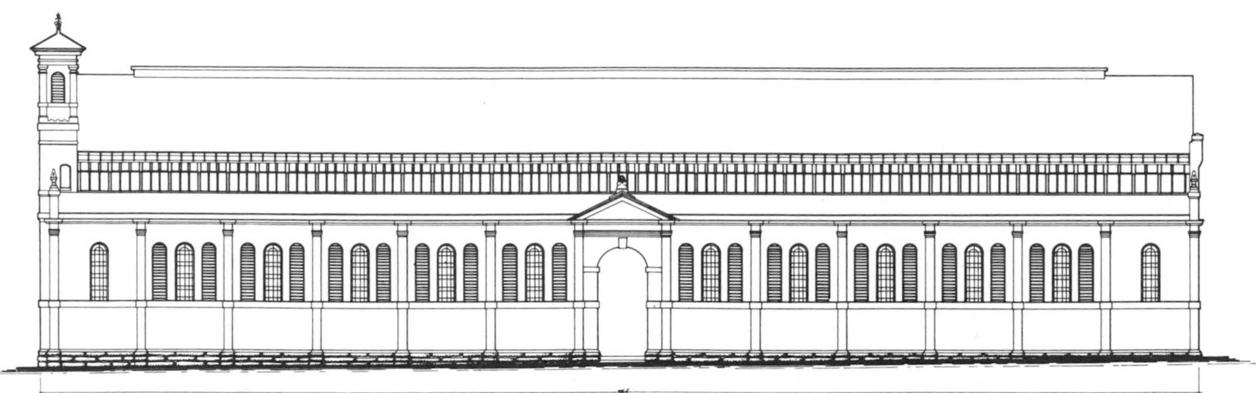

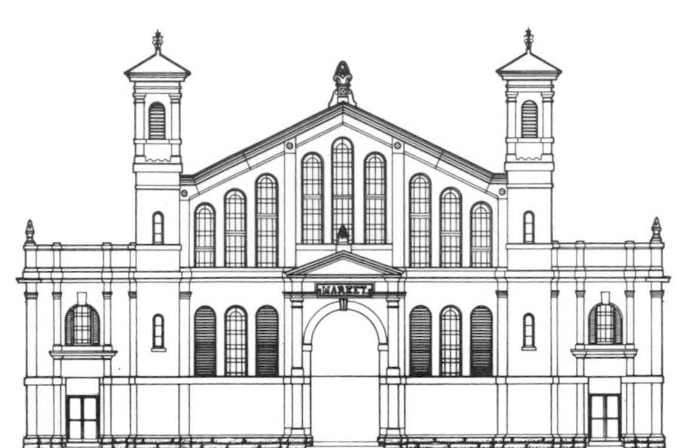

389, 390, 391 Indianapolis City Market. Indianapolis, Indiana. 1886. The visual importance of this market house expresses its significance as the focus of a rich agricultural region. Exterior walls are brick, interior spaces are spanned by lightweight iron trusses supported by cast-iron columns. The detail shows the elaboration that iron permitted without giving up its strength.

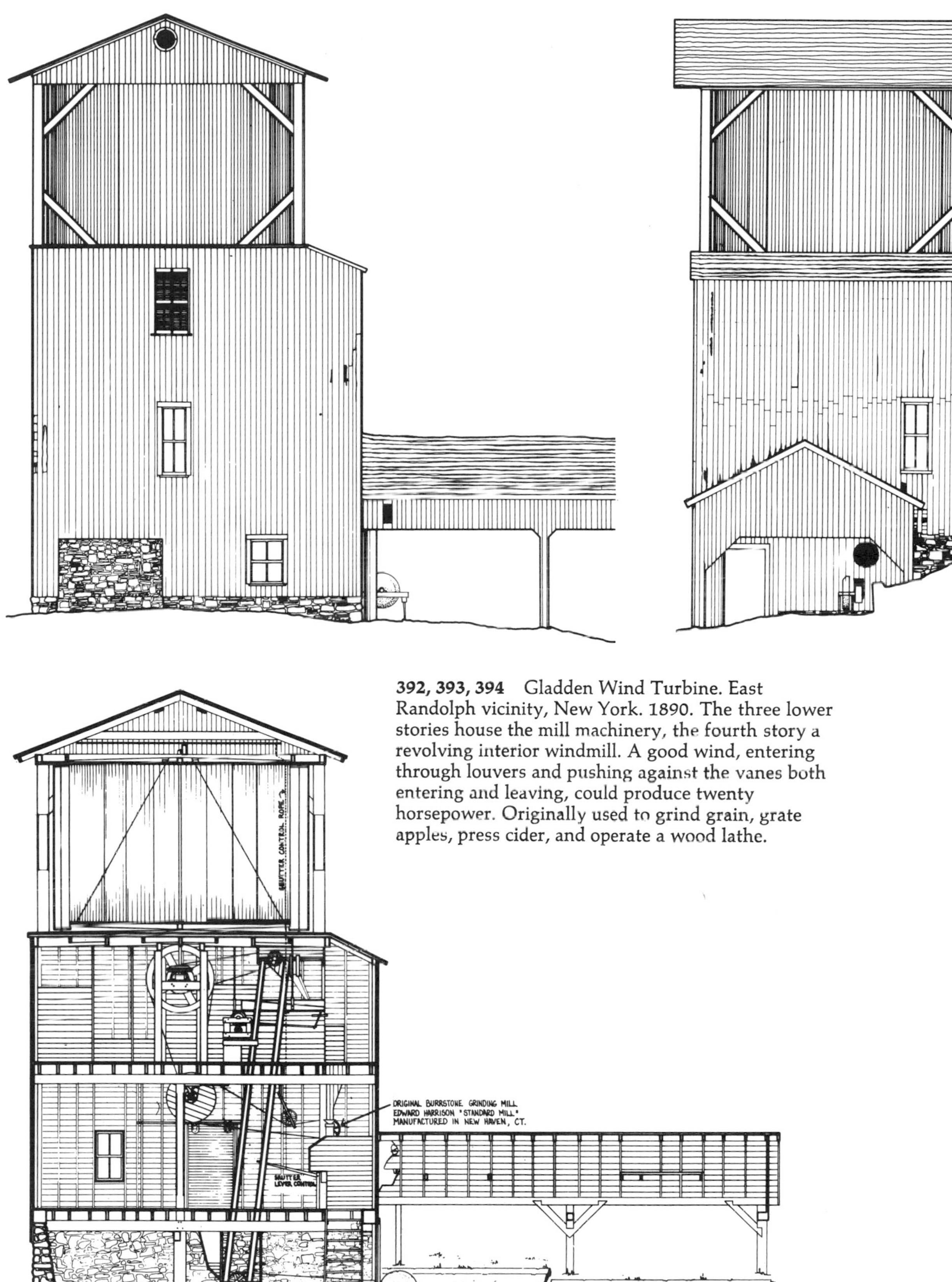

392, 393, 394 Gladden Wind Turbine. East Randolph vicinity, New York. 1890. The three lower stories house the mill machinery, the fourth story a revolving interior windmill. A good wind, entering through louvers and pushing against the vanes both entering and leaving, could produce twenty horsepower. Originally used to grind grain, grate apples, press cider, and operate a wood lathe.

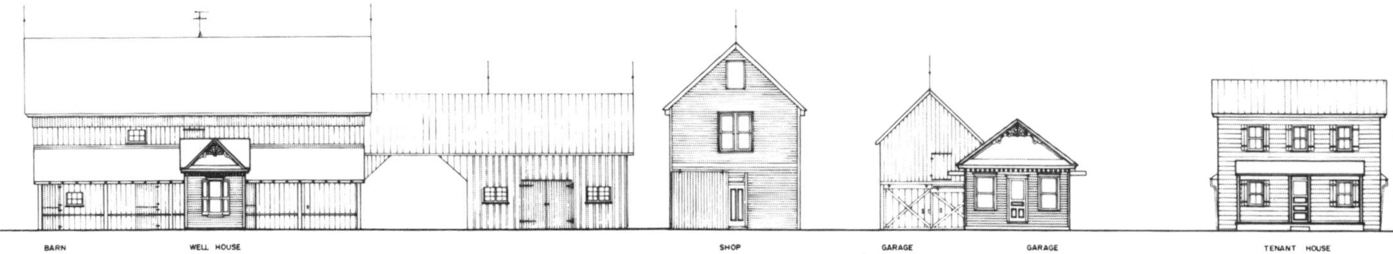

395 John Lindale Farm. Magnolia, Delaware. 1905. A peach-farm complex, reflecting the agricultural specialization and commercialization that took place during this period.

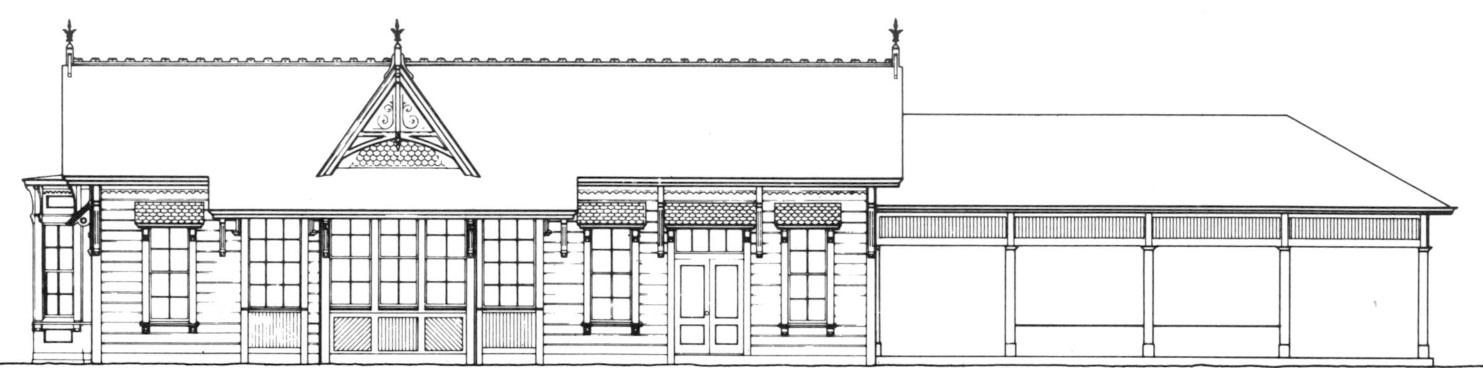

396 San Francisco and San Jose Railroad Station. Menlo Park, California. C.1890 renovation of 1867 structure. A picturesque railroad station typical of the post–Civil War period of suburban expansion, with characteristic West Coast fidelity to and enthusiasm for Stick Style ornament almost a generation after the vogue had had its heyday in the East.

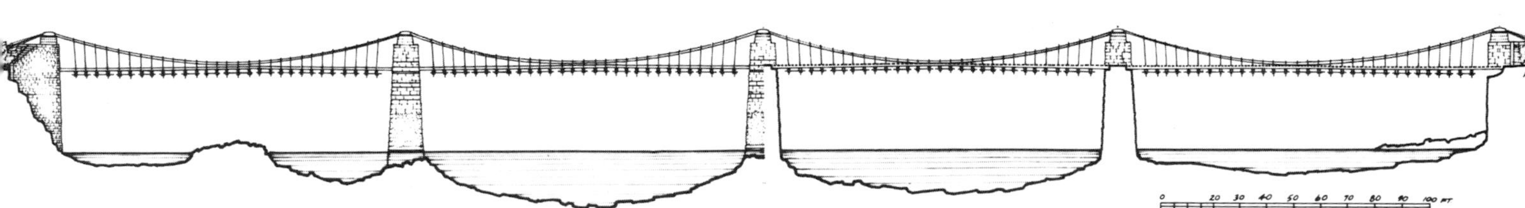

397 Delaware Aqueduct, Delaware and Hudson Canal. Highland Township, New York. 1847–1848, suspension bridge to carry the Delaware Canal; 1898, conversion to highway toll bridge. Designed by John A. Roebling, a pioneer in suspension-bridge design, who demonstrated the value of the suspension system for supporting heavy loads and its superiority over conventional masonry-arch or timber-truss bridges.

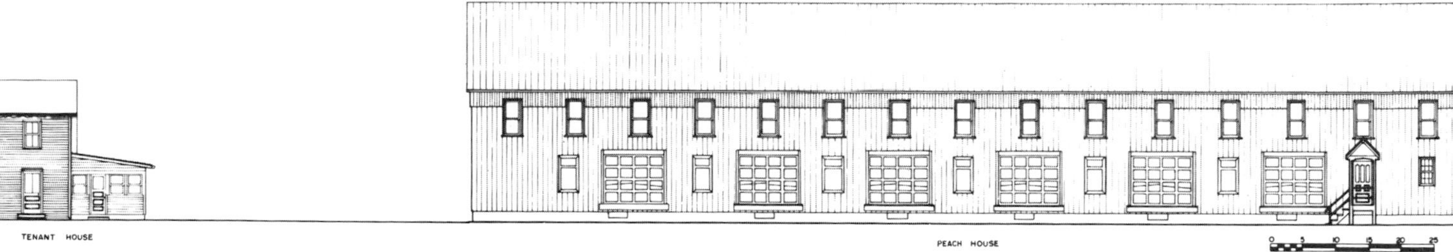

398 Fitch Depot and Office. Kingston, New York. 1870. An unusually fine example of the trackside depot, a once-thriving building type. It was constructed of bluestone, which was also the firm's product.

B&O station, Point O' Rocks, Maryland; 1875 (see 399, 400).

ORIGINAL STATION

399, 400 B&O station. Point O' Rocks, Maryland. 1875. A Victorian Gothic station, built as an addition to an 1860s station at the junction of the Baltimore & Ohio main line and the Washington branch.

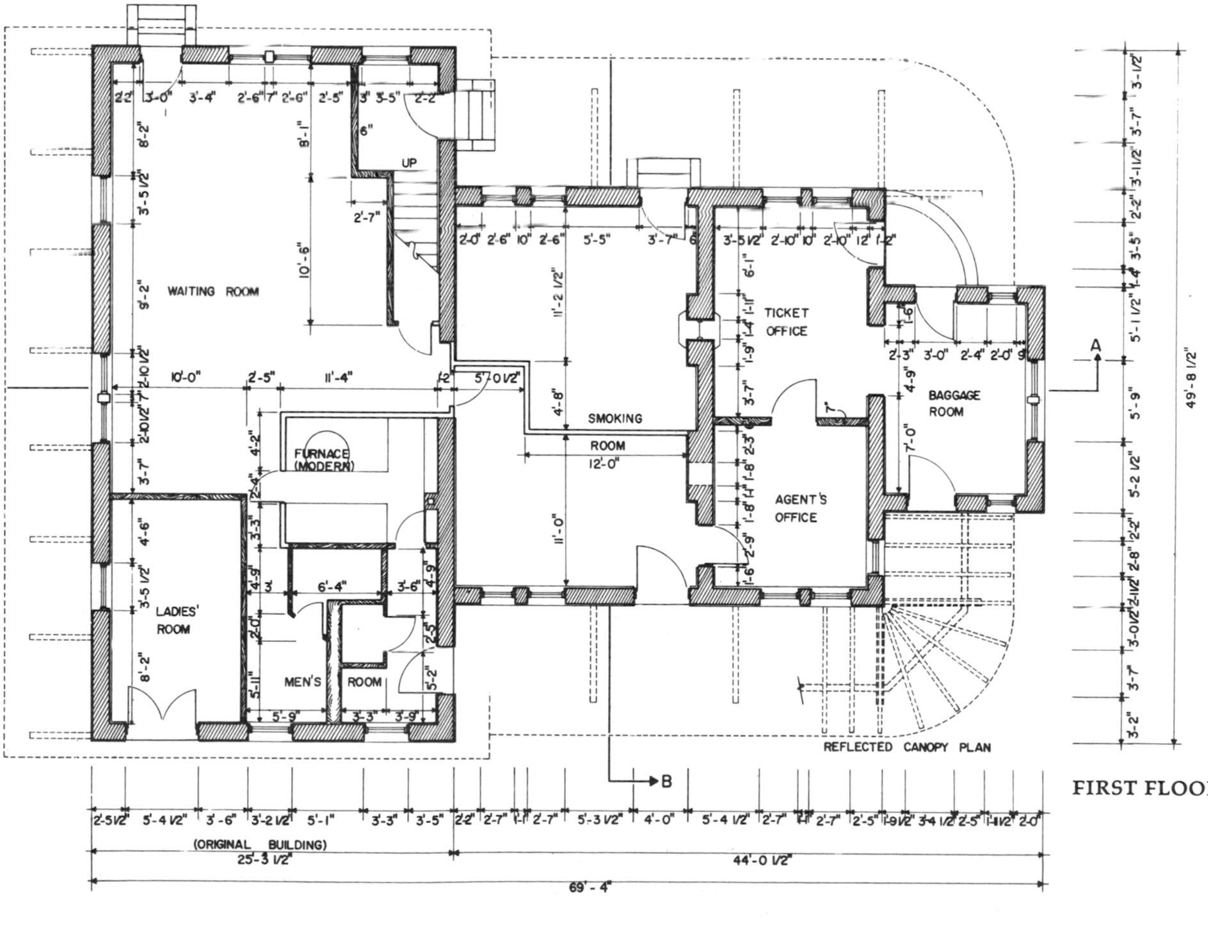

WAITING ROOM

UP

SMOKING ROOM

TICKET OFFICE

AGENT'S OFFICE

BAGGAGE ROOM

FURNACE (MODERN)

LADIES' ROOM

MEN'S ROOM

REFLECTED CANOPY PLAN

(ORIGINAL BUILDING)

25'-3 1/2"

44'-0 1/2"

69'-4"

49'-8 1/2"

FIRST FLOOR PLAN

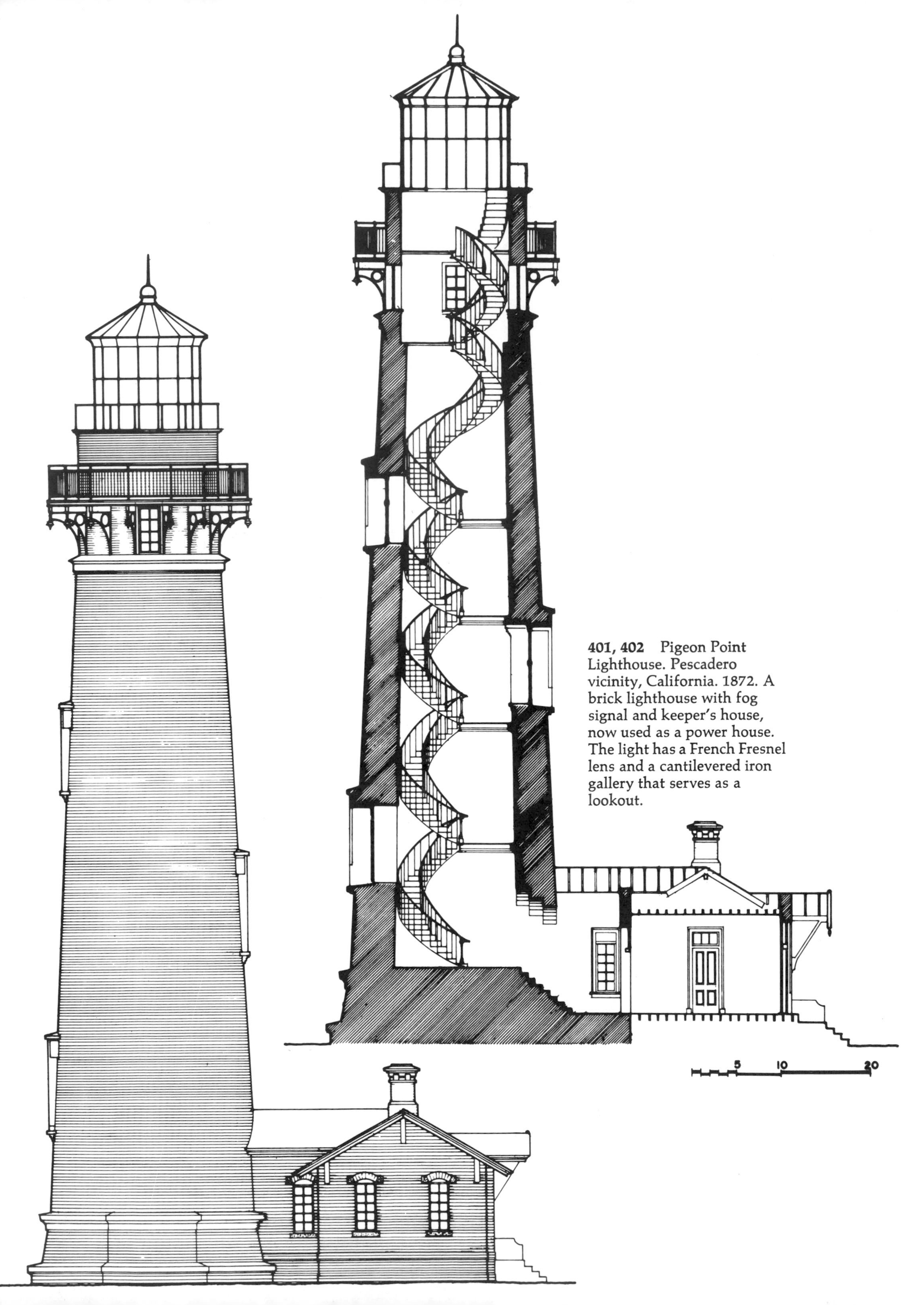

401, 402 Pigeon Point Lighthouse. Pescadero vicinity, California. 1872. A brick lighthouse with fog signal and keeper's house, now used as a power house. The light has a French Fresnel lens and a cantilevered iron gallery that serves as a lookout.

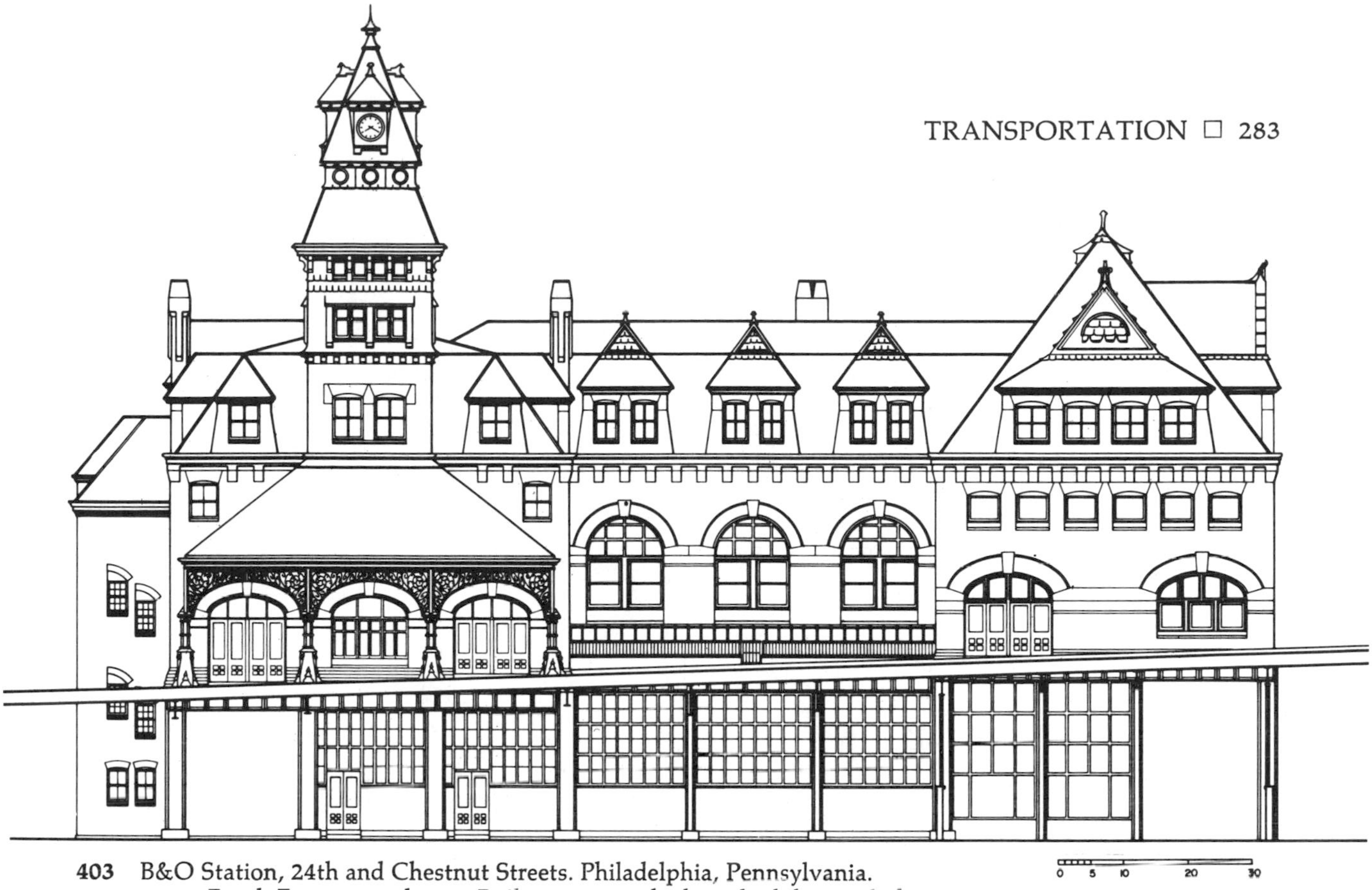

403 B&O Station, 24th and Chestnut Streets. Philadelphia, Pennsylvania. 1886–1888; Frank Furness, architect. Built at a time which exalted the symbolic significance of the station as a gateway to the city. It is a two-level design which separates the flow of arriving and departing passengers, with pedestrians entering the station through the portal beneath the clock tower and then descending to the tracks below. (Demolished, 1963.)

404 Railroad Station. Williamstown, Massachusetts. 1898. Representative of a type built during the peak years of rail modernization, electrification, and consolidation. Characteristic are the double-pitched roof and its canopy extensions.

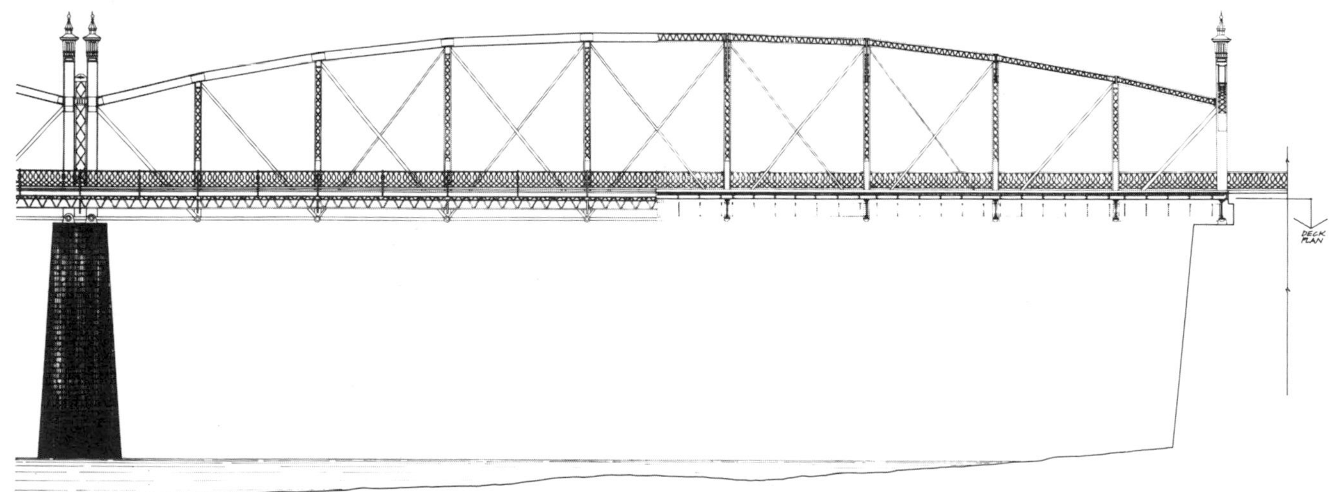

405 Bridgeport Bridge. Wheeling, West Virginia. 1893–1894. One section of a three-span steel truss bridge supported on two stone abutments and two piers. Sold by catalogue, it was typical of hundreds of railroad and highway bridges.

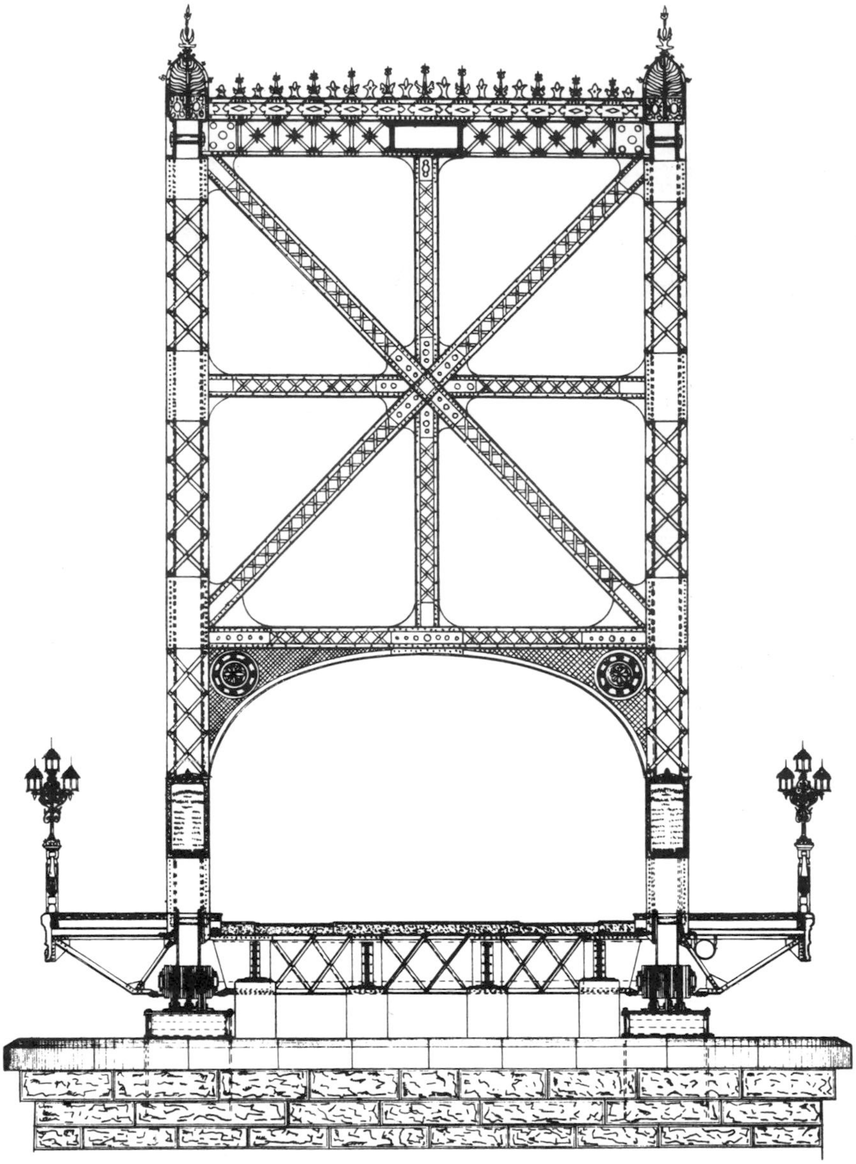

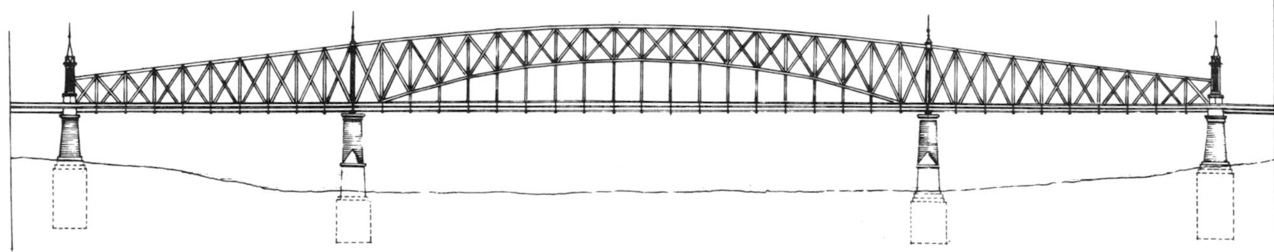

406, 407 South 22nd Street Bridge, at Brady Street. Pittsburgh, Pennsylvania. 1896. Steel construction on granite, an innovative design utilizing a truss-stiffened arch above the roadway.

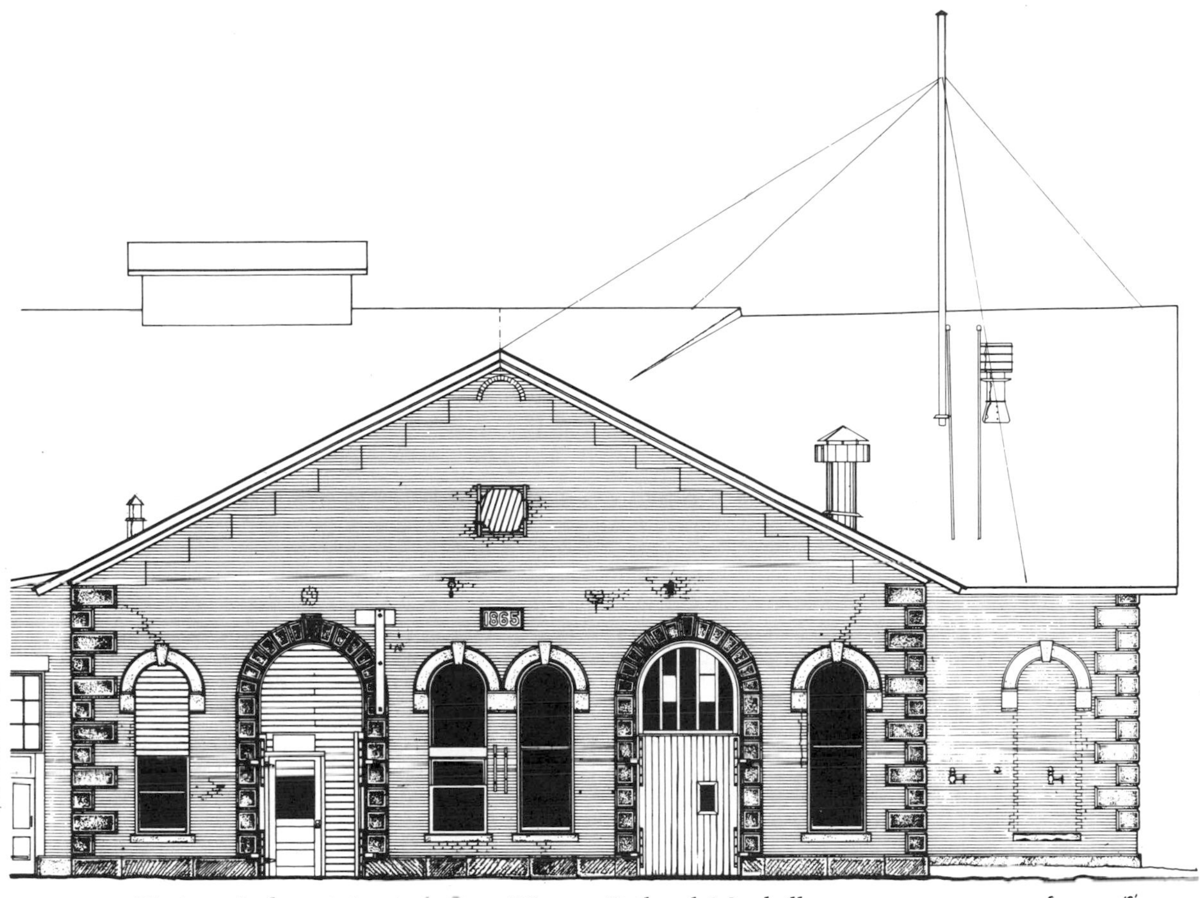

408 Blacksmith shop, Atlantic & Great Western Railroad. Meadville, Pennsylvania. 1865. Also included in this important repair complex are a machine and erecting shop and storehouse.

409 Appomattox Iron Works. Petersburg, Virginia. C.1810–1910, with alterations to serve an expanding ironworks operation, representing a series of pragmatic responses to increased demands for space. Left to right: 1880–1910, steel and pipe storage; c.1870s shopfront and facade alteration, office, storage, living space above; c.1825 machine shop, offices, living quarters.

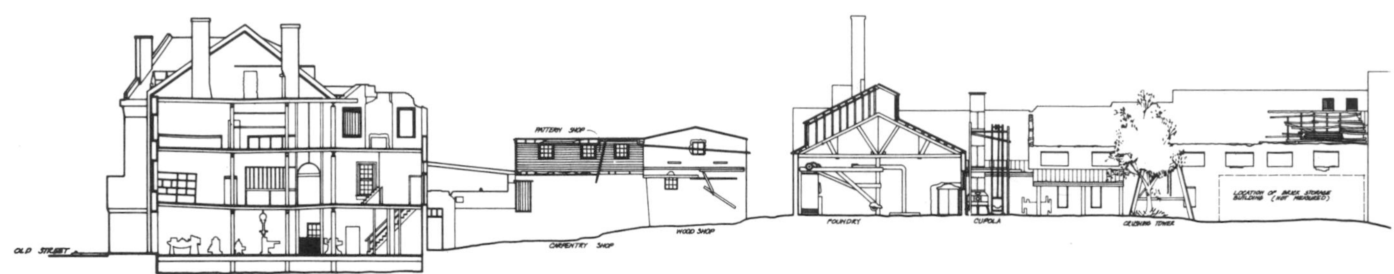

410 Appomattox Iron Works (section of drawing on preceding page).

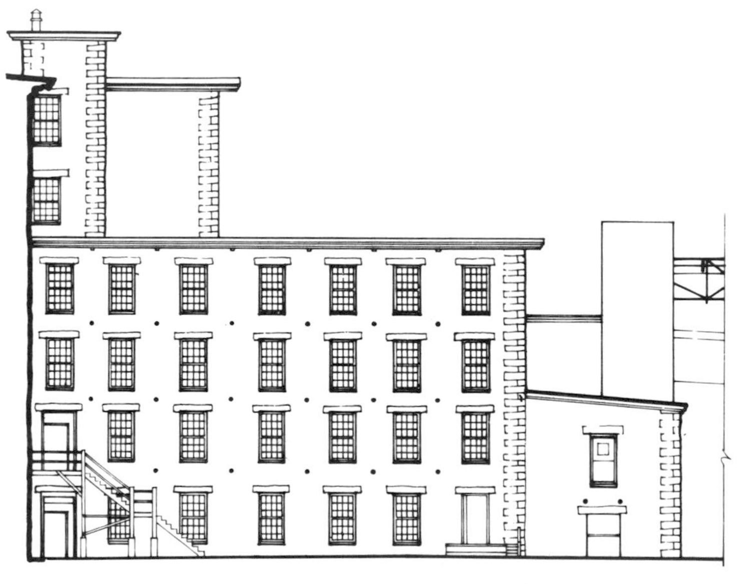

411, 412 Union Mills. Fall River, Massachusetts. 1859. A very large cotton mill for its time including picker house, waste house, engine house, mill. Exterior walls of locally quarried granite, with interior plank floors and iron column supports.

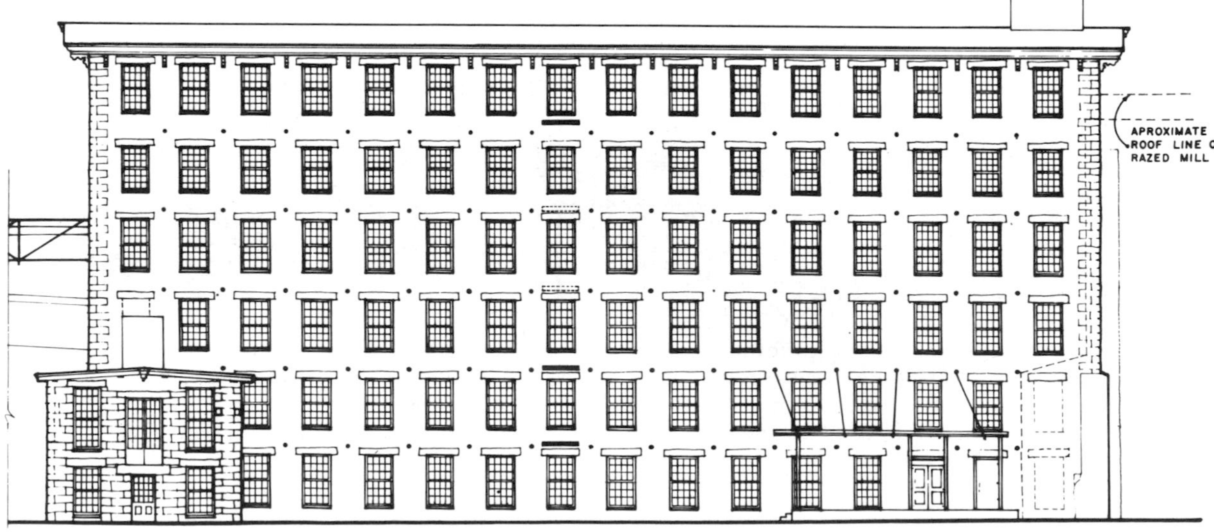

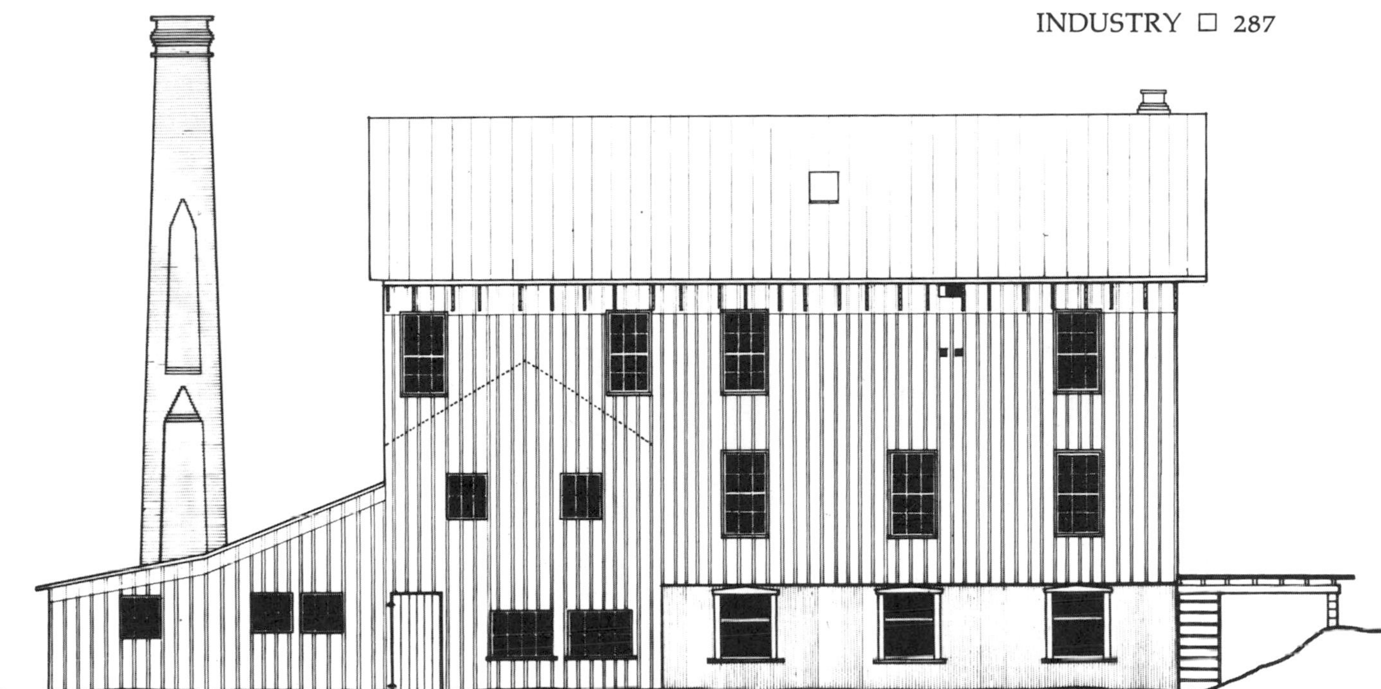

413 Easton Roller Mills. Easton, West Virginia. 1870; steam conversion, 1894. The installation of steam-powered roller mills was a major technological advance that accompanied the late-nineteenth-century agricultural revolution. Crushing the wheat kernels in several stages doubled the yield of high-grade flour and lowered its cost to the consumer.

Easton Roller Mills, Easton, West Virginia; 1870.

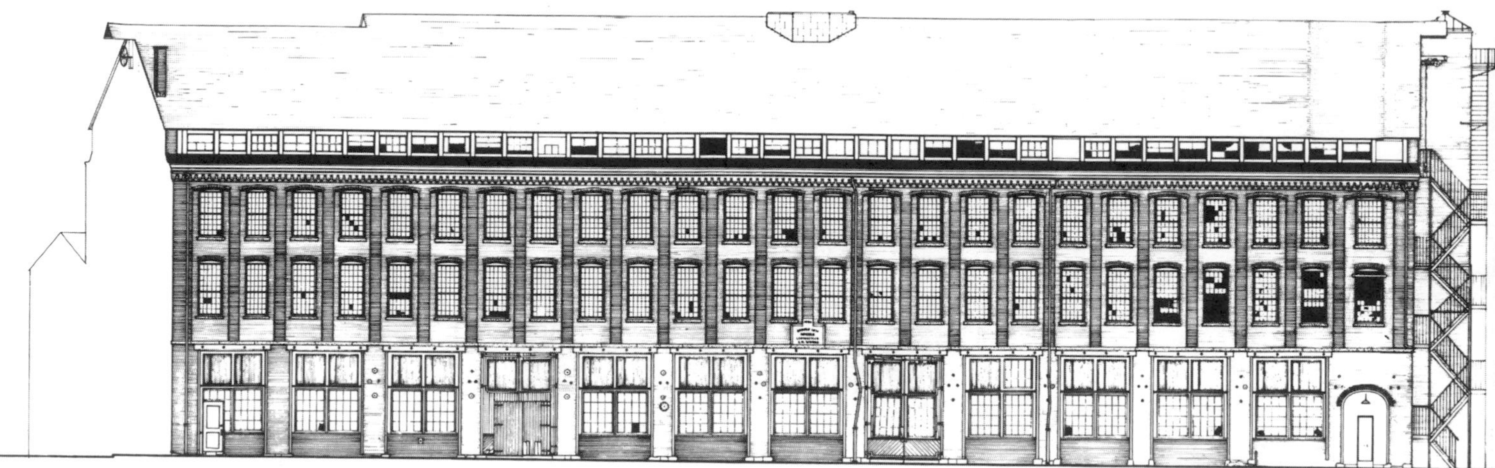

414 Rogers Erecting Shop, Rogers Locomotive Works. Paterson, New Jersey. 1871.
Upper stories served for the manufacture of locomotive components, the ground story for assembly.

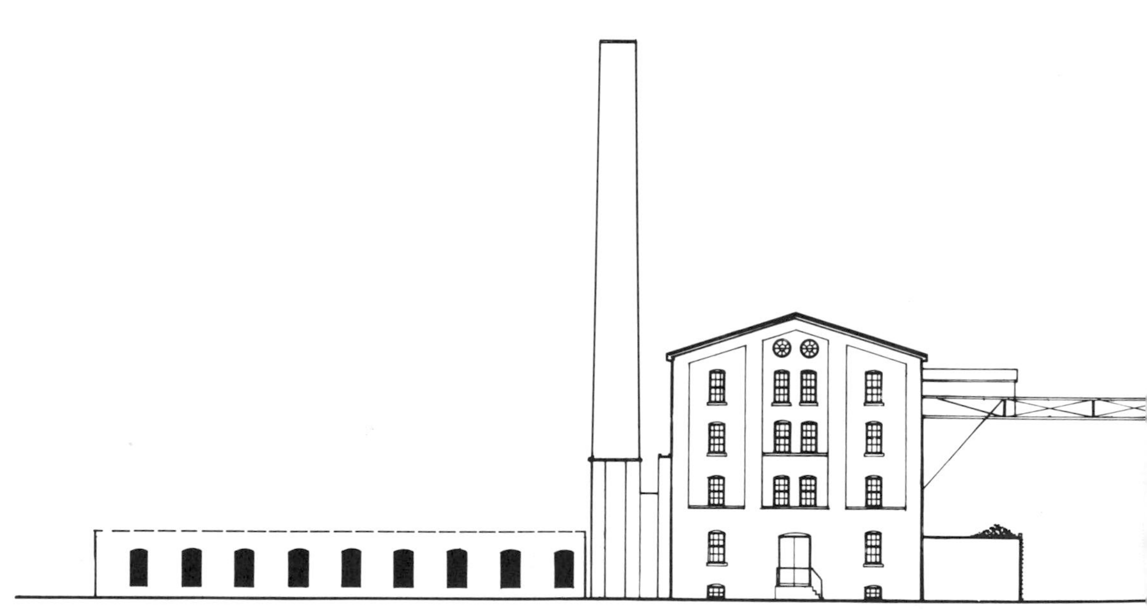

416 Cerealine Manufacturing Company, Mill A. Columbus, Indiana. C.1880. A typical roller mill, where experiments in the production process resulted in the development of a commercial packaged breakfast cereal.

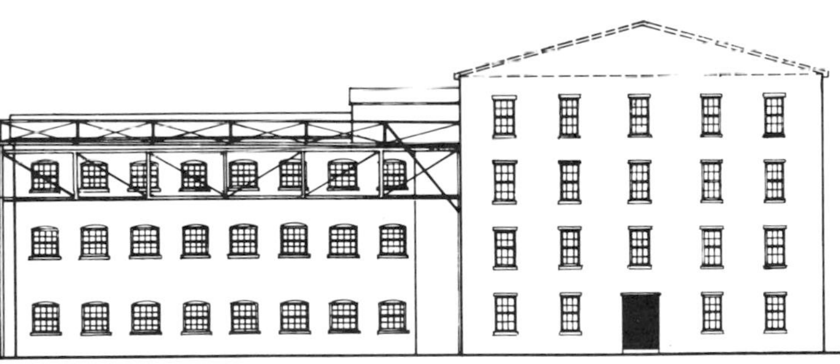

415 Munk and Roberts Furniture Company. Connersville, Indiana. Building at left, 1878; right, 1883. Factory space which has proved its adaptability. Constructed for the manufacture of furniture; c.1903, converted to buggy production; 1916, switched to the production of automobile tops.

417 Pillsbury "A" Mill. Minneapolis, Minnesota. 1880–1881. Sited on the St. Anthony Falls of the Mississippi, when built this water-powered mill was the world's largest.

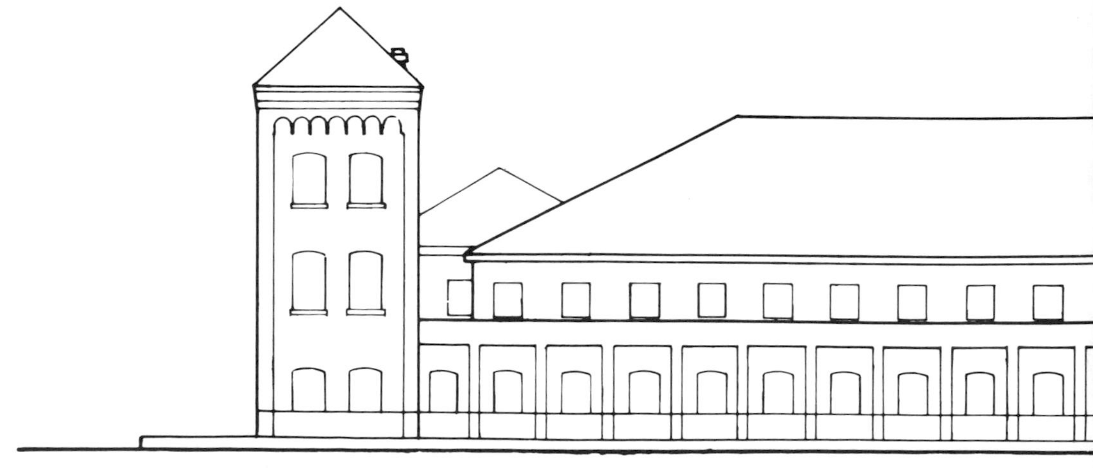

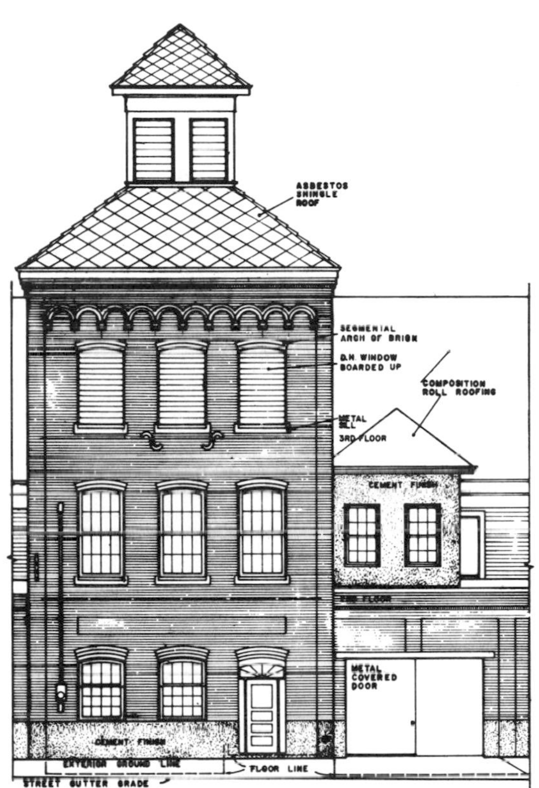

418, 419 Galveston Bagging and Cordage Factory. Galveston, Texas. 1888. A factory for the production of woven jute bagging, important for baling the Texas cotton crop. The extended floor plan permitted all cording, spinning, and weaving to be done under the supervision of a single foreman. Water tanks for the sprinkler system are located in the towers.

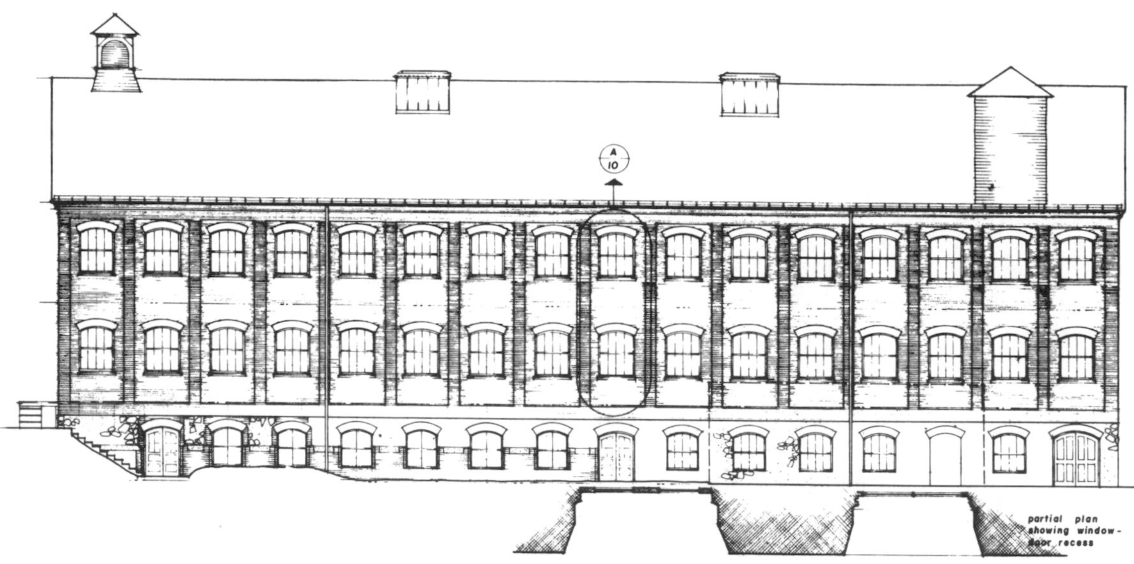

420 Thomas Kay Woolen Mill. Salem, Oregon. 1896. With dying and picking operations located in separate outbuildings, the production process resembled the English system, rather than the American process in which all activities were carried out under the same roof. The mill was water-powered, with wood, and after 1904, oil, used as auxiliary fuel.

421 Seneca Glass Company. Morgantown, West Virginia. 1896. Built for the production of hand-blown lead-glass stemware, a process resistant to mechanization at a time when the production of containers and windowpanes was becoming highly mechanized. The conical brick furnace stack is a reverbatory type common to other furnace industries and used wherever it is desirable to separate the flames of combustion from the object being heated.

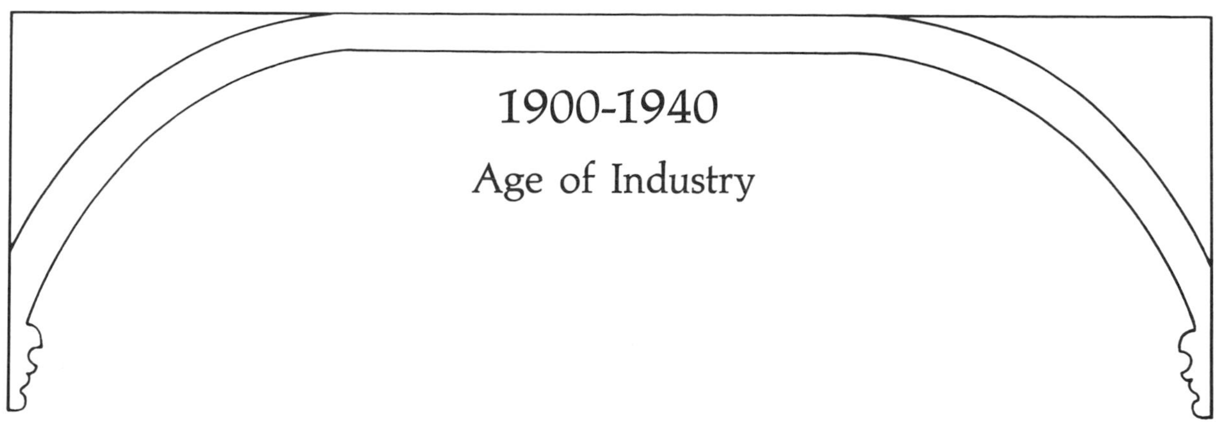

Materials

The twentieth-century builder had at his command a large number of new materials and new power over traditional building materials.

The first decade of the twentieth century saw enthusiastic use of and experimentation with concrete. Ultimately, a thorough understanding of its abilities to bear weight and withstand stress was achieved. Different types of concrete served for different uses: cast in hollow blocks, concrete proved to be economical; poured and reinforced with iron and steel rods, concrete could serve in many shapes and under a variety of conditions.

By 1920, with the development of transit or ready-mixed concrete, it all but replaced masonry as a structural component, although brick and stone remained popular as facing materials. (Except for a few types of utilitarian buildings the aesthetic possibilities of concrete were hardly exploited until after the Second World War.) Hollow clay tile also answered modern needs, saving half the weight of traditional brick masonry for a standard eight-inch wall. Vitreous glazed brick and terra-cotta were important as decorative cladding for steel-framed buildings.

The use of plate glass increased as framing methods reduced the bulk of the wall. In the 1930s, glass blocks were used in load-bearing walls and as translucent in-fill between structural framing members. Other new decorative materials were industrially polished granite, marble, and travertine.

Steel's triumph in framing the tall building was followed by its use as window sash, doors, and ornament. By 1910, galvanized corrugated sheet steel, sold and transported in standardized lengths, was ubiquitous.

After the late 1920s, stainless steel, low-alloy high-strength steel, corrosion-resisting metals, and light metals such as aluminum, magnesium, and beryllium were also commonly available as construction materials.

Modern technology even revolutionized the use of wood. Impregnated with synthetic resins, wood was resistant to fire, water, and termites. Wood laminated in thin layers as plywood had superior structural strength. And joined by metal connectors of modern design small-dimensioned wooden members could perform tasks equal to those of the tallest trees in native forests.

Construction Technology

Twentieth-century building technology provided America with extraordinarily effective means of manipulating her environment.

With concrete as a construction material, dams advanced from the earth-fill or gravity type to sophisticated multiple constructions of buttresses, domes, and arches. New regions came under cultivation as dams harnessed rivers, irrigated land, and generated electricity: Roosevelt, Coolidge, Wilson, and Wheeler in Arizona; Arrowrock in Idaho; Hoover in Nevada; Grand Coulee in Washington; Keokuk in Iowa, and many others.

An incessant demand for new bridges for river, road, and rail crossings and for western rail expansion could be met by bridges of the truss, suspension, and arch design that had mostly been developed by the early 1900s. As the highway triumphed over the railway in the 1930s, bridges of concrete arches and abutments were preferred. Depression-era Works Progress Administration bridges superseded many of obsolescent size, strength, or design.

In building construction, the tendency led to simplified and streamlined processes, including mass production, standardization, and prefabrication. Greater strength of materials yielded lighter construction—a development assisted by steel welding and synthetic adhesives. Ubiquitous in the first third of the twentieth century was the Guastavino system of thin-tile construction with heavy load-bearing capacity (characteristically seen in shallow vaults or domes laid with tiles in herringbone patterns).

Steel construction leaped forward in the Depression years with the incorporation of welding, rigid-frame trusses, and the cantilever. In concrete, continuous floor slabs supported by reinforced-concrete mushroom columns permitted heavy-load-bearing capacity in warehouse and freight-handling structures.

Behind twentieth-century technological advance was a modern machine-tool industry, with electrically driven high-speed welding and cutting tools, "super-speed" cutting tools of cemented tungsten carbide and tantalum carbide, heavy portable machine tools, and compressed-air tools. Although the nation had faced its geographical limits, its technological potential seemed without bounds.

Agriculture

By 1900 the frontier was closed. The nation was confronted by the fact that the land within existing borders would have to sustain and supply an ever-growing population.

Vast irrigation projects set in motion by the passage in 1902 of the National Reclamation Act made deserts bloom in a sixteen-state western and southwestern area. From the Imperial Valley in California and the lower Rio Grande in Texas, refrigerator rail cars (and after the mid-1920s also refrigerator trucks and ships) brought products of orchard and truck farm to big-city markets distant a thousand miles or more.

During the following decades, dam and canal projects cultivated rugged wilderness landscapes in intermountain deserts and in flood plains from the mountain streams of the Pacific Northwest to muddy southern bayous. On a scale as breathtaking as the nine-hundred-mile course of the Tennessee River, multipurpose Depression-era projects provided flood control and hydroelectricity along with irrigation, bringing entire regions into the economic mainstream.

While reclamation projects put new lands to the plow, the conservation movement put aside other millions of acres for future enjoyment and benefit. The Teddy Roosevelt generation accepted federal guardianship of water and forest resources; by the time the National Park Service was created in 1916, thirty-seven national parks and monuments had been established. Vast wilderness areas, eventually to exceed one-fifth of the nation's land surface, were withdrawn from the public domain to support conservation.

In the 1930s, when the Texas and Oklahoma dust storms shocked America, the government was committed to stand behind the farmer. Henceforth, the federal role in agricultural research, education, and management was to be major.

Even in the East, the agricultural picture changed beyond all recognition. While rich city dwellers seeking to build country houses sent rural land prices soaring, farmers retired on fat profits from the sale of their farms. At the same time, an influx of Italian, Greek, and other immigrants with traditions of intensive land cultivation brought back into use marginal farms in suburban and exurban areas.

On the Corn Belt landscape, as the electric line replaced the windmill, the farmer could no longer go it alone. In the first half of the century, some forty thousand farms were abandoned in Iowa alone when the economics of expensive electrically powered agricultural equipment dictated the necessity of farm consolidation. Tree and bush windbreaks grew dense around empty farmyards, while agricultural abundance built grain elevators that held ten million bushels and more.

The small farmer left his land. Vast agribusiness thrived. The nation led the world in food production and food consumption.

Transportation

Even as the twentieth century enters its closing decades, the landscape bears eloquent witness to the extraordinary effects of America's drive for mobility in its earliest years. At no time or place did more people move greater distances with more profound effects on the environment.

Two monuments—the great metropolitan train terminal and the endless highway ribbon—symbolize successive epochs, for which the year 1913 is perhaps the watershed. Because in that year, as a decade of construction culminated in the completion of New York City's Grand Central Terminal— queen of the majestic early-twentieth-century urban train stations — the number of registered automobiles exceeded one million.

About 1900 the use of electricity to power rails and automatic signals transformed transportation. Modernization yielded faster, lighter cars and heavier rails. The use of long-distance and commuter rail service increased many times over. Sturdy iron and steel bridges and viaducts and deep masonry-banked cuts, tunnels, and embankments were highly visible along the line of the tracks. Trolley-car service stretched ribbons of development beyond city limits, suburban rail lines strung out residential enclaves like beads on a necklace, and new tracks struck bold forays into yet unexploited southern and western lands.

The impact of the automobile was more dramatic still. At first, automobile use was limited to pleasure driving, and early scenic roads from New York's Bronx River Parkway to Oregon's Columbia River Highway took advantage of land contours and vistas to make driving enjoyable.

But in the post-World War I era, federal policy was committed to the completion of a connected system of highways, interstate in character, along which people and goods could be moved efficiently, safely, and speedily. Road engineering developed as a profession, expediting the construction of two-level automobile boulevards, grade separations of automobile and other traffic, and widened, straightened, and banked roadways.

Steel-truss bridges were replaced by modern concrete spans, and great suspension bridges carried automobile traffic across the Hudson River and San Francisco Bay. By the time of the Second World War, more than a million and a half miles of surfaced roadways crisscrossed the nation.

Today's observer may indeed find that hundreds of thousands of miles of roads have created one "longitudinal slum" after another. But there are also, for the romantic, fascinating survivals of the 1920–1940 era, when Americans were captivated by the automobile's promise of freedom and fun.

Roadside remains belonging to the realm of mass consumption and pleasure-seeking include tantalizing multihued neon-light graphics in fastastic shapes, frame and stucco tourist cabins (a half-million or more were built in the 1929–1934 period), streamlined bus terminals, shining steel and glass diners and other popular-food emporiums (a well-established type by the time the 1930s Moderne Style appeared), and gasoline service stations encased in white plastic and crowned by soaring logos.

Industry

Finance capitalists who dominated American industry at the beginning of the twentieth century were not bound by consideration for environmental amenity. A spectator described fourteen thousand tall chimneys silhouetted against the sky in the Monongahela Valley: "The realms of Vulcan could not be more somber or filthy . . . smoke begrimed . . . dirty, miserable. . . ."

Yet, scarcely a generation later, artists such as Charles Sheeler and Margaret Bourke-White could see beauty in the industrial landscape and poetry in the bright concrete factory cubes flanked by smoking chimney stacks. The application of electric power to industrial production helps to explain the difference. The first demonstration of high-voltage electrical-cable transmission was made in 1896; by 1920, almost one-third of the power in industry was electric.

Transmission lines ran to new industrial sites in the hinterlands, to onetime agricultural lands, to "industrial parks" near Lowell, Scranton, Youngstown, Chicago, St. Louis, Pittsburgh, and Detroit. Here, facilities integrated manufacture, storage, utilities, services, and transportation.

With the triumph of true assembly-line production after the development in 1913 of the overhead trolley to move materials mechanically, industrial sites expanded laterally instead of vertically. In formal campus-like arrangements, factory structures for light manufacturing seldom exceeded one or two stories.

A new component of the industrial scene was the tall steel-framed storage building that served a nation with vastly increased powers of production, consumption, and mobility.

Industry shifted its shape as well as its position. New scientific analysis of production flow, working conditions, and industrial output was applied to factory design. Novel configurations were dictated by contemporary products (chemical dyes, synthetic fabrics, cameras, automobiles, small electrical appliances, and metal alloys, including aluminum) and modern industrial processes (especially for paper, metal, and synthetics). Hydroelectric power moved industry from the North to the South, from old downtown waterfronts to deeper and more efficient harbors, and to remote western sites. Specialized production fueled the growth of dozens of American cities: Detroit (automobiles); New York (clothing and printing trades); Rochester (cameras and film); Schenectady and Cleveland (electrical appliances); Dayton (business machines and airplanes); Los Angeles (motion picture production).

Although besieged by economic depression and imminent war, the nation was buoyed by the promises of twentieth-century technology. America could look to the future with confidence.

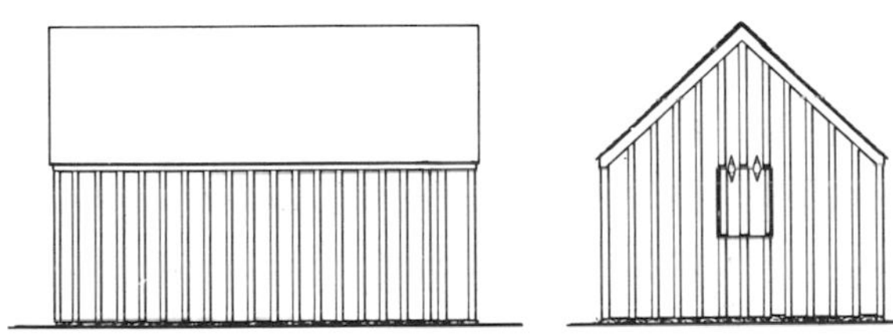

422, 423 Renderbrook-Spade Blacksmith Shop. Lubbock County, Texas. 1917.

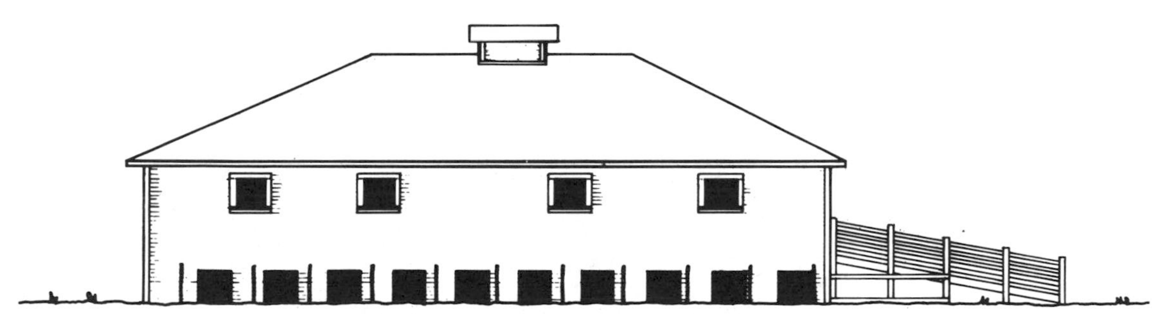

424 Sheep-shearing Shed. Moneta, Wyoming. 1917. Built to shear sheep by the Australian method of processing the wool of a large number of sheep at a single location. Wooden ramps lead sheep from a pen to a holding room, and thence to a shearing room with chutes to lower-level pens.

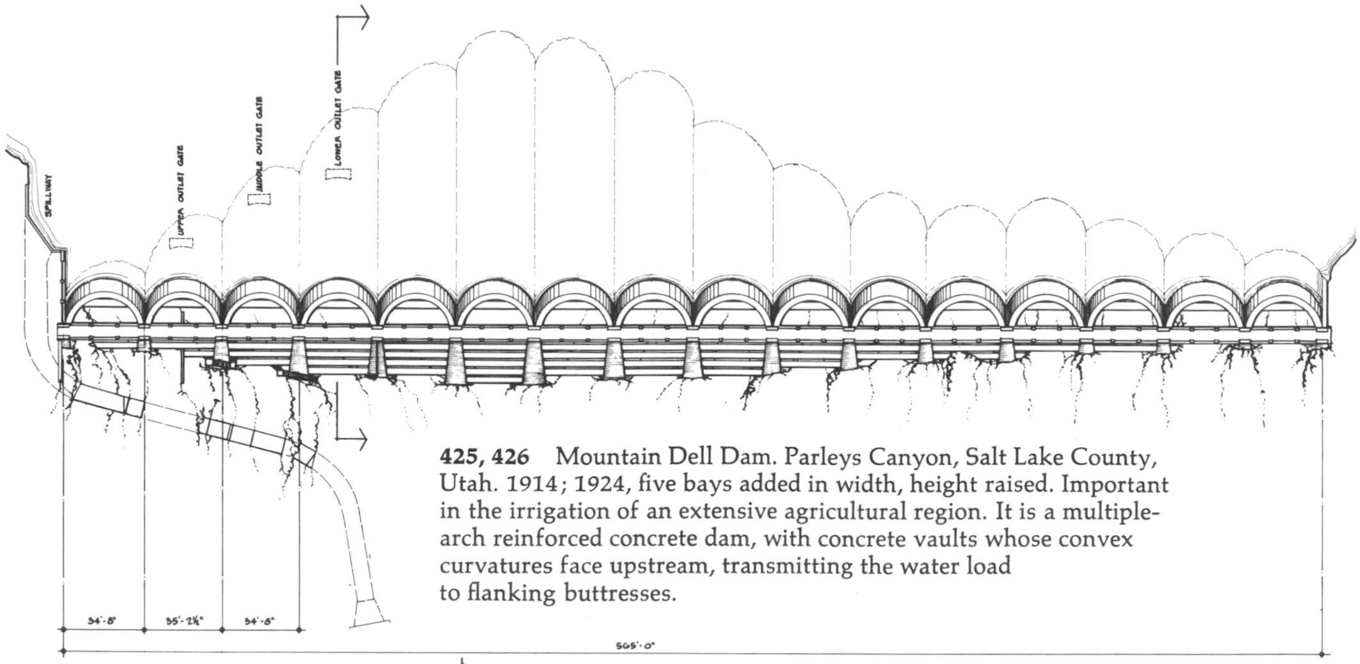

425, 426 Mountain Dell Dam. Parleys Canyon, Salt Lake County, Utah. 1914; 1924, five bays added in width, height raised. Important in the irrigation of an extensive agricultural region. It is a multiple-arch reinforced concrete dam, with concrete vaults whose convex curvatures face upstream, transmitting the water load to flanking buttresses.

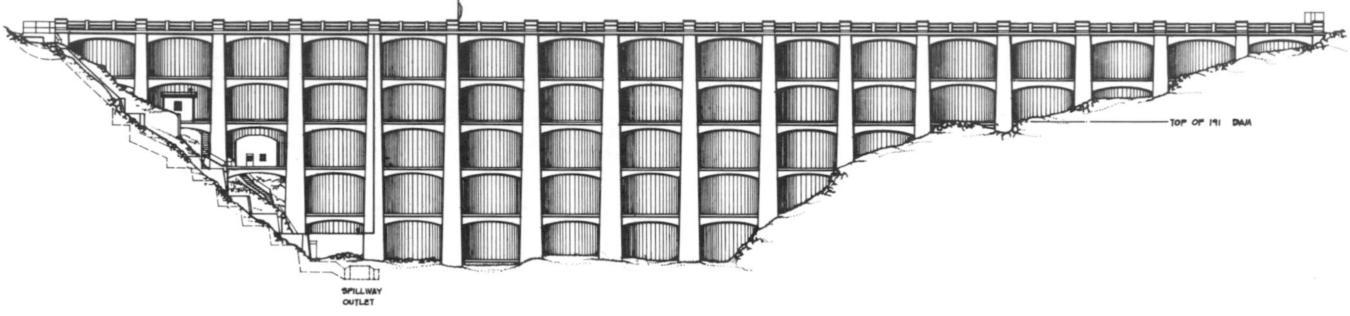

Mountain Dell Dam, Parleys Canyon, Salt Lake County, Utah; 1914–1924.

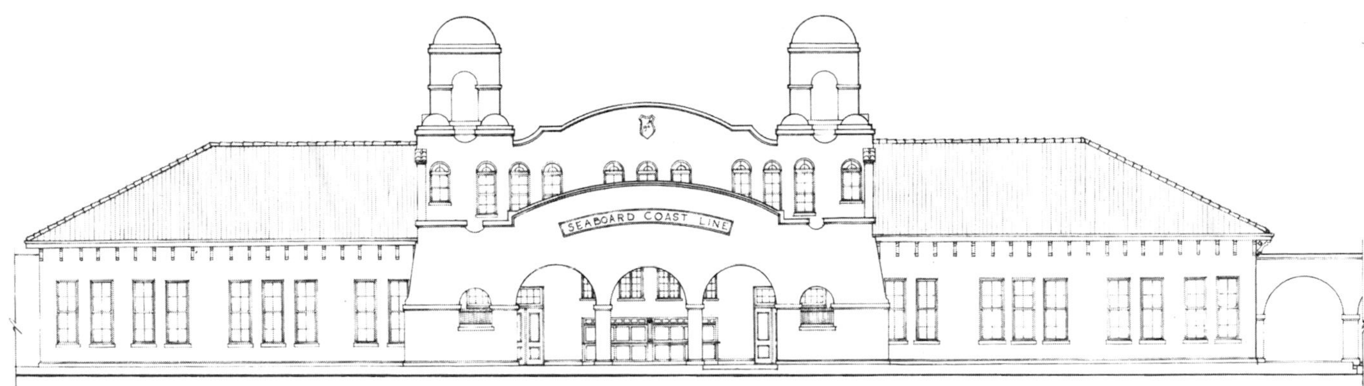

427 Orlando Train Station. Orlando, Florida. 1926. On the Seaboard Coast Line, built during the years of the great Florida boom. Spanish Mission in design, the station is of concrete, stucco, cast stone, and plaster with a terra-cotta tile roof.

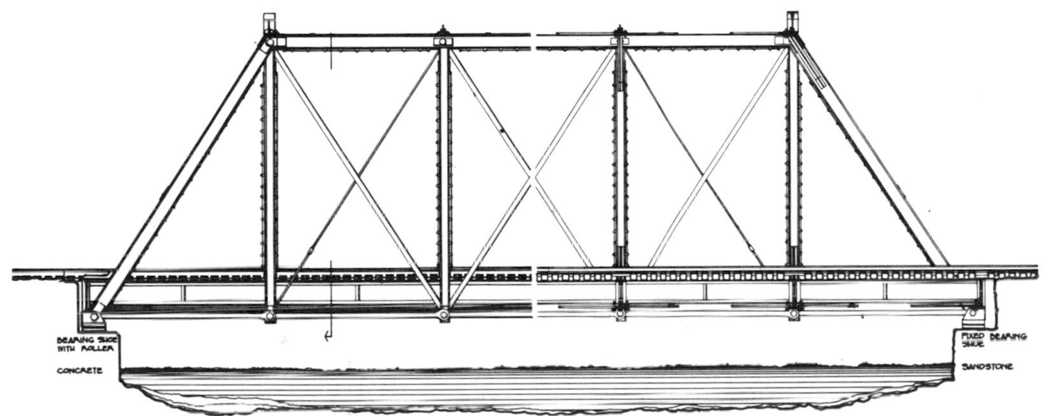

428 Iron Bridge, Delaware & Rio Grande Western Railroad. Provo vicinity, Utah. 1884–1919. An iron through-truss bridge, built originally for a narrow-gauge railroad, widened for standard-gauge equipment, then shortened and moved to its present site.

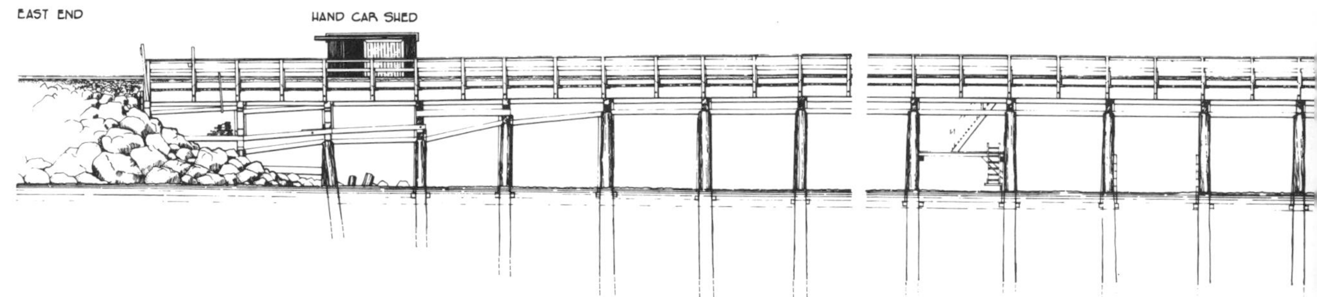

429 Southern Pacific Railroad, Ogden-Lucien Cut-off Trestle. Great Salt Lake, Utah. 1902–1904. In length eleven miles, the trestle is constructed of fir pilings and braces, crushed-rock ballasts, bolts with cast-iron washers, and a redwood deck.

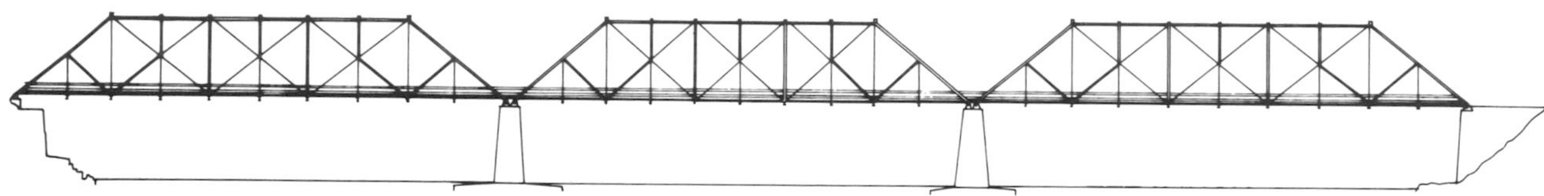

430 Dingmans Ferry Bridge. Dingmans Ferry, Pennsylvania. C.1900. A triple-span Pratt through-truss bridge, built by Phoenix Bridge Co.

Dingmans Ferry Bridge, Dingmans Ferry, Pennsylvania; c. 1900.

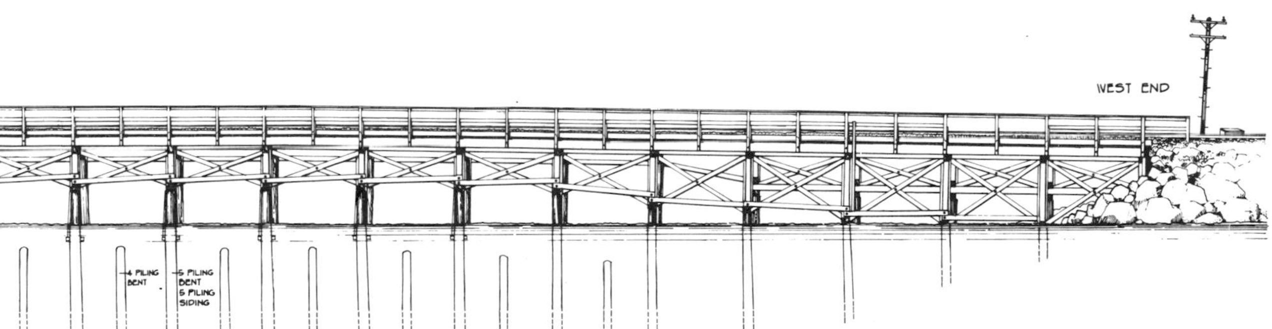

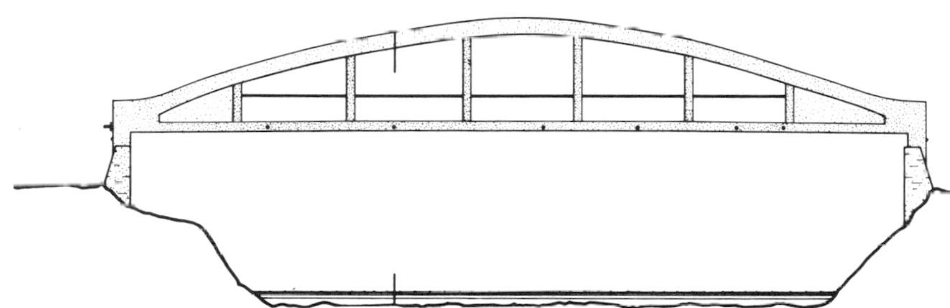

431 Bridge, Bridgeport Lamp Chimney Company. Bridgeport, West Virginia. 1924. A reinforced-concrete-arch bridge of unusual design, built to span a small creek separating a factory from a new warehouse.

432 Thames Tow Boat Company, Thames Shipyard. New London, Connecticut. 1900–1903. This was a construction and repair facility for wooden tugs and barges used to transport coal from Virginia to southern New England. It included a steam-powered sawmill, blacksmith shop, joiner shop, storage buildings, sail loft, boiler, and machine shops. Steam-powered marine railways hauled ships to dry ground.

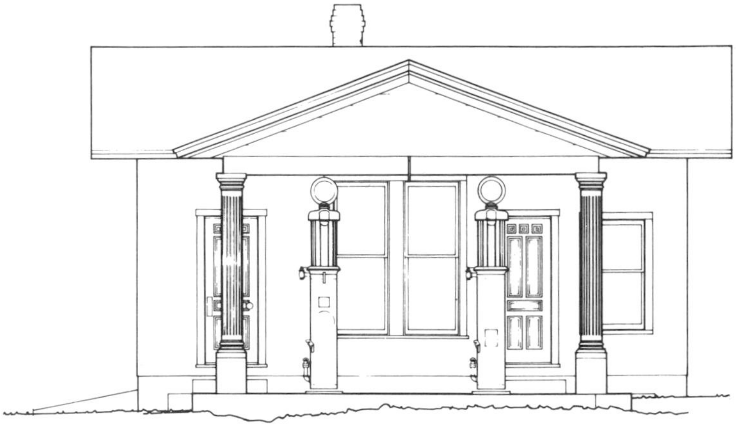

433, 434 Rockfish Service Station. Augusta County, Virginia. C.1925–1930. Representative of advanced service-station design in the decade that inaugurated the Automobile Age. Instead of purchasing cans of gasoline or pulling up to a curbside dispenser, the owner drove the car off the road and under the canopy where gas was pumped. At this time, service stations vied for new customers, offering an ever-wider range of services.

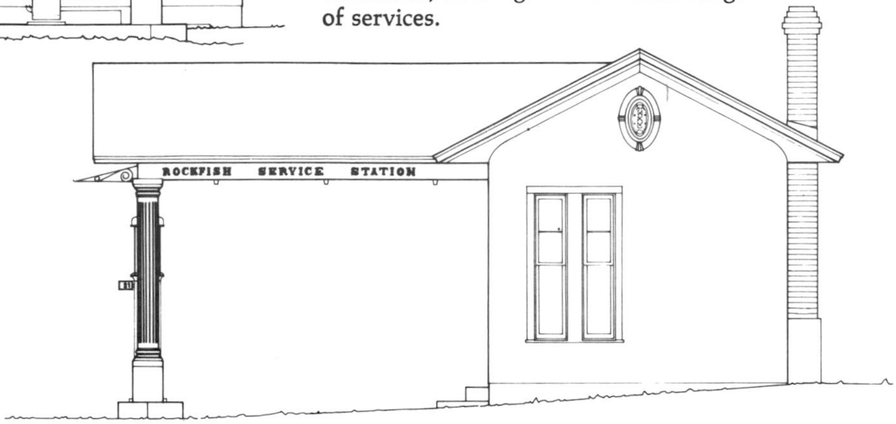

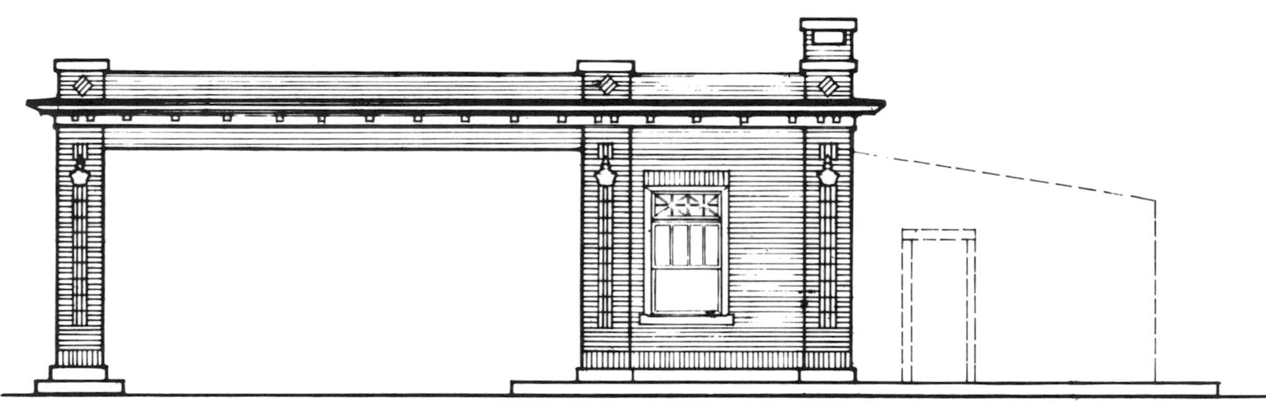

435, 436 Gulf Oil Company Service Station. Gainesville, Florida. 1925. Renaissance design.

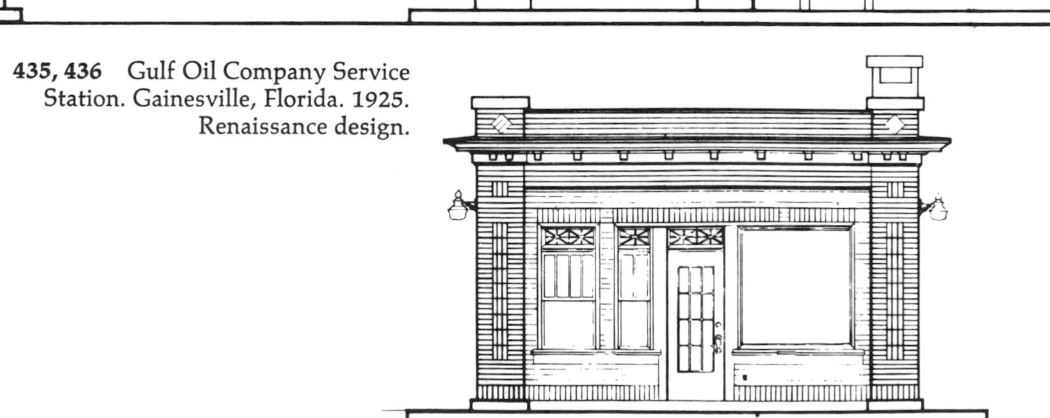

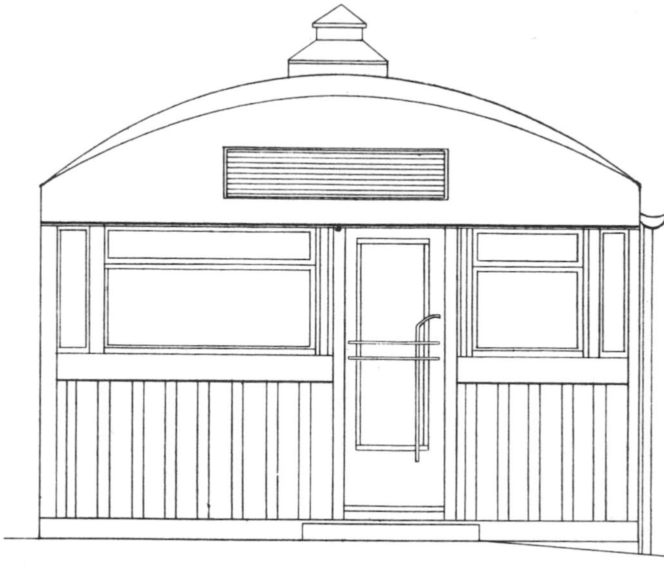

437 Mel's Diner. Queens, New York. An adjunct of Automobility, designed to symbolize speed and efficiency. The diner's greatest popularity occurred during the 1930s. Streamlined design and aluminum sheathing are characteristic.

438 Filling Station. Cleveland, Ohio. 1931. An example of standardization to achieve lower cost and establish a product image. Hundreds of units of this design were built annually, of concrete columns with continuous lightweight glass wall and enameled metal infill panels.

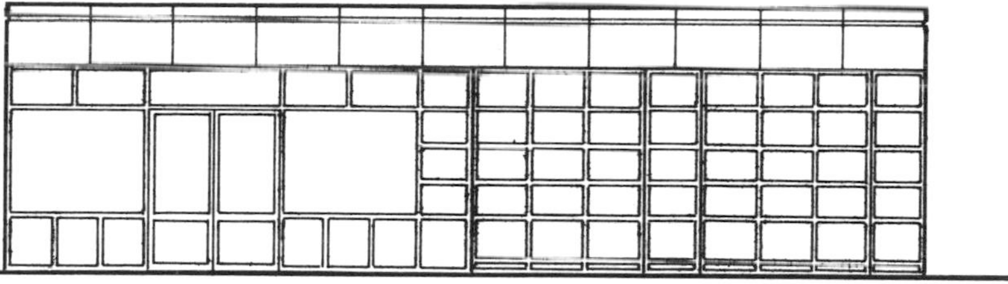

439 Greyhound Terminal. Dayton, Ohio. 1940. A symbol of the motor age, the porcelain enamel and aluminum sign scaled for easy visibility by the traveling public. Faced with limestone and blue terra-cotta, the structure is of reinforced concrete with steel sash windows.

440 Garland Beet Sugar Refinery. Garland, Utah. 1903. Part of an integrated agricultural production system, incorporating an irrigation canal, a hydroelectric generating system, a sugar-beet demonstration farm, and a railroad spur.

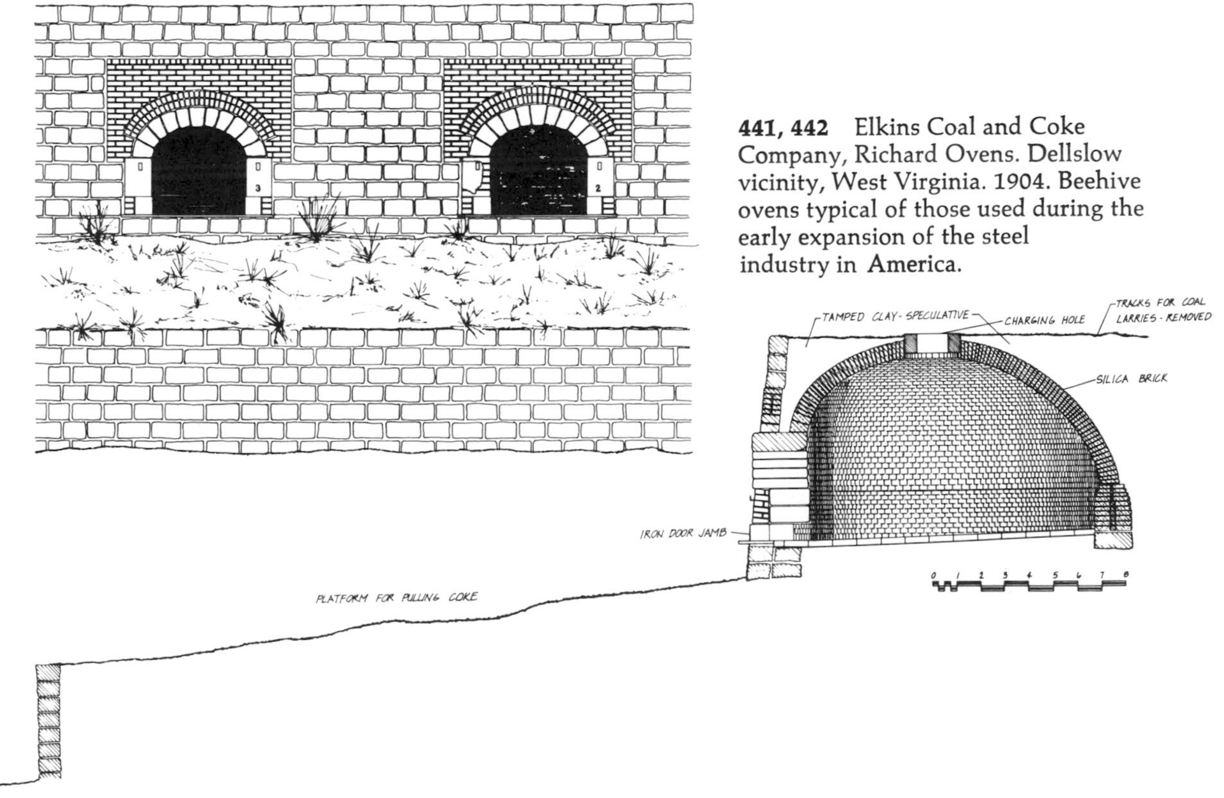

441, 442 Elkins Coal and Coke Company, Richard Ovens. Dellslow vicinity, West Virginia. 1904. Beehive ovens typical of those used during the early expansion of the steel industry in America.

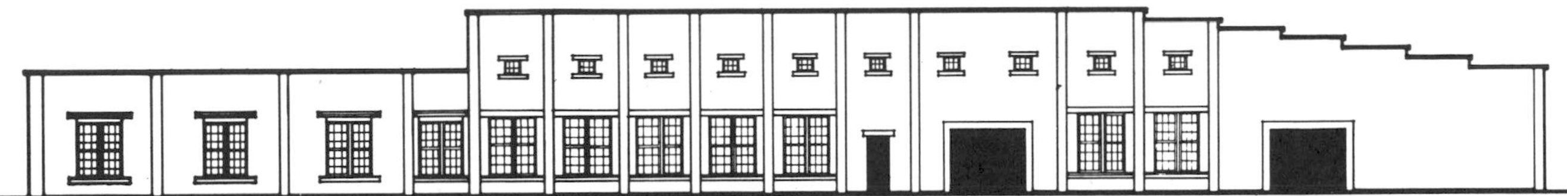

443 Buckeye Manufacturing Company. Anderson, Indiana. 1904. Built as a factory for gasoline engines, the one-story 524-foot concrete structure was enlarged in several stages in 1905–1917 to accommodate the manufacture of complete automobiles. About this time, concrete construction became virtually standard for factory structures.

Buckeye Manufacturing Company, Anderson, Indiana; 1904.

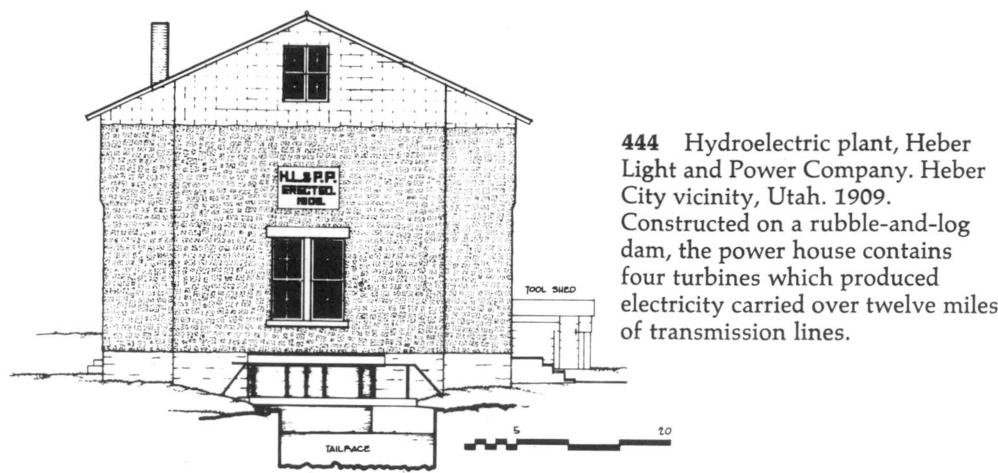

444 Hydroelectric plant, Heber Light and Power Company. Heber City vicinity, Utah. 1909. Constructed on a rubble-and-log dam, the power house contains four turbines which produced electricity carried over twelve miles of transmission lines.

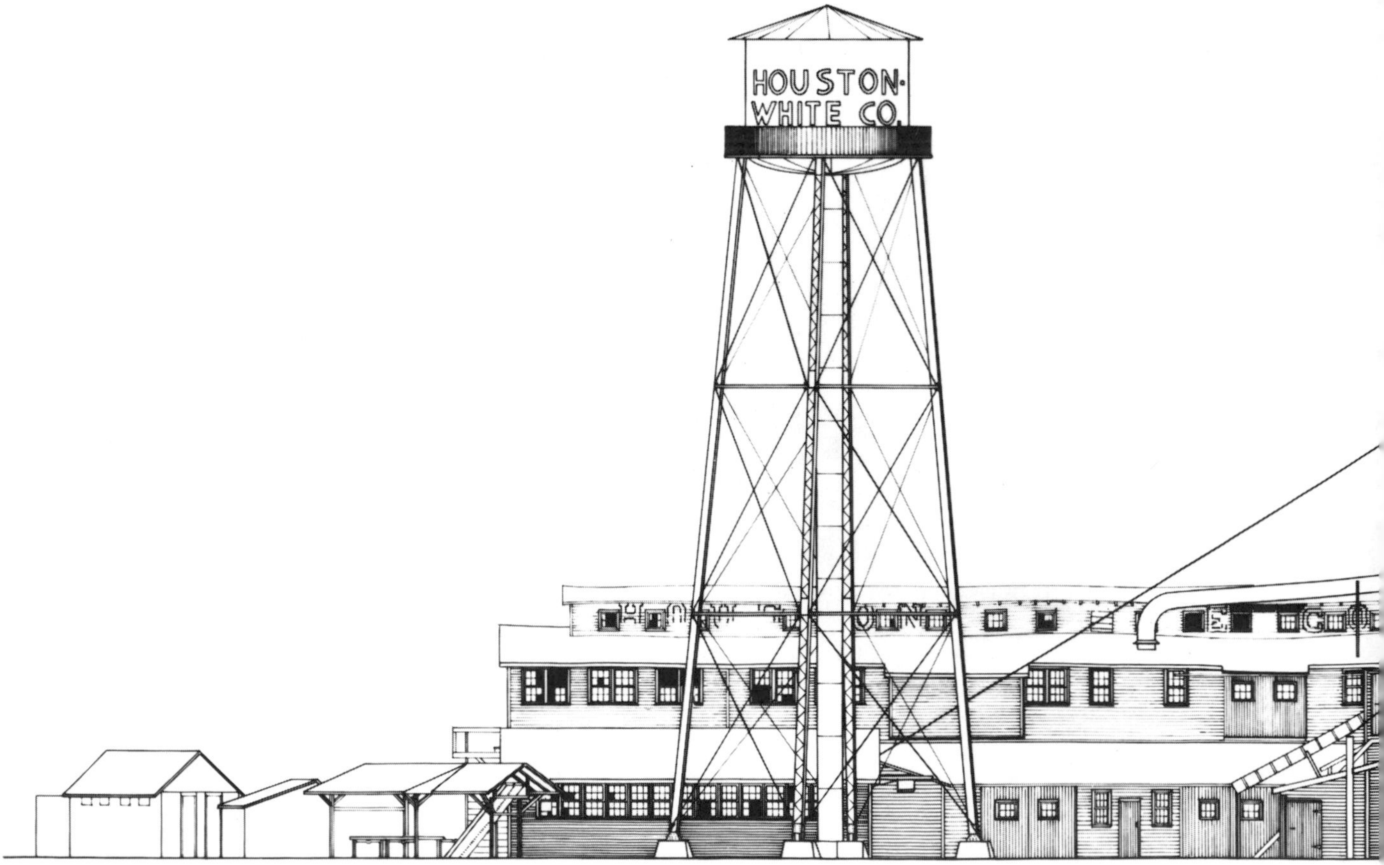

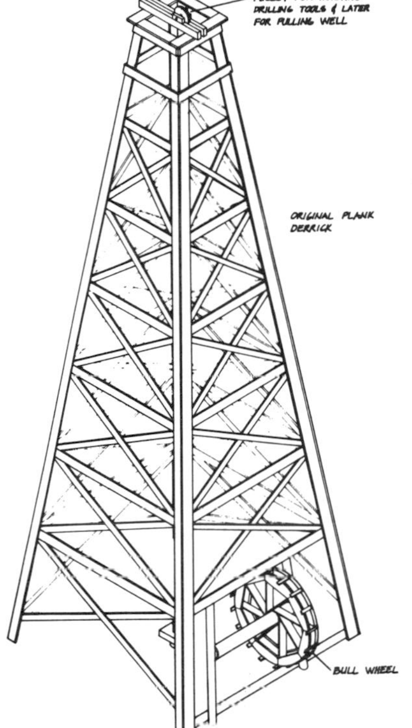

446 West Oil Company Endless Wire Petroleum Pumping Operation. Volcano vicinity, West Virginia. A late-nineteenth-century petroleum-pumping system. A single power source was used to pump oil from several wells by means of a continuous loop of cable connecting the power house to each of the wells.

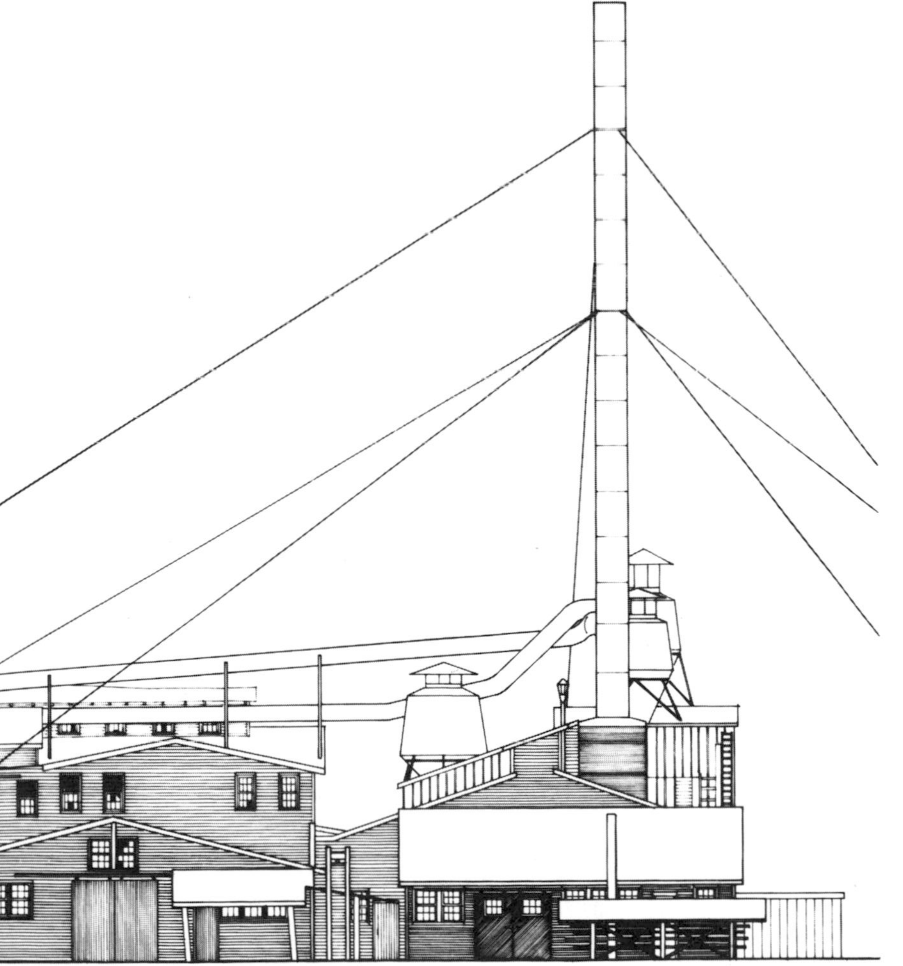

445 Houston-White Mill and Basket Factory. Hillsboro, Delaware. 1905. Built for the production of wooden produce baskets during a boom agricultural era. The long, low building at the rear holds the steam tank which loosened the bark of logs to be converted to veneer. The mill building at the right with the tall stack contains the veneer lathe. The tall tank is part of the water-sprinkler system. Power for the steam engine is obtained by burning waste woods.

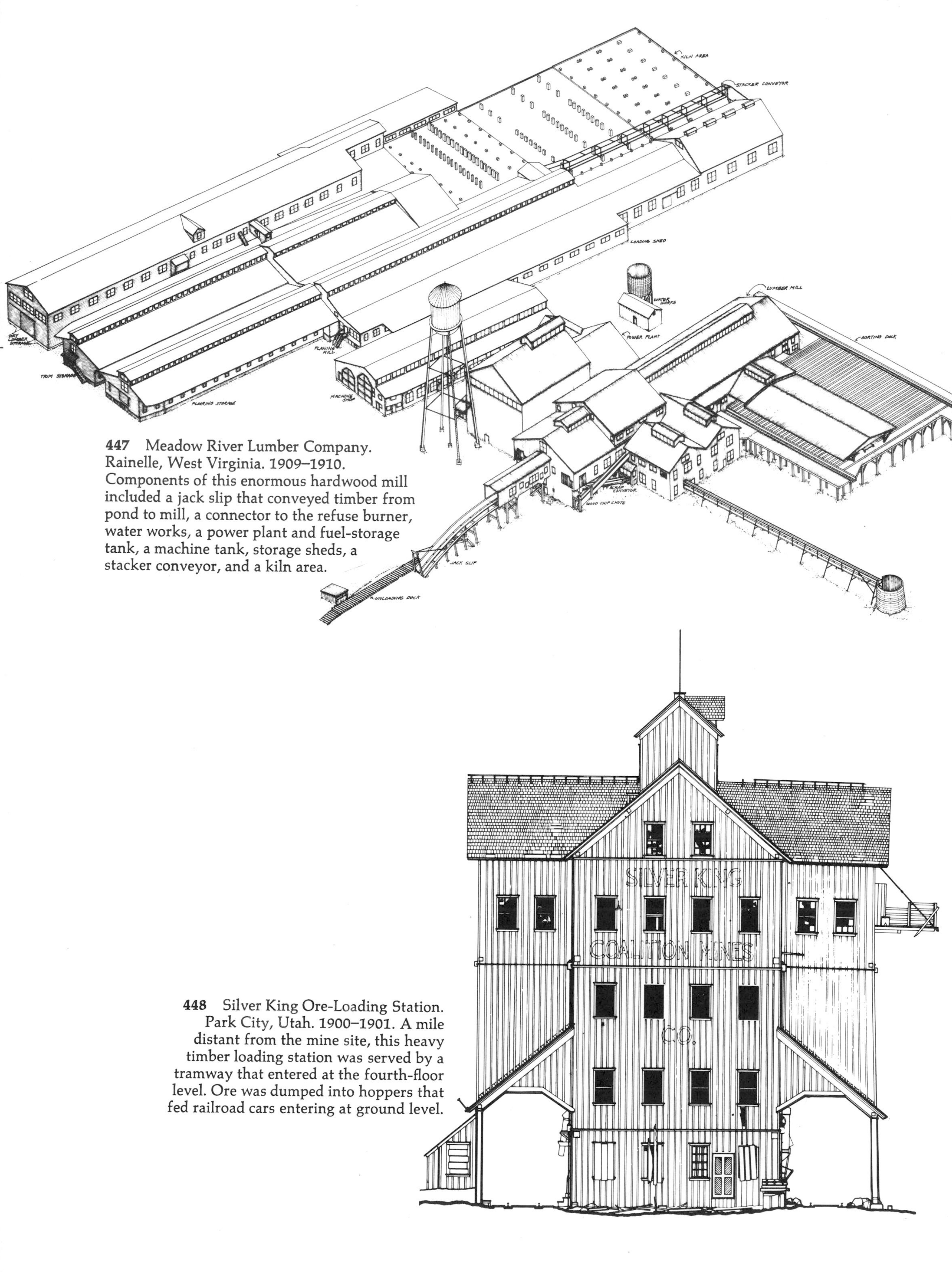

447 Meadow River Lumber Company. Rainelle, West Virginia. 1909–1910. Components of this enormous hardwood mill included a jack slip that conveyed timber from pond to mill, a connector to the refuse burner, water works, a power plant and fuel-storage tank, a machine tank, storage sheds, a stacker conveyor, and a kiln area.

448 Silver King Ore-Loading Station. Park City, Utah. 1900–1901. A mile distant from the mine site, this heavy timber loading station was served by a tramway that entered at the fourth-floor level. Ore was dumped into hoppers that fed railroad cars entering at ground level.

Pumping Station No. 2, San Francisco, California; 1912.

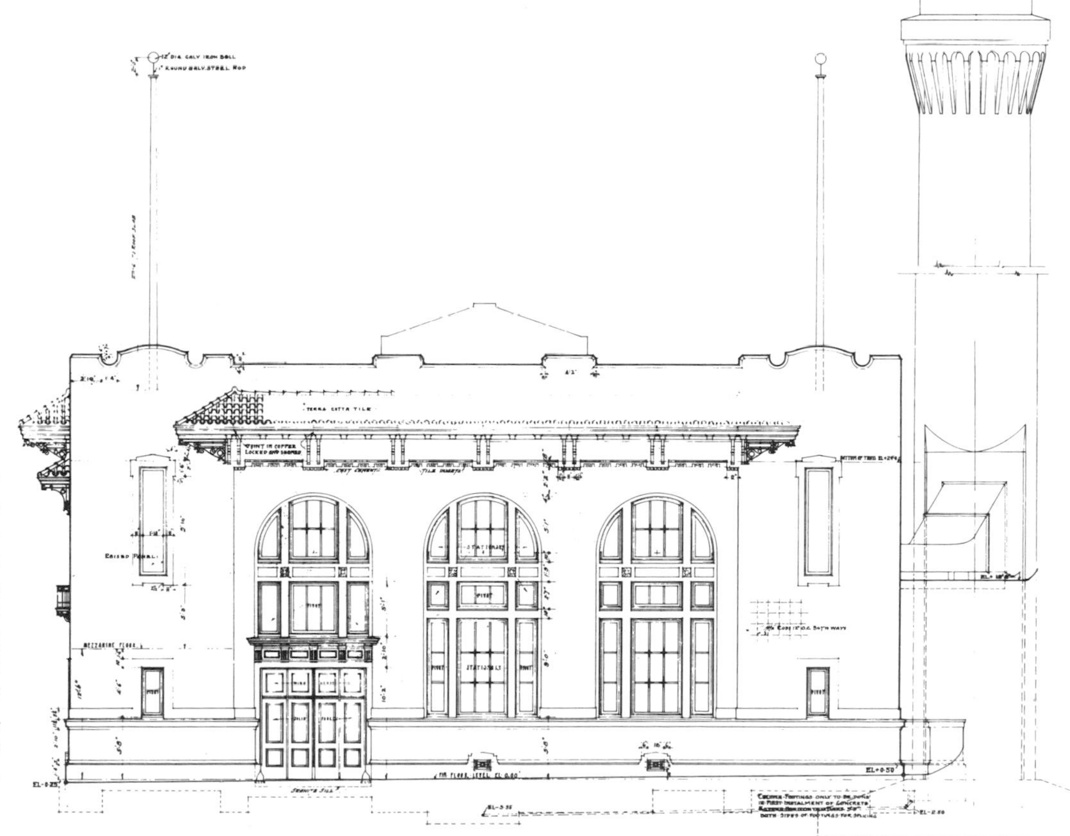

449 Pumping Station No. 2. San Francisco, California. 1912. Following San Francisco's Great Fire, this Spanish Mission concrete pumping station was constructed as part of an auxiliary fire-fighting system, independent of the domestic water supply.

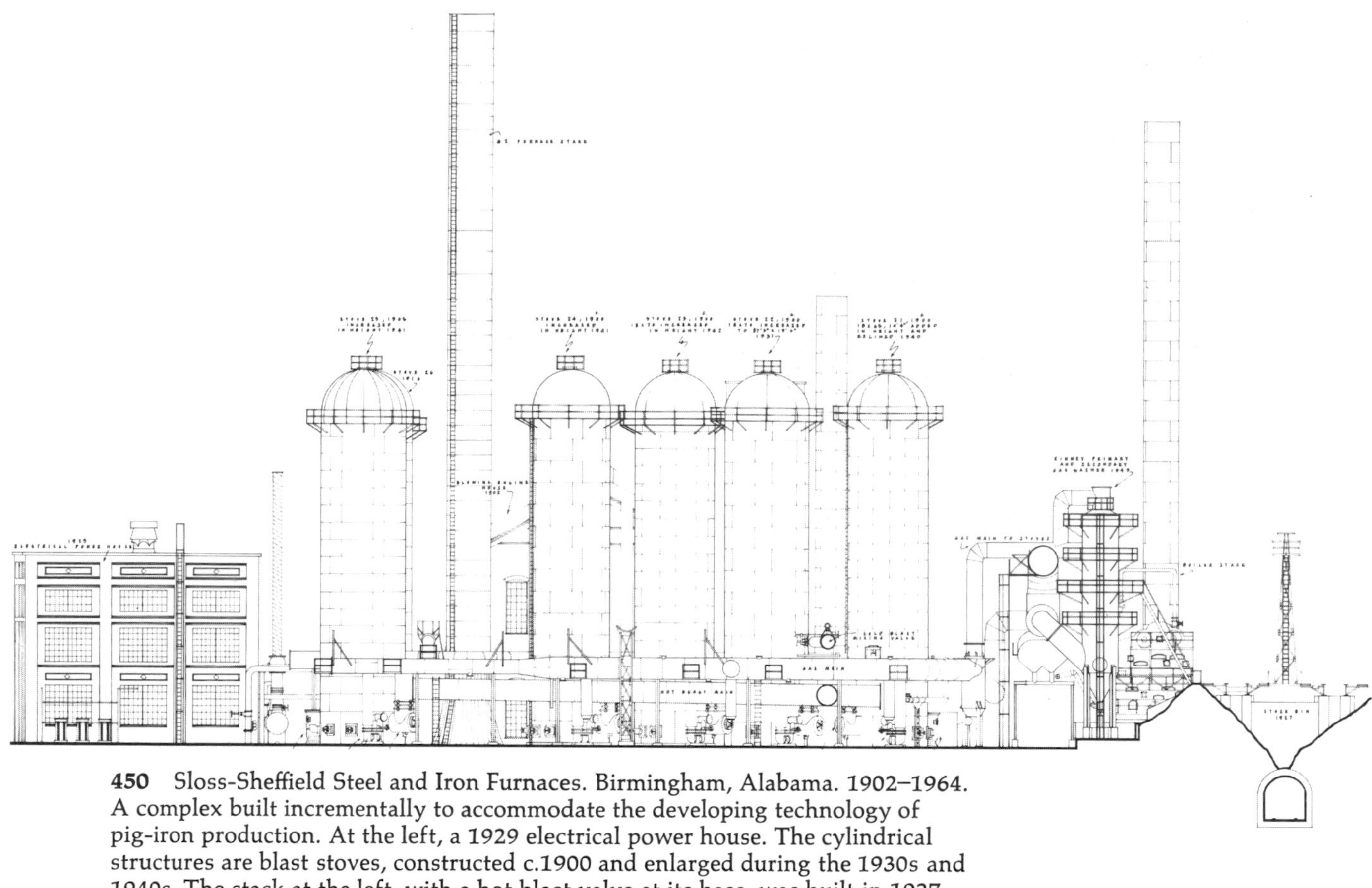

450 Sloss-Sheffield Steel and Iron Furnaces. Birmingham, Alabama. 1902–1964. A complex built incrementally to accommodate the developing technology of pig-iron production. At the left, a 1929 electrical power house. The cylindrical structures are blast stoves, constructed c.1900 and enlarged during the 1930s and 1940s. The stack at the left, with a hot blast valve at its base, was built in 1927. In this furnace, iron was melted and its impurities released.

451 Central of Georgia Railway Repair Shops. Savannah, Georgia. 1855–1926. Central of Georgia was the most important railroad line in the Southeast. This shop complex and depot provided complete facilities for passenger, freight, and repair services. The 1926 roundhouse at the left is of concrete, the 1855 smokestack of cast iron.

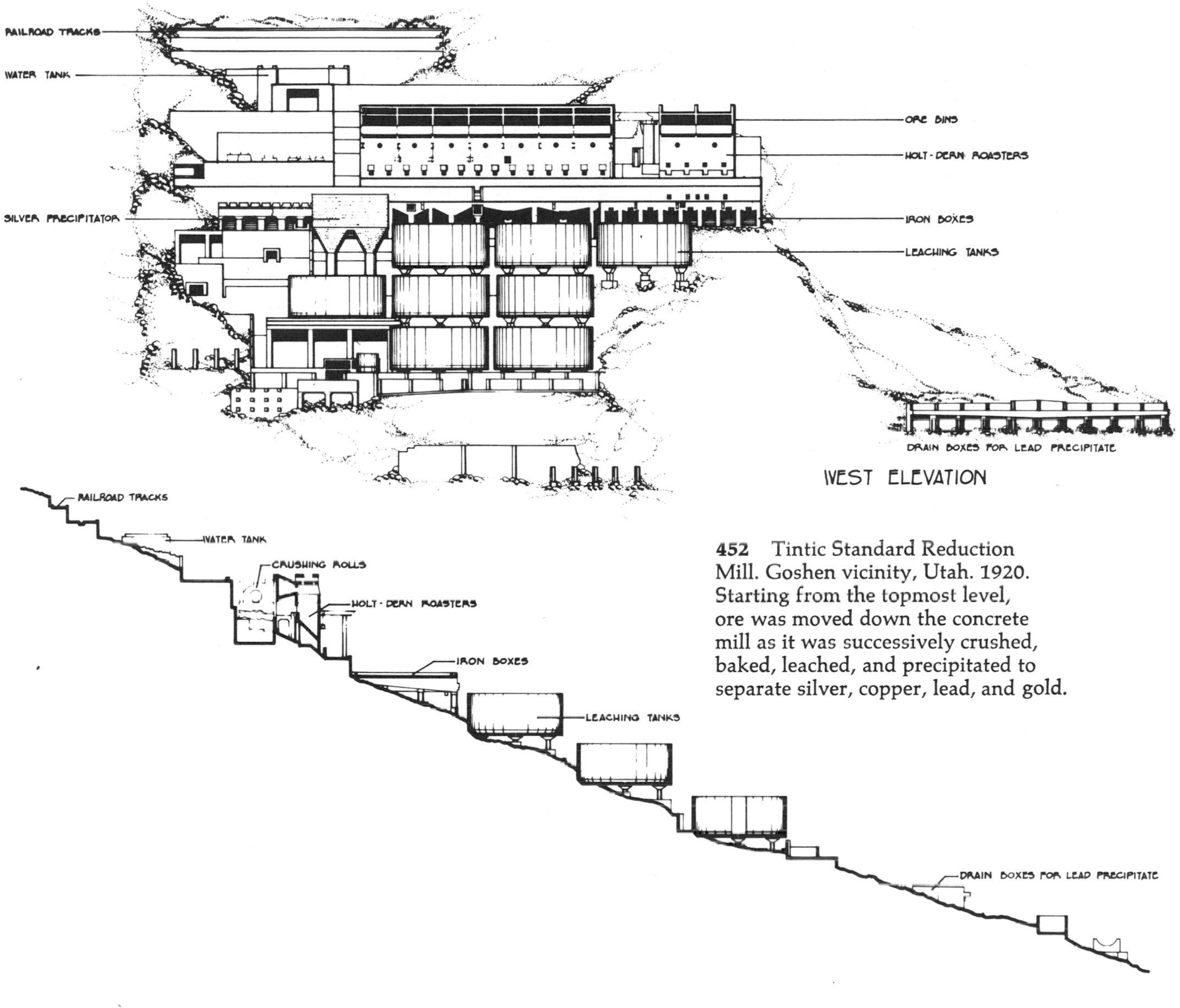

452 Tintic Standard Reduction Mill. Goshen vicinity, Utah. 1920. Starting from the topmost level, ore was moved down the concrete mill as it was successively crushed, baked, leached, and precipitated to separate silver, copper, lead, and gold.

453, 454 Sales and Service Building, Brooklyn Borough Gas Company. Brooklyn, New York. 1934. An Industrial-park type of design. It visually and functionally integrated gas-stove production on the site with retail sales and service facilities.

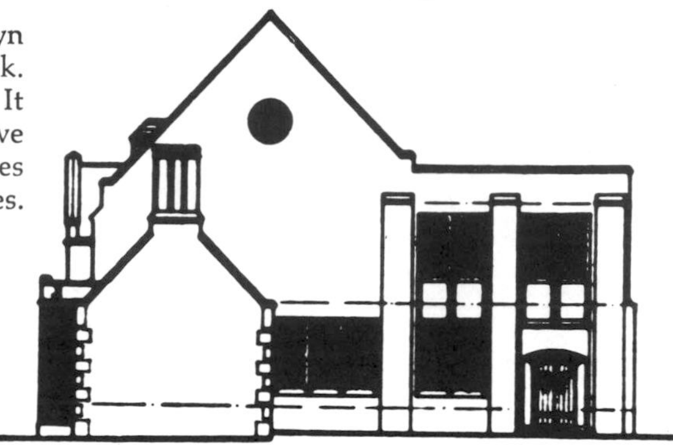

455 Lady Esther, Ltd. Clearing, Illinois. 1938; Albert Kahn Associated Architects and Engineers. Designed for a straight-line flow of materials through the production process, with clean, sweeping horizontal lines and wide windows for natural daylight. Glass blocks differentiate and illuminate the main reception area.

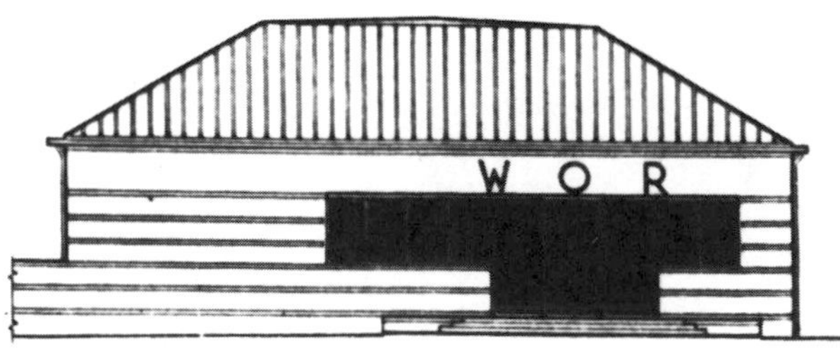

456 WOR Radio Transmitting Station. Carteret, New Jersey. 1935; Voorhees, Gmelin & Walker, architects.

Recommended Reading

Architecture—General

Blumenson, John J.-G. *Identifying American Architecture: Pictorial Guide to Styles and Terms 1600–1945.* Nashville: American Association for State and Local History, 1977.

Burchard, John, and Bush-Brown, Albert. *The Architecture of America: A Social and Cultural History,* abr. ed. Boston: Little, Brown, 1966.

Fitch, James Marston. *American Building 1: The Historical Forces That Shaped It.* 2d rev. and enl. ed. New York: Schocken, 1973.

———. *American Building 2: The Environmental Forces That Shaped It.* New York: Houghton Mifflin, 1972.

Fleming, John; Honour, Hugh; and Pevsner, Nikolaus. *The Penguin Dictionary of Architecture.* Baltimore: Penguin, 1969.

Gifford, Don. *The Literature of Architecture: The Evolution and Practice in Nineteenth Century America.* New York: E.P. Dutton, 1966.

Gowans, Alan. *Images of American Living: Four Centuries of Architecture and Furniture as Cultural Expression.* Philadelphia: J.B. Lippincott, 1964.

Hamlin, Talbot Faulkner. *The American Spirit in Architecture.* The Pageant of America Series, vol. 14. New Haven: Yale University Press, 1926.

Hammett, Ralph W. *Architecture in the U.S.: A Survey of Architectural Styles since 1776.* A Wiley–Interscience Pub. New York: John Wiley & Sons, 1976.

Harris, Cyril M., ed. *Dictionary of Architecture and Construction.* New York: McGraw-Hill, 1975.

Hitchcock, Henry-Russell. *Architecture: Nineteenth and Twentieth Centuries.* Paperback ed. Baltimore: Penguin, 1971.

———. *A List of Books, Portfolios, and Pamphlets on Architecture and Related Subjects Published in America Before 1895.* New York: Da Capo, 1976.

Kaufman, Edgar, Jr. *The Rise of an American Architecture.* New York: Praeger, 1970.

McKee, Harley J. *Recording Historic Buildings.* Washington, D.C.: Historic American Buildings Survey, 1971.

Mumford, Lewis. *Sticks and Stones: A Study of American Architecture and Civilization.* New York: Dover, 1955.

National Park Service, U.S. Department of the Interior. *The National Register of Historic Places.* Washington, D.C.: U.S. Government Printing Office, 1976, 1978, 1979.

Pevsner, Nikolaus. *A History of Building Types.* Princeton: Princeton University Press, 1976.

Poppeliers, John; Chambers, S. Allen; and Schwartz, Nancy B. *What Style Is It?* Washington, D.C.: Preservation Press, 1977.

Scully, Vincent. *American Architecture and Urbanism.* New York: Praeger, 1969.

Smith, E. Kidder. *Architecture in America: A Pictorial History.* Ed. by Marshall Davidson. An American Heritage Book. New York: W.W. Norton, 1976.

Whiffen, Marcus. *American Architecture Since 1780: A Guide to the Styles.* Cambridge, Mass.: M.I.T. Press, 1969.

Withey, Henry F., and Withey, Elsie Rathbone. *Biographical Dictionary of Architects (Deceased).* Los Angeles: New Age, 1956.

Wodehouse, Laurence, ed. *American Architects to*

the First World War. Gale Information Guide Library. Detroit: Gale Research, 1977.

Architecture—Specialized

Brooks, H. Allen. *The Prairie School.* New York: W. W. Norton, 1976.

Bunting, Bainbridge. *Early Architecture in New Mexico.* Albuquerque: University of New Mexico Press, 1976.

Cheney, Sheldon. *New World Architecture of 1930.* New York: Tudor, 1930.

Cram, Ralph, ed. *American Church Building of Today.* New York: Architectural Book, 1929.

Dorsey, Stephen P. *Early English Churches in America 1607–1807.* New York: Oxford University Press, 1952.

Egbert, Donald Drew. "Religious Expression in American Architecture," in A.L. Jamison and J.W. Smith, eds., *Religious Perspectives in American Culture.* Princeton: Princeton University Press, 1961.

Gayle, Margot, and Gillon, Edmund V., Jr. *Cast-Iron Architecture in New York: A Photographic Survey.* New York: Dover, 1974.

Hamlin, Talbot. *Greek Revival Architecture in America.* New York: Dover, 1964.

Hitchcock, Henry-Russell. *The Architecture of H.H. Richardson and His Times.* Rev. paperback ed. Cambridge, Mass.: M.I.T. Press, 1966.

———, and Seale, William. *Temple of Democracy: The State Capitols of the U.S.A.* New York: Harcourt Brace Jovanovich, 1976.

Jordy, William H. *American Buildings and Their Architects: The Impact of European Modernism in the Mid-Twentieth Century.* Garden City, N.Y.: Doubleday, 1972.

———. *American Buildings and Their Architects: Progressive and Academic Ideals at the Turn of the Twentieth Century.* Garden City, N.Y.: Doubleday, 1972.

Kimball, Fiske. *Domestic Architecture of the American Colonies and of the Early Republic.* New York: Dover, 1966.

McCoy, Esther. *Five California Architects.* New York: Praeger, 1975.

Mock, Elizabeth. *Built in U.S.A., 1932–44.* New York: Museum of Modern Art, 1944.

Morrison, Hugh. *Early American Architecture from the First Colonial Settlements to the National Record.* New York: Oxford University Press, 1952.

Newcomb, Rexford. *Architecture of the Old Northwest Territory: A Study of Early Architecture in Ohio, Indiana, Illinois, Michigan, Wisconsin, and Part of Minnesota.* Chicago: University of Chicago Press, 1950.

Pierson, William, H., Jr. *American Buildings and Their Architects: The Colonial and Neoclassical Style.* Garden City, N.Y.: Doubleday, 1970.

Van Ravenswaay, Charles. *The Arts and Architecture of German Settlements in Missouri: A Survey of a Vanishing Culture.* Columbia, Mo.: University of Missouri Press, 1977.

Rawlings, James Scott. *Virginia's Colonial Churches: An Architectural Guide.* Richmond, Va.: Garrett & Massie, 1963.

Robinson, Cervin, and Bletter, Rosemary Haag. *Skyscraper Style: Art Deco New York.* New York: Oxford University Press, 1975.

Rose, Harold Wickliffe. *The Colonial Houses of*

Worship in America Built in the English Colonies Before the Republic 1607–1789 and Still Standing. New York: Hastings House, 1963.

Scully, Vincent J., Jr. *The Shingle Style and the Stick Style: Architectural Theory and Design from Richardson to the Origins of Wright.* Rev. ed. New Haven: Yale University Press, 1971.

———. *Modern Architecture: The Architecture of Democracy.* New York: George Braziller, 1967.

Sinnott, Edmund W. *Meetinghouse and Church in Early New England.* New York: McGraw-Hill, Inc., 1963.

Stanton, Phoebe. *The Gothic Revival and American Church Architecture.* Baltimore: Johns Hopkins University Press, 1968.

Stoehr, C. Eric. *Bonanza Victorian: Architecture and Society in Colorado Mining Towns.* Albuquerque: University of New Mexico Press, 1975.

Waterman, Thomas T. *The Dwellings of Colonial America.* Chapel Hill: University of North Carolina Press, 1950.

Environmental and Urban History

Alsberg, Henry G., ed. *The American Guide: A Source Book and Complete Travel Guide for the United States.* New York: Hastings House, 1949.

Blake, Peter. *God's Own Junkyard: The Planned Deterioration of America's Landscape.* New York: Holt, Rinehart and Winston, 1964.

Chapman, Edmund H. *Cleveland: Village to Metropolis, a Case Study of Problems of Urban Development in Nineteenth Century America.* The Western Reserve Historical Society. Cleveland: The Press of Western Reserve University, 1964.

Clay, Grady. *Close-Up: How to Read the American City.* New York: Praeger, 1973.

Green, Constance McLaughlin. *American Cities in the Growth of the Nation.* Harper Colophon Books. New York: Harper & Row, 1965.

Jackson, John Brinckerhoff. *American Space: The Centennial Years, 1865–1875.* New York: W.W. Norton, 1972.

Lynch, Kevin. *What Time Is This Place?* Cambridge, Mass.: M.I.T. Press, 1972.

———. *The Image of the City.* Paperback ed. Cambridge, Mass.: M.I.T. Press, 1972.

McKelvey, Blake. *The Urbanization of America (1860–1915).* New Brunswick, N.J.: Rutgers University Press, 1963.

Mumford, Lewis. *The City in History.* New York: Harcourt, Brace & World, 1961.

Nairn, Ian. *The American Landscape.* New York: Random House, 1965.

Paullin, Charles O. *Atlas of the Historical Geography of the United States.* Washington, D.C.: Carnegie Institute of Washington, 1932.

Rifkind, Carole. *Main Street: The Face of Urban America.* New York: Harper & Row, 1977.

Robinson, William F. *Abandoned New England.* Boston: New York Graphic Society, 1976.

Sloane, Eric. *Our Vanishing Landscape.* New York: Ballantine, 1955.

Tunnard, Christopher, and Reed, Henry Hope. *American Skyline: The Growth and Form of*

Our Cities and Towns. New York: New American Library, 1956.

Tunnard, Christopher. *The Modern American City.* Paperback ed. Princeton, N.J.: D. Van Nostrand, 1968.

Vaughan, Thomas, and Ferriday, Virginia Guest, eds. *Space, Style and Structure: Building in Northwest America.* Portland: Oregon Historical Society, 1974.

Warner, Sam B., Jr. *Streetcar Suburbs: The Process of Growth in Boston 1870–1900.* Paperback ed. New York: Atheneum, 1968.

Weitzman, David. *Underfoot: An Everyday Guide to Exploring the American Past.* New York: Charles Scribner's Sons, 1976.

Industrial Archaeology and Building Technology

Condit, Carl W. *American Building: Materials and Techniques from the First Colonial Settlements to the Present.* Chicago: University of Chicago Press, 1968.

———. *Chicago, 1910–29: Building, Planning, and Urban Technology.* Chicago: University of Chicago Press, 1973.

Davey, Norman. *A History of Building Materials.* New York: Drake, 1971.

Peterson, Charles E., ed. *Building Early America: Contributions Toward the History of a Great Industry.* Philadelphia: Chilton, 1976.

Sande, Theodore A. *Industrial Archeology: A New Look at the American Heritage.* Brattleboro, Vt.: Stephen Greene Press, 1976.

Preservation

Grieff, Constance, ed. *Lost America: From the Atlantic to the Mississippi,* vol. 1. Princeton, N.J.: Pyne Press, 1971.

———, ed. *Lost America: From the Mississippi to the Pacific,* vol. 2. Princeton, N.J.: Pyne Press, 1972.

Huxtable, Ada Louise. *Will They Ever Finish Bruckner Boulevard? A Primer on Urbicide.* New York: Collier, 1972.

International Centre for Conservation, Rome, Italy, and the Internation Centre Committee of the Advisory Council for Historic Preservation. *Preservation and Conservation: Principles and Practices.* Washington, D.C.: Preservation Press, 1976.

Kidney, Walter C. *Working Places: The Adaptive Use of Industrial Buildings.* Pittsburgh: Ober Park Associates, 1976.

Kliment, Stephen A., ed. *Neighborhood Conservation.* New York: Whitney Library of Design, 1976.

National Trust for Historic Preservation; Wrenn, Tony P.; and Mulloy, Elizabeth D. *America's Forgotten Architecture.* New York: Pantheon, 1976.

Papageorgiou, Alexander. *Continuity and Change: Preservation in City Planning.* New York: Praeger, 1971.

Architectural Periodicals

American Preservation: The Magazine for Historic and Neighborhood Preservation. Little Rock, Ark.

Avery Index to Architectural Periodicals. 2d rev. ed. Boston: G.K. Hall, 1973.

Historic Preservation. Washington, D.C.: National Trust for Historic Preservation.

Journal of the Society of Architectural Historians. Philadelphia, Pa.

Landscape. Berkeley, Calif.

Society for Industrial Archeology Newsletter. Washington, D.C.: Smithsonian Institution, National Museum of History and Technology.

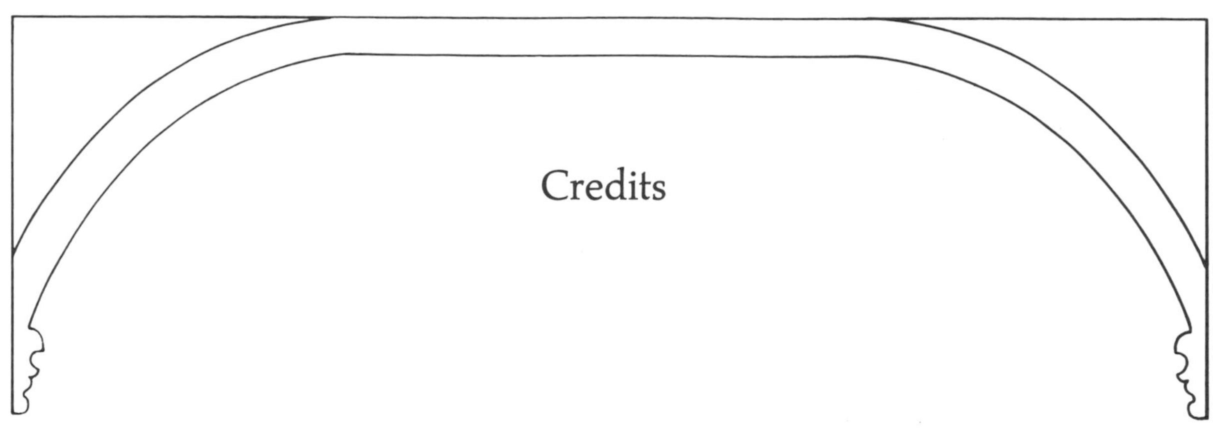

Credits

Drawing Credits

Most of the drawings are from the Historic American Building Survey, and the name listed below is that of the delineator. In other cases, the name of the publication or other source is given. In Part IV, many of the drawings are from the Historic American Engineering Record, as is noted.

The numbers listed below are those of the drawings.

1, 2, C. Morrison; 3, 4, 5, W. Schomburg; 6, H. Barnes; 7, M. Weil; 8, J. Crook, J. Blew; 9, D. Donivan; 10. R. Rogers; 11, J. Newson; 12, 13, G. Oman; 14, 15, C. Fraser; 16, 17, E. Pallme; 18, H. Willard; 19, E. Volk; 20, S. Habersham; 21, R. Keune, R. Swilley; 22, J. Reflogle; 23, J. Newsom; 24, F. Leslie; 25, D. Vandeven; 26, M. Hall; 27, 28, 29, K. Williams; 30, 31, M. Lewis; 32, 33, 34, G. Hodgkinson; 35, T. Waterman, R. Neale; 36, J. Burnett; 37, F. Clark, S. Raphael; 38, W. Stowell, A. Morrison; 39, R. Burkhart, A. Morrison; 40, H. Stevenson; 41, J. Waite; 42, A. Cook; 43, L. Chapin; 44, 45, T. Heindsman, F. Ferguson; 46, 47, J. Crytzer; 48, L. Thoch, J. Rauch; 49, R. Lewis, L. Ewald; 50, R. Lewis, C. Schott; 51, E. Rosenfeld; 52, H. Warfel; 53, P. Ward; 54, 55, F. Nichols, T. Herman; 56, J. Dudley; 57, 58, J. Roberts; 59, J. Burnett; 60, 61, 62, C. Brittain; 63, W. Tarbell; 64, C. Uthe; 65, P. Goiran; 66, H. Lawrence; 67, C. Eldridge; 68, 69, 70, H. McKinley; 71, 72, E. Nelson, P. Trolio, A. Towe; 73, R. Giebner; 74, S. Bauer; 75, L. Yost, A. Ledebuhr; 76, 77, R. Adams; 78, R. Schaefer; 79, T. Rachelle; 80, 81, E. Kusseraw, R. Adams, A. Wuchieri; 82, A. Easter, L. Pick; 83, L. Pick; 84, 85, M. Pease; 86, 87, H. Lansberry; 88, G. Embry, 89, R. Ferland; 90; T. Price, R. Ericson; 91, A. Caldwell; 92, 93, L. Van DeGraft; 94, T. Apostelaros; 95, P. Burkhart, S. Dornbusch; 96, 97, Chamberlain & Thomas; 98, T. Hauck, S. Tang; 99, S. Bauer; 100, A. Morrison; 101, A. McDonald; 102, T. McCormick; 103, J. Depeter; 104, M. Hall; 105, H. Hunderman; 106, T. Sanford; 107, R. Wyatt, W. Miller, R. Sharp; 109, P. Veeder; 110, D. Vyverberg; 111, D. Abramson; 112, J. Chimura; 113, H. McCauley; 114, S. Kinzy; 115, Large; 116, W. Petell; 117, S. Helene; 118, L. Eaton; 119, D. Yturralde; 120, H. McCauley; 121, P. Borchers, A. McDonald; 122, L. Hermsen, J. Burns; 123, 124, E. Popko; 125, L. Johnston; 126, J. Murphy, G. Rapp; 127, M. Wellen; 128, L. Hermsen; 129, P. Goiran; 130, P. Briggs; 131, T. Schubert; 132, B. Stokey; 133, 134, G. Dunn; 135, E. DeLony; 136, W. Fullerton, G. Hoffman, A. Reid; 137, *Monograph of the Works of McKim, Mead & White*, New York, 1915; 138, *Ibid.*; 139, *Carpentry and Building*, September 1900; 140, S. Smith; 141, D. Vyverberg; 142, T. Simmons; 143, L. Page; 144, E. Rabun; 145, *American Architect & Building News*, September 1877: adapted and delineated by S. Bauer; 146, B. Lee; 147, 148, 149, W. Klein; 150, 151, Juan Wilson; 152, A. Weinstein; 153, P. Ward; 154, J. Frins; 155, *Building Age*, November 1910; 156, S. Feller; 157, E. Popko; 158, S. Tate, F. Wiedemann; 159, R. Moje; 160, *American Country Houses of Today*, New York, 1912: adapted and delineated by S. Bauer; 161, R. Naugle; 162, 163, *American Architect*, November 1934; 164, J. Skelton; 165, 166, *American Architect*, May 1933; 167, 168, 169, *American Architect*, July 1935; 170, 171, *American Architect*, November 1934; 172, 173, S. Westfall; 174, J. Lentz; 175, 176, S. Udell; 177, 178, *The Modern House*, New York, 1933: adapted and delineated by S. Bauer; 179, Radford's Stores and Flat Buildings, Chicago, 1913: adapted and delineated by S. Bauer; 180, K. Hassin; 181, *Building Age*, November 1920: adapted and delineated by S. Bauer; 182, S. Westfall; 183, *Western Architect*, November 1926; 184, *American Apartment Houses of Today*, New York, 1926: adapted and delineated by S. Bauer; 185, W. Collier, L. Williams; 186, J. Schafer, K. Ahn; 187, H. Slocum; 190, W. Ellison, H. Holcomb; 191, 192, D. Spence; 193, H. Furman; 194, C. Rubira; 195, T. Syme; 196, W. Pigeon; 197, L. Robinson, W. Morton; 198, 199, H. Brodie; 200, 201, L. Crisson; 202, L. Nichols; 203, J. Depeter; 204, L. Eaton; 205, D. Woodrum; 206, J. Roberts; 207, 208, V. Gustafson; 209, W. McQueen; 210, A. DeCastro; 211, E. Villatoro, G. Rueblinger; 212, R. Dunnay; 213, 214, D. Woodrum; 215, G. Small, P. Wilday, E. Jenkins; 216, H. Tigner; 217, N. Brigham; 218, 219, J. Hansen; 220, 221, M. Thomas, D. McCoubrey; 222, C. Goldman, 223, H. Brack; 224, F. Mooberry; 225, R. Randall; 226, A. Weinstein; 227, F. Wiedenmann; 228, 229, M. Trumbo; 230, P. Wisley; 231, J. Tarr; 232, G. Anastes, E. Mills; 233, *American Architect*, October 1887: adapted and delineated by S. Bauer; 234, 235, J. Irwin, C. Garrick; 236, J. Poggenpohl; 237, *American Churches*, New York, 1915: adapted and delineated by S. Bauer; 238, 239, *Monograph of the Works of McKim, Mead & White*, New York, 1915; 240, *Western Architect*, November 1907; 241; *Architectural Record*, September 1931: adapted and delineated by S. Bauer; 242, R. Moje; 243, *American Churches*, New York, 1915: adapted and delineated by S. Bauer; 244, 245, *Amer-*

ican Architect, May 1933; 246, J. Rudd; 247, 248, *American Architect*, December 1936; 249, *American Architect*, October 1932; 250, M. Marshall, W. Jones; 251, 252, E. Phillups; 253, T. Herman; 254, 255, W. Cochran; 256, A. Newhouse; 257, 258, J. Waite; 259, D. Hall; 260, L. Nichols; 261, M. Halsey; 262, E. Smith; 263, E. Calloway; 264, A. Arbuckle; 265, S. Barnette; 266, M. Hall; 267, 268, 269, T. Rachelle; 270, W. Jahn; 271, V. Gustafson; 272, 273, J. Kelly; 274, F. Deboe, S. Tuminello, E. Murphy; 275, R. Paetz; 276, Restoration plan by Jonathan J. Woodman & Associates, Architects, R. Thimot; 277, 278, C. Dertrand, Z. Rike; 279, A. Morrison; 280, M. Moriarity; 281, J. Waite; 282, L. Johnston, G. Rapp; 283, F. West; 284, 285, 286, W. Schlarsic; 287, H. McKee; 288, G. Glaubinger; 289, R. Van Husen; 290, M. Bolte; 291, R. Dunay; 292, P. Borchers, M. Melragon, M. Fazlo; 293, E. Edwards; 294, H. Kesserling; 295, C. Alexander; 296, R. Lake; 297, C. Hellwig; 298, P. Borchers, M. Clouten; 299, 300, *American Architect & Building News*, May 1877; 301, D. Yturralde; 302, L. Roberts; 303, 304, S. Bauer; 305, Fitch, Kantrowitz, Ketterer, Shinhofen, Tomlinson; 306, C. Wyma; 307, 308, J. Robbins; 309, J. McIntire; 310, W. Edwards; 311, R. Giebner; 312, M. Wellen, J. Schafer; 313, T. Sanford; 314, C. Fraser; 315, R. Hartwig; 316, R. Ferland; 317, 318, 319, Jonathan J. Woodman & Associates, Architects, R. Thimot; 320, H. McCauley; 321, *Monograph of the Works of McKim, Mead & White*, New York, 1915; 322, J. Erins; 323, P. Borchers, N. Clouten; 324, Skidmore, Owings and Merrill; 325, P. Gardner; 326, *Monograph of the Works of McKim, Mead & White*, New York, 1915; 327, *American Architect*, February 1928; 328, R. Giebner; 329, J. Mackenzie; 330, J. Lentz; 331, J. Davis; 332, *American Architect*, March 1933; 333, *Monograph of the Works of McKim, Mead & White*, New York, 1913; 334, A. Weinstein; 335, L. West, J. Eley; 336, J. Smith; 337, R. Gillet; 338, C. Morrison; 339, C. Morrison; 340, *Monograph of the Works of McKim, Mead & White*, New York, 1915; 341, H. McCauley, H. Longnecker; 342, P. Borchers, H. Law; 343, *Monograph of the Works of McKim, Mead & White*, New York, 1915; 345, *American Architect*, September 1933; 346, A. Weinstein; 347, S. Bauer; 348, 349, R. Lake; 350, Jonathan J. Woodman & Associates, Architects; 351, *Architectural Record*, July 1931; 352, *American Architect*, January 1933; 353, Reproduced from architect's originals; 354, D. Hopping, R. Fleury; 355, 356, 357, R. Fernbach; 358, M. Rotsch; 359, G. Rogers; 360, H. Gulesian; 361, R. Mackellar; 362, 363, L. Nicoletti (HAER); 364, 365, B. Freeman; 366, 367, K. Hoeft (HAER); 368, N. Waxman; 369, D. Prycer, Yestadt (HAER); 370, 371, S. Cargol; 372, M. Marshall, W. Jones; 373, H. Maslow; 374, F. Bates, C. Harbison; 375, 376, F. Love (HAER); 377; J. DePasquale (HAER); 378, F. Hoggard; 379, D. Bouse (HAER); 380, 381, W. Gavzy (HAER); 382, T. Sanford; 383, D. Seale; 384, M. Boles, L. D. Schaaf (HAER); 385, D. Seale; 386, 387, F. Dings, A. Welch; 388, R. Perlmutter; 389, 390, J. Robinson (HAER); 391, D. Arbogast (HAER); 392, 393, A. Lubow (HAER); 394, A. Lubow (HAER); 395, M. Wellen; 396, S. Farneth; 397, F. DeLony (HAER); 398, P. Ward; 399, T. Wolosz (HAER); 400, D. Prycer (HAER); 401, 402, S. Farneth; 403, C. Morrison; 404, J. Tasker; 405, R. Meden (HAER); 406, 407, Albert, Burnham, Graves, Lawler (HAER); 408; F. Yestadt (HAER); 409, A. Jones, M. Chrisney (HAER); 410, B. Freeman, M. Chrisney (HAER); 411, 412, E. DeLony (HAER); 413, P. Flory, B. Freeman (HAER); 414, T. Ristau, W. Gavzy (HAER); 415, J. Reddick (HAER); 416, M. Boles (HAER); 417, D. Jacobson; 418, 419, M. Casey; 420, Hanns; 421, B. Freemar (HAER); 422, 423, W. Kilroy; 424, J. Uhlir; 425, 426, C. Ristau, Madgen (HAER); 427, J. Parks; 428, K. Bailey (HAER); 429, D. Bouse (HAER); 430, M. Rosenbloom (HAER); 431, W. Garrick, T. Ristau (HAER); 432, B. Freemont (HAER); 433, 434, D. Donovan; 435, 436, S. Tate, B. DelCueto; 437, B. Hoff; 438, *Architectural Record*, December 1931: adapted and delineated by S. Bauer; 439, *Railroad & Bus Terminal and Station Layout*, New York, 1945: adapted and delineated by S. Bauer; 440, J. McIntire (HAER); 441, 442, G. Nerburn (HAER); 443, M. Boles, J. Reddick (HAER); 444, T. Ristau (HAER); 445, D. Davis (HAER); 446, B. Carim, J. Esterson, G. Nerburn (HAER); 447, S. Hawks, K. Hoeft (HAER); 448, R. McNair (HAER); 449, Marsden Manson, Board of Public Works, San Francisco, 1912; 450, P. Stammer (HAER); 451, P. Dubin (HAER); 452, K. Bailey (HAER); 453, 454, *American Architect*, September 1934; 455, *The Architectural Forum*, August 1938: adapted and delineated by S. Bauer; 456, *American Architect*, June 1935.

Photograph Credits

P. 6, Old Ogden House, Library of Congress; p. 19, Dr. Upton Scott House, HABS; p. 35, Gadsden House, HABS; p. 37, Josiah Harris House, Library of Congress; p. 40, Dr. John Matthews House, Library of Congress; p. 41, Charles

Clapp House, HABS, J. Boucher; p. 53, Lyndhurst, R. A. Rifkind; p. 55, A. B. Austin House, Library of Congress; p. 67, Morse-Libby House, HABS; p. 74, Emlen Physick House, HABS, J. Boucher; p. 81, Ira Heath House, Library of Congress; p. 85, Brown-Donahue House, Library of Congress, G. Peterich; p. 89, Frederick Vanderbilt House, National Park Service; p. 92, Eisenhower Boyhood Home, Library of Congress; p. 103, T. S. Estabrook House, Library of Congress; p. 105, Marshall Morgan House, American Country Houses of Today; p. 120, Christ Church, Library of Congress; p. 128, First Church of Christ, Congregational, Library of Congress; p. 134, St. Mary's Church, HABS, J. Boucher; p. 139, Grace Church, Library of Congress; p. 143, Cape Island Presbyterian Church, HABS, J. Boucher; p. 149, Holy Trinity, Library of Congress; p. 152, St. Matthew's Episcopal Church, HABS, M. Rand; p. 163, First Congregational Church of Austin (now Our Lady of Lebanon), HABS; p. 169, Reynolds' Tavern, HABS, J. Boucher; p. 177, County Records Building, Library of Congress; p. 185, Old State Bank, Library of Congress; p. 189, U.S. Custom House, HABS; p. 198, Public Square, HABS, J. Boucher; p. 200, Hotel Florence, Library of Congress; p. 210, Bradbury Building, HABS, M. Rand; p. 216, Reliance Building, Library of Congress; p. 221, Richfield Oil Building, HABS; p. 222, Richfield Oil Building, detail, HABS; p. 232, Carnegie Library, HABS, W. Barrett; p. 251, Massachusetts Milestone, HABS; p. 253, Van Wyck-Lefferts Tide Mill, HAER, W. R. Ansteth; p. 261, Stone Barn, Library of Congress; p. 265, Schoharie Creek Aqueduct, Erie Canal, HAER; p. 267, Phoenix Mill, HABS, J. Boucher; p. 268, Steam Factory, HABS, J. Boucher; p. 280, B & O Station, HAER, W. E. Barrett; p. 287, Easton Roller Mills, HAER, W. E. Barrett; p. 298, Mountain Dell Dam, Parleys Canyon, HAER, J. Boucher; p. 300, Dingmans Ferry Bridge, HAER, G. Eisenmann; p. 305, Buckeye Manufacturing Company, HAER; p. 309, Pumping Station No. 2, HAER, J. Boucher.

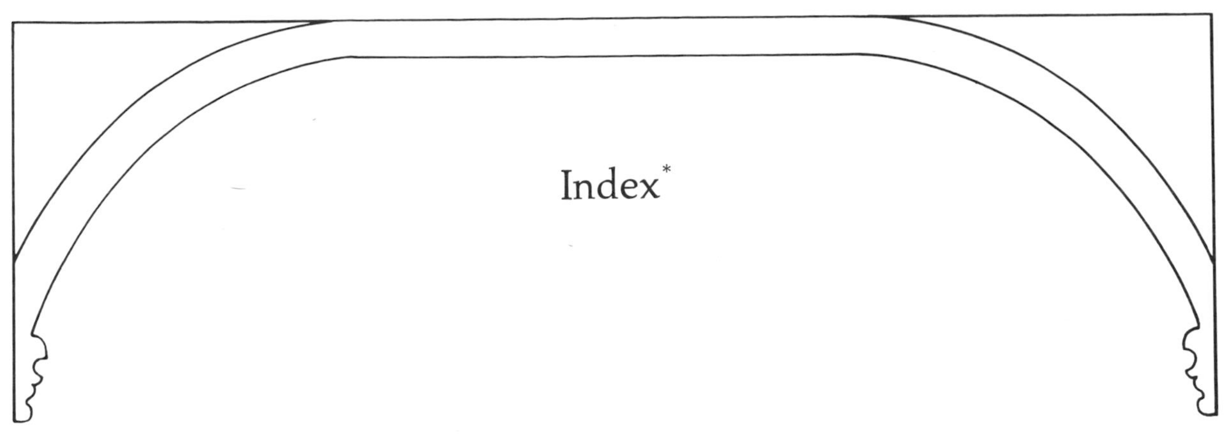

Index*

* NOTE: Numbers refer to pages in text on which terms listed in index are defined.